The Publicity Process

THIRD EDITION

Edited by **CHRISTINE FRIESLEBEN GOFF**

With Chapters by **EDMUND G. BLINN**
KENNETH L. EICH
KARL H. FRIEDERICH
KATHERINE TOLAND FRITH
VERYL FRITZ
BILL GILLETTE
CHRISTINE FRIESLEBEN GOFF
J. K. HVISTENDAHL
ROBERT C. JOHNSON
WILLIAM F. KUNERTH
DAVID L. LENDT
BARBARA M. MACK
JEROME L. NELSON
WALTER NIEBAUER
JANE WILLOUGHBY PETERSON
MARCIA PRIOR-MILLER

The Publicity Process

THIRD EDITION

1989

IOWA STATE UNIVERSITY PRESS / AMES

For Chad and Matthew

Manufactured in the United States of America

First edition, 1966 through five printings
Second edition, 1975
   Second printing, 1976
   Third printing, 1979
Third edition, 1989

Library of Congress Cataloging-in-Publication Data

The Publicity Process / edited by Christine Friesleben Goff — 3rd ed.
   p. cm.
   Includes index.
   ISBN 0-8138-1316-6
   1. Publicity.   2. Mass media.   I. Goff, Christine Friesleben, 1947-
HM263.S38 1989
   659.2 — dc19
                                       88-13618
                                         CIP

Contents

I   The Fundamentals of Publicity

II Selecting the Media Environments

III Creating Publicity Messages

IV Additional Publicity Tools

V Professional and Social Responsibility

Preface

THIS third edition of *The Publicity Process,* which was published first in 1966 and again in 1975, is long overdue but well worth the wait. The content is updated and effectively expanded so that it represents the best effort to date of providing students, consumers of the news, and nonprofessional publicists with a working knowledge of publicity methods.

As with the first two editions, this book is written by members of the Iowa State University journalism and mass communication department. The department has undergone numerous faculty changes in recent years; this time around, nine new contributing authors join seven veterans of the first two editions. Together they represent many years of experience in every communication field—print, broadcast, advertising, public relations, and photography. The end result is a book that uncomplicates the process of producing publicity and understanding the elements of mass communication.

Much of the material in this edition is new, including chapters on persuasion, information-gathering and interviewing techniques, developing a writing style, controlled publicity devices, and layout of publications. The inclusion of these topics makes this book a very practical how-to media guide.

Americans are deluged with communication messages almost every waking minute of the day. Typically, they rise in the morning to the sounds of their clock radios alternately playing songs, advertising products, and announcing the day's community events. The morning newspaper is on the stoop, and they either step over it on their way to work or spend less than fifteen minutes scanning the headlines and major stories or browsing through the ad inserts and comics.

CHRISTINE FRIESLEBEN GOFF

In their cars, Americans pass dozens of billboards and mass-transit advertising panels, some of which are so graphically well designed that the messages are hard to ignore. Bulletin boards in companies and factories hurl more messages. A stop at a doctor's office, business, grocery store, or service station will no doubt mean an encounter with a display of free brochures or flyers urging, "Take one," and many of those businesses will give out balloons, pens, yardsticks, or other trinkets with the company's name inscribed on the item.

Back home, Americans go through their mail, much of it unsolicited and usually referred to as junk, but surveys indicate that the word is a misnomer, as many of the messages in such mail are not ignored. Finally, a few people spend their evening relaxation time reading books, newspapers, or magazines, but the majority sit in front of the television, where more messages than they care to count interrupt the evening's entertainment programs.

This is what is meant by "information age," "segmented society," and "communication explosion," to name just a few of the current media buzzwords. It comes as no surprise that America leads the civilized world in the amount of entertainment, persuasion, and information proffered through both the mass media and controlled channels.

New technology—which changes so quickly that the word "new" is applicable for only a short time—is at least partially responsible for the tremendous increase in the amount of information thrown at us. Producing publicity, either by using a personal computer or by seeking the help of professionals with more sophisticated equipment, is now easier than ever before. The results are often cost-efficient and impressive.

No attempt is made here to expound on specific technology. Equipment and methods change so quickly that it would be futile to do so. But an explanation of the availability of such techniques allows the nonprofessional publicist to better grasp their significance and make use of them when possible.

Too often, individuals and organizations are intimidated by what they perceive to be an uncaring and uncooperating press in both the print and broadcast media. In reality, many who either avoid using the media or who fall into disfavor with them do so simply because they do not understand the news game.

One goal of this book, then, is to help both potential publicists and ordinary consumers of the news understand the functions of the various media. By paying full attention to the elements of mass communication, individuals can exercise more astutely their roles as media critics. Another goal is to help individuals identify themselves and their organizations as viable information sources. By learning how to identify when a publicity situation exists, when to use the media, and when to use alternative channels, publicists can work from a position of strength instead of weakness.

The book is divided into five parts. Part I explains the functions of publicity in terms of identifying audiences and issues, establishing the necessary communication links, and becoming successful information gatherers. Part II helps publicists and news consumers understand how the media operate and their strengths and limitations so that publicity messages can be channeled effectively. Part III provides general guidelines for understanding the elements of news, developing a writing style, and creating news releases and stories for print and broadcast. Part IV discusses the advantages and limitations of controlled media and specific photography, as well as layout, design, and advertising techniques. The two chapters in Part V evaluate the press's role in society and discuss the necessary ingredients for accountable journalism.

Although much of the material in this edition has changed, the audiences for which the earlier editions were written have not. The book is still appropriate for college and university students preparing for careers in which they expect to deal with representatives of the mass media, and also for students eager to know more about the nation's mass information systems. The material presented here will make them better-informed consumers and critics of the news. It is also an invaluable tool for organizations that must rely on their own members to produce publicity messages, members who are fearful of the task because of their inexperience. Finally, the book is a primer for anyone who would like to know more about how the nation's mass media operate: how news decisions are made, how information is distributed, how print and electronic media differ and how they are alike, and how ordinary citizens can obtain access to media services.

Appreciation is expressed to all the contributing authors who gave of their time and expertise to write chapters for this edition, especially Marcia Prior-Miller for being a sounding board for and a contributor of some of the ideas presented here. Thanks are due to J. K. Hvistendahl for giving me the opportunity to work on this project and to David L. Lendt, who edited the second edition and whose advice and encouragement were helpful and reassuring. My sincere gratitude goes to Robyn Hepker and Kelly Sargent, who did the odd jobs that helped tie the whole project together, and to Deloris Weigel and Sherry Smay, who let me on occasion take over the computers at their desks.

Contributors

All the chapter authors of this text are or were members of the Department of Journalism and Mass Communication at Iowa State University.

Edmund G. Blinn, professor emeritus, is a former reporter and editor for newspapers in Massachusetts, Connecticut, South Dakota, and Iowa and a former production editor for Iowa State University Press.

Kenneth L. Eich, associate professor, is a former radio reporter, editor, and news director for award-winning commercial and public broadcast stations. He has served on the board of directors of the Northwest Broadcast News Association, the Iowa Broadcast News Association, and the Iowa Associated Press Broadcasters.

Karl H. Friederich, professor, is a former Fulbright Lecturer and former editor of newspapers in Nebraska, California, and South Dakota.

Katherine Toland Frith, former associate professor, is a former copywriter for J. Walter Thompson, N. W. Ayer and Sons, and Grey Advertising in New York.

Veryl Fritz, associate professor, is a former copywriter, copy supervisor, account executive, and account supervisor for several agencies, including Campbell-Ewald Company and D'Arcy-MacManus and Masius. He also served as an advertising manager for Ralston-Purina and Massey-Ferguson and has held advertising workshops for retail merchants in a number of Iowa cities.

Bill Gillette, professor, has worked for magazines for 20 years and specializes in photography.

Christine Friesleben Goff, former instructor, is a free-lance writer and editor who specializes in news, features, and public relations. She has written and been a prospectus consultant for Iowa State University Press, has contributed to the writing of a career education communications and media guide, and is a former publication adviser.

J. K. (Jake) Hvistendahl, professor and former chairman, is a former newspaper editor and has published articles in *Journalism Quarterly,* the *Newspaper Research Journal, Quill,* and *Grassroots Editor* and has contributed chapters to several textbooks.

Robert C. Johnson, associate professor, specializes in photography.

William F. Kunerth, professor emeritus, is a former news editor, reporter, and advertising manager for several community newspapers in Wyoming and South Dakota, a former general manager of the Students Publishing Company at Northwestern University, and a former editorial faculty adviser to the *Iowa State Daily.*

David L. Lendt, director of university relations for the University of Missouri System and former director of university relations and associate professor of journalism and mass communication at Iowa State University. He is the author of *Demise of the Democracy* and author and editor of the second edition of *The Publicity Process,* also published by Iowa State University Press.

Barbara M. Mack, assistant professor, is a lawyer and member of Phi Beta Kappa, Order of the Barrister, and a former lawyer for the *Des Moines Register.*

Jerome L. Nelson, associate professor, was formerly a newspaper reporter, editor, and advertising representative in the state of Washington. He is a coauthor of a composition computer software program and the author of *Libel: A Basic Program for Beginning Journalists.*

Walter Niebauer, associate professor, has written for newspapers, magazines, and a university information service and has been an account executive for a public relations agency.

Jane Willoughby Peterson, assistant professor, is a former publication adviser with experience in public relations and public information. She is currently in charge of ISU's journalism education sequence.

Marcia Prior-Miller, assistant professor, has directed public relations and edited and produced printed media for nonprofit organizations in Texas and for a Kansas City book publisher. Her teaching and research interests include contemporary and historical magazine publishing and media institutions.

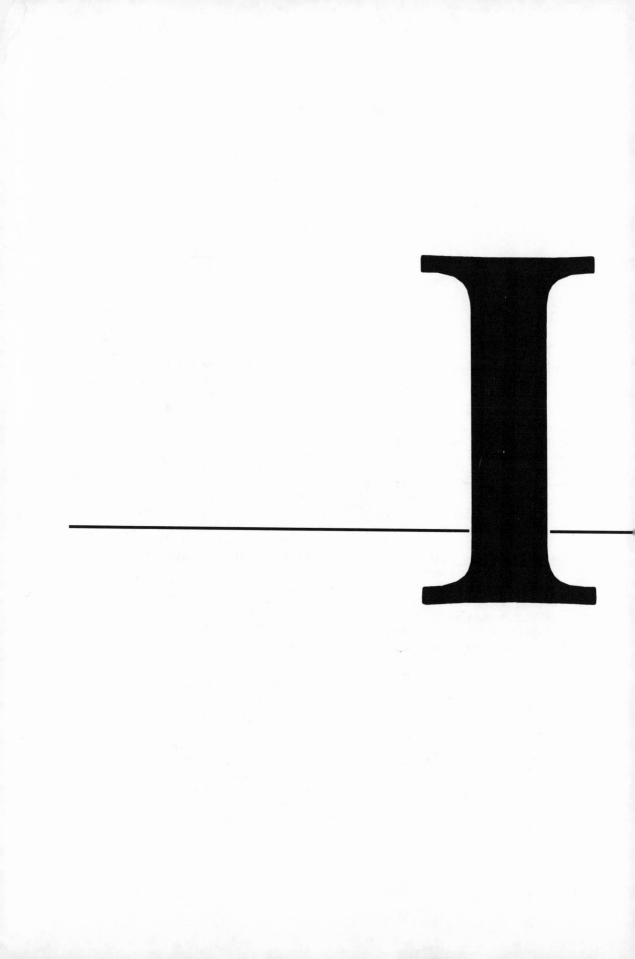

The Fundamentals of Publicity

APPLYING THE SKILLS demanded of publicists requires that those practitioners be well aware of the functions of publicity in a society that values self-government. The chapters in Part I explain those functions in terms of identifying the audiences and the issues, establishing the necessary communication links, and becoming successful information gatherers.

1 *Publicity and Public Relations*

DAVID L. LENDT

THIS BOOK is largely about publicity and the process involved in obtaining publicity for a political party, service agency, business, interest group, or idea. There are many meanings attached to the word "publicity." For some, it rouses visions of backslapping, cigar-smoking, martini-sipping "advance men" and of glitz and glitter and superficiality. This book, however, is addressed to the kind of publicity that is vital to the health of democracy, that bold experiment founded on the belief that well-informed, educated citizens are capable of governing themselves. Publicity of this sort is a critical ingredient in business, education, charity, and government.

The framers of the Constitution of the United States recognized that the need for a free flow of information in a democratic body politic was as great as the need for the free circulation of blood in the human body. When the flow of blood is restricted, the body's functions are seriously impaired. A part of society cut off from full access to the information necessary for wise decision-making will malfunction. It will make unwise decisions. Democracy will be in trouble.

In the First Amendment to the Constitution—the framers thought the issue was that important—are these words: "Congress shall make no law respecting an establishment of religion, or prohibiting the free exercise thereof; or abridging the freedom of speech, or of the press, or the right of people peaceably to assemble, and to petition the Government for a redress of grievances." It is one of the most important pieces of law in the history of humankind. It was and is a revolutionary idea that grew out of a revolutionary war. Insofar as publicity—the widespread and free exchange of information—helps the First Amendment to function, publicity also helps democracy to survive.

Admittedly, the "free marketplace of ideas" has not always functioned as smoothly as the founding fathers had hoped, although their fundamental good sense remains the foundation upon which all our opportunities and freedoms rest. All ideas do not flow through the democratic system with equal ease. Some people are more gifted publicists than others. (One purpose of this book, after all, is to make you a more effective publicist. It, too, is a contribution to the storehouse of human expression and to the marketplace of ideas.) Some groups and organizations and individuals have more talent and more resources than others, allowing them to do a better job of publicizing their accomplishments or ideas.

With all their wisdom and foresight, the founding fathers could not have imagined the influence of technological advancements on the distribution of information. They could not have dreamed of telegraph transmissions from one hamlet to another; and we have seen live video transmissions from the moon! Waves of technological change are transforming the nation from a society whose economy is founded on production to one founded on information. The rapidity with which the computer can assimilate, synthesize, and distribute that information threatens to put an even greater distance between interests with great resources and those without. It further threatens to restrict access to large audiences for those interests unable to afford the necessary technicians, hardware, and software.

When publicity is not flowing freely, when it appears that all sides of public questions are not being openly aired and debated, citizens grow uneasy and they eventually become alarmed. Well they might, for history and daily news accounts are sufficient reminders that dictatorial regimes consistently attempt to throttle the mass communications media to bring about an imbalance of information. Governance seems so much easier if opinions contrary to the government's can be silenced.

So the subject of this book is extremely important. Ideally, training in publicity will help a prospective publicist to do the best possible job of presenting ideas and causes in a professional, responsible way and in the best tradition of an open, democratic exchange of information and opinion. It should also help that person to communicate more effectively, to read and listen more critically, to understand the media more fully, and thus to operate more effectively in the broad democratic process.

Publicity versus Public Relations

Publicity, in its simplest terms, is a news story, a news release, a publicity release, or an article (the labels are interchangeable) that its author hopes to have printed or transmitted by one or more mass communications media (newspapers, magazines, radio, or television). This publicity also can be placed outside the spectrum of the mass media in the form of brochures, fliers, posters, displays, and a host of other options.

Publicity is usually a significant part, even the centerpiece, of a public relations program, but public relations is a broader concept. Public relations is everything a government agency, a corporation, a downtown store, or an individual candidate or entrepreneur does to present what is hoped will be an accurate and acceptable public image. Public relations may be affected by telephone etiquette or printed letterheads or computerized billing systems — or by the way a chief executive officer dresses or the kind of car a president drives. Virtually every facet of society — every state auditor and county sheriff, every brokerage office and gasoline station, every church and day care center, every school district and community college — is doing something deliberately to create or enhance a certain public image. (See Chapter 2 for a more detailed discussion of the public relations process.)

Although printed publicity releases are still heavily used, the trend is toward electronic transmission of stories created by computer (word processing) to the computers operated by wire services and by print and broadcast media outlets. New telecommunications technologies are making such arrangements more affordable while offering savings in time, paper, postage, and handling. (This chapter was electronically drafted and revised. It was electronically set in type as well.)

Another pervasive trend is making the publicity process more challenging than ever. Telecommunications technology not only has contributed to more high-speed computerized communication systems but also has subdivided audiences according to their specialized interests.

Cable television is the most conspicuous example of the trend, although it has been apparent in the publishing business for many years. National television programming used to be limited to one national public television network and three commercial networks. Now cable television outlets have proliferated to serve narrow, specialized slices of national audiences — those interested in the arts, movies, sports, or 24-hour news, for example — and commercial network ratings have reflected the incursion.

FM radio, to the amazement of those who considered it a "toy" medium just a few years ago, has become the dominant radio medium in most markets. But FM radio has also chopped up what had been a monolithic AM audience into several smaller audiences loyal to "their" FM station's format. (See Chapter 7 for a full discussion of the electronic media.)

Most of the nation's general-interest magazines have died. In their places are hundreds of magazines that cater to specialized commercial or avocational interests, from turkeys to personal computers, from commodities futures to auto repair. (Chapter 6 discusses the role of the magazine in the publicity process.)

The News Release

Although it may be addressed to a different outlet and although it may take the form of bits and bytes of data transmitted over a telephone line, the lowly news release remains the major product of the publicity effort. News releases are relatively inexpensive, do not require huge staffs to produce, and are generally easy to distribute. Thus, it is not surprising to find that news releases are being circulated by thousands of foundations, corporations, public service organizations, politicians, government agencies, schools and colleges, and softball and soccer teams. Everyone, it sometimes seems to some harried editors, is in the news release business.

When a publicist sends a prize release to the local newspaper, it will probably be delivered to an "In" box already cluttered with scores of other news releases from local sources as varied as the United Way, the League of Women Voters, and the County Republican Central Committee. Those releases may be joined with others from such far-flung sources as United Airlines, Digital Equipment Corporation, International Telephone and Telegraph, General Foods, the American Soybean Association, and the Presbyterian Church in the U.S.A. Each news release is one of many competing for valuable and limited time and space.

The job of a news release is to provide information through a medium to its listening or reading audience. A professionally written release will do that and no more. It will provide only information of substance and relevance to the story, the medium, and the audience. It will not waste the time of editors with insignificant details of interest only to the author of the news release, the author's organization, or like-minded colleagues.

The people who act as **gatekeepers** for the mass media—the editors of newspapers and magazines and the news directors of radio and television stations—are generally well-trained individuals who pride themselves on recognizing news when they see it. They object to being used by news release writers with axes to grind and no news to add to the inventory. (For a more thorough discussion of news values and the role of the gatekeeper, see Chapter 9.) If a news release doesn't deliver news to the editors, it won't get their time or attention—apart from the time and attention it takes to pitch the release into the nearest wastebasket.

The newsroom gatekeepers are like the rest of us in at least one respect: They appreciate it when someone is willing to help them do their job well. If information in a release has some news value, if the release is accurately and grammatically written, and if it avoids adjectives that try too hard to sell a point of view, it will stand apart from most news releases received in most newsrooms. Unfortunately, there are flacks and hacks and otherwise unprincipled practitioners in the news release business just as there are professionals who take pride in their literacy, accuracy, and objectivity.

Two inviolable rules apply to the writing of a professional news release:

1. It must be news.
2. It must be right.

The information contained in a news release must be scrupulously accurate. An editor may find that a release is newsworthy and may use it on that basis. If, however, the release is inaccurate, the editor is made to look incompetent, the publication or broadcast is made to look unreliable, and, worst of all, the public is misled.

Professional publicists take their responsibility to the public at large just as seriously as professional editors do. With the freedom accorded the press go several responsibilities, one of which is an uncompromising respect for the truth, insofar as the truth can be determined. A publicist who has been careless with the truth in a news release used by a trusting editor will likely get a cool response the next time around. Editors try to be objective, but an experience like that—depending on its consequences—can cause predictable responses. (See Chapter 18 for a detailed discussion of press responsibilities, and see the Code of Professional Ethics in the Appendix.)

Most editors are busy. They live with continual deadlines, and their work is made available for public scrutiny day in and day out. The professional publicist, in attempting to gain exposure for certain events or for certain data, attempts to help the editor meet those demanding deadlines.

Most editors are responsible. If there is any question concerning the information in a news release, they will check it out with someone in a position to know the facts. Most editors are also human beings, however, who in the rush of doing their jobs must frequently rely on the responsibility and honesty of others, including the publicists who provide unsolicited information to publications or stations. If, for whatever reason, a submitted news release is inaccurate, the publicist who sent the information may be in deep difficulty not only with editors but also with other publicists and the public. An immediate attempt should be made to correct the error with a phone call—if necessary, to every recipient of the release. If it is too late for that, the publicist should provide a correction notice to each recipient, apologizing for the error and including corrected information, for whatever use the editors might wish to make of it.

While factual accuracy is the most important part of making a news release "right," there is more to it than that. Most editors have a high regard for language. For that reason and others, news releases should reflect mechanical and grammatical accuracy. An obvious error, of whatever variety, tends to compromise the quality of the entire release.

In most advertising, public relations, and publicity offices, drafts of written materials are regularly circulated among several persons. The writers generally seek advice or consensus concerning expression or emphasis, rather than corrections of spelling or grammar; but even the professionals make occasional errors. It is a good idea to run news release copy by at least one other person before submitting it for possible publication.

Summary

Public relations is a broad concept, of which publicity is a significant part. For all practical purposes, publicity takes the form of news releases that are intended to be printed or transmitted by various communication outlets.

The lowly news release is an important part of the way things are done in a society that values self-government. It is the simplest way for organizations and individuals with widely divergent interests, goals, and ideas to gain access to the marketplace of ideas on a mass media scale. If the news release is to accomplish what it is intended to accomplish, it must be valuable as news and it must be precise and factual.

When the release is news and when it is correct, it is regarded not as a lowly thing but as the professional product of professional minds and hands. It is respected on the news desk, it is helpful to the public, and for these reasons it is far more likely to succeed in doing what the publicist hopes it will do.

Exercises

1. Have each member of the class ask five persons to define the terms "public relations" and "publicity." Compare the answers in a class discussion, and assess the misconceptions some people have concerning the concepts. What is the lesson to be learned as you begin preparing for your role as a publicist?
2. Make an appointment to visit with a public relations representative from a service agency or organization in your community, or invite that person to visit your class. Discuss the various methods of publicity the representative relies on to communicate the organization's messages to the targeted audiences. Find out how those choices are made. Ask the representative what other innovative promotional tools or activities the organization has used recently, and discuss the results. Also ask the representative to discuss the value of professional public relations activities.
3. Begin a class publicity file, the contents of which can be used throughout the course for discussion and analysis. Contact newspaper and information service personnel and ask them to save some news releases; then appoint someone to pick them up. Do the same with news releases from broadcast stations. Also, bring in pamphlets, brochures, fliers, posters, direct-mail pieces, and novelty items with a publicity message.

Suggested Reading

Baskin, Otis W., and Aronoff, Craig E. *Public Relations: The Profession and the Practice.* 2d ed. Dubuque, Iowa: Brown Publishers, 1988.

Crable, Richard E., and Vibbert, Steven L. *Public Relations as Communication Management.* Edina, Minn.: Bellwether Press, 1986.

Culligan, Matthew J., and Greene, Dolph. *Getting Back to the Basics of Public Relations and Publicity.* New York: Crown Publishers, 1982.

Ehrenkranz, Lois B. *Public Relations/Publicity: A Key Link in Communications.* New York: Fairchild Publications, 1983.

Klepper, Michael M. *Getting Your Message Out: How to Get, Use and Survive Radio and Television Air Time.* Englewood Cliffs, N.J.: Prentice-Hall, 1984.

Seitel, Fraser P. *The Practice of Public Relations.* 3d ed. Columbus, Ohio: Merrill Publishing Co., 1987.

Winston, Martin Bradley. *Getting Publicity.* New York: John Wiley, 1982.

2 *The Public Relations Process*

KARL H. FRIEDERICH

PUBLIC RELATIONS? What is it? Who needs it? How do you accomplish it? Any organization—government, business and industry, nonprofit groups such as the Red Cross or the local Y, hospitals, and educational institutions at all levels—should be asking and answering these questions. They are as important as budgets, policy-making and planning, and research and development. As a matter of fact, these terms should be as familiar to public relations practitioners as they are to the experts in the respective areas. Most successful organizations, in fact, put public relations on an equal basis with other segments of their operations. Thus, if there is a vice president for marketing and another one for research and development, there also is, in a successful organization, a vice president for public relations.

Why the stress on the equality of public relations on an organizational chart? The following definition of public relations provides some initial clues.

> Public relations is the management function which provides the professional skills necessary to communicate truthfully and effectively with concerned publics.

Added to this definition should be the element of bringing about mutual understanding between an organization and its relevant publics. As will be discussed shortly, only one of the four models that organizations follow in their practice of public relations truly works toward achieving this mutual understanding.

This definition, provided some time ago by Carl W. Hawver, then president of the Public Relations Society of America and vice president of public affairs for the Chrysler Corporation, implies two things about the term "management": (1) The management of an organization recognizes the proper role and philosophy of public relations, and (2) the process itself requires careful managing of all the professional skills necessary for a successful public relations policy. To accomplish this, the organization either hires individuals possessing these skills to work in-house—that is, as a member of the organization—or it retains a public relations agency for the provision of certain skills required by the organization.

As to the first point, it is important to realize that public relations for any organization begins with top management, and from there it must be diffused throughout the entire organization. In other words, public relations is an "all hands" job and not just the responsibility of the public relations practitioners.

Bringing about the main goal of communication efforts by the public relations professional—mutual understanding—requires the careful application of management skills to run an entire public relations department as well as to handle any public relations campaign, no matter how long its duration.

Communication skills referred to in the definition of public relations include the traditional ones, such as writing news and feature stories for print and broadcast media, taking pictures (still and motion or videotape), designing and laying out publications ranging from organizational newspapers and magazines to brochures and handbills, and writing speeches and scripts.

Among the newer skills required are the practitioner's ability to carry out meaningful research and evaluation, that is, a thorough investigation of a particular problem when it first arises and then evaluation of the outcome of a public relations campaign designed to deal with that problem. Thorough research and evaluation are the real distinguishing marks that differentiate public relations from publicity. The latter can be only an adjunct to, or a tool of, public relations. Publicity can never substitute for public relations in either a definitional or a practical sense.

The definition of public relations discussed here and the role of management in it are modern conceptions that are not yet practiced everywhere. When the public relations function is not integrated into the highest management echelons of an organization, much vital information about the human factors is often missing from management decisions.

Modern management and public relations philosophy call for public relations professionals to be part of the management team so these factors can be taken into account before decisions and policies are made final and binding. Otherwise, the role of the public relations practitioner is turned into that of a publicity hack who grinds out news releases, peddles them to various media, arranges open houses, and engages in other such peripheral activities. Under those circumstances the public relations practitioner becomes a member of the "boast and bucket brigade." The boasting consists of extolling the virtues of the organization for whom the practitioner works. On the bucket brigade side, a practitioner spends much time putting out brushfires in the form of community unrest or misunderstanding because management acted without the advice of public relations counsel.

Rather than spend so much time on these types of activities, public relations practitioners can contribute so much more to an organization if they can function in a preventive role. This can happen, however, only with management's proper recognition that a public relations philosophy must permeate an entire organization, from the top executive down to the most recent recruit.

Four Public Relations Models

If the readers could observe every public relations practitioner in the world in action, they could still not remember everything that had been observed. For that reason, and to simplify further discussion, four types of public relations are described here. These types are called models in order to emphasize that they are abstractions. Nevertheless, these models come close to describing reality – the way public relations has been practiced historically and contemporarily.

PRESS AGENT/PUBLICITY MODEL

When public relations activities were first undertaken, the main purpose was to use some form of persuasive communication. In the press agent/publicity model the practitioner's main concern is to spread the faith of the organization involved. Quite often, this results in incomplete, distorted, or half-true information. The communication model followed by this practitioner is strictly one way. The practitioner wants to *tell* about an organization; there is no interest in listening to those at whom this communication effort is directed. The diagram below depicts the communication model underlying the press agent/publicity model of public relations:

Source → Message → Medium → Receiver

The fact that all the arrows point in one direction is indicative of the way this public relations model functions. All activities, including communication, commence with a source and end with a receiver. Nothing travels the other way.

As discussed earlier, modern public relations practices include a major research and evaluation component. Not so in this public relations model. If the practitioners of the press agent/publicity model do anything of a research nature, it is merely to delineate the publics (more on that topic later) with whom they wish to communicate. In an evaluative sense they may also check whether the media used the material or whether the house or the stadium was successfully filled. In other words, did the people "buy" the messages that exhorted them to attend a promoted event?

PUBLIC-INFORMATION MODEL

About the turn of the century a second public relations method appeared. The only real difference between the public-information and the press agent/publicity models is that the former does not take any license with the truth the way a press agent might. The job of the public relations practitioner following the tenets of the public-information model is to objectively report information about an organization to its intended publics. Otherwise, the same communication model that was presented for the press agent/publicity model also applies here.

Research does not play a major role in the public-information model. There may be some readability and readership studies, but that's about it. Readability surveys measure whether messages are written at the appropriate level of difficulty for the intended audience. (See Chapter 10 for a readability formula and further discussion.) Readership studies measure whether an audience actually pays attention to and uses the information sent out by the public relations practitioner using the public-information model.

TWO-WAY ASYMMETRIC MODEL

Using the latest findings of modern social science, practitioners of the two-way asymmetric model of public relations are the real persuaders. Their main purpose is to get their intended publics to accept the point of view held by an organization. If successful, the practitioner helps people to change their attitudes and to behave in ways that are supportive of the organization. The end result of the model, which came into existence in the 1920s, is really no different from that of the press agent/publicity model, except that the two-way asymmetric practitioner is much more scientific about the approaches taken.

While the communication model underlying the press agent/publicity and the public-information models is identical, there is now a new wrinkle added to the communication model applicable for the two-way asymmetric model, namely feedback. The two-way asymmetric communication model looks like this:

$$\text{Source} \rightarrow \text{Message} \rightarrow \text{Channel} \rightarrow \text{Receiver}$$

Feedback

Under the two-way asymmetric model, communication now flows in both directions – from source to receiver and also from receiver to source. In its original application, the term "feedback" stems from cybernetic theory and has often been compared to the communication of a thermostat. All that the thermostat does is to monitor the room or building temperature and report to the "source" – that is, the furnace or air conditioner – calling for more warm or cool air, depending on the circumstances.

Despite the feedback, communication under the two-way asymmetric model of public relations is still essentially one-way because the effects of that communication and public relations program are still imbalanced in favor of the organization. While the organization using this model attempts vigorously to change the attitudes and behavior of those with whom it communicates, the communication that comes as a result of feedback seemingly has no impact on the organization's behavior and attitudes vis-à-vis the relevant publics.

The research function in the two-way asymmetric model takes on tremendous importance. The two types of research encountered are formative and evaluative. Two-way asymmetric practitioners use formative research to find out just what a given group of people will sit still for (more on this later). Practitioners then link their formative research findings to the policies and procedures of their organization and proceed to tell the world they are now operating in the public interest. Their evaluative research comes into play after a public relations campaign has run its course or while it is still going on. Having measured attitudes and/or behavior before they launched a public relations/communication campaign, these practitioners are now in a position to measure again. If they find changes in the desired directions, they pat themselves on the back and deem the campaign a success.

While the practitioners of the two-way asymmetric model think they utilize two-way communication, in reality this is merely an illusion. The organization practicing this model generally changes very little. In other words, it is still trying to get people to do its bidding as far as attitude or behavior changes are concerned.

TWO-WAY SYMMETRIC MODEL

Using this particular model for the practice of public relations provides the practitioner a new role. No longer is the public relations practitioner a persuader and one-way communicator. Rather, the practitioner now becomes the mediator between an organization and its publics. The goal is simply to bring about mutual understanding. Many forward-looking organizations are beginning to adopt this way of practicing public relations, which appeared in the late 1960s and early 1970s. Adherents of the two-way symmetric model also rely heavily on theory for their planning and evaluation of public relations programs. The social science–based theory that is subscribed to by practitioners of the two-way symmetric model leans heavily on modern communication theory rather than persuasion theory.

Under this model, the organization is just as likely to undergo major changes resulting from a public relations campaign as the relevant publics are. Dialogue, rather than monologue, is the order of the day. Most of the time, neither the organization nor the publics will change attitudes or behavior. The end result may well be that each side understands the other better and is willing to bring about an accommodation.

The earlier communication models, based largely on David K. Berlo's conception of communication (which will be discussed in more detail later), no longer apply for the two-way symmetric public relations model. Instead, the model looks like this:

Group   Group

Unlike the other communication models, this model strongly suggests that interaction is occurring between two groups—an organization and one or more of its publics. This is quite different from labeling one "source" and the other "receiver," the way the first three models conceptualized the communication process—one side initiating the communication and doing something to the other.

The research function in the two-way symmetric public relations model is also quite different from the other three. During formative research the practitioner intends to learn how the organization is perceived by the relevant publics and to determine what impact or consequences the organization has on those publics. Effective counseling with management, based on the formative research findings, will ultimately result in appropriate policies that are indeed in the public interest. The level of understanding of each side can also be measured as part of the initial formative research. In turn, this can be used to delineate communication objectives carefully. Evaluation research is primarily designed to measure the extent of mutual understanding present after a public relations effort.

Choosing a Model

The four models were presented in the chronological order in which they appeared on the American scene. But that is not to give the reader the erroneous impression that, as each new model was adopted, the preceding one(s) disappeared. Nothing could be further from reality. In the public relations world today all four models are indeed around and doing well. As a matter of fact, some organizations may use two or more of the models simultaneously in their day-to-day public relations endeavors, using the power of persuasion (press agent/publicity model) in some cases and the two-way symmetric model in others. (See Chapter 3 for a discussion of persuasion methods.) Which model is used depends entirely on the needs of the organization, which can be illustrated by examples.

A land-grant university in the Midwest has, as part of its auxiliary enterprises, major facilities such as an auditorium, a coliseum, and a 50,000-seat football stadium. It takes a monumental effort to fill the facilities for football and basketball games, concerts, and the like. The public relations model most likely used by the university's public relations practitioners (also referred to in the case of government and similar institutions as public information specialists) is the press agent/publicity model. There is nothing wrong with this model today as long as the practitioners stick to the truth.

On the same university campus, scholars and researchers constantly explore ways in which the human environment and condition can be improved. New findings in agriculture, home economics, engineering, and many other fields are reported almost daily. Old attitudes may change and new practices may be adopted as a result of this information, which is disseminated using the public-information model of public relations. (This is referred to as the adoption and diffusion process and will be discussed later.)

To understand the working of the last two models, envision the following: For years, Land-Grant U has been plagued by high enrollment, reduced allocations from the state legislature, reversion of budgeted funds ordered by the governor, and a reluctant administration and board of regents who would ask for and allow only minimal tuition increases. This situation has resulted in a concerned faculty, with a substantial number of its highly qualified members leaving for higher-paying jobs on other campuses or in business and industry. With a new president on the scene, the major priority becomes to increase faculty and staff salaries. He is very much in favor of substantial tuition raises. The public relations plan that can be put into effect to deal with this problem and the affected publics could indeed follow the two-way asymmetric approach if the new president simply wants to bully his way through to the desired end result. Or, as would be far more advantageous, the university's public relations practitioners could follow the two-way symmetric model, which would require a certain amount of accommodation and adaptation on the part of all involved publics, including the university administration.

Clearly, an organization can choose any of the four public relations models and the circumstances under which it is employed.

The Four-Phase Model of Public Relations

Regardless of which public relations model is being applied to a situation, but especially when the two-way asymmetric and symmetric models are involved, the practitioner goes through a series of distinct management steps. Public relations textbooks are replete with models outlining these sequential steps. They range from Marston's RACE formula to James Grunig and Todd Hunt's "Behavioral Molecule." For the sake of simplification, the model presented here (see Figure 2.1), which follows four specific steps or phases in dealing with a public relations problem, was developed by Cutlip and Center.

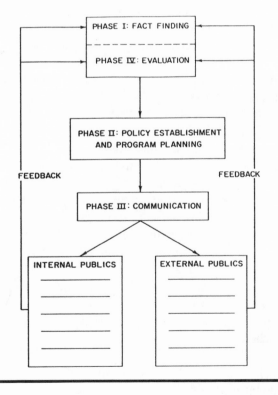

FIG. 2.1. The public relations process.

The four phases of the model are as follows:

I. **Fact-finding and research.** Analysis of the priority audiences, linkages, or publics of an organization; assessment of the attitudes and degree of understanding and support.

II. **Policy establishment and program planning.** Aligning an organization's policies with the concerns of publics, and planning a two-way communication program with the priority publics in order to deal effectively with what is important to both the publics and the organization, rather than dealing only with what is urgent.

III. **Communication.** Listening and telling an organization's story in terms compatible with the mix of the publics.

IV. **Evaluation.** Evaluating and assessing the effectiveness and outcome of all public relations activities of the organization.

PHASE I: FACT-FINDING AND RESEARCH

As a part of Phase I, the public relations practitioner is concerned with carrying out an inventory of the organization. Such an inventory should take into account manpower deployment, physical assets, past and present performance, and the kinds of programs and activities the organization has engaged in over time. The public relations practitioner should examine successful and unsuccessful activities and then attempt to isolate the reasons for each success and failure.

The fact-finding activities also lead to defining the constituent groups, linkages, or publics with which the organization has to deal. For example, a public school system can illustrate the variety of publics that might be encountered by a public relations practitioner.

The internal publics are those groups of individuals who reside or work within the organizational structure or are directly associated with the organization. External publics are those groups of individuals who are outside the organization but have direct relationships with it. For the school system illustration, the following are considered internal publics:

Students
Administrators
Members of the board of education
Teachers
Counselors
Teacher associates and other paraprofessionals
Student teachers
Student and adult volunteers

Secretaries and clerks
Grounds and custodial staffs
Other plant and transportation employees
Food service employees
School nurses

The following groups are part of the school system's external publics:

Parents of children in the school system
Parents of children not in the school system
Senior citizens
Other childless citizens
Athletics boosters
Churches
Civic groups
City, county, and state government officials
State and national legislators
Professional groups within the community
Business executives within the community
Labor unions
Suppliers and distributors of school-purchased services and goods
School officials and board members in other communities
PTA and other parental organizations
Social and civic agencies
Chambers of commerce
Patriotic groups
School visitors
Taxpayer groups
Local and regional mass media

The task of defining the school system's publics, their composition, and their attitudes and knowledge of the school goes beyond this simple classification scheme.

LINKAGES

Both internal and external publics are also part of an organization's linkages, of which there are four types.

Legislators and school board members are thought of as part of the **enabling linkages.** They provide the authority and control the resources that enable the organization to exist. That's why public relations departments deliberately plan programs in government relations and public affairs.

Functional linkages are subdivided into input and output linkages.

In the school district example, teachers and unions would be examples of **functional input linkages,** while students and employers of school graduates would be considered **functional output linkages.** For the input linkages, a public relations practitioner designs and implements employee and labor relations, or human relations, programs. Effective community relations programs would be developed for the functional output linkage groups.

Normative linkages for the school district would exist with other school districts in the state and across the country. The district would also have normative linkages with state and national associations of school board members. Public relations practitioners ordinarily do not develop special programs for the organization's normative linkage groups. Membership in these groups is intended for interaction with others who might face similar problems and for facilitation of communication.

The fourth type, **diffused linkages,** involves groups for which a program is often developed after a problem arises between the organization and one of the groups. The taxpayer group listed above as an external public generally doesn't complain until, for example, the school district officials call for the building of a new junior high school to be financed through bonds. In order to sell these bonds, the school district must first obtain approval from the district's voters. In the campaign period before election day the taxpayer group surfaces and speaks on behalf of the property owners in the district. Thus, the school district's public relations personnel will have to develop and implement a public relations plan to deal with the objections of and to counter the strategies advanced by the group. Under ordinary circumstances very little would be heard from this diffused group.

Our discussion of publics and linkages would be incomplete without mentioning that publics also need to be classified as **latent, aware,** and **active.** Publics come into being when a group of people face a similar problem, recognize that the problem exists, and organize to do something about it. At least one of these three conditions must be met before a public exists. For example, the taxpayer group previously mentioned does not surface until the school district announces the method of financing a new school.

Assume that before the financing of the new school was even discussed by the school board, only the need for the school had been discussed. At that point the taxpayers faced the same problem, but they did not consciously realize that the problem existed. Therefore, they were a **latent** public. Once the financing methods had been discussed by the board, the taxpayers became an **aware** public because they now recognized that a problem existed. They had thus met two of the three conditions spelled out above. Finally, when the taxpayers group held meetings and developed a strategy to convince the community not to increase taxes, they became an **active** public.

All three types of publics came into existence because of a problem created by the school district. The main point is that people are members of different types of publics and that their membership changes over time, depending on the situation.

FACT-FINDING AND RESEARCH METHODS

With the awareness of how constituent groups are defined, it is necessary to return to the fact-finding and research function in the first phase of the public relations process. The methods used to determine attitudes and other kinds of information within various publics necessarily vary from informal to sophisticated. One of the oldest informal methods is the practice of listening. This can be accomplished by keeping track of personal or telephone contacts, for example. However, reliance should not be placed solely on unsolicited contacts; some attempts should be made to initiate contacts and to use persons as sounding boards. A formal version of this method is the advisory committee or panel. Periodic analysis of an organization's incoming mail can also provide valuable information. If the organization has field representatives, then soliciting and evaluating their opinions about pending or past programs can provide valuable insights into the perceptions people have about the organization.

Monitoring the output of the mass media can also indicate what others are saying—or whether others are saying much of anything—about the organization. Press clippings and radio-television monitor reports are available from commercial sources in case the practitioner has neither the time nor the manpower within the organization's public relations department to obtain this information directly.

Conferences with those involved in a particular situation can reveal attitudes and knowledge in an informal manner. Careful analysis of opinion polls can further assist in gaining insights into public opinion on a broader level. Similarly, opinion polls carried out in other communities can alert the public relations practitioner to trends and possible problem areas. The speeches and writings of recognized opinion leaders and influentials in the community and the region can reveal concerns and problems with which an organization may have to contend.

These informal methods can be helpful to a public relations practitioner engaging in fact-finding or research for an organization, but all such informal methods lack the representativeness and objectivity necessary for sound attitude and opinion research. The formal methods that can be used to tap public attitudes, opinions, and knowledge are cross-section surveys, survey panels, depth interviews, content analyses, and mail questionnaires. Ideally, a public relations practitioner should be able to sit down with members of relevant publics and discuss, face-to-face, their views on particular problems and issues. This approach can work with some publics, such as employees; for others, however, it is impractical.

For this reason, the public relations practitioner may use scientifically designed sample surveys, administered in person or by telephone, of representative groups in each of the publics relevant to the organization's program. The idea behind using survey panels as a method of tapping knowledge, attitudes, and opinions is to find out what happens to the randomly chosen panel members under varying conditions and the passage of time. Whereas the well-administered cross-section survey will yield good quantitative information, the depth interview and the use of focus groups offer opportunities for probing the attitudes that underlie expressed opinions. Analyzing the content of the mass media can tell an organization what is being said about it, whether critical or laudatory. Such information, through the method of content analysis, can be codified and thereby quantified for various purposes.

Finally, the public relations practitioner who has to operate with a limited research budget can use the mail questionnaire method to survey attitudes and measure knowledge among relevant publics. The major drawback of this method is the often low return rate of completed questionnaires, which destroys, or at least impairs, the representative quality of the original sample. This approach generally yields adequate information when administered to largely homogeneous groups whose divergences of opinion are dramatic.

PHASE II: POLICY ESTABLISHMENT AND PROGRAM PLANNING

Once a close look at the setup of the organization has been taken, the various internal and external publics and linkages have been identified, and their mutual consequences analyzed, the practitioner can move to Phase II of the public relations process: establishing and aligning policy and planning a program of action.

A public relations program, if it is to succeed, must be based on sound policy (bringing an organization's policies into alignment with the concerns and needs of the different publics) and executed by capable personnel. Policy decisions must originate with or be endorsed by top management. Policy is often a nebulous or loosely formulated code of action. There is little point in activating a public relations program for an organization lacking direction.

Successful organizations, usually practicing some form of management by objectives, clearly enunciate their goals and objectives at all levels. The public relations practitioners then develop the appropriate public relations responses to lend proper support to the established goals and objectives. Goals are normally viewed as being broad, abstract, and not measurable. Objectives, on the other hand, are derived from goals; they are highly specific and measurable.

In the example of the school district, assume that the following goals and objectives have been set:

1. Establishing good rapport with teachers and other school employees, particularly in the area of salary negotiations
2. Getting support from at least 61 percent of the voters in local bond elections for new buildings or operating funds
3. Establishing or maintaining a favorable image of the schools in the community (through a favorable image of teachers, administrators, and school board members)
4. Maintaining and improving relations with adult and student interest groups

The planning of programs to meet objectives must take two general directions: long-range programs to achieve the objectives and short-term programs for particular projects.

In all of these activities, the role of the public relations practitioner undergoes a change as the process moves from the fact-finding to the program-planning phase. In Phase I the practitioner serves generally as an analyst; in Phase II the practitioner becomes an initiator and adviser. As the program moves toward the action (communication) stage of Phase III, the practitioner becomes an advocate. In Phase IV the practitioner once again assumes the role of an analyst. All of these have been traditional roles. In today's public-opinion climate, the two-way symmetric model of public relations suggests yet another role—that of moderator. Throughout all phases of the public relations process, the practitioner must act as a moderator and arbitrator, bringing together the various publics whose members may hold strong, but divergent, points of view.

The importance of the role of moderator is yet another argument for making public relations practitioners a party to policy decisions. Otherwise, they become glorified gofers, cranking out reams of publicity materials, speeches, or annual reports, preparing films or tapes, or putting together educational materials or exhibitions. These activities are all worthwhile, of course, but not when they are carried out in a vacuum created by excluding the public relations expert from policy planning and decision-making.

As part of Phase II, the practitioner is also responsible for securing and properly allocating resources—both personnel and money. The practitioner is assisted in these tasks by such methods as the PERT chart and the Critical Path Method, along with such traditional standby tools as zero-based budgeting. PERT and CPM have been developed by management scientists to help public relations practitioners define the network of interrelated events that have to be accomplished in sequence before a project is complete. These decision-making tools are used for channeling practitioners' limited time and money resources toward the projects with the greatest expected payoff.

PHASE III: COMMUNICATION

The word "communication" has its roots in Latin, where it means "common." The objective in communicating with various publics is to establish **commonality** between the organization and those for whom the message is intended. The process of communication is perhaps more easily understood if it is examined in the incremental steps given in David K. Berlo's model in Figure 2.2.

Referring to communication as a process simply means that it is an ongoing event or activity. As people interact with others, they are communicating. Communication thus becomes the process through which to transmit messages—thoughts, ideas, emotions—to other human beings. The goals and objectives of communicative efforts are indeed manifold and depend largely on the type of public relations practiced. At one time, and with a particular public, practitioners may be interested only in conveying accurate information about the organization to that public. At another time, the intent

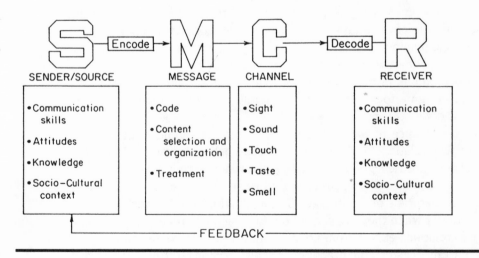

FIG. 2.2. Berlo's S-M-C-R model.

may be to persuade a public to support a hypothetical school district by voting in favor of a school bond issue. In other words, the practitioners want people to behave in a certain way, and accomplishing that is no mean task. As a matter of fact, the best results occur if the objective is merely to communicate. If the objective is to change people's attitudes or get them to behave in a desired way, the public relations practitioner should not expect to affect more than 20 percent of the target group.

The following elements occur in Berlo's communication model: source (or sender), message, channel, receiver, and feedback. All communication must come from somewhere: a **source** or **sender.** The source might be one person, a group of people, a corporation, a government agency, or any other organization or institution. Several factors determine how a source will operate in the communication process. One is the source's communication skills, both for sending and for receiving. Another consideration is the source's attitudes about himself or herself, about the subject matter of the message, and about the various publics to whom the message may be directed. How a source will operate also is affected by the source's knowledge of the subject and of the publics. (Analysis of the relevant publics, emphasized in the fact-finding phase, can pay dividends here.)

In Berlo's model, the **message** is what the public relations practitioner attempts to transmit to the publics. The process of putting the message together is called **encoding.** Several factors are involved in encoding, including the selection of a code; the message must be written or spoken in some language (set of symbols, such as English). For some kinds of communication, photography, film, music, and even gestures are possible codes. The level of difficulty of the code for various publics also must be considered. If, for example, the task is to communicate some scientific achievement to the publics consisting of scientists and elementary school children, the source obviously has to take into account their differences in intellect and education.

Once the message has been encoded, it is committed to a **channel** for transmission. Channels can be considered in several ways. Perhaps the simplest is to utilize the five senses to receive the message. Viewed in this manner, the channels of communication are ways of presenting a message so that it can be seen, heard, touched, tasted, or smelled. In a more practical sense, channels include public speech, discussion, and interviews; radio and recording; television and motion pictures; demonstrations and on-the-job training; and newspapers, magazines, and books.

The fourth element in the communication process is the **receiver**–the person or persons at the opposite end of the communication process from the source. The factors operating on the source (communication skills, attitudes, knowledge) also operate on the receiver, whose function is to decode the message.

As a sender (source) of messages, the public relations practitioner is interested in determining the effectiveness of the message via **feedback.** It is easier to obtain message feedback when the communication process takes place in a face-to-face conversation. Facial expressions, gestures, and verbal conversations can indicate how well the message is received. When the practitioner uses the mass media, however, feedback is not only delayed but usually incomplete as well. It often must be actively sought—for example, when the program is evaluated.

SOME IMPLICATIONS FOR SUCCESS IN COMMUNICATION

Berlo's S-M-C-R model provides us with a good framework within which to consider some of the factors that determine the success or failure of communication. After all, the public relations practitioner often communicates on behalf of a client or employer, sometimes with the intent of bringing about change in either a public or the organization represented.

Most individuals have had experiences with toy gyroscopes. Spin the wheel within its frame, and the gadget seems to take on a life of its own. Although the gyroscope is not impervious to outside forces, it is resistant to them. It has its own internal arrangement of energies in equilibrium. There seems to be an aura of magic attached to it, considering its partial independence from such a basic force as gravity. The operating gyroscope represents a dynamic system in equilibrium.

If public relations practitioners thought of individuals in various publics as gyroscopic organisms, the practitioners would do a more effective and realistic job of communicating. The gyroscopic organisms spin along, absorbing and consuming, resisting and casting off things in an impersonal, self-serving, and preoccupied process that selects from the environment those things (including information) that preserve and sustain their internal equilibrium.

Why the analogy of human beings with dynamic mechanical gadgets? Because an organization's public relations strategists should assume that individuals are actively preoccupied with their own concerns; that they are, in fact, actively resistant to becoming involved in the concerns of the organization; and that many view organizations and institutions, whether large or small, as impersonal, vague, peripheral aspects in their lives. Thus, a public relations message must often penetrate a field of resistance characterized by massive disinterest. The persuasiveness of a public relations message generally must rely exclusively on its appeal to the receiver's self-interest.

No message is received in its pure form. Receivers may magnify it, modify it, misinterpret it, or even ignore it altogether. These concerns are discussed at the end of this chapter with a look at the adoption and diffusion process. But first a brief look at the fourth and final phase of the public relations process.

PHASE IV: EVALUATION

The final phase is nothing more than a continuous application of the fact-finding and research phase. With evaluation, the practitioner reaches the so-called bottom line. By using the same research methods described in Phase I, the public relations practitioner can determine whether the objectives spelled out in Phase II have been met.

The Adoption and Diffusion Process

As a participant in the development of public relations programs, a practitioner is often required to influence opinions and actions through communication with sizable and distant groups. At an accelerating rate, modern society has been flooded with innovations for which information must be disseminated to those who need it.

To accomplish this, many practitioners use the adoption and diffusion process. **Adoption** refers to a person's behavior from the moment of awareness of a new product or idea to his or her acceptance or rejection of the innovation. **Diffusion** refers to the way the idea spreads through the system. Its emphasis is on the means and speed of the communication and on the rate of acceptance.

Whether the innovation is the adoption of the original hybrid seed corn by Iowa (and American) farmers, or whether it is the federal government's latest attempt to gain public acceptance of seat belts for the safety of motorists, the adoption of any of these new ideas can be described in five basic steps or stages—awareness, information (or interest), evaluation, trial, and adoption.

In the **awareness** stage an individual knows that an innovation exists but lacks detailed information about it. In this phase, research about new farm and home practices has shown that the mass media—radio, television, newspapers, and magazines—assume a preeminent role in the diffusion of the new idea, ahead of such other sources of information as government agencies, friends and neighbors, and dealers and salesmen. Figure 2.3 shows the rank order of information sources for the five stages in the adoption process.

In the second stage—**information (interest)**—a person develops more interest in the new idea. As a consequence, the person seeks more information about the innovation and considers its general merits. Dealers and salesmen replace the mass media in the second stage as the prime source of information.

During the **evaluation** stage, individuals make a mental application of the innovation to their present and future situation. Again they seek more

AWARENESS	INFORMATION	EVALUATION	TRIAL	ADOPTION
Learns about a new idea or practice	Gets more information about it	Tries it out mentally	Uses or tries a little	Accepts it for full-scale and continued use
1. Mass media— radio, T.V., newspapers, magazines	1. Dealers and salesmen	1. Dealers and salesmen	1. Dealers and salesmen	1. Friends and neighbors
2. Agricultural agencies, extension, vo-ag, etc.	2. Mass media	2. Friends and neighbors	2. Friends and neighbors	2. Dealers and salesmen
3. Friends and neighbors— mostly other farmers	3. Agricultural agencies	3. Agricultural agencies	3. Agricultural agencies	3. Agricultural agencies
4. Dealers and salesmen	4. Friends and neighbors	4. Mass media	4. Mass media	4. Mass media

FIG. 2.3.   Although mass media sources are most important at the awareness stage of the adoption process, friends, neighbors, and local dealers become more important at the evaluation and trial stages, as is shown here for the adoption of an agricultural innovation. Publicists must realize that it's important to coordinate the sending of messages to those sources most beneficial at each stage of the adoption process. (*Courtesy of Cooperative Extension Service, Michigan State University*)

information and decide either to try the innovation or not to try it. Dealers and salesmen play the dominant role of information providers in this stage, and the mass media are relegated to the place of least importance.

As part of the **trial** stage, a person actually applies the idea or practice, quite often on a small scale. Depending on what is at stake, the person is interested in the applicability and compatibility of the innovation. Once again, dealers and salesmen are the prime providers of information.

In the final stage—**adoption**—if the new idea or practice proves acceptable, a person adopts and decides to continue full use of the innovation. Personal experience is the most important factor in the continued use of an idea. The adopters are satisfied that the course of action being pursued is best for them.

Adoption of a new idea or practice does not occur all at once. The same research cited above has divided adopters into five categories, based on the amount of time it takes them to adopt a new idea or practice. Figure 2.4 shows the five adopter types based on the time of adoption. To illustrate how long it takes for a majority of individuals to become aware of and subsequently adopt a new practice, Figure 2.5 shows how long it took three American educational innovations to achieve universal adoption.

FIG. 2.4.   There are two major reasons some individuals are more innovative than others: (1) they become aware of the innovation earlier because
they are tuned in to the communication networks that promote the innovation, and (2) they require less time to make a decision. (*Courtesy of Cooperative Extension Service, Michigan State University and Iowa State University*)

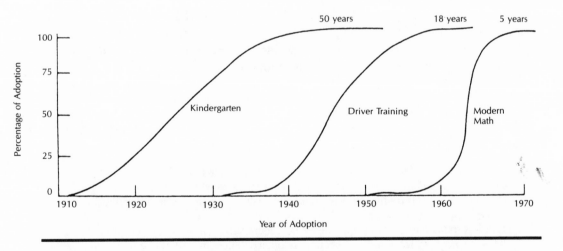

FIG. 2.5.   It took 50 years to obtain universal adoption of kindergartens in
the United States. Driver education started in the 1930s and took about 18
years to diffuse. But modern math was adopted by nearly all school systems during a period of only 5 years. Contributing to the quick adoption of
modern math were the ability of Americans to accept change as a positive
cultural value and Russia's launching of *Sputnik,* which forced America to
retrain its teachers. (*From Rogers and Shoemaker,* Communication of Innovations)

This brief discussion of the adoption and diffusion process makes it clear to any public relations practitioner, as well as any publicist, that communicating a new idea or practice is a long, tedious task. Different media are effective at different points and in different ways. The influence of the innovator or influential leader is great in every community. Communicators need to know what media and techniques to bring to bear in a given situation. Proceeding in an organized fashion, such as is suggested in this chapter, can make the end result much more effective.

Summary

There are four basic models of public relations—press agent/publicity, public-information, two-way asymmetric, and two-way symmetric. While all four models are in use today, only the two-way symmetric model suggests strong interaction between an organization and its publics.

Publicity is one part of the communication phase of the four-step public relations process. Professional public relations requires high standards of ethical behavior and consistent efforts to maintain a flow of communication, to adjust messages according to receiver feedback, and to keep in touch with institutional publics.

Communicating a new idea or practice is a process that evolves slowly over a long period of time. The public relations practitioner whose task is to accomplish public acceptance of a new idea or practice should consider dispensing that information through the adoption and diffusion process.

Exercises

1. Why is it imperative that a public relations practitioner have a role in the decision-making function of an organization? What happens when a practitioner's role is confined to performing the basic publicity tasks of producing and distributing news releases?
2. In a few explanatory paragraphs describe a local situation or problem that could be solved, or at least aided, through publicity. Then list all the internal and external publics that are in any way related to the problem or situation under discussion.
3. From your list in Exercise 2, identify the **key** publics to which you would direct your publicity and label them **latent, aware,** or **active.** Explain what needs to be done to move the latent and aware publics into the active category.
4. Cut out five publicity news releases from your local paper that have a feedback mechanism built into them. Describe what that feedback element is, and discuss its effectiveness.

Suggested Reading

Backstrom, Charles H., and Hursh, Gerald D. *Survey Research.* 2d ed. New York: John Wiley, 1981.

Berlo, David K. *The Process of Communication: An Introduction to Theory and Practice.* New York: Holt, Rinehart and Winston, 1960.

Grunig, James E., and Hunt, Todd. *Managing Public Relations.* New York: Holt, Rinehart and Winston, 1984.

Marston, John. *Modern Public Relations.* New York: McGraw-Hill, 1979.

Rogers, Everett. *Diffusion of Innovations.* 3d ed. New York: The Free Press, 1983.

3 *Using the Media to Bring About Change*

J. K. HVISTENDAHL

VIRTUALLY all college graduates, whether they recognize it or not, will find themselves in occupations in which one of their primary functions will be to bring about change – change in attitudes, beliefs, or behaviors. Home economists want to change health and nutrition habits, foresters want to get environmental messages across, teachers want their students to learn to write and spell, ministers want the members of their congregations to believe, and social workers want their wards to function more successfully in society by changing behaviors.

Change is often accomplished on a one-to-one or interpersonal basis. But the change referred to here is change encouraged by the mass media. In an ideal world perhaps all change would be brought about by interpersonal means – Johns Hopkins on one end of the log and a student on the other. Unfortunately, in mass society the number of personal contacts a professional person can make are limited by time and space. The mass media – television, radio, newspapers, magazines, and books – then become the most efficient delivery systems for messages designed to bring about personal and societal changes.

The Exaggerated Power of the Word

A commonly held belief is that the written word is a devilishly effective instrument of persuasion, a belief held especially by those who disagree with the persuasive message. A midwestern college professor once wrote to a congressman to protest a bill that would have shut off the flow of international mail, presumably to stop communist propaganda from entering the United States. The congressman indignantly replied, "You must certainly know . . . that anyone who is interested in getting this trash and tripe and filth and anti-American propaganda can receive it, but how can you ask that it be sent to high school kids and college students to be laid around on the desks of homes and campus dormitories polluting the minds of young Americans and propagandizing them into the belief that godless Communism is a good thing for the world?"

The congressman, like many others, imputes a potency to the printed word that teachers, ministers, foresters, and county extension directors could only hope for in their wildest dreams. If a few propaganda leaflets in a few moments could, as the congressman suggests, change students' lifetime beliefs, the job of those who are charged with bringing about change would indeed be simple.

Actually, bringing about change through the spoken or printed word is a long and complicated process. Nevertheless, the persuasion function does operate effectively in a democratic society. The free flow of information is vital to the change process; in the communist system the flow of persuasive information is limited to the government and to agencies approved by the government. The result is a system firmly rooted in the status quo with an economy that is barely able to feed and house the people. (It is ironic that the congressman was recommending government control of information, a facet of communism, in the name of anticommunism.)

The idea of a free flow of information, including persuasive messages, is founded in the First Amendment to the Constitution. The persuasive function is an honorable one, and those who employ persuasion in their work need make no apologies. Most Americans now accept the idea of a well-balanced diet; such words as "protein," "calorie," and "vitamin" have become household words. Americans are gradually beginning to believe in an environment free from pollution. And belief is the first step in the acceptance or adoption of a new practice. Even those who smoke cigarettes generally agree that the practice is a danger to their personal health. This level of acceptance was brought about through decades of education, supported and reinforced by countless newspaper and magazine articles, radio and television reports, and extension bulletins. In effect, there are two educational systems in a democracy: the formal system, of which virtually all Americans are a part, and the informal system through the print and broadcast media.

Persuasion Defined

Dr. Irwin Bettinghaus, a psychologist who has done much research in persuasion, defines **persuasion** as **"a conscious attempt by one individual to change the attitudes, beliefs, and behavior of another individual or group of individuals through the transmission of some message."**

That definition encompasses the work of the teacher, the preacher, the social worker, the extension worker, and virtually anyone who deals with people. All are engaged in a similar process—attempting to bring about change through the transmission of messages, oral or written. This definition also includes the propagandist. For this reason, the word "propaganda" is often applied to any persuasive message with which the recipient disagrees. By common usage, the word has come to have negative connotations. The word had honorable beginnings when in 1622 Pope Urban VIII launched a campaign to "propagate" the Christian faith in Europe. In that sense, the Pope was the first propagandist. But for all practical purposes the word has little meaning in modern persuasion research.

The modern view of persuasion is essentially this: Persuasive communication is a complicated process. Immediate success almost never occurs, and success of any kind is difficult to measure. Yet, in the long run, persuasion does take place, new ideas are accepted, and attitudes and opinions do change.

Aids and Barriers

Given that successful persuasive communication is hard to achieve, it is useful to look at some of the barriers between communicators and their audiences as well as some of the conditions under which success might be expected.

READERS ARE SUBJECT TO SELECTIVE EXPOSURE

Readership studies indicate that people tend to read articles with which they agree and to expose themselves only briefly or not at all to articles with which they disagree. Newspapers, although they may favor a particular political party in their editorials, frequently carry syndicated columnists of quite different political perspectives – columns by liberal Mary McGrory and conservative James J. Kilpatrick will often be found next to each other. Studies have shown that readers will read columns by the writer with whom they agree, ignoring the columnist who consistently presents viewpoints contrary to theirs.

Further, people who are deliberately subjected to material with which they disagree conveniently forget what they have read or distort the material so that it supports, rather than refutes, their views. The famous "Mr. Bigot" studies showed that racially bigoted people, in order to support their own biased views, consistently twisted the meaning of cartoons that showed the ironies of racial discrimination.

INFORMATION CAN STRENGTHEN ATTITUDES

Information is perhaps most effective when it supports or strengthens attitudes that already exist. In psychologists' language, information can have a **reinforcement** function. A manufacturing plant's public relations person who wants to build morale through the use of publications may have good success if the workers conceive that their relationship to management is at least fairly good. If, however, the workers conceive of their relationship to management as bad, information of any kind can be expected to have little effect until the underlying conditions of dissatisfaction are removed. A good information program could be expected to be useful in communicating to workers while the underlying conditions are being improved, of course.

INFORMATION IS EFFECTIVE IN ESTABLISHING NEW ATTITUDES

Information is perhaps most effective when attitudes about new subjects are first being formed. For this reason, modern publicists release unpleasant news immediately, rather than waiting until the information, liberally inflated with inaccuracies, has made its way through the grapevine and already established the attitudes and opinions of the employees or the general public.

For example, a company that must move one of its plant operations, perhaps laying off employees or requiring them to move to another city, releases the information as soon as the executive decision is made. By doing so, it can present the favorable, as well as the unfavorable aspects of the case. In short, the company can have at least a fair chance at shaping employees' attitudes, which otherwise surely would be formed in barbershops, beauty shops, bars, and cafes. For the same reason the management of the modern corporation has established employee orientation programs to reach the employee first with accurate information about company policies, benefits, and opportunities.

The emphasis on youth in such agricultural programs as 4-H, Future Farmers, and vocational agriculture is no accident. For youth, with their attitudes less firmly fixed than those of their parents, are more receptive to new ways of doing things. Many farmers in the 1920s and 1930s became interested in improved breeds of livestock only after their sons or daughters had started a 4-H calf project. The time and effort spent in informing youth is well spent, for when it comes to establishing new attitudes, the child frequently is indeed the father of the man.

INFORMATION CAN CHANGE LIGHTLY HELD ATTITUDES

New information, not surprisingly, can be expected to have a greater effect when attitudes are lightly held. Some hunters, for example, may have only slightly favorable attitudes toward the bounty system. They may think it's a pretty good idea. Authoritative information, perhaps originating from a state game biologist, may neutralize their lightly held attitudes. Further information from a source whom the hunters respect—perhaps a game warden speaking before a sports club—may convince some that the thousands of dollars spent in bounties might be used more profitably to provide habitat for game. Virtually the same process, of course, could be expected if the hunters were neutral about bounties.

The social psychologist describes attitudes that are lightly held as being **unstructured;** attitudes that are strongly held are described as being **structured.**

INFORMATION ALONE IS NOT LIKELY
TO CHANGE STRONGLY HELD OPINIONS

American propaganda aimed at the Russian masses could be expected to have little or no effect because of mistrust of the source. Similarly, Russian propaganda aimed at the American masses would probably be largely futile. However, a dissident or dissatisfied Russian might be influenced by the Voice of America; likewise, citizens of neutral countries or citizens of Russian satellite countries who are not happy with their lot would be likely targets for persuasion.

Political and social scientists Bernard Berelson, Paul Lazarsfeld, and

William McPhee made a classic study of how voters in Elmira, New York, made up their minds in an election campaign. They found that very few voters switched parties or candidates because of anything they had read or heard through the mass media. The effect of the media was much more likely to reinforce previously held opinions.

Similarly, the celebrated American soldier studies during World War II showed that American GIs would not change their negative attitudes about the fighting ability of the British even after they had seen the well-documented film *The Battle of Britain.* Tests showed that the soldiers had absorbed the knowledge, but their attitudes had remained exactly the same.

EMOTIONALLY FIXED ATTITUDES ARE DIFFICULT TO CHANGE

Attitudes that are closely associated with the emotions—fear, love, patriotism, hate, pity, and so forth—are difficult to change. No amount of reasoning or objective information can change the attitude of a small child who fears the dark, because of the overpowering effect of the emotion. Politicians have a way of using terms such as "American way," "freedom fighters," and "right-winger" to evoke emotion deliberately, to fix attitudes, or to promote favorable attitude change.

The addition of fluorides to drinking water to prevent tooth decay, for reasons psychologists do not fully understand, became largely an emotional issue. The preponderance of scientific evidence was on the side of fluoridation, but opponents launched an emotional (and often successful) campaign presumably based on the Constitution, the rights of the individual, Americanism, communism, religion, and implied dangers to unborn generations.

Philosophers of the seventeenth century such as John Locke and Thomas Hobbes were convinced that humans were rational creatures whose intelligence, if supplied with sufficient information, could come up with the right answers. Modern philosophers, especially the existentialists, believe that humankind is not nearly as rational as was once thought. And it doesn't take a philosopher to realize that many of the decisions made in life may be both emotional and rational, such as a person's decision to join a church, to go into debt to provide a needed operation for a child, or to build a farm for succeeding generations.

The communicator who sticks only to objective information with no appeal to emotions is likely to be only partly effective. Soil conservation and wildlife conservation are certainly related to a person's loyalty to country and fellow citizens; they are also related to the Judeo-Christian ethic of stewardship. The forester who preserves a forest of giant sequoias or a virgin stand of ponderosa pine is doing more than just exercising a technical skill.

Because emotional appeals often are based on false emotion or false feeling, many people with scientific training have rejected emotional appeals of any type as being unworthy or, indeed, as being unprofessional. Yet emotion can never be entirely separated from reason, and those who attempt to do so may be throwing the baby out with the bathwater. To deliberately play on the emotions of others to secure one's own ends is one thing, but to recognize that in virtually all areas of professional life there is a legitimate area of emotional appeal is quite another.

The argument of some members of the National Rifle Association that only criminals will own guns if handgun owners and handguns are licensed is demonstrably an emotional appeal. Both automobile owners and automobiles are licensed without discernible effect on the number of automobiles in the United States. There may be other reasons to oppose gun-control laws, but that isn't one of them.

On the other hand, an appeal for stewardship of the world's natural resources for the benefit of coming generations is an emotional appeal, but it is an acceptable one for those who believe in fairness and opportunity for all of humankind, present and future.

How Can the Publicist Persuade?

In view of the foregoing psychological obstacles to persuasion through the mass media, how *can* the media be used by the professional person to change attitudes or affect behavior? The mass media appear to be most effective in a reinforcement role but not very effective in conversion roles—changing Democrats to Republicans, for example, or union members to non-union members. Yet the reinforcement function is important and can be used to advantage by those who work with people.

Suppose a plant manager or public relations person wants to reduce the petty thievery of company property by instilling the attitude that "you just don't steal from the company you work for." Most Americans are *reasonably* honest (if they were not, no supermarket could stay in operation for long), but psychologists know that people are not *consistently* honest. Individuals who would not think of stealing a can of sardines from the supermarket or stealing the neighbor's garden hose may not believe they are stealing when they fill their pockets with nuts and bolts from the plant in which they work. Most Americans, even some of those behind bars, are honest most of the time and in general accept the ideal of honesty.

Because of that honesty, reinforcement of already existing attitudes against stealing—this time in the plant—can be made by applying established attitudes to new situations. One plant cut down petty thievery by a campaign in company publications that emphasized that "I don't steal from my parents, I don't steal from my neighbors, and I don't steal from the company which gives me my paycheck."

Farmers, like workers, have many existing attitudes that can be reinforced and channeled into new areas. Most farmers now believe in soil conservation at least to some extent, but the problem remains of making them believe in it strongly enough to change their behavior. This, too, is a job of reinforcement.

Persuasion can be effective in new situations when attitudes and beliefs are yet unstructured. When management is aware of this, it can use employee publications to "get there first" with accurate information on any changes of policy that affect workers in any way.

A midwestern packing plant once made an unannounced change in the brand name of one of its major products. The word got around the plant that sales had been dropping off because of "those babies who got poisoned in New York," forcing the company to rename the product. No babies had been poisoned in New York by the product of that, or any other, packing company. The company officials decided that a public denial of such a ridiculous rumor would only give the rumor more circulation. The public relations director printed a short, accurate story of the label change in the company publication. The belated article helped stop the rumor, no doubt, but even today some workers insist that the brand name was changed because of "those babies who got poisoned in New York." Information given to employees at the outset on even such a seemingly unimportant change as this one could have saved an unpleasant public relations problem.

Some Other Persuasion Hypotheses

The study of persuasion is still in its infancy. However, a number of hypotheses—or tentative statements—have been substantiated in research studies by psychologists Hovland, Janis, and Kelley. Readers should be warned, however, that these hypotheses cannot be accepted as being absolute or as being effective under all conditions. (The word "audience" is used in the broad sense, including audiences of both written and oral communication.)

1. **There will be more opinion change in the desired direction if conclusions are explicitly stated than if members of the audience draw their own conclusions.**

A commonly held theory is that if people are given the facts, they will make up their own minds because no one can tell them what to think. The weakness in this theory is that even intelligent audiences frequently fail to see the implications of the facts unless these implications are pointed out.

2. A mild threat may be more effective than a strong threat in influencing opinions.

Janis found that a strong fear appeal was less effective than a mild appeal in getting teenagers to practice good dental hygiene. Similarly, any-one who read the newspapers in the late 1950s was aware of the complete failure of the government program to persuade Americans to build bomb shelters. The response of most people was, "If the A-bombs are that bad, a little shelter isn't going to do any good" or "If things are going to be that bad, I don't want to survive."

3. Effects of persuasive messages tend to wear off after a lapse of time.

Even when persuasion is effective, the effect may not be permanent. Therefore, repeating the same information in different forms may be neces-sary to maintain attitude changes (parents and teachers know all about this). A county extension director cannot assume that the job is done after one or two articles on weed control appear in a newspaper column; plant manage-ment cannot assume that all workers know, understand, and accept a new policy after one or two announcements over the plant's speaker system. Reinforcement takes place when messages are repeated, preferably in a new form with different media.

4. The audience members most in need of the message are least likely to be there.

It is no secret that the parents who show up at the PTA meeting are likely to be those whose children are having little difficulty at school. Like-wise, the farmers who show up at an agronomy field day are likely to be those who are already the most progressive in the community. To reach the rest of the community, therefore, a publicist has to use all of the mass media—newspapers, radio, and television. A lazy or busy farmer might not attend a field day but might read about it in the local newspaper and most certainly would listen to a summary of the program on a favorite early-morning farm radio program.

5. A source who is trusted and can be believed (a high-credi-bility source) will have more effect than a source who cannot be trusted or believed (a low-credibility source).

Individuals know by experience that one source of information is often more reliable than another—the local minister versus the town gossip, for example. Thus, management personnel have a great stake in maintaining credibility with those with whom they communicate. If company management is caught in a lie—or even if the employees only *think* it is a lie—communication from that point forward will usually be less effective. Thus, it behooves everyone in public service and every person in management to act with absolute honesty, even though it might seem more expedient at the moment to cover up an unpleasant event with deception.

Examples of management's building credibility in the eyes of workers are many. W. A. Patterson, head of United Airlines, deliberately solicited employees' questions on hot issues in a personal column in the *Shield,* a company publication. Employees asked him if it was true that United Airlines had supplied presidential candidate Richard Nixon with free transportation. (It wasn't.) In a similar column General Electric employees asked what the salary of the company president was and whether he thought it was too large. (He told them what his salary was and that he didn't think it was too high.) The employees of both companies learned that the company treats them candidly and openly. Thus, when management communicates with employees, it is likely to find an audience that is receptive to the company's viewpoint rather than skeptical or openly opposed to any proposal from management, regardless of its merit.

6. An argument that has two sides is more effective if both sides are given and then reasons for accepting one side are presented.

This is the so-called inoculation effect. A one-sided argument is likely to arouse the intended audience to mentally structure the other side, which may then prevail. If communicators bring up the negative points along with the positive, they in effect inoculate the audience against countersuggestions.

For example, if an extension director is attempting to convince farmers that they should adopt a new crop (diversify), the director should present the difficulties as well as the advantages of the new crop. That approach is not only more honest but also more likely to be persuasive. Similarly, an office manager who is about to make a change in routine should be careful to point out the potential difficulties in the change as well as the advantages, thus inoculating the workers against all the reasons why the change won't work.

7. Group membership can heighten the effectiveness of a message.

Politicians have long recognized the importance of endorsements from groups organized along lines of special interests. Such **interest groups** are formed specifically to persuade the public and politicians to support a cause or causes. Students for a Democratic Society, the American Civil Liberties Union, the National Rifle Association, and many farm groups were formed for that purpose.

People who are strongly associated with a group are likely to accept and support the positions taken by the group. After all, they joined the group in the first place because they had similar interests. Therefore people who are attempting to promote a new practice in agriculture, health, environment, recreation, or any other field should not overlook any opportunity to appear before farm groups, service clubs, and other organizations to deliver their message.

Formal endorsements from a group may also be persuasive to people who ordinarily support the group's program even though they may not be members of the group. Social psychologists call such people **reference groups.**

8. Opinion leaders are a factor in persuasion.

Opinion leaders are very much like the early adopters in the adoption and diffusion process, discussed in Chapter 2. A different set of opinion leaders will be found in each area of interest—education, agriculture, business, health, and so forth. If a person's career involves working with groups of this kind, it is wise to identify the opinion leaders and take advantage of their singular ability to influence others. Influentials are almost always heavy consumers of information, which they often discuss at their places of employment or in their social circles. This process is often described as the two-step flow of communication—from the communicator to the influential and then to ultimate receiver.

Summary

It is safe to say people do not change easily. It is perhaps well they don't. If they changed as easily as the congressman believed, they would be subject to every influence from the media. But people do change as conditions change. The role of the professional person is to bring about changes that encourage people to adapt to new conditions and new situations. The role of persuasion, used for these purposes, is an honorable one, and the use of the mass media is almost the only way to reach the masses.

Exercises

1. Based on the information provided in this chapter, write a short paper outlining the psychological appeals you would *use* (and the reasons for your choices) for each of the following:
   a. Conducting a "Stop Smoking" campaign.
   b. Conducting a "Get Out the Vote" campaign.
   c. Conducting a campaign to reduce vandalism in state parks.
   d. Conducting a campaign to get people to reduce the amount of saturated fats in their diet.
2. Based on the information provided in this chapter, write a short paper outlining the psychological appeals you would *avoid* for each of the campaigns listed above. Be sure to substantiate the reasons for your choices.

Suggested Reading

Gordon, George N. *Persuasion: The Theory and Practice of Manipulative Communication.* New York: Hastings House, 1971.

Hovland, Carl I.; Janis, Irving; and Kelley, Harold. *Communication and Persuasion.* New Haven, Conn.: Yale University Press, 1953.

Rogers, Everett M. *Diffusion of Innovations.* 3d ed. New York: The Free Press, 1983.

Information-Gathering Techniques

JANE WILLOUGHBY PETERSON

OLID PUBLICITY begins with facts. Successful publicists recognize the importance of knowing their organization and their subject. Whether a publicist is responsible for promoting a service, an organization, an institution, or an idea, that person must be the expert.

Chapter 2 discusses the importance of taking inventory of an organization—manpower deployment, physical assets, past and present performance, and so on. Complete and informative fact-finding as it affects the organization and its publics is the first step in becoming the expert. Once that picture is clear, the publicist is ready to proceed with individual publicity efforts.

The publicist must learn as much as possible about the subject of the publicity and the source of the publicity. Information should also be gathered from other campaigns conducted for or related to the present publicity efforts.

In many ways, a publicist is a salesperson and representative for a product, service, or organization. When people want information, the publicist must be able to provide it. For example, if the goal is to promote the use of foods preserved by irradiation, the publicist first must know about the products and the process. Indeed, some people will be frightened at the prospect of consuming or serving foods that have been treated by radiation. If the publicist doesn't know enough about the process of irradiating foods, the levels of radiation used, and the safeguards of the procedure, the publicity campaign to promote the use of irradiated foods not only would fail to achieve its goals but also would most likely be damaged, all because of the publicist's lack of preparation.

Becoming the Expert

Background information is available from a number of sources—books, periodicals, newspapers, even personal contacts. With such a variety of sources, the publicist should remember that **backgrounding includes searching print and electronically recorded sources and direct interviewing.** The type of information needed for backgrounding also varies from statistics to personal biographies, from witnessing an event to gaining a basic understanding of an issue.

Whatever the publicist's product—fostering an acceptance of a new food-preservation process or promoting an organization, an institution, an idea, or an individual, just to name a few—the campaign's success will be directly related to the amount of time and effort put into learning about that product.

How does a publicist become an expert? Perhaps this can be explained best through an example. Suppose Rosemary Davies has been appointed a regional publicity director for Amnesty International, an organization concerned with the plight of political prisoners throughout the world. Davies and her publicity committee have planned a variety of messages and activities designed to create an awareness of the prisoners' circumstances.

One of the activities is a speech. The speaker will be Mary Ann Lundby, whom federal officials have named as an unindicted coconspirator for her involvement in the sanctuary movement. Lundby was named at the same time twelve sanctuary workers in Arizona were arrested for their activities in aiding people fleeing to the United States from Central and South America. Members of the sanctuary movement call these people refugees; federal officials call them illegal aliens. Thus, Lundby was called as a witness in the trial of the twelve workers, and she refused to testify.

Davies has invited Lundby to speak to Amnesty International members and guests about the sanctuary movement and her related experiences. To prepare the publicity for the event, Davies must learn more about both the speaker and the sanctuary movement.

One of a publicist's best friends in fact-finding is the reference librarian of a public or school library. The publicist should get to know that person and become familiar with what types of information can be found in the reference section. If there is a college or university library nearby, so much the better. But if not, most librarians will help obtain sources of information not on their shelves.

Reference sections contain printed and electronically recorded information ranging from general, government, and statistical information sources to newspaper, television, and current events sources (see Figure 4.1). At the library, Davies would first look in the general resource books, such as *Readers' Guide to Periodical Literature.* In the *Readers' Guide* she most likely would find listings of several articles on the sanctuary movement in general but very little about the speaker, Mary Ann Lundby.

A publicist learns to play detective when searching through reference books. With the help of a librarian, Davies can search through the titles to find specific articles about Lundby and others who were either arrested or called as witnesses in the government trial.

FIG. 4.1. The reference books shown here are just a few of the many resources available through which to gather information. Reference librarians are more than willing to help publicists become familiar with the resources most suited to their needs. (*Ross Fuglsang*)

GENERAL INFORMATION SOURCES

There are a number of general sources that provide ready reference to articles approaching a topic from a variety of angles—from historical and philosophical to social and economic. Some of these sources are listed below.

Readers' Guide to Periodical Literature. This index provides handy reference to authors and subjects of articles that have appeared in general-circulation magazines, such as *Time, Newsweek,* and *Better Homes and Gardens.*

Magazine Index. This helpful guide indexes popular magazine titles.

Business Periodical Index. Arranged alphabetically by subject, this index refers to articles that have appeared in general and specialized business publications.

Social Sciences Index. Basic journals in the social sciences of anthropology, economics, geography, law, public administration, political science, psychology, and sociology are listed in this index.

Humanities Index. Referenced in this index are basic journals in the humanities, including classics, history, literature, philosophy, religion, and the arts.

Public Affairs Information Service (PAIS) Bulletin. This useful index for political science, government, economics, and social legislation contains listings of books and government documents as well as periodicals.

Yearbooks and almanacs. These books include information such as government and industry statistics, lists of associations and societies, population figures, and chronologies of important events for the year.

BIOGRAPHICAL INFORMATION SOURCES

After exhausting the general sources, Davies would look for more information on the individuals involved in the sanctuary movement. She could do that by using biographical sources, such as the *Current Biography Index,* which contains information on individuals in the news. The following are some useful sources.

Who's Who in America. This source is a collection of information about people in America who have distinguished themselves in some way and are considered prominent.

Biography and Genealogy Master Index. This index lists biographies in more than 350 sources, including *Who's Who* volumes.

Biography Index. All types of biographical materials, such as pure biographies, critical materials, autobiographies, letters, and diaries published in books and periodicals, are contained in this guide.

Current Biography. More than 300 biographical sketches of newsmakers of various nationalities are referenced annually in this source.

STATISTICAL SOURCES

Now that Davies has general background information as well as information on individuals involved in the sanctuary movement, she can use statistical sources to get some idea of the magnitude of the movement. Statistical sources will help Davies find out how many people enter the United States legally and even estimates on how many enter illegally. The publicist who studies current and past statistics can better understand the trends of a topic. Some statistical sources are given below.

Statistical Abstract of the United States. This collection of statistics on every aspect of life in the United States also contains some foreign statistics. Some of the categories covered are population, agriculture, education, health, business, and science.

United Nations Statistical Yearbook. Basic statistics from countries around the world are listed in this source.

American Statistics Index (ASI). Statistical information in any subject area appearing in U.S. government publications can be found in this index.

Statistical Reference Index (SRI). This source contains an indexing of statistics from publications of private organizations and state governments.

GOVERNMENT INFORMATION SOURCES

Armed with general, biographical, and statistical information, Davies next would search through government sources to learn about the agencies and officials who work in identifying and processing immigrants. Information about the officials and agencies involved in the prosecution of illegal aliens and people who aid their entry into the United States also could be found. Some sources of this information are given here.

The United States Government Manual. This directory of the federal government includes descriptions of each agency and its officials. Also provided are the addresses and phone numbers of current federal officials.

Washington Information Directory. This directory of government agencies and officials lists the publications of each branch of the government.

Congressional Staff Directory. Published annually in this directory is a listing of all members of Congress and their staffs. Biographical information is given for many of the people listed.

State Official Register. Similar to the *United States Government Manual,* this source is state-specific.

Monthly Catalogue of U.S. Government Documents. This official register of federal publications includes indexes by subject and agency.

Congressional Information Service (CIS) Annual Index. This detailed index to congressional publications and public laws is an excellent source for government and legal information.

NEWSPAPERS, TELEVISION, AND CURRENT EVENTS SOURCES

There is still another information source that Davies could tap. To find out if and how the media in other cities have covered the sanctuary movement activities, she would look at newspaper and television reports. Libraries carry selected indexes to newspapers such as the *New York Times* and the *Wall Street Journal.* The information in such indexes varies from brief synopses to detailed references of articles appearing in the paper. A number of these indexes are listed below.

New York Times Index. This subject index gives brief synopses with exact references to the page, date, and column of the story.

Wall Street Journal/Barron's Index. Detailed references to articles appearing in the two major financial papers are provided in this source for stories on business, finance, and trends in society.

The Washington Post Index. This subject index is a major reference source for political and government stories.

Facts on File. In this reference, world news facts are indexed by subject and by people as they appeared in newspapers, magazines, broadcasts, and government reports.

CBS News Index. The subject and headline for transcripts of CBS network news broadcasts are provided in this index.

Television News Index and Abstracts. This subject index to the evening news broadcasts of CBS, NBC, and ABC leads to summaries of the transcripts, including commercials.

At this point, Davies has a great deal of background information on the sanctuary movement in the United States, but something is still missing. As the regional director for Amnesty International, Davies must be knowledgeable about any local activities that relate to the movement or to the refugee situation. The most efficient way to find that information is to check local media coverage of any such happenings. Some libraries provide indexing for newspapers in the area. Local articles not only provide more information on the topic but also supply names of individuals either involved or interested in the movement. Davies will want to interview those persons to obtain even more information.

Local involvement in an issue is a strong component in any publicity campaign. The publicist can capture audience interest in the more global issues if local activities and individuals are highlighted. (This is the news element **proximity,** which is discussed in Chapter 9.)

The background sources listed above are not exhaustive. But they should give the publicist an idea of the types and variety of sources available for finding information about the product. Publicists who are committed to the success of their campaigns recognize the importance of thorough backgrounding.

Interviews as a Source of Information

Once the publicist has exhausted all of the reference backgrounding possibilities and has a command of the subject, it is time to talk to the people involved. Direct interviewing of sources includes talking to people who are recognized as experts about the issue, as well as those people who are or have been involved in the issue.

INTERVIEWING DEFINED

Interviewing has been defined as conversation with a purpose. Using the sanctuary movement as an example, the purpose may be to find out more about the history of the movement, individual involvement in the movement, or future directions of the movement—but the point is, there is always a purpose. Therefore, the publicist must plan, organize, and prepare for the interview. Part of the planning and preparing is the work already done in backgrounding the topic, idea, or organization. Intelligent questions can be asked of the person (referred to as the **source**) only if the interviewer is knowledgeable about the subject.

KNOWING WHAT TO ASK

Preparing a list of questions is vital to accomplishing the interviewer's objective—soliciting interesting and important information. A prepared list increases the interviewer's self-confidence because he or she has a predetermined plan in mind. Off-the-cuff interviewing usually invites disaster. Taking advantage of an interviewer's lack of direction, some sources evade the issues they don't want to discuss or cut the interview short to resume their often busy schedules.

There is one danger in the prepared list, however. Interviewers must not be so bound to prearranged questions that they miss an opportunity to explore other avenues that come up unexpectedly. If a source introduces a point or topic that the interviewer senses might be pertinent, the list should be set aside temporarily and the new topic discussed.

A number of helpful books are available that discuss interviewing techniques, two of which are listed at the end of this chapter. At the risk of oversimplification, though, the normal procedure is to begin with the easier questions (often called the icebreakers) and work up to the more difficult ones. Generally speaking, the more comfortable the sources are with interviewers, the more cooperative they are in answering questions.

The publicist should keep several pointers in mind when organizing a list. Questions should be specific, not vague, for vague questions reap vague generalizations for answers. Questions should be short, not long, for a long question is often confusing and the source may forget to answer part of it.

Finally, questions should be open-ended, not closed, for open-ended questions encourage the source to explain, describe, or justify a point. Closed questions can be answered with a simple yes or no.

ARRANGING AND CONDUCTING THE INTERVIEW

The publicist rarely needs to conduct hurriedly arranged interviews. Therefore appointments can be set up well in advance of the actual meeting. When phoning to request an interview, a publicist should introduce himself or herself, identify the group or organization represented, and finally, explain the purpose of the interview and how the information will be used. As a matter of courtesy, publicists should estimate the amount of time needed for the interview so the source can plan accordingly.

The etiquette of conducting the interview is self-evident. Publicists make a point of dressing appropriately and arriving promptly. They are ever aware that the source is doing them a favor. They acknowledge this by thanking the source for taking time out of a busy day to be interviewed. They also are careful to conclude the interview within the allotted time.

Some interviewers use tape recorders; others do not. The decision is strictly personal. Generally speaking, though, if the topics discussed are complex or controversial, it is a good idea to have a tape recorder on hand. Most sources don't object to this anymore because they are as concerned about accuracy as the interviewers are. Recorders are relatively unobtrusive in size nowadays and therefore are not the inhibiting factor they once were.

There is one circumstance, though, in which the tape recorder usually is not used, and that is in a personality interview. In order to capture the true essence of a source's demeanor, most interviewers forgo the use of a recorder, which might cause the source to behave differently.

Even if a tape recorder is used, the publicist should take adequate notes because machines are not always reliable. Note-taking requires interviewers to hone their listening skills. It is important to know how to listen and write at the same time, not always an easy task. But the skill is invaluable, as the source may say something vitally important while the interviewer is writing. If the comment is missed, so too an important part of the story might be missed.

One other imperative skill publicists must develop is that of being observant. The effective writer helps the reader visualize the person as well as hear the specific words. Many times the surroundings are as important as the source and what is being discussed. The same is true of what the source is wearing or what gestures and facial expressions are made. Descriptive writing is one way to entice readers to continue with the story rather than abandon it in boredom.

When closing an interview, it is always a good idea for interviewers to ask three final questions:

1. The source should be asked if there is anything else he or she would like to add. This gives the source an opportunity to fill in any blanks the interviewer inadvertently left unfilled.
2. The source should be asked if there is any other person knowledgeable about the issue who might also consent to an interview. Sources will usually know of people who share the same interests and concerns and of others who disagree with them.
3. The source should be asked if he or she may be contacted later if there are further questions. This demonstrates personal interest in the subject, and it also keeps open the lines of communication.

Summary

Having done adequate backgrounding and comprehensive interviewing, the publicist is now armed with more than enough information about the people and issues from which publicity is generated. Other chapters detail the specifics of particular publicity techniques. But it is important to realize that the individual messages the audience sees or hears are only a small part of what the publicist has learned through thorough backgrounding efforts. When the publicist has become the expert, he or she is confident that the messages released are detailed and accurate. Additionally, the publicist-expert now is prepared to answer any questions that surface throughout the campaign.

Exercises

1. Select an organization, institution, or charity to represent as a publicist. Using the backgrounding techniques outlined in this chapter, go on a fact-finding mission in order to become an expert ready to represent the chosen product. When you have compiled the information, write a report that clearly explains what the product is all about. The report should include information from each of the source categories listed in the chapter.
2. Building on Exercise 1, identify an appropriate expert source to be interviewed on the background information gathered. Prepare a list of questions you would ask the source.
3. Identify sources of information on the local level (surveys and chambers of commerce, for example) for finding background information on organizations, institutions, and so on. Also, identify the type of information that could be found in each source.

Suggested Reading

Biagi, Shirley. *Interviews That Work*. Belmont, Calif.: Wadsworth Publishing Co., 1986.

Metzler, Ken. *Creative Interviewing*. Englewood Cliffs, N.J.: Prentice-Hall, 1975.

Rivers, William L. *Finding Facts*. Englewood Cliffs, N.J.: Prentice-Hall, 1975.

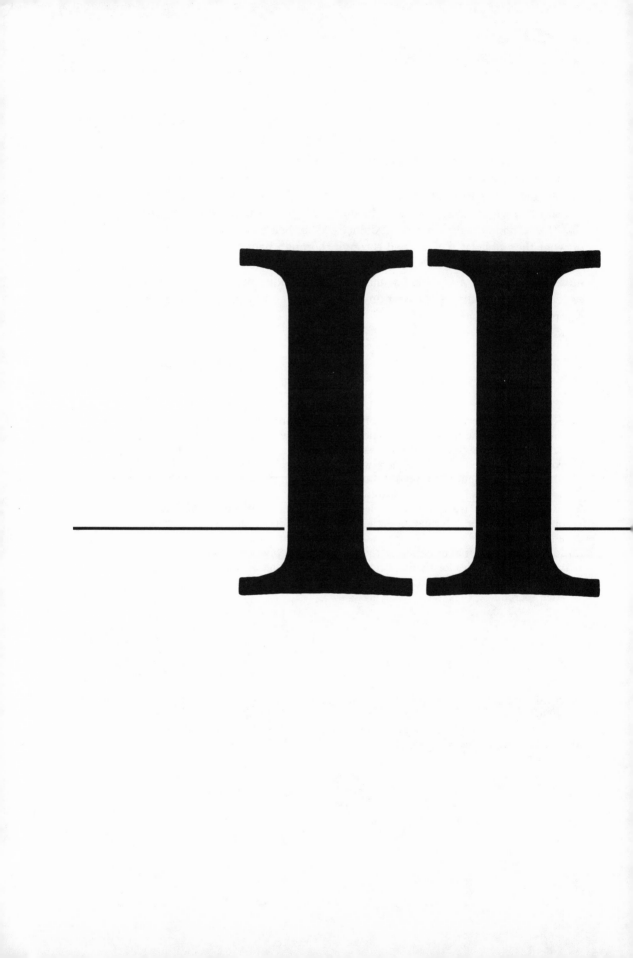

Selecting the Media Environments

BOTH publicists and consumers must understand how the various media operate, their strengths and limitations, their capabilities and their handicaps, so as to channel publicity messages effectively. The first three chapters in Part II discuss publicity options available in the mass media; the last chapter explores advertising alternatives in those media.

5 *Newspapers: The Medium That Provides Heavy Local Coverage*

WILLIAM F. KUNERTH

NEWSPAPERS are the backbone of most publicity campaigns. They maintain that position in the face of media research studies showing that the American public (1) spends more time attending to the electronic media—especially television—than to newspapers, (2) gets most of its news from television, and (3) places greater credibility on news offered by the broadcast media than that read in newspapers.[1]

Many newspaper partisans will argue with the accuracy of those findings, particularly points (2) and (3) as they relate to local news. But even if the research results are completely accurate, today's publicist still considers newspapers the basic vehicle for the transmission of messages.

1. The Roper Organization, *Trends in Attitudes Toward TV and Other Media: A 24-Year Review, 1959–1982* (a series of studies in conjunction with the Television Information Office).

Why Use Newspapers?

Of the numerous reasons for the newspaper's continued popularity, the most important probably are (1) **access,** (2) **content and capacity,** and (3) **coverage.**

ACCESS

The 1,705 daily newspapers in the United States have a combined circulation of about 63 million. The 7,700 weekly, semiweekly, and triweekly newspapers have a combined circulation of about 50 million. These general-content publications are meant to serve all readers in their circulation areas. In addition, several hundred specialized newspapers are aimed at ethnic, religious, political, and other target audiences. In numbers and geographic spread, newspapers are the most accessible of the media.

CONTENT AND CAPACITY

The newspaper is a favorite of publicists because it is the basic information medium and because it has a huge appetite for news. As was mentioned in Chapter 1, the bulk of the material that publicists feed into information channels is in the form of news called **news releases.** Newspapers concentrate more on informing and less on entertaining than do any of the other mass media, and they can accommodate much more information in their pages than can the competing media. For example, the stories covered in a typical network newscast will fit easily onto a newspaper's front page.

As a result, newspapers—even the metropolitans—find room for relatively minor items. Most papers try to find room for a brief story or at least a calendar item on the upcoming meeting of the camera club or the flower lovers' annual exhibit. An event need not be exceptionally newsworthy to merit bulletin-board treatment in a newspaper. (To obtain more prominent exposure, the publicist must be mindful of news values, writing techniques, and editors' individual requirements, all of which are discussed in Part III.)

COVERAGE

In general, newspapers are unequaled in their ability to cover specific markets. The typical hometown daily without competition is delivered to about 80 percent of the households in the city it serves. It is read daily by about two-thirds of the adults in the community. This appears to be the case, regardless of the editorial quality of the publication. It is a long-established habit for most families to subscribe to the local paper. Even a newspaper's sharpest critics are likely to consider it an essential ingredient in their lives. Anyone who has worked in the circulation department of a community newspaper is familiar with the enraged readers who in a pique cancel their subscriptions, only to renew them a week or two later. Some of the more stubborn or angered readers may hold out for a month. During this period, more often than not they are reading a copy of the paper at work or mooching one from a neighbor.

Although newspaper penetration varies from city to city, the medium does offer the highest degree of individual market saturation of any of the mass media. In competitive, metropolitan areas, where residents are served by more than one newspaper company, city coverage may be as low as 30 percent of the households. In monopoly-newspaper cities, it might be 80 percent or more. For example, Standard Rate and Data Service reported that in 1983 the *New York Daily News* reached 38 percent of the households within the city; the *Omaha World-Herald,* 71 percent; and the *Huron* (S.Dak.) *Plainsman,* 97 percent.

Although free papers, shoppers, and advertising papers have been around for 50 years, they have experienced their sharpest growth in the past decade. According to the National Association of Advertising Papers, about 4,000 of these publications—with a circulation of 70 million—are now being published. In recent years, many of them have been termed TMCs (total market circulation), for one of their two common characteristics. First, they offer saturation coverage (to every home) of their circulation areas. Second, they are distributed free. The content of these publications varies from 100 percent advertising to an advertising-news mix similar to that of a conventional newspaper. These papers have made deep inroads into the advertising revenues of paid-circulation daily and weekly newspapers. Many publishers of the latter have established their own shopper or TMC publications.

It is important that the publicist recognize the opportunities presented through these papers, many of which make widespread use of publicity releases. To use these papers effectively, the publicist must determine whether or not they carry news.

In dealing with paid-circulation newspapers, the publicist should find out if the publisher offers additional outlets such as specialized publications (farm supplements, for example), special editions (fashion, gardening, auto care, and so on), shoppers, or cable television. Many of today's newspaper publishers are moving into these areas, and each may offer publicists an outlet for their material.

Although about 98 percent of American homes are equipped with television and radio receivers, broadcast stations cannot claim the same kind of local-community coverage that a newspaper can, because of the competitive situation. The broadcast audience is highly fragmented in almost every market and is becoming more so with the spread of cable television and satellite delivery.

That is not the case with newspapers. In 1986, the American Newspaper Publishers Association reported that 1,534 U.S. cities had daily newspapers, 128 cities had more than one daily, and 48 cities had two or more dailies under separate ownership.

Most communities are served by one newspaper publishing company whose output may be a weekly, a single-edition (morning or evening) daily, or a morning-evening-Sunday combination. In recent years, there has been a loss of afternoon papers in several metropolitan communities and a switch from afternoon to morning papers in medium-sized markets. The decline of afternoon newspapers is attributed to the heavy viewership of television from 5 p.m. through the prime-time evening hours.

An exception to the one-newspaper towns exists in many suburban communities where intensive publisher competition to extend coverage in growing markets has resulted in a plethora of regional suburban newspapers. In the Chicago area, for example, residents of some of the northern and western suburbs may be served by three or four area papers.

Although proponents of widespread free expression have reason to be concerned about the monopolistic aspects of the newspaper industry in the United States, the situation does allow for efficient, near-saturation coverage of most communities and their environs through a relatively small number of publications. (See Chapter 17 for further discussion of media monopolies.)

OTHER ADVANTAGES

Other advantages of the newspaper as a publicity medium include the following:

1. **Its broad socioeconomic audience.** Newspaper readership cuts across most occupational and income groups, although it falls off sharply among people of very low economic status.

2. **Its varied fare.** In addition to straight "nuts and bolts" news, the newspaper contains a smorgasbord of information about business, agriculture, sports, family life, and social affairs. No matter what area of activity the publicist's firm or organization is engaged in, newspapers probably cover it.

3. **Its ability to handle complex, lengthy material.** Statistical reports, financial statements, and research studies can usually be presented more effectively by newspapers than by the electronic media. A reader who is concerned about grasping the details of a complex story can read it carefully the first time around and reread portions if necessary. The radio or TV story cannot be slowly perused or recaptured.

4. Its permanence and reproducibility. As with other print media, messages in newspapers can be saved and referred to repeatedly. They can also be easily copied and distributed to interested parties. Publicists often find it useful to order reprints of articles favorable to their interests.

DISADVANTAGES

1. Hasty and selective reading by some readers. According to the Newspaper Advertising Bureau, about two-thirds of newspaper readers say they page through entire issues, but many people are quick and selective in their reading of newspapers. A typical pattern is to scan the front page, take a thorough look at sports or social news, and then read favorite comics.

2. Mediocre reproduction. For economic reasons, newspapers are printed on low-quality paper and on high-speed presses that use fast-drying inks. Naturally, the quality of reproduction suffers, especially when compared with that of magazines. The problem is most acute in reproducing full-color photographs, especially of food. Most people can recall seeing pictures of green cheese and blue meat in newspaper photo spreads.

3. Lack of appeal to youth. Although they do offer a varied fare, studies reveal that readership is relatively low among youth. The very young tend to become addicted to television, and most teenagers appear partial to radio.

4. Lack of a broad-coverage national newspaper. Although most newspapers provide heavy coverage of their own markets, no single newspaper dominates the national market. There are no strong national newspapers in the United States comparable to those in many other countries, especially the densely populated European nations and the countries whose press is controlled by the government.

Only a handful of general-circulation newspapers have coast-to-coast distribution in the United States—*USA Today,* the *Wall Street Journal,* the *Christian Science Monitor,* and the *New York Times.* Their circulations, ranging from 140,000 to 2 million, are spread thinly across the country relative to competitive national media such as network television and mass-circulation magazines. Audiences of prime-time television shows reach upwards of 15 million homes, and the circulation of *Reader's Digest* is more than 17 million.

If publicists must reach impressive audiences throughout the entire country over broad regions, and if the message is to be spread through newspapers, the publicists must deal with a large number of units.

5. Short life of daily newspapers. Although weekly newspapers tend to be kept around the home until the next issue, daily papers usually go into the next day's trash.

Working with Newspaper Editors and Reporters

In working with newspapers, the publicist may supply material to publications of vastly different sizes, from the *Ree Heights* (S.Dak.) *Review* (circulation of 274) to the *New York Daily News* (Sunday circulation of 1.8 million).

The news operation of many of the ma-and-pa weeklies is often taken care of by one person—the editor. This individual may also carry the title of publisher and may be the advertising salesperson, printer, circulation manager, bookkeeper, and janitor as well. The publicist can be sure that a release will reach the proper person on a small weekly (circulation of 2,000 or less).

At large weeklies (circulation of 3,000 to 5,000) and small dailies (circulation of 5,000 to 20,000) the person in charge of the news operation may be called the editor, the managing editor, or the news editor. It is best to send releases to the managing editor. Often the editor is in charge of the editorial page, and the news editor may handle national news only. Medium-sized and large dailies (circulation of 25,000 and up) usually have a raft of specialized or departmental editors and reporters in addition to the sports and family section staffs, which are usually found even on small papers.

Although publicists should not pester editors, most editors welcome an initial visit from the publicist during which the news policies of the paper, the format preferred for news releases, the use of pictures, and other business details are discussed. Also, the publicist can probably find out from the editor under what circumstances the paper might send its own reporter and photographer to cover events. This initial visit should be set up by phoning for an appointment. Editors are busy people, and a surprise visit might not be appreciated.

If possible, the publicist should attempt to establish a long-term professional friendship with local editors. Although a few editors discourage this and should not be pressed, most enjoy talking shop with another professional. But such relationships will not substitute for well-written, newsworthy releases.

Compiling a Media List

Some publicists send most of their material to the same basic list of newspapers. Others vary the list according to the nature of the information contained in the release. A publicist may be concerned about covering a specific geographic area or reaching individuals with a special interest. On occasion, a publicist may send a news release to only one newspaper.

Compiling a list of newspapers that might use a publicist's material is relatively easy because of the comprehensive media directories available. The most useful is probably *Editor and Publisher Yearbook*. It contains the most complete directory of daily newspapers available. Basic data include a list of staff members as well as population, circulation, and trade area statistics (see Figure 5.1). Of particular interest to the publicist is information about special editions and specialized writers and editors. Therefore, if a press release relates to farming, food, education, or any other specific area, a publicist may be able to send it to the newsperson responsible for that coverage.

Editor and Publisher Yearbook also carries an abbreviated listing of weekly newspapers, foreign dailies, and black, college, and special-interest newspapers. The latter category includes papers that concentrate on entertainment, labor, real estate, sports, and many other topics (see Figure 5.2). Another section of the same directory that may be of interest to publicists lists journalistic organizations. Included are associations of writers who specialize in agriculture, food, sports, the outdoors, and numerous other subjects (see Figure 5.3). It is important to establish contacts with professional groups whose members are providing news coverage of the publicists' areas of interest. State newspaper associations publish directories of daily and weekly newspapers. A complete listing of these associations is also found in this directory.

Another helpful general reference is the *Gale Directory of Publications,*[2] which contains a thorough rundown of most print media—newspapers, magazines, professional journals, and specialized publications. *Gale* is cross-referenced by region, by frequency of publication, and by subject (farm, business, and sports, for example). Chapter 6 provides illustrations and more information on this reference book, as well as the addresses of various media directories.

Circulation Is Not the Only Criterion

One might assume that publicists are interested only in reaching the largest number of people possible. With that thought in mind, consider the newspaper statistics in Table 5.1. If publicists are intent on numbers only, they are unlikely to bother with the 7,700 nondaily newspapers that deliver an audience of only 50 million. With less than one-fourth as many publications (1,705), daily newspapers reach a larger audience—almost 63 million.

2. Formerly and popularly known as the *IMS/Ayer Directory of Publications,* this reference book changed its name to *Gale Directory of Publications* in 1987.

ALABAMA

ALEXANDER CITY
Tallapoosa County
'80 U.S. Census-13,807; E&P'86 Est.144,485

Alexander City Outlook
(m-tue to fri; S)

Alexander City Outlook, 139 Church St., Alexander City, AL 35010; tel (205) 234-4281; Boone Newspapers group.
Circulation: 4,086(m); 4,086(S); Sworn Sept. 30, 1985.
Price: 25¢(d); 25¢(S); $4 / mo.
Advertising: Open inch rate $5.35(m); $5.35(S). **Representative:** Landon Associates, Inc.
Politics: Independent. **Established:** 1892.
Not published: Christmas.
Special editions / sections: Chamber of Commerce (Jan); Parade (Feb); Spring Fashion (Mar); Bridal Edition (Apr); Wind Creek State Park, Graduation (May); Newcomers (June); Back-to-School, Football (Aug); Fall Fashion (Sept); Holiday Cookbook, Gift Guide (Nov).

CORPORATE OFFICERS
President	Lon Williams
Vice Pres	James B Boone, Jr

GENERAL MANAGEMENT
Publisher	Lon Williams

ADVERTISING
Manager	Billy McGhee

NEWS EXECUTIVES
Editor	Les Ernst

EDITORS AND MANAGERS
Business	Les Ernst
Editorial Page Editor	Lon Williams
Food / Religion / School	Dorothy Foshee
Sports	Pat Lewandowski
Women's / Travel	Dorothy Foshee

PRODUCTION
Manager	Paul Jackson

Market information: Total market coverage; SAU.
Mechanical available: Offset; black and 3 ROP colors; inserts accepted — preprinted, hi-fi, SpectaColor.
Mechanical specifications: Type page 13" x 21 1/2"; E - 6 cols, 2 1 /16", 1 /8" between; A - 6 cols, 2 1 /16", 1 /8" between; C - 6 cols, 2 1/16", 1 /8" between.
Commodity consumption (estimated): Newsprint 240 short tons; widths 27 1 /2", 13 3 /4"; single pages printed 3,040; single plates used 1,700.
Equipment: EDITORIAL: All-electronic cps — 1-COM / 12; 5 VDTs. CLASSIFIED: All-electronic cps — 1-COM / 12; 1 VDTs. DISPLAY: Layout — 1-COM / Dek Unisetter, 1-COM / 7200.
PRODUCTION: typesetters — 2-COM / Unisetter, 1-COM / 7200; plate exposers — N; direct to plate imaging — 3M / Pyrofax; cameras — Clydedale.
PRESSROOM: Line 1 — 4-KP. MAILROOM: Counter stackers — BG / Count-o-veyor 104A; bundle tyers — 1-Carlson. COMMUNICATIONS: facsimile — QWI / II. receiving dishes —AP.

ANDALUSIA
Covington County
'80 U.S. Census- 10,415; E&P '86 Est. 10,410

The Andalusia Star News
(m-tues to sat)

Andalusia Star News, 209 Dunson St., Andalusia, AL 36420-0403; tel (205) 222-2402, Boone Newspapers group.
Circulation: 3,982(m), Sworn Sept. 30, 1985.

Price: 25¢(d); $3 / mo, $36 / yr.
Advertising: Open inch rate $5.53(m).
News Services: AP, NEA. **Politics:** Independent. **Established:** 1939.

GENERAL MANAGEMENT
Publisher	Joel Starling

ADVERTISING
Manager	Henry Burt

NEWS EXECUTIVES
Editor	David Moore

PRODUCTION
Supervisor	Paul Jordan

Market information: Total market coverage; SAU.
Mechanical available: Offset; black and 3 ROP colors; inserts accepted — preprinted, hi-fi, SpectaColor.
Mechanical specifications: Type page 13" x 21 1/2"; E - 6 cols, 2 1 /16", 1 /8" between; A - 6 cols, 2 1 /16", 1 /8" between; C - 6 cols, 2 1/16", 1 /8" between.
Equipment: EDITORIAL: All-electronic cps — COM / MDT 350.
PRESSROOM: Line 1 — 4-G / Community. WIRE SERVICES: low speed — AP. BUSINESS COMPUTERS: RSK; applications: Bookkeeping, Circulation.

ANNISTON
Calhoun County
'80 U.S. Census- 29,523; E&P '86 Est. 28,435
ABC-CZ (80): 69,476 (HH 24,651)

The Anniston Star
(e-mon to fri; m-sat; S)

Consolidated Pub. Co., 216 W. 10th St., Anniston, AL 36201; tel (205) 236-1551.
Circulation: 30,891(e); 32,650(m-sat); 32,334(S); ABC Sept. 30, 1985.
Price: 25¢(d); 25¢(sat); 75¢(S); $7 / mo, $84 / yr.
Advertising: Open inch rate $11.15(e); $11.15(m-sat); $11.15(S). **Representative:** Branham / Newspaper Sales.
News Services: AP, NYT. **Established:** 1883.
Advertising not accepted: Alcoholic beverages; vending machine copy.
Special editions / sections: Vacation; Winston 500 Race; Financial; Football; Holiday Cookbook; Physical Fitness; Bride.
Supplements: USA Weekend(S).

CORPORATE OFFICERS
President	Phillip A Sanguinetti
Vice Pres	H Brandt Ayers
Secretary / Treasurer	Almus J Thornton
Consultant	Ralph W Callahan

GENERAL MANAGEMENT
Publisher	H Brandt Ayers
General Manager	P A Sanguinetti
Business Manager	John Childs
Credit Manager	Almus Thornton
Purchasing Agent	P A Sanguinetti
Marketing Director	John O'Mara

ADVERTISING
Director	John O'Mara
Manager-Retail	Hershel Victory
Manager-National	John O'Mara
Manager-Classified	Dean Youngblood

CIRCULATION
Director	Sam Ogle

NEWS EXECUTIVES
Editor	H Brandt Ayers
Exec Editor	Paul Rilling
Editor-in-Chief	Cody Hall

EDITORS AND MANAGERS
Action Line	Sue Vondracek
Amusements	Ellen Morrison
Books	Cody Hall
Columnist	George Smith
Editorial Page Editor	Chris Waddle
Editorial Writer	Paul Rilling
Food	Ellen Morrison
Metro Editor	Bill Cornwell
Radio / Television	Ellen Morrison
Sports	Charles Goldberg
Wire Editor	George Evans
Women's	Ellen Morrison

PRODUCTION
Superintendent	Albert Heard

Foreman-Composing	Jerry Thornton
Foreman-Pressroom	James Weaks
Foreman-Camera Room	Stewart Ridgeway

Market information: Split run; Total market coverage; SAU.
Mechanical available: Offset; black and 3 ROP colors; inserts accepted — preprinted, hi-fi, SpectaColor.
Mechanical specifications: Type page 13" x 21 1/2"; E - 6 cols, 2 1 /16", 1 /8" between; A - 6 cols, 2 1 /16", 1 /8" between; C - 8 cols, 1 1/2", 1 /8" between.
Commodity consumption (estimated): Newsprint 2,382 short tons; widths 27 1 /2", 13 3 /4"; black ink 48,015 pounds; color ink 4,223 pounds; single pages printed 11,671; single plates used 21,382.
Equipment: EDITORIAL: All-electronic cps — 1-Ik / 320; 25-Ik / 50 VDTs. CLASSIFIED: 4-Ik / 50 VDTs. DISPLAY: 2-Ik / 50 VDTs.
PRODUCTION: OCR readers — 1-EC / 5200 typesetters — 2-Ik / Mark VIII; plate exposers — 1-N / FT40LNS; plate processors — 1-Nat / A-340; cameras — 1-R / 480, 1-C / Spartan 2; automatic film processors — 1-LE / 2600; film transporters — 1-C; shrink lenses — 1-19"CK / 7 1 / 4%; color separation equipment(conventional) — 1-C / EZ Color.
PRESSROOM: Line 1 — 6-G(1 folder); reels / stands — 6-Cline. MAILROOM: stuffers — 2-M; bundle tyers — 1-SA. COMMUNICATIONS: facsimile — 3M / Telecopier, 5-RSK / 100, 2-Commodore / 64. satellite / microwave — Scientific Atlanta. WIRE SERVICES: high speed — AP; low speed — AP (66 wpm); receiving dishes —AP,NYT. BUSINESS COMPUTERS: IBM / 34; applications: Financial statements, Payroll, Accts receivable, Accts payable, Circ, billing; PCs & micros networked.

ATHENS
Limestone County
'80 U.S. Census- 14,558; E&P '86 Est. 14,811

Athens News Courier
(m-tues to fri; S)

Athens News Courier, 410 W. Green St.; PO Box 670, Athens, AL 35611; tel (205) 232-2720; Bryan Newspapers group.
Circulation: 7,941(m); 7,941(S); Sworn Sept. 30, 1985.
Price: 25¢(d); 50¢(S); $30.50 / yr (local); $40.50 / yr (elsewhere).
Advertising: Open inch rate $4.68(m); $4.68(S).
News Service: AP. **Politics:** Independent. **Established:** 1968.
Special editions / sections: Football; Spring Fashion; Cattlemen; Home Improvement; Graduation; Christmas.

CORPORATE OFFICERS
President	Robert Bryan
Secretary-Treasurer	Betty Bryan

GENERAL MANAGEMENT
Publisher	Robert Bryan
General Manager	W R Nelson
Office Manager	Pam Bryan

ADVERTISING
Director	W R Nelson
Director-Classified	Connie Tucker

CIRCULATION
Manager	Bill Murrell

NEWS EXECUTIVES
Editor	Craig Beasley

EDITORS AND MANAGERS
Editorial Page Editor	R C Bryan
Librarian	Patty Holland
News Editor	Sonny Turner
Photo Director	Liz Kimbrough
Political	Curtis Robinson
Sports	Neil Chittam
Women's	Edna Pendergrass

PRODUCTION
Supervisor	Ann Greene

Market information: Zoned editions; Total market coverage; SAU.
Mechanical available: Offset; black and 3 ROP colors; inserts accepted — preprinted, hi-fi, SpectaColor.

FIG. 5.1. This section of *Editor and Publisher Yearbook* lists newspapers by the city in which they are published and also includes a listing of their editors and specialized writers (farm, sports, and business, for example). It contains circulation information and identifies the special sections regularly produced by each newspaper.

AGRICULTURE

NJ (Toms River 08754-0389) PO Box 389; (201) 240-5330.
URNER BARRY'S PRICE-CURRENT (mon to fri); Agricultural market news; Est.1858
Circ.2,000; $272/yr.; Adv.$17.00 p.c.i.
President — Paul B. Brown
Vice Pres — Bud O'Shaughnessy
Secretary — Rick Brown
Treasurer — Paul B. Brown, Jr.
General Manager — Paul B. Brown, Jr.
Director — Michael O'Shaughnessy

APPAREL, CLOTHING, AND TEXTILES

NY (New York 10003) 7 E. 12th St.; (212) 741-4340.
WOMEN'S WEAR DAILY (mon to fri); Est.1910
Circ.63,018; ABC Sept. 30, 1986; $1/copy; $69/yr; Adv.$149 p.c.i.
Prop — Fairchild Publications
Board Chairman/Publisher — John B. Fairchild
Sr. Vice Pres/Editor/Group Pub — Michael Coady
Group Vice Pres/Exec Editor/Assoc Pub — Patrick McCarthy
Vice Pres/Adv Director — Olivia Thompson

BUILDING, CONSTRUCTION, AND ENGINEERING

CA (Los Angeles 90013) 448 S. Hill St.; (213) 623-1477.
DAILY CONSTRUCTION SERVICE (mon to fri)
Circ.955; Sworn Dec. 31, 1985; $60/mo; $165/3 mo; $450/yr; Adv.$5.25 to $2.75 per inch
Publisher/General Manager — William Wallace
Managing Editor — Otis Tyson

CA (Monterey Park 91754) 2 Coral Circle; (213) 727-0120.
DODGE CONSTRUCTION NEWS (mon to fri); Construction; Est.1865
Circ.4,100; Sworn Dec. 31, 1986; $8/copy; $1,045/yr; Adv.$21.45 p.c.i. (display); $3.75/line (class., min. 10 lines)
Publisher — F.W. Dodge/Div. McGraw-Hill
Adv Manager — Donald Gale
News Manager — Gordon Watkins
Editor (Engineering) — Don Gale, Sr.

CA (San Francisco 94110) 2450-17th St.; (415) 864-8600.
DAILY PACIFIC BUILDER (mon to fri); Construction; Est.1890
Circ.5,497 (special ed., 18x/yr-15,000); Pub. Sworn Statement July 1, 1986; $10/copy; $387/qtr; $666/6 mo; $1092/yr; Adv.$19.75 p.c.i.
Publisher — F.W. Dodge Co./Div. McGraw-Hill
Publisher/Editor — David A. McDonald

CO (Denver 80206) 101 University Blvd., Suite 260; (303) 393-8100.
DAILY JOURNAL (mon to fri); Construction, Legal, General business; Est.1897
Circ.3,760; $10/copy; Adv.Display-$19.25 p.c.i.; Classified-$25.65 p.c.i.
Publisher — Jeanne L. Schuler
Sr. Editor — Rosalie Merzbach
Circ Manager — Omar Medlin

IL (Chicago 60606) 230 W. Monroe St., #1200; (312) 368-6500.
DODGE CONSTRUCTION NEWS (a McGraw-Hill publication)(mon to fri); Construction, Architecture; Est.1946
Circ.2,000 pd. (mon to fri), 4,500 free (mon only); June 30, 1986; $4.50/copy; Adv.$3.50/line
Editor/Publisher — Jeff S. Krieter
Senior Editor — Gene Ice
Managing Editor — Kurt N. Wehrmeister
Assoc Editor — Bob Christensen
Art Director — H. M. Thompson
Regional Sales Manager — Alex A. Radwan

LA (New Orleans 70152) PO Box 52031; (504) 368-8900.
DAILY JOURNAL OF COMMERCE (mon to fri); Building and Construction Municipal Bonds
Circ.3300 (approx.); $270/yr; Adv.$10 p.c.i.
Editor/Publisher — Carlo Ragusa
Adv Director — Paul Serpas

CANADA (Willowdale, ON M2S 4Z6) 280 Yorkland Blvd.; (416) 494-4990
DAILY COMMERCIAL NEWS (mon to fri); Construction & Building; Est.1927
Circ.6,082; ABC Sept. 30, 1985; $269/yr. (Canadian); Adv.$1.79/line (Canadian)
Publisher — Southam Communications Ltd.
Editor — Scott Button
Publisher — Alan Helsey
Circ Manager — Josie Vogel
Sales Manager/Display Adv — Dave Watson
Tel. Sales Supervisor — Susan Steele
Associate Publisher — Ian Hardy

COURT, LEGAL, BUSINESS, COMMERCIAL, AND FINANCIAL

CA (Fresno 93707) PO Box 126; (209) 237-0114.
FRESNO DAILY REPORT (mon to fri); Business, Court & Financial; Est.1886
Circ.1,300; 75¢/copy; Adv.$6.00 p.c.i.
Managing Editor — Gordon M. Webster, Jr.
Production Manager — Norman G. Webster

CA (Los Angeles 90012) 210 S. Spring St.
DAILY COMMERCE See Real Estate category, this section.; or Los Angeles, CA Daily Section

CA (Los Angeles 90012) 210 S. Spring St.; (213) 625-2141.
DAILY JOURNAL (mon to fri); Court, Legal, Business, Commercial and Financial; UPI, Reuters; Est.1888
Circ.22,967; VAC Sept. 29, 1986; 25¢/copy; $161/yr; Adv.$11.06 p.c.i.
Publisher — Gerald Salzman
Editor — Ken Jost
Business Manager — John Babigian
Advertising Director — Burt Mann

CA (Los Angeles 90013) 304 S. Bway, Suite 210; (213) 628-4384.
METROPOLITAN NEWS m w f; Court, Legal, Business, Commercial and Financial; Est.1945
Circ.2,000; Sworn Oct. 31, 1986; 25¢/copy; $50/yr; Adv.$6 p.c.i.
Editor & Publisher — Rodger M. Grace

CA (Oakland 94607) P.O. Box 30157 (415) 465-3121.
INTER-CITY EXPRESS (mon to fri); Court, Legal, Business, Commercial and Financial; Est.1909
Circ.1,200; 50¢/copy; $9/mo; $65/yr
Editor — Steve Ball
Business Manager — Guy Everingham

CA (Palo Alto 94304) 1701 Page Mill Road
WALL STREET JOURNAL See New York, N.Y. Daily Section.

CA (Sacramento 95814) 1115 H Street; (916) 444-2355.
THE DAILY RECORDER (mon to fri); Government & Legal; Est.1911
Circ.1,864; Sworn Sept. 25, 1985; 50¢/copy; Adv.$4.20/in. display; $4/in. classified
Publisher — The Daily Journal Co.
Editor — John Hayes
Business Manager — Patricia Cabano

CA (San Diego 92138) PO Box 85469; (619) 232-4381
SAN DIEGO DAILY TRANSCRIPT (mon to fri); Est.1886
Circ. 8,431 ABC 9/30/86; 50¢/copy; $78/year; Adv $17.45 p.c.i.
Publisher — Keith Lister
Ad. Manager — Ted Diekman
Managing Editor — Gary Shaw
City Editor — Priscilla Lister Schupp
Comptroller — Robert Johnson
Production Manager — David Showley
Real Estate Editor — Bill Burris
Classified & Legal Advertising Mgr. — Dean Abbot

Circulation Manager — Tom Valentine
Editor — Martin Kruming

CA (San Francisco 94103) 99 S. Van Ness; (415) 621-5400.
THE RECORDER (mon to fri ex holidays); Court, Legal; Associated Press, ACCN, McClatchy News Service; Est. 1877
Circ.6,500; Sworn Oct. 1, 1985; 50¢/copy; Adv.$5.80 p.c.i.
Publisher — George G. McDonald
Vice Pres/Business Mgr — Paul J. McDonald
Controller — David Jewell
Adv Manager — Randy Goldner
Production Manager — Steven Redinger
Circ Manager — Randy Goldner
Managing Editor — Richard P. Hine
News Editor — Monica Bay

CA (San Jose 95113) 76 W. St. John St.; (408) 287-4866.
POST-RECORD (mon to fri); Court, Legal, Business, Commercial and Financial; Est.1917
Circ.1,000; 25¢/copy; $59/yr; Adv.$3.75 p.c.i.
Publisher — Earle T. Rose
Business Manager — Seymour T. Rose

CA (Santa Rosa 95402) 1818 Fourth St., PO Box 8777; (707) 545-1166.
SONOMA COUNTY DAILY HERALD-RECORDER (mon to fri); Legal, Court News & Recordings; Est.1899
Circ.487; Sworn Sept. 13, 1985; 55¢/copy, $145/yr; Adv.$4 p.c.i.
Managing Editor — Winifred (Teddie) Sipe
Publisher — Dale Sipe
Rep — ACCN Advertising Service
Proprietor — Herald Pub. Co.

CO (Colorado Springs 80903) 22 N. Sierra Madre; (303) 634-1593.
DAILY TRANSCRIPT(mon to fri); Legal; Est.1927
Circ.500; Sworn Jan. 1, 1987; 20¢/copy, $20/yr; Adv.$4 p.c.i.
Editor — E. Dale Steward

FL (Ft. Lauderdale 33302) PO Box 14366; (305) 463-1432.
BROWARD REVIEW (mon to fri); Business/Legal; Reuters, PR Newswire; Est.1962
Circ.4,200; Publisher's Statement Sept. 26, 1986; 50¢/copy; $99/yr; Adv.$20.46 p.c.i./$1,267 full page
Publisher — Lucia Robinson
Editor — Michael Huber
Vice Pres./Assoc. Pub. — Ruth H. Brown
Editor-In-Chief — Edward Wasserman

FL (Miami 33132) 100 N.E. 7 St.; (305) 377-3721.
MIAMI REVIEW & DAILY RECORD (mon to fri); Business/Legal; UPI, PR Newswire; Est.1926
Circ.15,500 (95% paid); ABC Dec. '86; 50¢/copy; $99/yr; Adv.$47.09 p.c.i.; $2,917 full page
Editor-In-Chief — Edward Wasserman
Editor — Richard Westlund
Publisher & Gen. Mgr. — Richard Roffman
Assistant to the Editor-In-Chief — Richard L. Papiernick
Executive Editor, Miami — R.L. Papiernik
Executive Editor, Broward — Michael Huber
Executive Editor, Palm Beach — Robert Douglas

FL (West Palm Beach 33401) 328 First St.; (305) 832-0386.
PALM BEACH REVIEW/COMMERCIAL RECORD (mon to fri); Est. 1954
Circ. 3,100; 50¢/copy; $70/yr; Adv. $16.14 p.c.i./$1,000 full page
Publisher — Lucia Robinson
Assoc Publisher — Ruth Brown
Adv. Manager — Mandy Cantor

GA (Atlanta 30303) 190 Pryor St., SW; (404) 521-1227.
FULTON COUNTY DAILY REPORT (mon to fri); Court & Commercial News; Est.1890
Circ.1,900; $1/copy; $110/yr; Adv.$21.50 p.c.i.
Publisher — Shayla Keough
President — Frances K. Beck
Vice Pres/Treasurer — Walter G. Nale
Vice Pres/Secretary — Earl H. Higgins

IL (Chicago 60610-4674) 415 N. State St.; (312) 644-7800.
CHICAGO DAILY LAW BULLETIN (mon to fri ex holidays); Legal & Credit; AP, ACCN; Est.1854
Circ.6,075; Sworn Oct. 1, 1985; 50¢/copy; Adv.$16.00/inch
President — Lanning Mac Farland, Jr.
Assoc Publisher — Stephen Anderson
Editor — Brian Owen
Plant Manager — William Hohs
Printing Sales — Jack Ruggles
Classified — Pam Kristie
Controller — James Banich
Counsel — Arthur Wilkins
Display Adv. — Earl Kogen
Display Adv. — Greg Cederlund
Subscriptions — Margaret Junker

IL (Chicago 60606) 1 S. Wacker Dr. (312) 750-4000.
WALL STREET JOURNAL (mon to fri); See New York, N.Y. Daily Section.; Est.1888 50¢/copy; $119/yr; Adv.$47.67 p agate line
Assoc. Publisher — Peter Kahn
Editor — Robert Bartley

IN (Indianapolis 46268) 3500 DePauw Blvd., #2070; (317) 636-3303.
INDIANAPOLIS COMMERCIAL (mon to fri); Est.1895
Circ.900; 50¢/copy, $68/year; Adv.$4.90/inch
Publisher — Scott Bemis
Editorial Dir. — Nancy A. Cotterill
Editor — Liz Main
Office Mgr. — Glenda Jones
Public Affairs Manager — Kenneth Vann
Circulation Dir. — Jacque Griffin
Subscription/Advertising Acct Exec. — Stephanie Smith
Production Dir. — Doug Garrison
Typographer — David Underwood
Composition — Judy Smith
Composition — Linda Blaylock
Composition — Brenda Schuessler

IA (Sioux City 51101) 706 Pierce St. (712) 255-8829.
DAILY REPORTER (mon to fri); Legal, Commercial; Est.1896
Circ.415; Sworn Sept. 30, 1986; 55¢/copy; $110/yr; Adv.$3.00 p.c.i.
Chairman — Lawrence S. Slotsky
President — Jeffrey S. Slotsky
Business Manager — Larry Forbes

KS (Topeka 66608) 1935 N. Topeka Ave.; (913) 232-8600.
TOPEKA LEGAL NEWS (m w f); Court, Legal, Business, Commercial and Financial; Est.1897
Circ.400; 50¢/copy, $80/yr; Adv.$4.75 pci
Owner/Publisher — Hall Directory

KS (Wichita 67201) PO Box 3179; (316) 263-5277
DAILY RECORD (mon to fri); Legal;
Circ. 750; 15¢/copy, $52.50/yr (includes Wichita Journal); Adv. $3 p.c.i.
Publisher — Harper Publishers, Inc.
Editor — William Krause

KY (Louisville 40201) 116 W. Market St., PO Box 1062; (502) 583-4471.
DAILY RECORD (mon to fri); Court, Legal, Business, Commercial and Financial; Est.1901
Circ.477; $45/qtly, $80/semi-annual, $140/yr; Adv.$50/line legal
Publisher — J.B. Garwood
Treasurer — J. William McMurray
Managing Editor — Leslie Wills

LA (Baton Rouge 70815) 8252 West El Cajon Drive; (318) 926-6882.
DAILY LEGAL NEWS (mon to fri); Court, Legal, Business, Commercial and Financial; Est.1925
Circ.675; 88¢/copy; Adv. $3./p.c.i.
Publisher — Legal News, Inc.
Editor — J. M. Mike Cannon

LA (Shreveport 71101-5413) 501 Texas St., Rm. M-103; (318) 222-0213
DAILY LEGAL NEWS (mon to fri); Court, Legal, Business, Commercial and Financial
Circ.875; 75¢/copy; Adv.$35 mon/4"X 1"
Publisher — Daily Legal News, Inc.
Editor — Lee Ann Bryce

FIG. 5.2. This *Editor and Publisher Yearbook* list identifies newspapers that do not have general circulations but cater to specialized audiences such as farmers, business people, and ethnic populations. Other lists in this publication include college newspapers, the foreign press, and photo and feature syndicates.

CANADIAN DAILY NEWSPAPER PUBLISHERS ASSN.—HQ.: 321 Bloor St East, Suite 214, Toronto, ON M4W 1E7; (416) 923-3567. John E. Foy, Pres.; Jean-Robert Belanger, Chmn.; David R. Hunter, Sec. Elections held in April.

RADIO-TELEVISION NEWS DIRECTORS ASSOCIATION OF CANADA— P.O. Box 235 - Clarkson Station, Mississauga. ON L5J 3Y1. (416) 977-2221. Ian Glenday, CBC-TC, Toronto, For TV, Pres.; Eric Rothschild. Newsradio, Toronto. For Radio, Vice Pres.; Mike Donegan, CFCF-TV, Montreal, Vice Pres.; Barrie Hussey, Toronto, Exec. Sec.; Dave Rogers, Toronto, Sec.-Treas.; Barry Hamelin, BN Toronto, Treas. Elections held in Nov.

CANADIAN MANAGING EDITORS' CONFERENCE— HQ.: Box 5020, Ottawa, ON K2C 3M4, (613) 829-9100. Bob McAleer, Windsor Star, Pres.; Nelson Skuce, Ottawa Citizen, 1st Vice Pres.; Murray Burt, Winnipeg Free Press, 2nd Vice Pres.; Peigi Kirby, Ottawa Citizen, Exec. Sec. Elections held in May.

CANADIAN MEDIA DIRECTORS COUNCIL— 130 Adelaide St. W., Suite 2000, Toronto, ON M5H 3P5. J. Patterson, Pres.; H. Dow, Vice Pres.; S. Bonfield, Sec.; B. Elliott, Treas. Elections held in June.

THE CANADIAN PRESS— 36 King St. E., Toronto, ON M5C 2L9; (416) 364-0321. Arthur E. Wood, Chmn.; Keith Kincaid, Pres.; Donald Jarrett, Sec. Elections held in April.

CANADIAN PRINTING INK MFRS. ASSN.— Box 294, Kleinburg, ON L0J 1C0, (416) 893-1689. Ian Nicol, Pres.; Henry Wittenberg, Sec.-Treas. Elections held in Feb.

CENTER FOR FOREIGN JOURNALISTS— 11690-A Sunrise Valley Dr., Reston, VA 22091; (703) 620-5984. Thomas Winship, Pres.; James D. Ewing, Vice Pres./Treas.; George A. Krimsky, Vice Pres./Exec. Dir.

CATHOLIC PRESS ASSOCIATION— 119 North Park Ave., Rockville Centre, NY 11570; (516) 766-3400. Rev. Owen F. Campion, Pres.; James A. Doyle, Exec. Dir.; Albina Aspell, Vice Pres.; Rev. John T. Catoir, Sec.; Arthur Runnels, Treas. Elections held in Mar.

CCAB, Inc. (Canadian Circulations Audit Board)— HQ.: 44 Eglinton Ave. W., Toronto, ON M4R 1A1; (416) 487-2418. D. Follis, Chmn.; H. J. Bray, Vice Chmn.; Patrick Sweeney, Pres./Gen. Mgr. Elections held in Mar.

COLLEGE MEDIA ADVISERS— Department of Journalism, Memphis State University, Memphis, TN 38152. David Knott, Dept. of Journalism, Ball St. Univ., Muncie, IN 47306, Pres.; Richard C. Lytle, Texas Student Publication, P.O. Box D, Austin, TX 78713-7209, Vice Pres.; David L. Adams, Kedzie Hall 103, Kansas St. Univ, Manhattan, KS 66506, Vice Pres.-Member Svcs.; Les Hyder, Students Publishing Co., Box 134, Dallas, TX 75275, Sec.; Reid Montgomery, South Carolina Press Association, P.O. Box 11429, Columbia, SC 29211, Treas. Elections held in Oct.

COMMUNITY COLLEGE JOURNALISM ASSN.— HQ.: Dept. of Journalism, Midland College, 3600 N. Garfield, Midland, TX 79705; (915) 684-7851. M. M. Jacobson, 17149 Strathern St., Van-nuys, CA 91406, Pres.; Ralph L. Sellmeyer, Midland College, TX, Exec. Sec.-Treas. Elections held in Aug.

COUNCIL FOR THE ADVANCEMENT OF SCIENCE WRITING, INC.— HQ.: 618 N. Elmwood, Oak Park, IL 60302; (312) 383-0820. Barbara J. Culliton, Pres.; Joann Rodgers, Vice Pres.-Sec.; Dr. Robert F. Murray, Jr., Vice Pres.; Jerry Bishop, Treas. Elections in May-June.

COUNCIL OF BETTER BUSINESS BUREAUS, INC.— 1515 Wilson Blvd., Arlington, VA 22209; (703) 276-0100.

William H. Tankersley, Pres.; Richard L. Bullock, Sr. Vice Pres. Elections held in Oct.

COUNCIL FOR ADVANCEMENT AND SUPPORT OF EDUCATION— Suite 400, 11 Dupont Circle, Washington, DC 20036; (202) 328-5900. Raymond E. Willemain, Chmn.; James L. Fisher, Pres.; Virginia Carter Smith, Vice Pres.; Michele Wiley, Sec. Elections held in July.

CUVIER PRESS CLUB— HQ.: 126 Wm. H. Taft Rd., Cincinnati, OH 45219; (513) 861-5500. James E. Duffy, Pres.; William J. Plogstead, Vice Pres.; Robert C. Porter, Jr., Sec.; Richard L. Vance, Treas. Elections held in April.

DIRECT MARKETING ASSN., INC.— 6 E. 43rd St., New York, NY 10017; (212) 689-4977. Jonah Gitlitz, Pres.; Robert J. Teufel, Rodale Press, Inc., Chmn.; William C. Johnson, Fingerhut Corp., Vice Chmn.; Paul Leblang, Saks Fifth Avenue, Vice Chmn.; Stephen E. Toman, Grolier Enterprises, Inc., Treas.; Richard C. Wolter, Columbia House, Sec. Elections held in Oct.

DOG WRITERS' ASSN. OF AMERICA— 66 North McKinley, Hamilton, OH 45013; (513) 863-2870. Harold W. Sundstrom, 9800 Flint Rock Road, Manassas, VA 22111, Pres.; Pat Dresser, 1462 Granger Road, Medina, OH 44256, Vice Pres.; Edith E. Munneke, 66 North McKinley, Hamilton, OH 45013, Sec. Elections in Feb.

EDUCATION COUNCIL OF THE GRAPHIC ARTS INDUSTRY, INC.— 4615 Forbes Ave., Pittsburgh, PA 15213; (412) 621-6941/Ext. 229. H. Wayne Warner, Pres.; Jack Simich, Man. Dir.; Bonnie Bokor, NSTF/Educ. Council Coordinator. Elections held in Oct.

FOOTBALL WRITERS ASSN. OF AMERICA— HQ.: Volney Meece, Exec. Dir., Box 1022, Edmond, OK 73083; (405) 341-4731. Jack Gallagher, Houston Post, Pres.; Dan Foster, Greenville News, 1st Vice Pres.; Gordon White, New York Times, 2nd Vice Pres.; Volney Meece, Daily Oklahoman and Times, Exec. Dir. Elections held in June.

FOREIGN PRESS ASSN.— 18 E. 50th St., New York, NY 10022; (212) 826-4721. Roy Murphy, TV of New Zealand, Pres.; Gianni Capra, La Voce Repubblicana, Italy, 1st Vice Pres.; A. Balu, Press Trust of India, 2nd Vice Pres.; Andrei Arkhipov, New Times, Moscow, Gen. Sec.; Monique Rubens, Gemini News Svc., London, Asst. Gen. Sec.; Robert Miko, Pacific Dialogue, Tokyo, Treas. Election held in Dec.

GRAPHIC ARTS TECHNICAL FOUNDATION, INC.— 4615 Forbes Ave., Pittsburgh, PA 15213; (412) 621-6941. Calvin W. Aurand, Pres.; John C. Wurst, Vice Pres.; Jerry Marler, Sec.; Dennis E. Watt, Treas. Elections held in Oct.

GRAPHIC COMMUNICATIONS INTERNATIONAL UNION— 1900 L St. NW, Washington, DC 20036; (202) 462-1400. James J. Norton, Pres.; Sol Fishko, Pres. Emeritus; Michael P. McNally, Sec.-Treas.; William Moody, Information Dir. Elections held quadrennially.

GRAPHIC PREPARATORY ASSN.— 501 North Wesley Ave., P.O. Box 2, Mount Morris, IL 61054; (815) 734-4178. James L. Martin, Jr., Pres.; Frank E. Benham, Vice Pres.; Ray D. Williams, Sec. Elections held in Jan.

GRAVURE RESEARCH INSTITUTE— 22 Manhasset Ave., Port Washington, NY 11050; (516) 883-6670. Walter A. Voss, Meredith/Burda, Des Moines, IA, Pres.; Harvey F. George, Exec. Vice Pres.; Valfrid Palmer, Alco Gravure, Inc., Rochelle Park, NJ, 1st Vice Pres.; Donald M. Hackbert, R.R. Donnelley & Sons, Chicago, IL, 2nd Vice Pres. John R. Shaw, Photo-Engravers & Electrotypers Ltd., Toronto, ON, Sec.-Treas. Elections held in Nov.

GRAVURE TECHNICAL ASSN.— 60 E. 42 St., Suite 1545, New York, NY 10165; (212) 661-8936. McKinley M. Luther, Exec. Vice Pres.; Normand B. Dufour, Pres.; Walter A. Voss, 1st Vice Pres.; John J. Collins, 2nd Vice Pres.; Stan Pinover, Sec./Treas.; Roland Gravenkemper, Treas. Elections held in Apr.

IFRA (INCA-FIEJ) RESEARCH ASSOCIATION— Washingtonplatz 1, D-6100 Darmstadt, 06151/76057. Odd Ronnestad, Pres.; E.J. Winnington-Ingram, Vice Pres.; Dr. F.W. Burkhardt, Man. Dir.

INTER AMERICAN PRESS ASSOCIATION— HQ.: 2911 N.W. 39th St., Miami, FL 33142; (305) 634-2466. Edward H. Harte, Harte-Hanks Newspapers, Corpus Christi, TX, Pres.; Alejandro Miro Quesada, El Comercio, Lima, Peru, 1st Vice Pres.; Ignacio E. Lozano, Jr., La Opinion, Los Angeles, CA, 2nd Vice Pres.; Oliver F. Clarke, The Daily Gleaner, Kingston, Jamaica, Treas.; Hector Davalos, Novedades, Mexico, DF, Sec.; W. P. Williamson, Jr., Exec. Dir. Elections held in Oct.

INTERMARKET ASSOCIATION OF ADVERTISING AGENCIES— Communications Center, 1605 N. Main St., Dayton, OH 45405; (513) 278-0681. Walter Ohlmann, Pres.

INTERNATIONAL ADVERTISING ASSN. INC.— 475 Fifth Ave., New York, NY 10017; (212) 684-1583. William O'Neill Sweeney, Exec. Dir.; A. E. Pitcher, Ogilvy & Mather Ltd., London, England, World Pres.; Hideharu Tamaru, Dentsu Inc., Tokyo, Japan, Vice Pres., Asia/Pacific; Dino Betti van der Noot, B Communications, Milan, Italy, V.P., Europe. Jose Daniel Nasta, Publicitaria Nasta S.R.L., Asuncion, Paraguay, Vice Pres., Latin America; Samir E. Fares, SSC & B Lintas Worldwide, Dubai, United Arab Emirates, Vice Pres., Middle East/Africa; John Cunningham, Westinghouse Electric Corp., Pittsburgh, PA, Vice Pres., U.S./Canada. Elections held in May every two years.

INTERNATIONAL ASSOCIATION OF BUSINESS COMMUNICATORS (IABC)— HQ.: 870 Market St., Suite 940, San Francisco, CA 94102; (415) 433-3400. Norman G. Leaper, Pres.; Clara Degen, Vice Pres.; Christopher Bunting, Chmn.; Jean G. Cormier, Finance. Elections held at International Conference.

INTERNATIONAL ASSN. OF PRINTING HOUSE CRAFTSMEN, INC.— HQ.: 7599 Kenwood Rd., Cincinnati, Ohio 45236; (513) 891-0611. Caesar V. Fontana, Pres.; James E. Lorentz, Vice Pres.; Patricia A. Milligan, Exec. Vice Pres. Elections held in Aug.

INTERNATIONAL CHAIN OF INDUSTRIAL & TECHNICAL ADVERTISING AGENCIES— 2700 Route 22, Union, NJ 07083; (201) 688-2700. Elections held in May.

INTERNATIONAL CIRCULATION MANAGERS ASSN.— HQ.: P.O. Box 17420, Dulles Airport, Washington, DC 20041; (703) 620-9555. Russell A. Bancroft, Pres.; Richard J. Lakus, Exec. Vice Pres.; Joseph B. Forsee, Gen. Mgr.-Treas., 11600 Sunrise Valley Drive, Reston, VA 22091. Elections held in June or July.

INTERNATIONAL FEDERATION OF ADVERTISING AGENCIES, INC.— Suite 1115, 1605 Main St., Sarasota, FL 33577; (813) 366-2902. Kurt Gabel, Pres.; Griffin Watkins, Exec. Vice Pres.; Gerald Popejoy, Vice Pres.; Kenneth Hill, Sec./Mgr. Dir.; Dianne Martin, Asst. Sec.; Robert Pinne, Treas. Elections held in Jan.

INTERNATIONAL LABOR COMMUNICATIONS ASSOCIATION (AFL-CIO/CLC)— HQ.: AFL-CIO Bldg., 815-16th St. N.W., Room 404, Washington, DC 20006; (202) 637-5068. Carolyn Jacobson, Pres.; James M. Cesnik, Sec.-Treas. Elections held biennially.

FIG. 5.3. This section of *Editor and Publisher Yearbook* lists state and regional press associations (groups composed of newspaper editors, publishers, and business personnel). It also identifies press associations that deal in specialized areas.

Table 5.1. Newspaper Numbers and Circulation

	Number	Total circulation
Morning dailies	485	36,279,000
Evening dailies	1,220	26,444,000
Total morning/evening	1,705	62,723,000
Sunday editions	800	58,816,000
Nondailies (weeklies, semiweeklies, triweeklies)	7,700	50,098,000

Source: Facts About Newspapers '86, American Newspaper Publishers Association.

Even more efficient are the 800 Sunday papers that have a circulation of nearly 59 million.

The fact is, publicists do bother with weekly newspapers even though such papers do not offer as many readers as the dailies. Numbers are not the only criterion of farsighted publicists. They may submit material to weeklies for any of several reasons:

- **The likelihood the paper will use the material.** Many weeklies are understaffed and often have trouble filling the **news hole** (the space in the newspaper allotted to news, illustrations, and other non-advertising material) for each issue, whereas most daily editors are faced with selecting a small portion of the editorial material available to fill each day's issue.
- **The likelihood the release will be read if it is used.** Readership of weekly newspapers is intensive. The 8- to 20-page edition of the typical weekly will be checked from cover to cover by a large share of its readers, while readers of the 60- to 100-page metropolitan daily devote an average of only 30 minutes to it.
- **The importance of the audience composition.** Weekly newspapers reach a large segment of rural, small-town, and suburban populations. On certain occasions, publicists might consider these audiences to be vital targets. A publicist might be working for a politician who is promoting a piece of farm legislation or a company selling equipment to care for large lawns and gardens.

So, publicists are concerned with more than audience size. In selecting media, they most often are interested in the chance that the material will be used and read and in the nature of the audience it will reach.

Specialized Newspapers

Publicists generally use newspapers to reach broad segments of the socioeconomic spectrum, but they also use specialized publications with highly tailored audiences. About 60 black newspapers, 185 foreign-language publications, and 100 professional, business, and special-service dailies are listed in *Editor and Publisher Yearbook*. As was mentioned earlier, there are also newspapers for particular religious, political, age, and occupational groups. Thus, the publicist can use newspapers to reach highly homogeneous audiences—the black community in New York City or Baltimore, members of the Episcopal church across the United States, Republicans in the Midwest, or labor unions in Illinois.

Other Opportunities

Although most of the publicist's efforts are aimed at placing news releases in newspapers, the medium offers other opportunities for expression. In addition to supplying editors with already written stories, the publicist may suggest story ideas, especially to the editor of the local newspaper. Naturally, the bulk of such ideas should be related to the publicist's area of interest. However, a publicist who has a professional attitude about news (and that certainly should be the case) may supply an editor or a reporter with story suggestions outside the publicist's bailiwick.

The same applies to editorial ideas, although this is a more sensitive area than news. A publicist should not pester editors with suggestions that they write editorials supportive of an organization or a project. But if a significant issue arises that the publicist believes deserves editorial comment, the idea can be relayed to editors. Editors are individuals. Some will be receptive; others will not. The publicist has to play the situation by ear.

One of the major obligations of the press is to serve as a sounding board for its readers. The letters-to-the-editor section provides that forum. Occasionally a publicist may find it helpful to write a letter to the editor or to encourage someone else to do so. Certainly, this outlet should not be overused, but it should be considered when a publicist believes that it is important to impart a point of view that probably would not be expressed in the news columns. The most effective letters are restrained, factual, and brief. Long, emotional diatribes seldom persuade and may be counterproductive. In recent years, corporations, government officials, and other public figures have become regular users of the letters columns.

A variation of the letter to the editor is another editorial-page article often referred to as **op-ed** (opposite or next to editorials). Op-ed articles focus on issues of public concern and are usually written by a person with special expertise or insight about the issue. Because the content is often more in-depth and is presented in a succinct writing style, op-ed articles usually carry more prestige than do letters to the editor.

Many publicists overlook the op-ed choice when in fact such articles provide excellent opportunities to put newsworthy topics before the public. A publicist might, for example, write an op-ed piece on the local effects (either positive or negative) of a proposed family-law bill under consideration by a state legislature. Or perhaps an organization working for more stringent groundwater control measures could have an expert on the issue write an op-ed article on the deadly long-range effects of contaminated water. The possibilities are endless for the publicist who is simply aware of the potential benefit of the op-ed outlet.

Local columns written by newspaper staff members tend to receive high readership and provide a comfortable climate for the discussion of sensitive issues. This seems to be true regardless of the quality of the column. The publicist should be alert to situations in which a column item might be helpful, but he or she should not pressure columnists to run self-serving items. Such suggestions or requests should be restricted to significant or high-interest issues.

Sometimes publicists or specialists such as county extension directors may be offered a chance to write their own columns. If such an opportunity presents itself, a publicist would be wise to take it but also should seek the advice of a professional journalist about editorial content and writing style.

Most newspapers run calendars of events. The publicist may use them instead of, or as a supplement to, news coverage of an event.

In addition to their news sections and departments, many newspapers carry regular and seasonal supplements. Most large dailies offer a Sunday or weekend feature magazine and a television or entertainment supplement. Seasonal editions often cover fashion, real estate, business, education, sports, gardening, and home furnishings and improvements. A publicist should check with local editors to determine which special sections their papers publish and when the copy deadlines are. Most dailies include special sections in their listing in *Editor and Publisher Yearbook.*

Photographs and Artwork

Although graphics are discussed in Chapter 14, it is important to note that good, relevant photographs or artwork (maps, graphs, cutaways, sketches, and so forth) almost always increase the chance that a news release will be used. Occasionally, a photograph and cutline (the descriptive or explanatory material below the picture) may adequately cover a news event and need not be accompanied by a release.

Criticisms and Corrections

Veteran publicists offer a mixture of advice about criticism of press coverage and the policy to follow when journalists make mistakes. At one extreme, the advice is "Don't argue with people who buy ink by the barrel." Other publicists suggest that journalists should be notified of their every goof. A realistic approach probably lies somewhere in the middle. Like anyone else, journalists are inclined to react negatively to nitpickers but will usually listen to people who have a reasonable concern. The publicist should probably limit criticisms and requests for corrections to significant issues. If a reporter is involved, he or she should be contacted first. If no satisfaction is gained, then an editor may be notified.

For example, if a reporter identified an officer in your company as chairman of the board rather than chief executive officer, the publicist should probably just drop him a friendly note pointing this out. However, if the reporter mistakenly included or left out the word "not" in a quote, this should be corrected because the mistake reversed the meaning of the statement.

Wire Services and Syndicated News

Newspapers—especially the large dailies—rely heavily on professional services not provided by their own staffs. Such services include the two major wire services, the Associated Press (AP) and United Press International (UPI); news syndicates operated by major newspapers, such as the Log Angeles Times/Washington Post News Service and the New York Times News Service; and a host of feature syndicates that provide comics and cartoons, household features, religious, and other material. Wire service bureaus and newspaper and feature syndicates are all listed in *Editor and Publisher Yearbook.*

Seldom will the publicist deal with any of those agencies. But a publicist with a major story or a prize-winning news picture should query a newsperson at the nearest AP and UPI bureaus to determine if they are interested. Because the material filed by the newspaper syndicates is staff-written, those outlets are seldom open to the publicist.

The business manager of a major news-feature syndicate says, "Millions of dollars in public relations money is wasted by sending press releases to syndicates. We throw away bushel baskets of press releases every week." He advises publicists to send their material to the authors of the syndicated features—food news to the cooking columnist, garden news to the garden columnist, and financial news to the money management writer.

Summary

Newspapers remain the backbone of most publicity campaigns for several reasons—their access, coverage, content, and capacity to accommodate the material offered by publicists. Although most newspapers reach a broad socioeconomic audience, they also can be used to reach target groups.

In addition to providing news releases, publicists should be alert to opportunities offered by other newspaper features—columns, editorials, and letters to the editor. Only under unusual circumstances should the publicist attempt to place material with the wire services or the news and feature syndicates.

Exercises

1. Choose a particular problem that can be addressed through publicity sent to newspapers. Define the geographic area in which you will work—for example, a campaign to increase the number of organ donors in central Iowa. Compile a list of newspapers through which to deliver your messages. For each selection, identify the audience addressed, the circulation of the paper, and the person to whom you would submit your material.
2. Make a list of the possible publicity messages you could provide to the papers listed in Exercise 1. Think beyond the standard news release, but be sure your selections are practical for the papers and their audiences. Explain the reasons for your choices.
3. Apply the chapter discussion on the disadvantages of newspapers to your issue. What are the apparent weaknesses of the newspapers you have chosen for your campaign? What can you do to minimize these weaknesses?

Suggested Reading

Simon, Raymond. "The Basic Press Release," "Timing and Dating Releases," and "There's No Interest Like Local Interest." Units 1–3 in *Publicity and Public Relations Worktext.* 5th ed. Columbus, Ohio: Grid Publishing, 1983.

Walsh, Frank. "Understanding the Mass Media." Chapter 2 in *Public Relations Writer in a Computer Age.* Englewood Cliffs, N.J.: Prentice-Hall, 1986.

6

Magazines: A Way to Reach Almost Everyone

MARCIA PRIOR-MILLER

MAGAZINES—bright, lively, colorful, informative, and influential—occupy a unique place among the mass media. As a result they can be a strong link in the publicity process. In the second edition of *The Publicity Process,* Richard Disney noted that "the magazine's special virtues—its versatility, intensity of readership, ability to pinpoint special audiences" are the publicity planner's strongest allies. "Whatever your interest," he wrote, "there is a magazine to match it, with a ready-made audience waiting to hear what you have to say, if you say it well enough."

Indeed, as Disney suggests, magazines are an ideal complement to newspapers in a publicity campaign. The newspaper's weaknesses are the magazine's strengths. Magazines appeal to a narrower socioeconomic audience, but that audience is more highly educated and has a higher average income. Magazine reading is intense, and magazine coverage is national or regional rather than local. The majority of magazines have high visual appeal and use some of the best reproduction technology available.

Unfortunately, publicists sometimes overlook magazines for reaching audiences. In most cases, this neglect occurs either because publicists are unaware of the broad spectrum of available magazines that might reach their audiences or because they are uncertain about how to gain access to magazines.

But working with the editors of magazines and newsletters differs only slightly from working with newspaper editors. Magazine editors often rely as heavily as newspaper editors do on news releases to keep abreast of developments in the fields their publications cover.

Ways to Use Magazines for Publicity

When planning media choices for publicity, a publicist may consider using magazines in any one or combination of the following three ways:

1. For news releases. The same releases that alert newspaper editors to upcoming or past events, personnel changes, or background information may be useful to magazine editors. Although proportionately fewer releases may appear in their original or rewritten form in a magazine than in a newspaper, editors use the information from releases for news columns. They also use releases for ideas for feature articles or in other areas of their magazines.

2. For articles or features. Some publicists write and submit articles themselves. If publicists lack the time to write features or have no experience in writing for specific audiences in the styles used by diverse magazines, professional free-lancers can be hired to write articles on assigned topics.

3. As a primary medium for distributing information. Publicists may produce their own magazines. An increasing number of medium-sized and large organizations publish one or more magazines. In many cases publicists hired by an organization are directly responsible for editing and producing magazines. Organization publications are typically targeted to readers inside and/or outside the organization.

Small organizations often adopt a newsletter format. The editing of newsletters is, in many respects, an extension of the skills of both magazine and newspaper editing. (See the bibliography at the end of this chapter for additional information on publishing and editing magazines.)

A publicist's ability to use magazines best begins with an understanding of the types of magazines that are published and their purposes and audiences. Publicists must also become familiar with the resources available for obtaining information about magazines.

Getting to Know Magazines

Magazines vary widely in size, shape, and visual appeal. Richard Disney has noted that "the first things about the magazine field that are likely to strike an acute observer are the volume, the range of content, and the utter lack of uniformity among American magazines. . . . Some are color-splashed; some are drab. Some are works of art; some are shabby."

Yet, in the midst of this great diversity, a few broad groupings of magazines and their close relatives—newsletters and magapapers—are commonly used in the industry. (Gaining in popularity in recent years, the magapaper is a newsletter that incorporates some of the best editorial, visual, and production features of the newsletter and the magazine. It often looks like a high-quality newsletter but reads like a magazine.)

Knowing the basic three categories into which most magazines fall (discussed below) and where to find information about individual magazines are first steps toward identifying the purpose for which a given magazine is published, the audience that reads the magazine, and the subjects covered in the magazine. By understanding the purpose, audience, and subjects of a magazine, a publicist can learn how information is treated in the magazine. These are the keys to using magazines for effective publicity.

Magazine Reference Books

A number of directories that provide basic information about magazines, including their addresses and telephone numbers, are listed at the end of this chapter. No single resource provides an exhaustive listing of the magazines published within a given subject area. Most directories include publications from any or all of the basic three categories of magazines, but some directories are more useful than others for locating information on magazines in a particular category. Those directories are highlighted in the sections below. A publicist should become familiar with each of the directories. The more these references are used, the more skillful the publicist becomes in identifying that magazine or group of magazines that will reach a target audience for a specific publicity purpose.

Various magazine directories use slightly different categories for grouping magazines, but this should not be a barrier. Most directories use subject categories or market groups, such as farm, sports, or women's magazines. Once the subject category has been determined, magazines can be further identified by the primary purpose of their editorial content.

Categories of Magazines

The three primary categories of magazines as they relate to publicity are **lifestyle** or **consumer magazines, trade magazines,** and **organization publications.**

LIFESTYLE OR CONSUMER MAGAZINES

The most visible and best known of magazines, consumer magazines are written and edited for the general public. They are designed to enhance the lifestyles of their readers. Most are circulated nationwide, and some are circulated internationally. A few are distributed locally, such as city and regional magazines and Sunday magazines that are circulated in newspapers. Magazines are usually sold at retail outlets: drugstores, grocery stores, newsstands, and convenience stores. The majority carry advertising for retail products (consumer goods—hence, the name "consumer magazine"). The titles are legion and to most people are household names: *Time, Newsweek, Good Housekeeping, Vogue, Sports Illustrated, The New Yorker, Reader's Digest.*

Of the three types of magazines, consumer magazines may be the least useful to publicists working with information that is local in interest or timely. Editors of these publications want information with broad regional or national appeal. Planning for issues occurs months in advance. A publicist should give careful thought to which information would be of value to these editors.

Two types of consumer magazines are commonly recognized: **general** and **specialized.** There is no general consensus as to the precise differences of these categories, but historically the majority of consumer magazines were general magazines—they carried information of interest to almost anyone, anywhere. The popular *Reader's Digest,* with a circulation of more than 17 million, is a good example. In recent years an increasing number of consumer magazines have narrowed their subject areas, becoming more specialized. As a result, they appeal to smaller audiences. Like the material in the majority of general consumer magazines, the writing in specialized magazines is not highly technical, but topics are covered in greater depth.

The differences between general and specialized magazines are illustrated by comparing a general magazine like *Sports Illustrated* with a specialized magazine like *Runner's World. Sports Illustrated* covers all types of sports, giving news and features about personalities and events throughout the world. *Runner's World,* on the other hand, treats one sport in great depth. Although *Sports Illustrated* might include articles about jogging, *Runner's World* focuses exclusively on the subject. Articles in *Runner's World* include not only features on major personalities who run but also technically oriented articles on selecting shoes for running, avoiding injuries while jogging, and so forth.

Several directories provide information about lifestyle or consumer magazines, their purposes, and their audiences. Among the most useful are *Bacon's Publicity Checker, Writer's Market,* the *Consumer Magazine and Agri-Business* edition of the Standard Rate and Data Service directories, and the *Gale Directory of Publications* (formerly known as the *IMS/Ayer Directory of Publications*).

Compiled specifically for the publicist, *Bacon's* lists magazines in more than 160 market groups. Each magazine entry includes the name of the publication, its address and telephone number, a designated contact person, the frequency of publication, and the name of the publisher. Especially useful to the publicist is *Bacon's* key to the types of releases that the publications typically use (see Figure 6.1).

More-detailed information about the audiences and editorial content of consumer magazines is readily available in two sources: *Writer's Market* and the *Consumer Magazine and Agri-Media Rates and Data* edition of the Standard Rate and Data Service directories. Available through many libraries, both directories classify magazines by subject.

The *Gale Directory,* one of the most readily available of directories that list U.S. magazines, also lists publications by subject (see Figure 6.2). Information on Sunday magazines is given in newspaper media directories, which are discussed in Chapter 5.

TRADE MAGAZINES

Also known as business or professional magazines, the more than six thousand trade magazines in the United States are written for people in specific businesses, industries, or professions. They are edited to enhance the growth of these trades and, secondarily, the professional development of the people who work within them. Although trade publications, like consumer magazines, have broad national and regional audiences and are planned months in advance, the relatively narrower interests of the readers and the more specialized treatment of information in these magazines make them excellent avenues for publicity when that publicity is matched with the goals of the magazines. The many scientific and academic journals can be considered a subcategory of trade magazines and are good channels for reaching scholars and researchers.

Trade magazines can also be divided according to whether they cover

92 — General Magazines (340)

92A — GENERAL INTEREST MAGAZINES-U.S.(90)
92B — MEN'S MAGAZINES-U.S.(11)
92C — YOUTH MAGAZINES-U.S.(17)
92D — GENERAL MAGAZINES-METRO-U.S.(171)
92E — SENIOR CITIZENS-U.S.(15)
92F — EPICUREAN-U.S.(9)
92Z — GENERAL MAGAZINES-CAN.(27)

92A — General Interest Magazines-U.S. (publications: 90)

92A-1B   16 MAGAZINE, 157 W. 57th Street, New York, NY 10019; Ms. Randi Reisfeld, Editor; Monthly; Phone: (212) 489-7220.   3,7,9,14

92A-1E   ABOUT TIME, 30 Genesee Street, Rochester, NY 14611; Ms. Carolyne S. Blount, Editor; Monthly; 18,500; Phone: (716) 235-7150.
3,4,5,6,7,9,11,13,14

92A-1H   AFTER DARK, 175 Fifth Avenue, New York, NY 10010; Mr. Lee Swanson, Editor-In-Chief; Monthly; 50,000; Phone: (212) 929-5940.
1,5,11,13,14

92A-1I   AMERICAN HERITAGE, 10 Rockefeller Plaza, New York, NY 10020; Mr. Byron Dobell, Editor; Bi-Monthly; 130,000; Phone: (212) 399-8900.   6,11   ★✔

92A-1J   AMERICAN HISTORY ILLUSTRATED, 2245 Kohn Road, P.O. Box 8200, Harrisburg, PA 17105; Mr. Ed Holm, Editor; 10 Times/ Year; 120,000; Historical Times, Inc.; Phone: (717) 657-9555. 6,7,9,11   ▲

92A-1L   AMERICAN WEST, 3033 N. Campbell Avenue, Tucson, AZ 85719; Mr. Thomas W. Pew, Jr., Editor; Bi-Monthly; 150,000; American West Publishing Co.; Phone: (602) 881-5850.   3,5,6,7,9,11   ▲

92A-1N   AMERICANA, 29 W. 38th Street, New York, NY 10018; Mr. Michael Durham, Editor; Bi-Monthly; 400,000; Phone: (212) 398-1550.
5,6,7,9,10,11

92A-1M   AMERICAS, 19th & Constitution Ave., N.W., Washington, DC 20006; Mr. Winthrop P. Carty, Editor-In-Chief; Bi-Monthly; General Secretariat Of The Organization Of America.   6,7,9,11,13,14   ★✔

92A-1Q   AMPERSAND, 1680 N. Vine Street, #900, Hollywood, CA 90028; Mr. Byron Laursen, Editor; Quarterly; 1,500,000; Alan Weston Communications, Inc.; Phone: (213) 462-7175.   6,7,13,14   ★

92A-1O   ANIMAL KINGDOM, New York Zoological Park, Bronx, NY 10460; Mr. Eugene Walter, Jr., Editor-In-Chief; 6 Times Year; 132,000; New York Zoological Society; Phone: (212) 220-6860.
3,5,6,7,9,11,13,14

92A-1P   ASIA, 725 Park Avenue, New York, NY 10021; Ms. Joan Dim, Editor; Bi-Monthly; 18,000; Asia Society, Inc.; Phone: (212) 288-6400.   3,4,5,6,7,9,11,13,14   ■

92A-2   THE ATLANTIC, 8 Arlington Street, Boston, MA 02116; Mr. William Whitworth, Editor-In-Chief; Monthly - 25th Prec.; 500,000; The Atlantic Monthly Company; Phone: (617) 536-9500.   6,7,9,11

92A-2N   ATTENZIONE, 152 Madison Avenue, New York, NY 10016; Ms. Lois Spritzer, Editor; Monthly - 15th Prec.; 160,000; Adam Publications, Inc.; Phone: (212) 683-9000.   1,3,5,6,7,9,11,13,14   ✔

92A-3   AUDUBON, 950 Third Avenue, New York, NY 10022; Mr. Les. D. Line, Editor; Bi-Monthly - 1st; 425,000; National Audubon Society; Phone: (212) 546-9100.   6,7,9,11   ▲

---

1. New Products   2. Trade Literature   3. General News   4. Personnel   5. Events   6. Articles, By-lined
7. Articles, Staff   8. Financial   9. Letters   10. Questions & Answers   11. Books   12. Contracts
13. Films   14. Entertainment   ■ Newsletter Format   ★ New listing since previous edition
● Charges for cuts   ✔ Uses color publicity photos   ▲ Does not use publicity photos

---

FIG. 6.1.   A quick glance at an entry in *Bacon's Publicity Checker* can save a publicist the frustration of spending time organizing and writing publicity items that don't conform to a magazine's content or format.

TRADE, TECHNICAL AND CLASS PUBLICATIONS

VIRGINIA
Mount Vernon
Water Gardening Journal (quar.) Gardening

NEWSLETTERS

EDUCATIONAL
See Educational under General Magazines, also
Anthropological & Ethnological; Physical Education &
Entomological; Eugenics & Genetics; Geographic;
Speech; Historical & Genealogical; Music & Musical

CONVENTIONS & FAIRS

COMMERCIAL &

CONGRESSIONAL
GOVERNMENT

AGRICULTURAL PUBLICATIONS GROUPED ACCORDING TO CLASSIFICATION

FARM NEWSPAPERS Continued		
WISCONSIN Continued		Circ.
Kewaunee		
Statesman (wkly.) .... 1895...		‡2,650
Waupaca		
Wisconsin State Farmer (wkly.)		
	Ind. Agric...	‡25,659
	Free...	‡7,064

CANADA

ALBERTA
Edmonton
Alberta Farm Life (wkly.)
  Special for farmers...
  Free... 25,000
Red Deer
Giant, The (mo.) ....Farm News...
  Non-paid... ⊛73,028

MANITOBA
Birtle
Eye - Witness (wkly.)
  Agriculture, community news...
Boissevain
Recorder (wkly.) .... Ind. & Agric... ‡2,100
Brandon
Manitoba Farm Express News (bi-mo.)
  Manitoba's farming community...
  Non-paid... ‡36,300
Westman Rural (wkly.)
  Agric. community news...
  Free... ‡20,000
Carberry
News - Express (wkly.)
  Agriculture, community news... ‡1,409
Gilbert Plains
Maple Leaf Press (wkly.)
  Agriculture, community news...
Grandview
Exponent (wkly.) .... Ind. Agric... ‡2,161
Rossburn
Review (wkly.)
  Agricultural community news... ‡1,942
St. Pierre
Farm Bulletin (mo.) .... Agriculture...
  13,900

ONTARIO
Alliston
Farming Today (Simcoe County Edition)
  (mo.) .... Agriculture...
  Non-paid... ‡11,000
Dresden
Voice of the Elgin Farmer (s-mo.)
  Farm News & Views...
  Non-paid... ‡6,856
Voice of the Essex Farmer (s-mo.)
  Farm News & Views...
  Non-paid... ‡9,536
Voice of the Kent Farmer (s-mo.)
  Farm News & Views...
  Non-paid... ‡8,009
Voice of the Lambton Farmer (s-mo.)
  Farm News and Views...
  Non-paid... ‡7,759
Voice of the Middlesex Farmer (s-mo.)
  Farm News & Views...
  Non-paid... ‡10,286
Voice of the Oxford Farmer (s-mo.)
  Farm news & views...
Elmira
Farm Gate, The (mo.) ....Farm News...
  Non-paid... ‡17,400
Mount Forest
Farming Today (Wellington-Waterloo-Perth
  Edition (s-mo.) .... Agriculture...
  Non-paid... ‡15,999

QUEBEC
Lennoxville
Townships Sun, The (mo.)
  Environment, agriculture regional... 2,700
Longueuil
Terre de Chez Nous, La (Fr.) (wkly.)
  Agriculture... ⊛48,320
Ste. Agathe Des Monts
Quebec Farmer's Advocate (12 ti. a yr.)
  Farming... ‡5,000

SASKATCHEWAN
North Battleford
North West Farmer-Rancher (s-mo.)
  Agriculture...
  Non-paid... ‡11,235
Saskatoon
Express News-Farm Edition (s-mo.)
  Farm oriented...
  Free... ‡69,000
Western Producer (wkly.)
  Farm Home & Gen'l News... 138,563

FUR FARMING		
CANADA		Circ.

ONTARIO
Bewdley
Fur Trade Journal (mo.)
  Fur Trade & Fur Farm's... ‡500
  Non-paid... ‡300
Rabbits in Canada (bi-mo.) .... Rabbitry... ‡200
  Non-paid... ‡300

GENERAL (Agriculture)
See also Farm Newspapers.

ALABAMA
Birmingham
Progressive Farmer (mo.) ...... Agricultural... ★557,337
Montgomery
Neighbors (mo.) .... Agric. Gardening...

ARKANSAS
Fayetteville
Arkansas Farm Research (bi-mo.)
  Agricultural Research...
  Non paid... ‡9,100
Little Rock
Farm Bureau Press (11 ti. a yr.)
  Gen. Farm... ‡97,936

CALIFORNIA
Berkeley
Agricultural History (quar.) .....Agric. Hist... ‡1,280
Dixon
Tribune (wkly.)
  Independent, agric. business... ‡2,900
Indio
Desert Rancher (wkly.) .... Agriculture... ‡15,532
  Non-paid... ‡5,500
Napa
Napa County Record (s-wkly)
  Local news & selective... ‡2,100
San Francisco
California Farmer (s-mo.) ...... Agricultural... ★56,633
Redwood Rancher (6 ti. a yr.)
  Agric. wine grapes industry...
Santa Fe Springs
Aerial Applicator Farm, Forest & Fire (9 ti.
  a yr.)..... Aerial Agric. & Fire Control...
  Controlled... ‡8,214

COLORADO
Denver
Colorado Rancher and Farmer (14 ti. a yr.)
  Farming & Ranching... 18,215
Rocky Mountain Union Farmer (10 ti. a
  yr.) .... Agriculture... * ‡8,600

CONNECTICUT
Putnam
Ag - Review (mo.) .... Agriculture... 9,500
  Non-paid... 36,000

DISTRICT OF COLUMBIA
Washington
Agricultural Outlook (mo.)
  Food and Marketing, farm income... ‡1,917
Extension Review (quar.)
  Agriculture, Home Econ., Rural
  Devel'mt, Youth... ‡312

FLORIDA
Gainesville
Florida Agriculture (12 ti. a yr.)
  Agriculture... ‡71,000
  Non-paid... ‡1,200
Independent Farmer and Rancher (wkly.)
  Agricultural... ‡7,500
Orlando
Florida Grower and Rancher (mo.)
  Agriculture...
  Controlled... ‡28,000

GEORGIA
Atlanta
Ornamentals South (6 ti. a yr.)Agriculture...

IDAHO
Boise
Idaho Farmer-Stockman (s-mo.)
  Agriculture and Livestock... 16,394
Cottonwood
Farm & Ranch Chronicle (mo.)
  Farm & Ranch News...
Idaho Falls
Potato Grower of Idaho (mo.)
  Potato Grower Shipping-Processing...
  Non-paid... ‡18,000

ILLINOIS
La Salle
Illinois Agri-News (wkly.)
  Farm & Rural Community... ‡28,964
  Non-paid... ‡24,547
Lombard
Prairie Farmer-Illinois (s-mo.) Agricultural... 167,996
Prairie Farmer - Indiana (s-mo.)
  Agricultural... ★167,996
Wallaces Farmer (s-mo.) .... Agricultural... ★91,627

MASSACHUSETTS		
Mascoutah		
Farm Impact (4 ti. a yr.)		
	Local Agriculture News...	
	Non-Paid...	‡16,000

IOWA
Ankeny
Journal of Soil and Water Conservation
  (bi-mo.)
  Land & Water use & Natural Resources
  Management... ‡13,448
Des Moines
Successful Farming (14 ti. a yr.)
  Agricultural... ★521,754
Hampton
U. S. Farm News (mo.) ...... Farmers Union... ‡5,415
Newton
Daily News Plus (wkly.)..... Farm & Home...
  Non paid... ‡10,100

KANSAS
Belleville
Farmer Stockman of the Midwest (wkly.)
  Farm news... ‡7,862
Overland Park
Agricultura de las Americas (Span.) (mo.)
  Farming (Inter'l)... >3,842
  Non-paid... >36,623
Topeka
Kansas Farmer (s-mo.) ...... Agricultural... ★52,504

KENTUCKY
Bowling Green
Kentucky Farmer (mo.) .... Agriculture... ★31,901

MAINE
Freedom
Farmstead Magazine (6 ti. a yr.)
  Home Gardening & Small Farming... ‡175,000
  Non-paid... ‡2,000

MARYLAND
Baltimore
Georgia Farmer (mo.) .... Agriculture... ‡3,100
  Non-paid... ‡24,000
Maryland Farmer (mo.) .... Agriculture... 13,000
  Non-paid... ‡18,000
Virginia Farmer (mo.) .... Agriculture... ‡4,000
  Non-paid... ‡24,000

MICHIGAN
Hazlett
Michigan Patron (mo.) .... Agriculture... ‡2,200
Saint Joseph
Transactions of the ASAE (bi-mo.)
  Agricultural Engineering... ‡2,250
Sparta
Great Lakes Fruit Growers News (mo.)
  Agriculture... ‡2,625
  Non-paid... ‡582
Great Lakes Vegetable Growers News (mo.)
  Agriculture... ‡1,176
  Non-paid... ‡2,877

MINNESOTA
Lakeville
Farm Show (bi-mo.)
  New Products & Product Evaluations... ‡150,000
Saint Paul
Farmer/Dakota Farmer, The (s-mo.)
  Agricultural... ★138,025
Farm Industry News (10 ti. a yr.)
  High Income Farmer... >301,045

MISSISSIPPI
Jackson
Mississippi Farm Bureau News (10 ti. a yr.)
  Farm People... ‡146,000
Madison
MFC News (mo.) .... Farm People... ‡83,684

MISSOURI
Columbia
Missouri Ruralist (21 ti. a yr.) Agriculture... ★60,688
Today's Farmer (10 ti. a yr.) Agricultural... ‡60,000
Kansas City
Acres U.S.A. (mo.) ...... Farm economics... ‡15,000
Farmland News (s-mo.)
  Agriculture and Cooperatives... ‡285,000
Bozeman
Montana Agriculture (mo.) ...... Agriculture... ‡6,200

NEBRASKA
Lincoln
Nebraska Farmer (s-mo.) ...... Agriculture... ★58,139
Tekamah
Midwest Messenger (wkly.) .... Agriculture...
  Non-paid... ‡84,000

NEW HAMPSHIRE
Concord
Weekly Market Bulletin (wkly.)
  Agriculture... ‡10,000
  Non-paid... ‡10,000

Circulation— ★★ = Sept. A.B.C. Statement; ★ = June and March A.B.C. Statement; ☆ = A.B.C. Audit; ⊛ = C.C.A.B. Qualified Audit; ◆ = C.A.C. Audit; ± = V.A.C. Statement; > = B.P.A. Aud
‡ = Publisher's Report; § = P.O. Statement; Bold face figures—sworn; Light face figures—estimated.

1178

FIG. 6.2. The *Gale Directory of Publications* (formerly known as the *IMS/ Ayer Directory of Publications*) provides one of the better listings of all publications—newspapers and magazines—by both geographic and subject categories.

topics in general or specialized ways. Trade publications that are edited for general audiences are referred to as **horizontal publications,** and magazines that specialize are referred to as **vertical publications.**

A horizontal publication is edited for people with similar interests or jobs in all types of businesses and industries. Thus, people who are responsible for advertising might read the horizontal publication *Purchasing Magazine* regardless of whether they work for an advertising agency or such diverse businesses as a shoe manufacturer, a retail car dealership, or the advertising department of a local newspaper. These same people might also read vertical publications for their respective industries: *Leather and Shoes, Automotive News,* and *Editor and Publisher.*

Trade magazines include information that is more technical than that found in consumer magazines. Editors of trade publications assume that the reader understands the jargon of the profession, and they seek to provide information about products and developments in the field long before the general public becomes aware of those innovations.

Although consumer-product advertising appears in some trade publications, most advertising is for wholesale products and business-related services.

Information about trade magazines can be found in *Bacon's Publicity Checker,* the *Business Publications Rates and Data* edition of the Standard Rate and Data Service directories, and the *Gale Directory of Publications. Ulrich's International Periodicals Directory* provides information on academic journals. Agriculture-related periodicals are included in both the *Consumer Magazine and Agri-Media* and *Business Publications* editions of Standard Rates and Data Service. In the former, agriculture publications are given in a separate section. In the latter, as in most other directories, agriculture publications are listed as a subject category or market group.

ORGANIZATION PUBLICATIONS

Organizations produce publications to promote the organizations' growth. The magazines provide information of interest to members of the organizations as well as to people who are interested in, but are not members of, the organizations. This group includes association publications as well as in-house journals and public relations magazines. So many of these publications exist that no accurate count is possible.

Of the three major types of magazines, organization publications may be the most accessible to publicists. The publications cover narrowly focused subject areas. Their audiences can be local, regional, or national. Some organization publications have long lead times; others have short planning periods. A publicist may have to work harder to identify the publications that reach a specific audience—particularly those that do not have national audiences and therefore are not listed in standard media directories. However, consumers of such publications are highly committed readers with equally high levels of involvement in the subjects and activities of the organizations served by the publications.

Organization publications are sometimes categorized with trade publications, but viewing them as a separate group can be useful for the publicist for several reasons. There are many types of organizations besides business—religious, fraternal, and leisure, to name just a few. The audiences for organization publications often are much more narrowly defined than the audiences of either business or consumer magazines. The information that readers seek from organization publications differs from the information they seek from other trade selections, even when the organization publications are business-related. Finally, organization publications include, in addition to some well-known, highly prestigious selections, publications that use nonmagazine formats: newsletters and magapapers.

Association magazines are produced by associations primarily to keep their members posted on organizational activities. How an organization goes about this task varies widely. Compare, for example, the official journal of the National Geographic Society, *National Geographic,* with the weekly newsletter of a local school.

Public relations magazines are edited primarily from the perspective of the management of a particular profit or nonprofit organization. Unlike business and trade publications, however, a key purpose of public relations magazines is often to promote a positive image of the organization. To accomplish their purposes and to reach their primary audiences, editors of public relations publications may target their magazines to their inside (in-house journals) or outside constituencies or occasionally both.

Relatively little advertising appears in most organization publications. Many association and public relations magazines are supported by the dues of members or by the organizations that produce them, so they carry no advertising at all.

Information about association and public relations magazines is provided by *Bacon's Publicity Checker* and volume 5 of the *Working Press of the Nation.* The newsletters and magazines of many associations are published for so narrow an audience that they may not be listed in some of the standard periodicals directories. The publicist wanting to reach the maximum number of people interested in highly specialized information might also consult *The Encyclopedia of Associations.*

Matching Publicity Needs with Editorial Interests

There are three keys to successfully meshing a magazine's editorial requirements with specific publicity needs. The first and most critical key is matching the purpose and content of information to the editorial purpose and content of the magazine. The second key is matching the target audience for publicity with the target audience of the magazine. The third key is timing.

On a conceptual level, these factors are similar to those that might cause a publicist to select a particular newspaper, radio, or television station to reach a specific audience. What distinguishes a magazine from other media is its ability to match information on a subject with an audience's desire for that information, regardless of where those readers live.

Magazines carve out audiences first by subject matter—for example, sports in general or skiing in particular. Should a magazine decide to do so, it might further narrow that audience to teenage cross-country skiers in Canada.

Almost every magazine knows in great detail the demographics of its readership: sex, age, income, and education, occupation, and more. The publicist who knows the target audience for which a particular item of information is best suited can, with a bit of careful research, select one or more major or minor magazines that can help get that information to that audience.

As has already been noted, magazine editors usually work with longer lead times than do newspaper editors. Not long ago few people would have considered the magazine a likely target for publicity releases with short-range deadlines, especially announcements about events. If a publicist needed to place an article for the upcoming weekend, only a few magazines and newsletters would be able to reach that audience in time. However, the technological advances that began changing the publishing world in the 1970s and 1980s have changed the magazine editor's deadlines as well.

For example, Figure 6.3 shows a calendar of events listed in *Road Rider* magazine. Not only is an entire page devoted to upcoming events and regular meetings, but the magazine's editors also asked publicists to send information about motorcycle events with the promise of publication. Thus, a bit of long-range planning can link publicity with a magazine's publication date and a particularly suitable editorial environment for that information.

A magazine's frequency of publication in relation to an event is a major consideration. Six months' or even three months' advance notice for publicity may not be a prerequisite for having a release be timely for a magazine.

WHAT'S HAPPENING

For a listing of your motorcycle event in this column please send the details to: ROAD RIDER — WHAT'S HAPPENING, P.O. Box 6050, Mission Viejo, CA 92690. Please include all information possible — dates, locations, starting times, where to write sponsoring group, and phone number. To be sure of a listing, please let us know AT LEAST 120 days before the 1st of the month in which the event occurs.

August 15

Chapter "C" Freewheelers of Englewood, Colorado, 3rd Annual "1000-in-24", 1000 miles in 24 hours. Ride will start and end in the Denver area, but will include parts of Wyoming and Utah. For more information contact: Bill Gillespie, 3435 S. Dexter St., Denver CO 80222, (303) 758-8804.

September 1-5

Americade — Rockies, Estes Park, Colorado. Contact Bill and Gini Dutcher, Americade — Rockies, P.O. Box 2205B, Glens Falls, New York 12801. Call 24-hour hotline: (518) 656-6396 for 60 seconds of information and 20 seconds to leave your name and address.

September 1-12

The 4th Annual Iron Butt Rally. This 10,000 mile competition starts and finishes at Montgomeryville Cycle Center in north suburban Philadelphia. The rally around the perimeter of the United States includes timed checkpoints in Maine, Wisconsin, Washington, California, and Florida. Entry fees received before August 1, 1987 are $595.00, after August 1: $695.00. This year's rally is limited to forty participants. Contact: Jennifer Simons, Montgomeryville Cycle Center, 980 Route 309. Montgomeryville, PA 18936, (215) 699-7511 or George Egloff (201) 859-3788.

September 3-7

Finger Lakes BMW Club, Annual Finger Lakes BMW Rally, Hidden Valley Campground, Watkins Glen, New York. Contact: Finger Lakes BMW Club, 5035 Ridge Road, East Williamson, NY 14449.

September 4-6

Antique Motorcycle Club of America, 16th Annual AMC Davenport Midwest "Grand National", Mississippi Valley Fairgrounds, Davenport, Iowa. Contact: R.B. McClean, 2411 Middle Rd., Davenport, IA 52803, (319) 324-8137.

GWRRA, 3rd Annual Region "D" Rally, WINGATHON, Twin Plaza Motel, Benton Harbor, Michigan. Field events, bike judging and many extras. Contact: Kathy Kurth, Rally Coordinator, 6608 Oakbrook, Whitehouse, Ohio 43571, (419) 877-5743.

BMW Club of Houston, Ltd., 17th Annual South Central Reunion, a gathering of friends and neighbors at New Ulm, Texas. Contact: Ron Goodall, (713) 367-1620 or Floyd Crow, (409) 866-5323, before 9:00 p.m. CST.

September 4-7

Christian Motorcyclists Association, Ohio State Rally, United Missionary Campground, Ludlow Falls, Ohio, U.S. 48 and U.S. 55 Northwest of Dayton. Contact: Dave Smith, 2057 Decker Ct., Worthington, OH 43085, (614) 764-2548.

GWRRA Chapter "B", WING WHIRL '87, Ottawa, Ontario, Canada, two hours west of Montreal: four hours northeast of Toronto; one hour from New York state. See the Parliament Buildings, the Changing of the Guard, the Byward Market and Gatineau Park. Tour to nearby historic towns and explore the motorcycle roads of western Quebec. Contact: Roger LeBlanc, 890 Elsett Dr., Ottawa, Ontario, Canada, K1G 2S5.

1987 Three Flags Classic, Mexico to Canada. If you weren't one of the entrants drawn in April, there is a possibility of cancellations. Call sign-in coordinator, (818) 334-6742, Ride information numbers, (213) 863-5016, (818) 609-8179, (714) 539-8025, or write, Three Flags Classic, SCMA, P.O. Box 487, Norwalk, California 90651-0487.

September 5-6

The greatest show on earth! The Kansas City all British car and cycle meet, Kansas City, KS. Contact: Jack Turner, 12908 West 67th St., Shawnee, KS 66216, (913) 268-4401.

Washington Ninety-Niners, AMA District 27 Rally. Contact: Jim Allyn, 719 S. Donovan, Seattle, WA 98108, (206) 927-5134.

September 5-7

Spirit of Alabama, National Championship Poker Run and Field Meet, Oxford Lake Civic Center, Oxford, Alabama. Contact: Spirit of Alabama, c/o Mike Cova, P.O. Box 1846, Anniston, AL 36201, (205) 237-0680, (AMA/Dunlop Elite G/T Touring Series).

Road Rider Division of AMA District 36, Northwest Regional Road Riding Convention, San Jose Family Camp, Groveland, California. Contact: Road Rider Division 36, c/o David Schiller, 42866 Parkwood St., Fremont, California 94538, (415) 657-2087, (AMA/Dunlop Elite G/T Touring Series).

GWRRA, Labor Day Weekend Region "F" Rally III, Vail, Colorado: rally headquarters, Raintree Inn Hotel. For GWRRA rally hotel rates call 7:00 a.m. to 7:00 p.m. daily MST (800) 824-3662, in Colorado (800) 423-0633. Camping first come first serve in the National Forest. Mini-Tours, prospector poker run, poker walk, meal (first 500 registrants), field events, drill team competitions, seminars, exhibitors and much more. Contact: GWRRA Region "F" Rally, 1001 Wagonwheel Dr., Fort Collins, CO 80526, (303) 223-3387.

Wheels of Man MC, AMA District 31 Tour. Contact: Jean Sandburg, P.O. Box 14854, Phoenix, Arizona 85063, (602) 933-0108.

September 6

Red Rock Riders, 4th Annual Poker Run, South Overlook at Red Rock Dam, near Pella, Iowa. Sign-up from 9:00 a.m. to 1:00 p.m. For more information contact: Red Rock Riders, P.O. Box 282, Pella, IA 50219, (515) 628-1677.

The Fellowship M.C. Ltd., 3rd Annual Poker Run for Muscular Dystrophy, 10:00 a.m. Highway 53, LaCrosse, Wisconsin, in the city park behind Bridgeview Plaza. Questions, call Mike, (608) 781-2353.

September 10-13

Blue Comet MC, AMA District 6 Tour. Contact: Rodney Shultz, P.O. Box 234, Menach Rd., Skippack, Pennsylvania 19474, (215) 723-8518.

September 11-13

The BMW Motorcycle Club of Hampton Roads, 10th Annual Surf and Sand Rally, KOA Kampground, Virginia Beach, Virginia. Contact: BMW Motorcycle Club of Hampton Roads, 3804 North Landing Road, Virginia Beach, VA 23456.

The Wisconsin BMW Motorcycle Club, Inc. Wisconsin Dells BMW Rally, Eagle Flats Campground near Wisconsin Dells, Wisconsin. Featuring all the amenities of a great rally, enough to do and see for the entire weekend. For BMW riders and their guests only. Contact: Shirl Wozniak, 183 W. Tripoli Ave., Milwaukee, WI 53207, (414) 744-1753.

The 9th Annual Davis Rally, New Hampton, Iowa. Grand Prize 1987 Kawasaki Voyager X11 and featuring Kawasaki Team Tour. Poker-Run Grand Prize, a Time-Out Tent Camper. AMA and District 22 Sanctioned. For more information contact: Gene & Luci Davis, 713 E. Hamilton, New Hampton, IA 50659, (515) 394-2311.

13th Annual International M/C Aftermarket Expo., Las Vegas, Nevada.

September 12-13

Monmouth Shore Points M.C., 2nd Annual Garden State Tour, through historic New Jersey. AMA sanctioned District 2. Preregistration $25.00 per person before August 15 gets free camping: $30.00 per person at sign-in. For more information call MSPMC, (201) 493-9806 or Beth Tewhill, 389-3964. Write or send checks to M.S.P.M.C., P.O. Box 372, Oakhurst, New Jersey 07755.

September 13

Ohio Road Riders M.C., 3rd Annual Charity Poker Run for the Handicapped, Medina County Fairgrounds, West Smith Rd., Medina, Ohio. All bikes welcome. For more information contact: O.R.R.M.C., P.O. Box 1294, Medina, OH 44258, or call Dave Sprouse, (216) 725-2634.

The Lost Wheels Motorcycle Club, 12th Annual Poker Run. Starts at 9:00 a.m. from Dutchess Mall, I-84 and Rt. 9, Fishkill, New York, $12.00 per person. For more information call: Ed Jensen, (914) 896-7756.

September 15-20

The ultimate rally for touring and sports bikes, Ozark Motorcycle Jubilee, Branson, Missouri. Seminars, clinics, programs and Poker Runs to Eureka Springs, Arkansas, and Fantastic Caverns, Springfield, Missouri. Contact: Ozark Motorcycle Jubilee, P.O. Box 674, Colby, Kansas 67701, (913) 462-6871 or 462-7252.

September 17-19

The International Northeastern Harley-Davidson Dresser Touring Association, Inc., 1987 Fall Rally "Christmas with your Harley friends", Canaan Valley Resort, Davis, West Virginia. With the assistance of the Chamber of Commerce, and the Resort, the surrounding community will reflect the spirit of the Yuletide season, allowing members and guests to share the joy of Christmas during weather which still permits riding. For more information contact: Del Austin, R.D. #1 Box 36, Randolph Road, Great Bend, Pennsylvania 18821, (717) 879-2709.

September 18

Jerseypine Cruisers, AMA District 17 Tour. Contact: Ken Wyant, 510 W. Higgins Rd., Park Ridge, Illinois 60068, (312) 696-4131.

September 19

Lea County Roadriders, AMA District 25 Tour. Contact: Joann Staggs, P.O. Box 691, Hobbs, New Mexico, (505) 397-2824.

Central Cal BMW Riders, 2nd Annual Autumn Beemer Bash, approximately 25 miles east of Modesto, California in the historic gold rush area foothills on the Tuolumne River. Lots of activities. Contact: Central Cal BMW Riders, P.O. Box 3517, Modesto, CA, (209) 522-2118.

September 19-20

2nd Annual Arizona "See It All" Grand Tour, sponsored by the London Bridge Rotary Club, Budweiser — Bud Light, and Blue Water Riders Motorcycle Club of Lake Havasu City, AZ. Adventure in the old west — travel the highways and byways of Arizona. Contact: Arizona Grand Tour, P.O. Box 549, Lake Havasu City, AZ 86403, (602) 855-4604.

September 20

Blue Ridge Road Riders of Frederick, Maryland, Charity Poker Run. Ride benefits Big Brothers/Big Sister of Frederick County. Ride begins at Frederick Shopping Center, W. 7th St., Rt. 15 at 12:00 noon. Contact: Janine Woodward, (301) 694-8310.

Lodi M/C, AMA District 36, 50th Anniversary Parade & Bar-B-Q. Contact: Lodi M/C, Lodi, California, (209) 368-7182.

September 23-26

Til Thompson's Aspencade Motorcyclists Convention, The Midway Exposition Center, Columbia, Missouri. Contact: Gene Taylor, Aspencade '87. 3035 W. Thomas Rd., Phoenix, Arizona 85017, (800) 237-5450 or in Arizona: (602) 272-2900.

Golden Aspen Rally, 18th Annual Southwest Tour, Ruidoso, New Mexico. Contact: Ron Andrews, P.O. Box 1458, Ruidoso, NM 88345, (505) 257-4031.

September 25-27

Chicago Region Rally, Lake Alexander Campground, Momence, Illinois. For BMW riders and their guests only. Field events, tech sessions by CHITECH, sidecar seminar, camping, campfires, hot showers, fishing and more. Contact: Madelynn Wilharm, 2N935 Elodie, Elburn, IL 60119, (312) 377-2703 or 932-9699.

GWRRA, North Carolina State Rally "Wings Over The Smokies", Cherokee, NC. Poker runs, field events, self-guided tours, twilight parade, bike show, and play bingo for the grand prize, a 1987 Honda Interstate. No trophies for transported bikes. Contact: Norma Freedle, Route 14, Box 405, Lexington, NC 27292, (704) 787-4876.

BMW Motorcycle Owners of Vermont, 8th Annual Green Mountain Rally, Camp Betsy Cox, Pittsford, Vermont. Friday night chili, Saturday Continental breakfast, Saturday night dinner, tours, field events, bottomless pot of Vermonts famous Green Mountain Coffee Roaster Coffee, Vermont's fabulous fall foliage and more. Contact: BMWMOV, 38 Crescent Street, Rutland, VT 05701.

R & E Colorama, AMA District 16 Tour. Contact: Richard Lofquist, P.O. Box 296, Rhinelander, Wisconsin 54501, (715) 369-4723.

12th Annual Maggie Valley BMW Rally, Winngray Family Campground, at I-40 twenty mile marker, located three miles south of I-40 on Hwy. 276, Maggie Valley, North Carolina. BMW riders and invited guests only. For more information contact: Paula Scruggs, 16 West Baird Mountain Road, Asheville, N.C. 28804, (704) 645-3123.

September 26-27

New England Motorcycle Dealers, Inc., Northeast Regional Road Riding Convention, Sturbridge, Massachusetts. Contact: New England Motorcycle Dealers, Inc., c/o Bob Frink,

---

FIG. 6.3.   Shorter lead times and the increased popularity of specialized magazines have greatly improved magazines as useful targets for publicity releases. (*Reprinted with permission of* Road Rider *magazine,* © *1987.*)

Asking an editor about editorial and production deadlines for a magazine may be the only way to determine how to time the distribution of releases.

To match a release with magazines of interest, a publicist starts by looking closely at what is to be publicized and how the audience might use the information. If interested, for example, in distributing information about a new process that makes leather better able to withstand harsh winter temperatures, the publicist might plan a campaign aimed at both shoe manufacturers and consumers.

For the first audience the publicist would identify a group of trade publications for shoe manufacturers and wholesale shoe buyers. Releases to manufacturing publications might focus on details about how the method is used in manufacturing, its impact on manufacturing costs, and the ability to use existing technology versus the demand for new technology. Distribution of the releases would account not only for the magazine's editorial lead time but for seasonal manufacturing cycles as well. Releases to magazines read by shoe buyers would focus on benefits to consumers, impacts on costs to retailers, and potential enhancement of retailers' ability to sell a high-quality product.

To reach consumers, the publicist would identify fashion magazines for men and women. Releases to these magazines might focus on the process's impact on shoe-leather durability under stressful weather conditions. Other releases might emphasize potential effects on design or identify for consumers the manufacturers that are currently using the process and how it will change their products. These releases might be distributed later than those to the manufacturers and buyers but in time for the fall issues preceding the distribution of shoes manufactured with the process.

In the sports world, a publicist for the annual Boston Marathon might send releases to both *Sports Illustrated* and *Runner's World* to attract spectators and participants and to maintain national and international interest in the marathon. A publicist working for a local marathon, on the other hand, might send releases to *Runner's World* to attract big-name runners and to build interest in the marathon outside the local community. The publicist for the local marathon could also publicize heavily in magazines and newsletters distributed to members of sports clubs and athletic associations. However, because of the limited interest in an event without national prominence, and because a smaller community might not be able to accommodate the large crowd that national publicity could draw, releases would not be sent to a magazine with the national scope of *Sports Illustrated.*

News Releases and Features in Magazines

Although the differences between newspapers and magazines have become less pronounced in recent decades, some basic differences still exist. The difference in the way these two print media use and write news stories and features is important for the publicist. Although readers may never have articulated that difference, most recognize that newspapers and magazines have different priorities.

Newspapers emphasize news—late-breaking news of interest to people living in a specific region. Publicity about past or future events, background on events relevant to local businesses and industry, personnel changes, and other local information is important to newspaper editors because they know it is important to their readers. Furthermore, the most important news is presented on the first pages of the newspaper.

A newspaper's second priority is articles of general human interest. Such articles and features entice the casual reader and add notes of interest to the daily or weekly news. Because features are considered less important than news stories, they usually appear on later pages.

Magazines reverse the priorities of newspapers. Features and articles are given the most prominent place in the magazine, and news items are secondary. Most magazine readers select their favorite magazines for the articles and features that cover topics in depth. Although readers expect magazines to provide the latest information on the subject at hand—be it fashion, farming, or fishing—news items per se are usually secondary reasons for reading the magazine. Even readers of news magazines typically get headlines from the local newspaper, radio, or television; they read the magazines for analysis and background on the news.

Faced with selecting print media for news releases, a publicist should look at the news of newspapers and the features of magazines and distribute news releases accordingly—that is, send releases about events to newspapers and send feature articles to magazines. However, the discerning publicist will take advantage of the magazine editor's interest in both news and features to make the most effective use of magazines in a publicity campaign.

Most magazines have departments or columns that provide news items: announcements about coming events, new products or trends, and people in the forefront of the field. A careful look through a copy of any magazine will indicate where a magazine staff might use a news item. For example, Figure 6.4 illustrates how *Road Rider* magazine highlights news releases from organizations. As in the "What's Happening" column illustrated in Figure 6.3, publicists are encouraged to send information for possible publication.

Regardless of where a specific magazine is published, the size of its

FYI

On the Euro-front, **Moto Guzzi is finalizing its 1987 plans,** but chances are the U.S. will see the SP1000 Mark II, which will come stock with saddlebags in order to qualify for the burgeoning sport-touring marketplace; two versions of the LeMans 1000, the standard and the Special Edition (special by virtue of paint, graphics, close-ratio transmission and radial tires); two 744cc V75 models with four-valve heads; and the dual purpose V65 NTX. All these bikes have cleaned up their emissions acts so that they pass the stringent California requirements, where Moto Geese have not been legally sold since 1984... **The other Italian V-twin, Cagiva/Ducati is also well represented,** starting with two versions of the Alazzurra 650, the standard and the SS; two varieties of the dual-purpose Elefant 650, the standard and the SE; then there is the quick and nimble and smooth Paso 750; and the even quicker and nimbler but not nearly so smooth F-1; and finally, a direct assault on the bastions of chopperdom, the Delta. As soon as we get press kits and all, we'll tell you more about these models.

The British International Motorcycle Association, that keeper of the Triumph and Norton and Matchless, etc., faith, has now taken under its wing the 2,000 members of the Triumph International Owners Club. They're

---

OOOPS!!!
Great America Show Correction

In the December FYI column we only made two mistakes concerning the **Great America Motorcycle Show** for the Los Angeles area; both the dates and the place were wrong. Here is the right information: The show will be held January 9-11 at the Los Angeles County Fairgrounds. Other Great America Motorcycle Shows will be seen at New York, San Francisco, Philadelphia, Chicago and Atlanta. Call (714) 675-0312 for details.

---

planning the second "British In The Blue Ridge" rally sometime this July, and it will probably be at the T.W.O. Motorcycle Resort in Suches, Georgia. All you Brit Bike Buffs can get ahold of B.I.M.A. at P.O. Box 28713, Atlanta, Georgia 30358; (404) 252-0070. Don't forget your gudgeon pins and spare half-links... **More Blue Ridge notes: up north a bit the High Country Cycle Camp** will officially open this coming May. The H.C.C.C. is a campground strictly for motorcyclists, just 20 miles off the Blue Ridge Parkway, near Ferguson, North Carolina. The Camp will provide lots of tenting space, plus chalets for those who don't want to stretch the canvas. Only two-wheel vehicles will be allowed within the camping grounds. Sounds like owner Tom Thompson has a great future; you can get in touch with him and High Country Cycle Camp by writing to Route 1, Box 216, Ferguson, North Carolina 28624; or call (919) 973-7522. We'll give the place a try the next time we're in that neck of the woods.

Who is John Ulrich? He's the editor and publisher of *American Roadracing.* He's been a few other things in his life, but John has just been named by Motorsport Organization and Management, Inc., to head their monthly publication. The tabloid newspaper is dedicated to "high performance street motorcycles and road racing." By the way, AR is no newcomer, as it has been published continuously since 1973. As we like to say in the small world of moto-journalism, the more the merrrier. *American Roadracing* is distributed to all members of the Western Eastern Roadracers Association (WERA), but we imagine the circulation will expand greatly before long. Interested types can contact the editorial offices at 41 U.S. Highway 17 South, Hardeeville, South Carolina 29927... **Another editorial change is Clark Stivers becoming the editor of the Riders of Vision** newsletter. He has also been appointed coordinator, treasurer, backhoe operator and window cleaner of the organization, and he'd like to spread the word that the new address is RoV, P.O. Box 469, Bar Harbor, Maine 04609.

On the newsfront, a big round of applause for *The Wall Street Journal,* which ran a nice page-one story on the GWRRA Michigan rally. The point of the exercise was to tell the reader that motorcycling has become a popular pasttime for all walks of life. And for the affluent. "Price: $10,598. Enthusi-

---

STOP THE PRESSES!!!
V-Daze '87
Goes To Tennessee!
"AN AFFAIR
TO REMEMBER"

We just received word that the Venture Touring Society's 3rd Annual V-Daze International Motorcycle Rally, in conjunction with the 8th Annual Yamaha Family Affair (Southeastern Region), will be held at Pigeon Forge, Tennessee, from June 8th through the 12th.

This event has been sanctioned by the AMA and District 32, and is part of the AMA/Dunlop Touring Elite series. Headquarters will be at the Grand Hotel in Pigeon Forge, with a big trade show attached.

Lots of entertainments in the area, with Dollywood just around the corner, the Great Smoky Mountains National Park on the horizon, and good riding in every direction.

Info on V-Daze is available from:
Venture Touring Society
1615 South Eastern Ave.
Las Vegas, NV 89104
For lodging in the area, write or call:
Chamber of Commerce
105 Mill Creek Road
Pigeon Forge, TN 37863
(615) 453-5700
And any Yamaha dealer can tell you all about the Family Affairs. See you there!

---

asts have added thousands of dollars in sidecars, camper trailers that pop up to sleep four and hitches that haul canoes." This is the sort of press we can use lots of; our thanks to WSJ staff reporter John Bussey for a good job... **At the irresponsible end of the spectrum we have Jack Anderson's column** titled "U.S. Motorcycle Gangs Export Thugs And Drugs," dealing with — who else? — the Hells Angels. Nobody will question the fact that there are various scruffy types who are more interested in illegal activities than in motorcycling, but we do question featuring that sort — which probably comprise less than 1/10th of one percent of our motorcycling fraternity — in a nationally read column. How about a column on the nice people that go motorcycling, Jack?

This column is made up of items mostly culled from RR's mail — clippings, articles, letters, announcements and, of course, the monthly mountain of press releases. For those who have asked who "writes" FYI, the answer is: You do. Do keep that mail coming in, folks — and thanks.

FIG. 6.4.   By carefully examining several issues of a selected magazine, a publicist can determine how an organization's information can best be used by that publication. (*Reprinted with permission of* Road Rider *magazine,* © *1987.*)

circulation, or the degree of its specialization, news releases can play a part in developing the lively editorial product that readers expect. As was mentioned earlier, a release can be not only an item for a news column but also an idea for an editor to develop into a feature article. If the publicist wants to be certain that a feature is written about a particular subject, he or she should take the initiative. Many magazine articles and features are written not by staff members but by publicists and free-lancers who submit the articles to the magazine.

There are two primary ways in which a publicist can initiate the writing of a feature: The publicist can write it, or a free-lance writer can be hired. Writing feature articles for audiences of specific magazines is a professional skill that can be learned just as a publicist can learn to write quality news releases. Feature writing is, however, more time-consuming and draws on a broader range of skills. Even if a publicist has the basic skills or is interested in learning the ropes of feature writing, the time needed to do that writing may not be available. Therefore, a publicist might contract with a free-lance writer to have one or more feature articles written.

Publicists can contact free-lancers in several ways. The *Working Press of the Nation,* available in many large libraries, lists the names and addresses of free-lance photographers and writers. Local free-lance writers can often be contacted through local media. Newspaper editors and radio and television news producers often know members of their own staffs or individuals in the community who do free-lance work. Finally, a careful study of the writers of articles in publications can reveal potential free-lancers, as their names do not appear in publication mastheads. The editor can then provide a telephone number or address or, to protect the author's privacy, forward a letter to the writer. This approach is particularly useful because a writer who has already successfully written for a particular publication has a greater chance of having additional articles published in it.

It is not an accepted practice for a publicist to ask an editor to write a feature. Indeed, such a request would be perceived as unprofessional.

Making Contact with Editors

The editorial offices of magazines are widely dispersed geographically. However, that is not a problem because there is little need for personal visits to those offices. Once the publicist has become familiar with a magazine by consulting the appropriate media directories, *Writer's Market,* and recent issues of the magazine, if personal contact with the editor is necessary, it can be made by a phone call. This contact serves not only to introduce the publicist but also to confirm the accuracy of information in the directories, to check on publication deadlines, or to request copies for more careful study of a magazine not available locally.

News releases should be sent directly to the editor, but feature articles should not. Convention requires that a letter to the magazine editor precede the submission of feature articles. Called a **query letter,** it should mention the proposed subject of the article, the angle of the story, and a basic outline of the content. In most cases publicists will want to send a query letter prior to writing an article. For a variety of reasons, the editor may not be interested in the idea, or the editor may suggest a different way to develop the article. In either case, time spent writing is saved and aimed in the most effective directions. Additional information about writing query letters, articles for magazines, and the business of free-lance writing is available in the references at the end of this chapter.

Summary

Magazines complement newspapers in the distribution of information. Giving priority to subject over geographic location, magazines have audiences with both general and highly specialized interests in almost every imaginable subject. For the publicist who knows which audience is to be reached and the ways in which that audience might conceivably use the information, the magazine page offers brilliant reproduction, prestige, and in-depth information presented either as news or in a feature format.

Exercises

1. Choose a particular problem that can be solved with publicity. Then, using the references given in the chapter, make a list of the magazines that would be good channels for reaching your target audience. Identify the magazines by primary category: a) consumer magazines; b) trade magazines; c) organization publications.
2. Identify the source of the information you obtained on each magazine listed in Exercise 1. Note the patterns of reference sources that are most helpful for your purposes. Describe briefly your reason for selecting each magazine.
3. Project a realistic and appropriate schedule of release mailings to coincide with the production and publication deadlines of the chosen magazines in relation to the publicity campaign. When possible, allow for editorial delays that might necessitate publication in a later issue.

Suggested Reading

MAGAZINE MEDIA DIRECTORIES

Bacon's Publicity Checker. Bacon's, 332 S. Michigan Ave., Chicago, IL 60604. Annual.

Editor and Publisher Yearbook. Editor and Publisher, 850 Third Ave., New York, NY 10022. Annual; Sunday magazines.

The Encyclopedia of Associations. Gale Research Co., Book Tower, Detroit, MI 48226. Annual.

Gale Directory of Publications (formerly *IMS/Ayer Directory of Publications*). Gale Research Co., Book Tower, Detroit, MI 48226. Annual.

Standard Rate and Data Service directories: *Business Publications Rates and Data, Consumer Magazine and Agri-Media Rates and Data,* and *Newspaper Rates and Data* (Sunday magazines). Standard Rate and Data Service, 5201 Old Orchard Dr., Skokie, IL 60076. Monthly.

Ulrich's International Periodicals Directory. R. R. Bowker Co., 1180 Avenue of the Americas, New York, NY 10036. Annual.

Working Press of the Nation. National Research Bureau, 474 N. Third St., Burlington, IA 52601. Annual.

Writer's Market. F&W Publications, 9933 Alliance Rd., Cincinnati, OH 45252. Annual.

WRITING ARTICLES AND FEATURES

Graham, Betsy. *Magazine Article Writing: Substance and Style.* New York: Holt, Rinehart and Winston, 1980.

Rivers, William L., and Work, Alison R. *Free-lancer and Staff Writer: Newspaper Features and Magazine Articles.* 4th ed. Belmont, Calif.: Wadsworth Publishing Co., 1986.

Spikol, Art. *Magazine Writing: The Inside Angle.* Cincinnati: Writer's Digest Books, 1979.

Writer's Market. See listing above.

QUERY LETTER REFERENCES

Biagi, Shirley. "How to Write an Effective Query." Chapter 5 in *How to Write and Sell Magazine Articles.* Englewood Cliffs, N.J.: Prentice-Hall, 1981.

Graham, Betsy P. "The Query Letter." Chapter 8 in *Magazine Article Writing: Substance and Style.* New York: Holt, Rinehart and Winston, 1980.

Schoenfeld, Clay A. *Effective Feature Writing.* New York: Holt, Rinehart and Winston, 1982.

Spikol, Art. *Magazine Writing: The Inside Angle.* Cincinnati: Writer's Digest Books, 1979.

PUBLISHING AND EDITING MAGAZINES

Click, J. William, and Baird, Russell N. *Magazine Editing and Production.* 4th ed. Dubuque, Iowa: Wm. C. Brown Publishers, 1986.

Hubbard, J. T. W. *Magazine Editing.* Englewood Cliffs, N.J.: Prentice-Hall, 1982.

Mogel, Leonard. *The Magazine: Everything You Need to Know to Make It in the Magazine Business.* 2d ed. Chester, Conn.: The Globe Pequot Press, 1988.

Rivers, William L. *Magazine Editing in the '80s.* Belmont, Calif.: Wadsworth Publishing Co., 1983.

Williams, W. P., and Van Zandt, Joseph. *How to Start Your Own Magazine.* Chicago: Contemporary Books, 1978.

7

The Electronic Media: Radio, Television, Cable, and Beyond

KENNETH L. EICH

IF any publicists, individuals, or groups seeking publicity ignore broadcasting and cablecasting in their media mix, they could be overlooking a significant portion of the available audience that does not regularly read newspapers, magazines, or other printed materials. Surveys by the Burns W. Roper Organization have claimed since 1959 that most Americans receive most of their news from television. Those same surveys indicate that most Americans consider television to be the most reliable and believable medium of communication. In addition to that, mid-1980s figures from the American Newspaper Publishers Association (ANPA) showed that a smaller percentage of Americans and fewer younger Americans read newspapers than did previously.

Even allowing for the inevitable bias in interpreting survey research conducted by or for the print and broadcast industries (the Roper surveys are commissioned by the Television Information Office, for example), most publicity campaigns will want to include a mixture of appropriate media messages such as news, paid advertisements, and free public service announcements rather than rely on only one or two formats and media outlets.

The Technology

Perhaps no other communication medium has expanded more dramatically than broadcast and cable in the last decade. By the mid-eighties there were more than 10,500 radio and 1,500 television stations in the United States. There were also 7,300 cable television (CATV) systems and dozens of cable services ranging from news and information to arts and entertainment to sports to music videos. Also, several hundred low-power television (LPTV) stations were broadcasting to very limited areas such as small communities or sections of metropolitan areas.

All of these broadcast and cable services were designed to cater to parts of an audience that became increasingly fragmented as more and more stations and channels became available in most American cities and towns, thanks to the links provided by satellite distribution, coaxial cable, and even fiber optics. The proliferation of broadcast stations and networks now permits publicists to select the most appropriate outlets for their messages and to target those messages to the most desirable audiences.

Many changes at the network television level—the June 1980 launching of Atlanta broadcaster Ted Turner's Cable News Network (CNN), the expanded early-morning newscasts by ABC, CBS, and NBC, the late-evening ABC news program "Nightline," the increasing popularity of newsmagazine programs such as CBS's "60 Minutes" and ABC's "20/20," and the continuing commitment to public affairs programs such as ABC's "This Week With David Brinkley," CBS's "Face the Nation," and NBC's "Meet the Press"—had their scaled-down counterparts at many local stations. By the mid-1980s, television in many of the nation's large, medium-sized, and even small markets offered viewers several hours of news and public affairs programs each weekday.

Despite considerable deregulation of radio by the federal government in the early 1980s, radio news and public affairs programs continued at about the same level at almost nine out of ten stations responding to a nationwide survey conducted by the Radio-Television News Directors Association (RTNDA). By the mid-1980s, however, cutbacks were reported at some small and medium-sized stations.

Many of those stations apparently thought that their network or audio service affiliation was sufficient to provide listeners with information. National radio networks—including six at ABC, two each at CBS, NBC, and United, as well as Mutual, Associated Press (AP) Network News, and

United Press International (UPI) World News—continued to have hundreds of member stations. But as in television, local radio programming still offered numerous opportunities for individuals and groups to communicate their messages in various forms to target audiences.

Some Easing of Government Regulations

By the early 1980s, the Federal Communications Commission (FCC), the government agency that regulates American broadcasting, eliminated minimum guidelines for radio news, commercials, and public service announcements as a percentage of overall station programming. The FCC believed that the increasing number of radio stations in the country allowed the marketplace to determine how much news, advertising, and public service a particular station provided its listeners.

On the other hand, the relatively small number of TV stations still prevented the FCC from eliminating such programming guidelines for television. That situation may change soon as network and cable television become more diversified. The important point here is that radio and television, unlike newspapers, magazines, and other print communications, continue to be regulated by the federal government regarding overall programming, particularly the treatment of political candidates. These restrictions and others are outlined later in this chapter for consideration with respect to different forms of broadcast publicity.

Broadcast News

Unlike print media, which theoretically can add more pages to provide more news coverage, electronic media cannot add more time to their program schedules. In fact, many radio, television, and cable stations do not operate 24 hours a day. For example, daytime-only AM (amplitude modulation) radio stations can legally operate only from sunrise to sunset, although the federal government eased this restriction somewhat in the early 1980s to include time just before sunrise and just after sunset.

Generally, AM radio is more information-oriented than FM (frequency modulation) radio for several reasons, including AM's news-coverage tradition that began in the 1930s and provided the latest details during World War II. FM's later development and clearer reception, including stereo sound, have given it a more music-oriented image when compared with AM radio.

It's important to remember that audiences for broadcast news and public affairs programs often are easily distracted or are doing other things while listening to radio and television. The portability of the radio has made it a companion medium in the car, truck, van, or tractor for years. Similarly, TV news audiences often are reading the newspaper or eating a meal while trying to absorb what their favorite anchorperson is telling them. Neither radio nor television can assume that its audience is captive. Too many other activities compete for the time and attention of busy people.

EXPLORING SOME BROADCAST OPTIONS

With some exceptions, AM radio will probably provide more news opportunities than FM in a typical broadcast market. The ability to reach target audiences, insomuch as is possible by knowing the format of broadcast stations, works to the advantage of the publicist. For example, the opening of a local youth center is likely to be an important news story on a contemporary-hit radio station, whether it's AM or FM. The local TV station might do a soft feature report about the opening, and the local cable operation might have a public access channel available for a program produced by the center's own people.

Broadcast reference books, such as those listed at the end of this chapter, provide basic information about stations and programming. To find out whether a publicity opportunity exists, a publicist should contact the news directors at local radio and TV stations. They are in charge of the daily operation of the news departments at their stations. They may be the entire news staff at a small or medium-sized radio station, or they may direct a staff of 25 or more in medium-sized and larger TV stations.

Too often, publicists forget to look into broadcast options beyond the most obvious and often-used ones. To see how a publicist should take advantage of all the broadcast possibilities in a particular area, consider the alternatives if the youth center mentioned above was located in Cincinnati. Figures 7.1 through 7.3 highlight various entries for Cincinnati in broadcast reference books.

For example, the *Spot Radio Rates and Data* page in Figure 7.1 indicates that WCKY in Cincinnati programs for a general-interest radio audience through its news-talk-information format. The listing includes numerous consumer-oriented programs, ranging from financial and personal advice to car care. Several shows are listener phone-in programs. WCKY's programs offer opportunities for the publicist to have appropriate messages broadcast about the activities of the new youth center.

Figure 7.2, from the *Broadcasting Cablecasting Yearbook,* lists the communities served by Warner Amex Cable Communications in and around

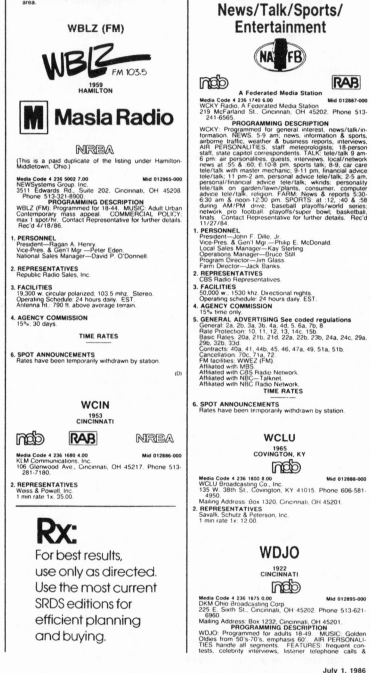

FIG. 7.1.   Listings in *Spot Radio Rates and Data* provide the publicist with such information as the station's programming format, personnel, and spot announcements. The book also includes media market maps and market data for each state.

Ownership: Charles Dolan.

Cheviot. Continental Cablevision. 3511 Glenmore Avenue 45211. (513) 661-6500. Tom Peters, mgr-chief tech. Atty: Smith & Schnacke.
  Serves Cheviot. Hamilton county. Top-100 TV market.
  Subscribers: 1,400; homes passed: 4,000; total homes in franchised area: 4,000 Started 1980. Length 21 mi.
  Ownership: Continental Cablevision Inc. (see MSO).

Chillicothe. Chillicothe Cablevision. 38 East Water St. 45601. (614) 775-4300.
  Serves Chillicothe and surrounding Ross county. Outside all TV markets.
  Subscribers: 6,520; homes passed: 10,500; total pop in franchised area: 24,957. Started 9/64. Length 90 mi. Franchise fee $5,000/yr.
  Ownership: McDonald Group Inc. (see MSO).

Cincinnati. Warner Amex Cable Communications Inc. 11252 Cornell Park Drive 45242. (513) 489-5000. Robert L. Montgomery, gen mgr. Tom Navaro, chief tech. Atty: In-house counsel, New York.
  Serves Cincinnati, Amberley, Anderson, Blue Ash, Colerain, Columbia twp, Crosby twp, Deerfield twp, Deer Park, Delhi twp, Elmwood Place, Evendale, Fairfax, Forest Park, Glendale, Goshen, Greenhills, Hamilton twp, Harrison Village, Harrison twp., Indian Hill, Lebanon, Lincoln Heights, Lockland, Loveland, Madeira, Mariemont, Mason, Miami twp, Milford, Montgomery, Mount Healthy, Newtown, North College Hill, Norwood, Reading, St. Bernard, Sharonville, Silverton, South Lebanon, Springdale, Springfield, Sycamore, Symmes twp, Terrace Park, Union (Butler), Union (Clermont, Woodlawn and Wyoming, all Ohio; West Harrison, Indiana. Hamilton, Clermont, Butler and Warren counties, Ohio; Dearborn county, Indiana. Top-100 TV market.
  Subscribers: 145,000; homes passed: 305,015; total homes in franchised area: 332,000. Started 1/80. Length 2,700 mi. Charges: instal $10 up; $3.95 up/mo. Franchise fee 3-5%.
  Channel usage: total ch capacity 60; TV chs 15; pay cable 9; basic cable 24; automated 4; access 8; other origination programing 3. Total radio stns 23 FM; 1 weather.
  ■ Pay cable: 9 chs (HBO, Showtime, Movie Channel, Cinemax, Bravo, Disney; $13.95 each); (Viewer's Choice 1, 2, 3; pay-per-view).
  Origination–automated: 4 chs (weather radar, color test, NYSE ticker, EPG); access: 8 chs (public, govt, educ, leased); other: 3 chs (free previews, local classified).
  Basic cable: 24 chs (A&E, BET, CNN, CNN Headline, CBN, Country Music TV, C-SPAN, ESPN, EWTN, FNN, Learning Channel, MTV, TNN, NJT, Nickelodeon, PTL, SPN, Silent Network, Trinity, USA, VH-1, TWC, WGN-TV, WOR-TV, WTBS).
  Advertising accepted.
  Other services: Two-way capability.
  Ownership: Warner Amex Cable Communications Inc. 100% (see MSO).

Clarington. Bates Communications Corp. Box 396, New Martinsville, W. Va. 26155.
  Serves Clarington, Sardis. Monroe county. Top-100 TV market.
  Subscribers: 508; homes passed: 600; total pop in franchised area: 770. Started 9/57. Length 8 mi.
  Ownership: Bates Communications Corp. (see MSO).

Clay. Tele-Media Co. of Southern Ohio. Box 39, Bellefonte, Pa. 16823.
  Serves Clay. Scioto county.
  Subscribers: 155; homes passed: 225; total pop in franchised area: 680. Started 7/76. Length 2.4 mi. $13; $7/mo.

Clyde. Continental Cablevision of Ohio Inc. 101 W. Main St., Bellevue 44811. Joe Helms, mgr; Dave Phillips, chief tech.
  Serves Clyde. Sandusky county. Outside all TV markets.
  Subscribers: 910; homes passed: 1,763; total pop in franchised area: 6,000. Started 3/71. Length 23 mi.
  Ownership: Continental Cablevision Inc. (see MSO).

Columbiana. TCI Media of Addil. 139 N. Main St. 44408.
  Serves Columbiana, Leetonia, Fairfield twp, Washington twp, Washingtonville. Columbiana county. Top-100 TV market.
  Subscribers: 1,400; homes passed: 3,200; total pop in franchised area: 18,100. Started 12/69. Length 35 mi. Franchise fee 3%.

Ownership: Tele-Communications Inc (see MSO)

Columbus. All American Cablevision Co. 1980 Alum Creek Dr 43207 (614) 445-7141 Bruno Masdea. sys mgr; David Bay, chief tech.
  Serves Columbus, Bexley, Hamilton, Groveport, Obetz and Westerville. Franklin county. Top-100 TV market.
  Subscribers: 32,900; homes passed: 72,900 Started 12/73. Length 555 mi. Charges instal $25; $9.95/mo.
  Channel usage: total ch capacity 30; TV chs 8 (1 shared); pay cable 4; basic cable 15 (2 shared), automated 4 (1 shared); access 1; other origination programing 1 shared.
  ■ Pay cable: 4 chs (HBO, Cinemax, each $10.95/mo.; Playboy, Disney, each $9.95/mo.). 29,200 subscribers.
  Origination–automated: 4 chs (natl/fin news, job bank, color radar, program guide); access: one ch (govt, pub); other: one ch (community programing).
  Basic cable: 13 chs (CNN, ESPN, CBN, Nickelodeon/A&E, Nat Jewish/Learning Channel, Lifetime, Fin News/BET, CNN Headline, Weather Channel, USA, C-SPAN, SPN, WTBS, MTV, Nashville)
  Ownership: American Television & Communications Corp., 100% (see MSO).

Columbus. Coaxial Communications 3770 E. Livingston Ave. 43227. (614) 236-1292. Leo Brennan, gen mgr; Doug Grace, chief tech.
  Serves Columbus, Reynoldsburg, Whitehall, Pickerington, Canal Winchester, Violet twp, Franklin City and surrounding Franklin county. Top-100 TV market.
  Subscribers: 40,000; homes passed: 70,000; total homes in franchised area: 200,000. Started 11/70. Length 500 mi. Franchise fee 6%.
  Ownership: Coaxial Communications Inc , 98%

Columbus. KBLE Ohio Inc. 124 S. Washington Ave. 43215. (614) 221-0692. William Johnson, pres. Pat Birney, chief tech. Atty: William Johnson, Columbus.
  Serves Columbus. Franklin county. Top-100 TV market.
  Subscribers: 6,300; homes passed: 18,500; total homes in franchised area: 38,000. Started 10/78. Length 184 mi. Franchise fee 3%.
  Ownership: William Johnson, 100%.

Columbus. Warner Amex Cable Communications Inc. 930 Kinnear Rd. 43212. (614) 481-5000. Jerry Murray, VP & gen mgr; Arnold Maki, chief tech.
  Serves Columbus, Dublin, Grove City, Marble Cliff, Minerva Park, Norwich twp, Perry twp, Riverlea, Worthington, Gahanna, Grandview Heights, Hilliard, Upper Arlington, and surrounding Franklin county. Top-100 TV market.
  Subscribers: 62,500; homes passed: 140,019; total homes in franchised area: 160,000. Started 12/71. Length 1,400 mi. Charges: instal $25; $9.95/mo. Franchise fee 3%.
  Channel usage: total ch capacity 34; TV chs 6; pay cable 5; basic cable 14; automated 2; access 1; other origination programing 3. Total radio stns: 30 FM.
  ■ Pay cable: 5 chs (HBO; 17,200 subscribers; $12.25/mo.); (Showtime; 4,500 subscribers; $12.25/mo.); (Movie Channel; 16,800 subscribers; $12.25/mo.); (Disney; 2,500 subscribers; $12.25/mo.). (Playboy; 3,400 subscribers; $12.25/mo.
  Origination–automated: 2 chs (weather, program guide); access: one ch (govt, pub, educ); other: 3 chs (studio, pay-per-view, commercial production).
  Basic cable: 14 chs (Weather Channel, USA CNN, ESPN, Nickelodeon, A&E, Lifetime, C-SPAN, CNN Headline, Fin News, SPN, Nashville, MTV, CBN, WTBS).
  Ad accepted; annual volume $1 million.
  Other services: Two-way capability; pay-per-view billing, system diagnostics.
  Ownership: Warner Communications Inc./American Express, 50% each (see MSO).

Concord twp. TCI of of Lake County. Box 380, Painesville 44077. (216) 354-8000. Ed Williams, mgr; Jerry Snyder, chief tech.
  Serves Concord, Kirtland, Chester, Waite Hills, M.O.T.L., Painesville, Perry twp, Perry Village, N. Perry. Lake county. Top-100 TV market.
  Subscribers: 10,500; homes passed: 18,800; total homes in franchised area: 20,000. Started 9/81.

FIG. 7.2. *Broadcasting Cablecasting Yearbook* has radio, television, and cable sections with information about ownership, personnel, and advertising rates. One section lists radio stations according to formats and special programming.

OHIO

OHIO
See SRDS Consumer market map and data at beginning of the state.

THIS STATE OBSERVES DAYLIGHT SAVINGS TIME.

Akron
Summit County—Map Location F-4
See SRDS Consumer market map and data at beginning of the state.

See Cleveland-Akron-Canton
(Including Lorain, Shaker Heights)

Canton
Stark County—Map Location F-5
See SRDS Consumer market map and data at beginning of the state.

See Cleveland-Akron-Canton
(Including Lorain, Shaker Heights)

Cincinnati
(Including Newport, KY)
Cincinnati, Hamilton County—Map Location A-8
Newport, Campbell County—Map Location H-3
See SRDS Consumer market map and data at beginning of the state.
Stations located within the combined coverage area are consolidated under multiple city headings. This is not to imply that all of the stations provide equal coverage of the entire area or cities involved. It is part of the time buying function to determine the extent of individual station coverage, audience delivered, etc. within the area.

WCPO-TV
(Airdate July 26, 1949)
CINCINNATI

CBS Television Network
ncb
A Scripps-Howard Station

Media Code 6 236 0100 2.00   Mid 007665-000
500 Central Ave., Cincinnati, OH 45202. Phone 513-721-9900, TWX, 810-461-2690.

1. PERSONNEL
General Manager—Terry Connelly.
Ass't. Gen'l & Gen'l Sales Mgr.—J. B. Chase.
National Sales Manager—Jeff Sales.
Local Sales Manager—Ruth Ackerman.
Director of Operations—Rick Reeves.

2. REPRESENTATIVES
Blair Television.

3. FACILITIES
Video 316,000 w., audio 58,900 w.; ch. 9.
Antenna ht.: 1,019 ft. above average terrain.
Operating schedule: 24 hours daily. EST.

4. AGENCY COMMISSION
15% to recognized agencies; no cash discount.

5. GENERAL ADVERTISING See coded regulations
General: 2a, 3a, 4a, 5, 6b, 7a.
Rate Protection: 10i, 11m, 12m, 13m, 14f.
Contracts: 20c, 25, 26, 27a, 32c, 34c.
Basic Rates: 40b, 41b, 41d, 42, 45a, 46, 47c.
Cancellation: 70b, 70i.
Prod. Services: 83, 84, 85, 86.
(*) Service charge for splicing and/or editing multiple product commercials will be 10.00.
Affiliated with CBS Television Network.

6. TIME RATES
Rates have been temporarily withdrawn by station.

11. SPECIAL FEATURES

COLOR
Schedules network color, film, slides, tape and live.
Equipped with high and low band VTR.

13. CLOSING TIME
Closing time on all scripts, film, slides and other program material is 72 hours prior; 1 week film, slides and artwork.

June 15, 1986

WIII-TV
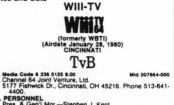
(formerly WBTI)
(Airdate January 28, 1980)
CINCINNATI

TvB

Media Code 6 236 0125 9.00   Mid 007664-000
Channel 64 Joint Venture, Ltd.
5177 Fishwick Dr., Cincinnati, OH 45216. Phone 513-641-4400.

1. PERSONNEL
Pres. & Gen'l Mgr.—Stephen J. Kent.
Sales Manager—Tim Bennett.
Business Manager—Greg Curvall.

2. REPRESENTATIVES
Independent Television Sales.

3. FACILITIES
Video 1,000,000 w., audio 200,000 w.; ch 64.
Antenna ht.: 777 ft. above average terrain.
Operating schedule: 6-2 am. EST.

4. AGENCY COMMISSION
15% to recognized agencies on time; no cash discount.

5. GENERAL ADVERTISING See coded regulations
General: 2a, 2b, 3a, 3b, 3c, 3d, 4a, 5, 6a, 8.
Rate Protection: 10m, 11m, 14m.
Contracts: 20b, 21, 22a, 25, 26, 31b, 32c, 34a.
Basic Rates: 40a, 41b, 41c, 42.
Cancellation: 70f, 71, 72, 73a, 73b.
Prod. Services: 80, 81, 82, 83, 85, 86.

6. TIME RATES
Rates have been temporarily withdrawn by station.

11. SPECIAL FEATURES

COLOR
Schedules color film, slides, tape and live.
Equipped with high band VTR.

13. CLOSING TIME
72 hours.

WKRC-TV
(Airdate April 4, 1949)
CINCINNATI

mmt SALES INC

ABC Television Network
ncb   TvB
A Taft Station

Media Code 6 236 0150 7.00   Mid 007666-000
Taft Television & Radio Co., Inc., a subsidiary of Taft Broadcasting Company
1906 Highland Ave., Cincinnati, OH 45219. Phone 513-651-1200, TWX, 810-461-2606.

1. PERSONNEL
Vice-Pres. & Gen'l Mgr.—John Rose.
General Sales Manager—John Dawson.

2. REPRESENTATIVES
MMT Sales, Inc.
Taft Stations.

3. FACILITIES
Video 316,000 w., audio 31,600 w.; ch 12.
Antenna ht.: 1,000 ft. above average terrain.
Operating schedule: 6-2 am. EST.

4. AGENCY COMMISSION
15% to recognized agencies on net time charges.

5. GENERAL ADVERTISING See coded regulations
General: 2b, 3a, 4a, 5, 6a, 7b, 8.
Rate Protection: 14h, 16.
Contracts: 20c, 21, 22a, 23, 25, 26, 27a, 28, 30, 31b, 32c, 32d, 34e.
Basic Rates: 40a, 40b, 41c, 41d, 42, 43b, 44b, 45a, 46, 47a, 47b, 49, 51a, 51e.
Comb.: Cont. Discounts: 60a, 62b.
Cancellation: 70d, 70n, 71, 72, 73a.
Prod. Services: 83, 84, 86, 87b, 87c.
Affiliated with ABC Television Network.

6. TIME RATES
Rates have been temporarily withdrawn by station.

11. SPECIAL FEATURES

COLOR
Schedules network color, film, slides, tape and live.
Equipped with high and low band VTR.

13. CLOSING TIME
72 hours prior film, slides; 1 week artwork; 3 days musical content and commercial copy.

WLWT
(Airdate February 9, 1948)
CINCINNATI

Katz American

NBC Television Network
ncb   TvB
A Multimedia Station

Media Code 6 236 0200 0.00   Mid 007667-000
Multimedia of Ohio, Inc.
140 W. Ninth St., Cincinnati, OH 45202. Phone 513-352-5000, TWX, 810-461-2610.

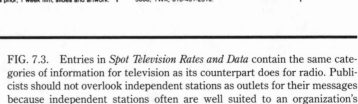

FIG. 7.3. Entries in *Spot Television Rates and Data* contain the same categories of information for television as its counterpart does for radio. Publicists should not overlook independent stations as outlets for their messages because independent stations often are well suited to an organization's needs.

Cincinnati. Eight access channels are listed as part of the cable system, including channels reserved for the general public and local governments and schools. The youth center publicist might be able to cablecast the center's various activities and programs on some of these access channels. Two-way communication between the program participants and the cable audience may even be possible.

Depending on its programming format and target audience, an independent (nonnetwork-affiliated) television station, such as WIII-TV in Cincinnati (see Figure 7.3), might be a potential publicity source for the youth center. Independent stations usually have more scheduling flexibility than network TV affiliates do, although other factors (such as WIII's Channel 64) sometimes limit their potential audience, viewer awareness, and even the relative strength of their signals. But the channel *is* available, and the publicist should find out if it is a viable publicity option for the youth center.

Nowadays, assignment editors handle more duties and responsibilities, especially in TV news operations. The assignment editor can be a particularly important contact in arranging coverage of an event or activity. Currently, cable news staffs at the local level are rare. A publicist should probably contact the program director, the public access coordinator, or, in a small cable company, the general manager. The United States Supreme Court ruled in 1979 that cable operators could no longer be required to provide public access channels, but many companies continue to offer the service as part of their programming package when bidding for an exclusive franchise in a city or town. Local cable channels don't have relatively high viewerships yet, but their status could change when cable reaches more households than the approximately 50 percent penetration achieved by the mid-1980s.

BROADCAST STORY COVERAGE

Electronic news coverage may vary significantly from the print media's evaluation and handling of the same event. News coverage may also vary among several stations in a given broadcast market, depending on a station's news commitment, staff size, frequency and length of newscasts, and facilities and equipment available for live or taped broadcasts in a studio or at the scene of the event.

Smaller radio and television stations with limited staffs are more likely to use audio or video materials produced by an outside person or organization. Larger broadcast operations are more likely to use such handouts as news tips or ideas to generate their own stories. A professional broadcaster is unlikely to air poor-quality tape, just as a provided news release will probably not be read over the air word for word. Publicists not only should monitor their local media but also should personally contact the appropriate people at those stations to determine possible coverage.

As will be discussed in more detail in Chapter 9, news is generally defined as what is new and newsworthy. These qualities are especially important in the broadcast media, where most stories are happening now, have just happened, or will happen in the immediate future. The news value of one story may depend on how each particular station wants to include the story in its overall coverage or on whether the story is interesting or important enough to its target audience to be covered at all.

Broadcasters try to make the news sound fresh or current. By constantly updating stories or providing continuous coverage of them, broadcast newscasts avoid sounding like a repeat of the morning newspapers, which are filled with yesterday's news. Unlike news in the print media, broadcast news generally avoids stories that are as much as 24 hours old. Much of broadcasting's immediacy is lost if the news is old or even old-sounding.

Broadcast news and public affairs programs generally have time for local information, though. Professional news departments always look for worthwhile local stories or angles for national and international stories to make their broadcasts meaningful to their audiences.

Many stations provide interview, panel discussion, or other public affairs programs to allow more detailed coverage of a story. Features such as personality profiles or light, humorous pieces can be extremely useful for broadcasters, especially on weekends and holidays. During these traditionally slow times, there is not much hard news such as government meetings, but newscasts and other information programs have time to fill. A publicist should monitor a station's programming to determine how to take advantage of such opportunities.

Broadcast Ads and Public Service Announcements

If a publicity campaign has an advertising budget, the publicist should consider spending at least part of it on appropriate electronic media. The National Association of Broadcasters (NAB) suspended its guidelines concerning the maximum number of commercial minutes per hour on radio and television after a federal appeals court ruled in 1981 that such voluntary limits violated antimonopoly laws and restrained trade. The ruling allowed broadcasters to program as many commercial minutes as the marketplace will bear and their stations' audiences will tolerate.

Despite that ruling, many radio stations continued to limit the number of commercial minutes per hour, although some significantly increased their commercial load. Monitoring local stations allows publicists to compare the

number of commercial breaks and commercial lengths among the radio stations in any broadcast market.

A sales manager at a radio or TV station quotes ad prices based on a
rate card, although some stations are willing to negotiate. Generally, increasing the number of ads placed with a particular station will decrease the price
per ad. Political advertisements, as noted later in this chapter, cannot be
charged more than a broadcast station's lowest unit rate. Naturally, the
emphasis for publicity should be on achieving the greatest impact for the
available advertising budget. For this reason, a publicist is more likely to
buy time on the radio rather than on television, with cable TV advertising
still being relatively limited at the local level.

In a given market, radio ads may still sell for as little as a few dollars
each while ads on the local TV station may cost several hundred dollars
apiece, depending on when they are run. Television production costs and
talent fees are also considerably higher than in radio because of the need for
more staff, equipment, and broadcast facilities.

However the broadcast advertising budget is allocated, a publicist
should cluster ads within a reasonable time frame or during specific parts of
a station's schedule. Such grouping of ads is more effective for audience
exposure and recall than widely scattered commercials throughout the
broadcast schedule or over a long time. Of course, if the budget allows, a
saturation campaign with many ads broadcast over a longer time can be
effective, such as for a relatively unknown political candidate who is trying
to establish name recognition. (See Chapter 8 for more discussion of broadcast advertising.)

If a publicist has no budget, or a limited one, many stations will air free
public service announcements (PSAs) for nonprofit organizations or worthy
causes. However, broadcasters are unlikely to provide free time, as well as
free use of their staff and production facilities, if a publicist buys advertising
space in any local print media.

Public service announcements should be produced as professionally as
paid commercials, including the use of station announcers, music, and appropriate sound effects. Straight narration without any additional production
is usually not the most effective communication technique and could easily
be missed among the countless ads and PSAs aired. By working closely with
broadcast stations, a publicist can produce professional PSAs, as well as
avoid wasting time and effort submitting PSAs that are unacceptable in
content, style, or format.

Advertising copy should be written in broadcast style, using strong
verbs and clear, concise language. Spots should run no more than 30 seconds
unless a particular station still runs 60-second commercials or PSAs. Nationwide surveys in the mid-1980s showed that almost nine out of ten broadcast spots were 30 seconds or less, although some cable ads ran as long as 2

minutes. (See Chapter 12 for a complete discussion of broadcast writing style.)

PSAs should be submitted to a station's public service director, program director, or general manager, depending on the station staff size. Such free ads should emphasize a worthy cause or a community service or spirit with the local angle highlighted. Because of deregulation, national and regional PSAs are less likely to be used on radio stations, so a locally produced spot with a local spokesperson talking about a local service is more likely to be aired—if it is well done. Television PSAs, like TV commercials, are considerably more expensive and time-consuming to produce, even though the station's broadcast time is free.

Be aware that broadcast PSAs are aired at generally less desirable times than commercials, which buy time within or adjacent to a particular TV program or during a premium time on radio. A publicist may want to monitor local media to determine which, if any, broadcast stations run PSAs during radio drive times (morning and afternoon commuting periods) or TV prime time (three hours each weeknight before the late local newscast).

As with any media mix, the chances of successfully using electronic media to publicize something increase when a publicist takes advantage of as many opportunities as possible. Broadcast news, features, public affairs programs, and public service announcements can all provide free publicity, while commercials can provide paid exposure during highly rated entertainment programming on radio, television, and cable.

Broadcast Regulation

As was mentioned earlier, the broadcast and cable industries in the United States are regulated by the federal government through the Federal Communications Commission. Congress established that agency through the Federal Communications Act of 1934. The president of the United States nominates the commissioners, who are approved or rejected by the Senate. During President Ronald Reagan's first term, the number of commissioners was reduced from seven to five, and Mark Fowler, Reagan's appointee as FCC chairman at that time, hastened the deregulation of radio as part of the president's effort to reduce the federal bureaucracy and government restrictions on free enterprise.

Critics of FCC moves to deregulate radio and, to a lesser extent television and cable, fear that public access to the airwaves will be restricted if broadcasters and cable operators are governed only by the marketplace. Groups representing churches, minorities, parents, and women, to name a few, oppose the easing or elimination of laws and rules that grew out of technological chaos during the early days of radio. But restrictions on content are often of the most concern to broadcasters, and publicists should be aware of these restrictions.

THE FAIRNESS DOCTRINE

One of the most controversial restrictions on broadcasting content is the fairness doctrine, which requires that broadcasters cover all sides of controversial issues of public importance. The FCC judges how well broadcasters have adhered to the fairness doctrine by considering overall programming, including newscasts, news interviews, on-the-spot news coverage, news documentaries, and any other programs that broadcasters consider necessary in order to cover all sides of such issues.

What is or is not a controversial issue of public importance varies among broadcast markets. Such issues may range from local option taxes to fluoridation of drinking water. But the FCC has decided that broadcasters must make a good-faith effort to cover the issues rather than avoid covering all sides by ignoring such issues entirely.

The FCC has also decided that broadcasters must seek out opposing viewpoints rather than assume there are no other sides to an issue. The constitutionality of the fairness doctrine was upheld by the U.S. Supreme Court in 1969, when the court ruled that the airwaves belong to the public, not to the broadcasters who merely rent those airwaves for the length of their licenses (renewable every seven years for radio and every five years for television). In 1987, the FCC voted 4–0 to abolish the fairness doctrine. President Reagan supported that action by vetoing congressional efforts to make the doctrine law. Congress also failed to reinitiate the doctrine as part of an appropriations bill as this book went to press. However, there are indications that such efforts to revive the fairness doctrine will continue.

SECTION 315

Section 315 of the 1934 Federal Communications Act governs how all legally qualified political candidates for public office may use a broadcast station's facilities. This part of the 1934 law is often erroneously referred to as the equal-time provision. But in reality, Section 315 has nothing to do with so-called equal time.

The FCC has defined use of a station's facilities to include any way a political candidate appears over the air except in newscasts, news interviews, on-the-spot news coverage, and documentaries in which the candidate's appearance is only incidental. For example, after President Reagan officially announced he was running for reelection in 1984, television stations that then broadcast any of his old movies or TV shows were required to provide equal opportunities for all other legally qualified candidates for that same office who requested such opportunities.

Equal opportunities include comparable time during that station's broadcast schedule, depending on when the original use was made of that station's facilities. Candidates must request equal opportunities within one week of the original use, according to a 1959 amendment that prohibits candidates from accumulating "equal time." That amendment also exempts the above-mentioned news categories from Section 315's equal opportunities.

The FCC does not decide which political candidates are "serious," "viable," or "electable." All legally qualified candidates for a particular office are entitled to equal opportunities under the provisions of Section 315.

As was previously noted, broadcasters are prohibited by law from charging more for political advertising than their lowest unit rate. They may charge even less than that rate, but they must offer the same rate to all legally qualified candidates for that same office. Section 312 of the 1934 law requires broadcasters to provide airtime for political ads, and the U.S. Supreme Court has ruled that broadcasters cannot censor political candidates' uses of their broadcast facilities.

If a publicity campaign involves a controversial issue, the publicist should be prepared for some broadcasters to balk at providing much coverage, because they will then have fairness obligations to cover all sides. Keep in mind that the doctrine considers a station's overall performance, including news, paid ads, free public service announcements, and any other programming pertaining to that controversial issue.

If the publicity campaign involves a legally qualified political candidate for public office, equal opportunities under Section 315 may arise. But unlike the fairness doctrine's obligation to seek out other views on controversial issues, Section 315 makes each candidate responsible for monitoring the broadcast media and asking for equal opportunities whenever another legally qualified candidate for that same office uses a station's facilities.

Summary

Electronic communications have several strengths and weaknesses relative to print media.

Broadcasting is immediate. It can transmit the latest information, including last-minute changes, more quickly than other media. However, broadcasting's message can often be missed by the listener or viewer, and there is usually no opportunity for an instant replay except in sports coverage.

Broadcasting is fast. It can transmit information as that information becomes available, not hours or days later as in print media. But broadcasting's message can be incomplete or lack the perspective of a newspaper or magazine article about the same topic.

Broadcasting is flexible. It can integrate all program elements into a professional package, with information and entertainment blending smoothly and almost unnoticed. Overcommercialization and undue emphasis on the show-business aspects of broadcasting may, of course, alienate at least part of an audience.

Broadcasting can repeat a message or its key points often, even within a short time. Remember, however, there's a difference between repetition and redundancy. Broadcast audiences can tune messages out physically or mentally quite easily.

Exercises

1. Monitor your local electronic media for one week, keeping track of their news, public affairs, and public service programming. Consult *Broadcasting Cablecasting Yearbook* and other sources listed in the Suggested Reading to find out basic information about the stations' personnel, format, and programming.
2. Choose a particular local problem that can be solved with publicity. Then, based on the information gathered in Exercise 1, make a list of broadcast stations that you would most likely use to air your messages. Justify your choices by pointing out the criteria on which you based your decisions.
3. Decide how you would like to use the facilities at one of the stations listed in Exercise 2 to produce a publicity message for your problem. Then contact the appropriate person at the station and discuss the feasibility of your suggestions. Write up a short report of your visit with the station's representative.

Suggested Reading

MEDIA DIRECTORIES

Broadcast Advertisers Reports. 142 W. Fifty-seventh St., New York, NY 11019. Lists companies' and products' expenditures on radio and television programs and networks during specific times.

Broadcasting Cablecasting Yearbook. 1735 De Sales St. NW, Washington, DC 20036. Lists agency and station sales representatives plus program and equipment suppliers.

Standard Rate and Data Service directories: *Spot Radio Rates and Data* and *Spot Television Rates and Data*. Standard Rate and Data Service, 5201 Old Orchard Dr., Skokie, IL 60076. Lists broadcast station ownership, network affiliation, facilities and equipment, hours of operation, advertising rates, and advertising copy guidelines.

Television Advertising Bureau and *Radio Advertising Bureau*. 485 Lexington Ave., New York, NY 10017. Fact books listing strengths of each medium compared with other media of mass communication.

Television and Cable Factbook. Television Digest, Inc., 1836 Jefferson Pl. NW, Washington, DC 20036. Lists United States and Canadian commercial stations, their facilities, personnel, coverage area, and total audience circulation.

BROADCAST MAGAZINES

Advertising Age. Publishes a weekly roundup of ad industry news.

Broadcasting. Publishes a weekly roundup of industry news, including radio, television, and cable.

Television/Radio Age. Publishes every other week on radio, television, and cable developments.

8 *Advertising: Publicity You Pay For*

VERYL FRITZ

BY the mid-1980s, businesses in the United States were investing an estimated $100 billion in advertising. This huge figure includes money spent in all of the popular media – newspapers, television, magazines, radio, outdoor, and direct mail – that advertisers use to promote their products, services, and ideas. The $100 billion, according to advertising trade journals, also includes estimated expenditures by advertisers in a wide range of promotional activities.

Although the amount invested in advertising might seem an extremely large sum, it represents only about 2 percent of the nation's gross national product, or GNP (see Fig. 8.1). That percentage has remained relatively steady since the 1950s even though the amount of money devoted to advertising has shown sizable increases.

FIG. 8.1. Advertising expenditures, expressed as a percentage of gross national product, remained at or near the 2 percent level from 1950 through 1980. (*Data prepared by Robert H. Coen, vice president, McCann-Erickson Advertising Agency, Inc., New York, N.Y.*)

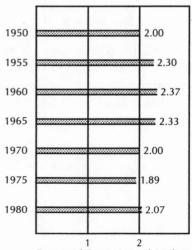

1950	2.00
1955	2.30
1960	2.37
1965	2.33
1970	2.00
1975	1.89
1980	2.07

Percent of Gross National Product

105

The annual advertising budget for many of the leading corporations is likewise impressive. Procter and Gamble Company, consistently one of the leading spenders, reported expenditures in the mid-1980s of approximately $1.5 billion annually. The other companies ranking in the top five leading advertisers are Philip Morris Companies; Sears, Roebuck and Company; RJR/Nabisco; and General Motors Corporation.

The amount of money that individual companies invest in advertising depends on the type of products being sold and the objectives set for the firm's advertising efforts. For example, the advertising budget of Kellogg Company, a leading marketer of ready-to-eat cereals, represented an estimated 16.5 percent of their U.S. sales in 1986. On the other hand, the estimated $839 million that General Motors spent in U.S. advertising that same year was less than 1 percent of its U.S. sales of more than $91 billion.

The Role of Advertising

Why do companies invest so much money in advertising? Today's marketers recognize advertising as an important part of the promotional mix. Companies advertise to communicate with their customers and prospects.

Advertising is essentially the voice of marketing. As such, it is just one of the many marketing tools that can help move goods or services from the company to its target market.

Some products, of course, lend themselves to advertising more than others, and the importance of advertising varies from business to business and from company to company. The role that advertising should play is a major decision in the marketing planning process.

Although there are many definitions of advertising, a common one is this:

> Advertising is the nonpersonal communication of information, usually paid for and usually persuasive in nature, about products, services, or ideas by identified sponsors through the various media.[1]

To the publicist, advertising may seem similar to other communication techniques. It contains many of the qualities associated with news, publicity, and propaganda, and it is used widely by public relations specialists. Advertising does have at least three distinguishing characteristics:

---

1. Courtland L. Bovée and William F. Arens, *Contemporary Advertising*, 3d ed. (Homewood, Ill.: Irwin, 1989), 5.

1. Advertising is almost always purchased (or provided in return for services of value).
2. The buyer of advertising is assured the message will be printed or broadcast.
3. Advertising is displayed in such a way that it can be identified as having been paid for.

In some ways, advertising is the most straightforward of all publicity techniques. Whereas the source of a planted news story, a public relations gimmick, or a propaganda device may be hidden, the advertisement is marked as a persuasive message paid for by an individual or organization with a direct interest. The purpose of an advertisement is seldom mysterious.

Advertising Takes Many Forms

Over the years, a number of specialized forms of advertising have developed. Individual forms of advertising are designed to communicate with specific audiences and to meet specific advertising objectives. The average consumer may not be aware of some of the different forms, but the publicist should understand the purpose of the different types and the audiences served.

Consumer advertising in one of the mass media familiar to most people may be scheduled nationwide and thus be regarded as national advertising. Or it may be regarded as local advertising when done by retail stores and businesses and scheduled in local media.

Robert Coen, senior vice president of McCann-Erickson Advertising Agency, is widely recognized as an expert in forecasting and measuring media expenditures. He estimated U.S. advertising spending for 1986 at more than $101.9 billion. Of this total, slightly more than 56 percent was identified as national advertising, with the remainder classified as local advertising. (See Figure 8.2 for estimates from 1950 through 1980.)

FIG. 8.2. Approximately 55 percent of advertising expenditures in 1980 were identified as national advertising. Since 1960, however, the share attributed to local advertising has increased while the share of national advertising has declined. (*Data prepared by Robert H. Coen, vice president, McCann-Erickson Advertising Agency, Inc., New York, N.Y.*)

Percent of Total Advertising Expenditures

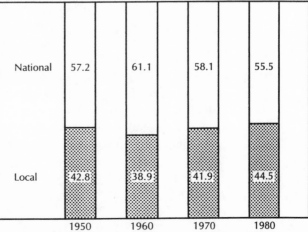

	1950	1960	1970	1980
National	57.2	61.1	58.1	55.5
Local	42.8	38.9	41.9	44.5

Consumer advertising may be product advertising, with a message that provides consumers with information about a product or service. Other consumer advertising may be promotional in nature. Such advertising is designed to create immediate action and announces a sale, carries a coupon, provides information about a contest, or gives details about some other offer.

Trade advertising persuades retailers or wholesalers to stock a certain item for resale to their own customers. It helps gain distribution for consumer products or enlists retailer cooperation in a product promotion.

While the greatest share of all advertising is aimed at selling products and services, a steadily increasing share of the nation's advertising dollars is devoted to selling ideas. Thus **corporate** or **institutional advertising** is used to enhance the reputation of a corporation or business or to influence public opinion.

Likewise, **public service advertising,** with which the publicist is most concerned, is used to support social causes. Forest fire prevention, United Way, and American Red Cross messages are familiar examples of this kind of advertising.

Selecting a Medium

The planning for a series of advertisements, or for a single message, involves a number of steps. When an advertising opportunity has been identified, the publicist develops advertising objectives that outline the basic message to be delivered and the audience to be reached. Many advertising efforts fail because the advance planning was inadequate and the objectives were not clearly established.

Once appropriate objectives have been set, planning proceeds simultaneously in a number of areas:

- An advertising budget is established.
- A strategy for creating interesting and effective messages is developed. (This creative process is covered in Chapter 16.)
- The advertising medium or media are determined, and a media plan developed.

It is essential that planning in these areas be coordinated because the advertising message often dictates the type of media to be used. Also, the size of the advertising budget influences media decisions.

The identification of the target market, or audience, is a critical factor in the success of any advertising effort. Information on the target market guides the media selection process. The media used depend to a great extent on matching the target audience with the audience of a specific medium. Knowledge of individual lifestyles and reading, viewing, and listening habits is extremely helpful to the person responsible for selecting the appropriate media. Thus a publicist must have a general understanding of the characteristics of the various media, as well as the advantages and disadvantages of each medium.

NEWSPAPERS

The newspaper industry has survived the emergence of magazines, radio, and television and remains the leader among the mass media in advertising revenue, accounting for more than 25 percent of the advertising dollars. As was mentioned in Chapter 5, the 1,705 daily newspapers in the United States have a total circulation of about 63 million. Even the largest dailies are essentially community-oriented, serving at most a major metropolitan area, a state, or a region. In addition, smaller communities are served by more than 7,700 weeklies, semiweeklies, and triweeklies.

Although not used by national advertisers to a great extent today, newspapers are the primary promotional vehicles for local retail advertisers, which accounted for almost 85 percent of all newspaper advertising revenue in 1980 (see Figure 8.3). Newspapers with larger circulations are often used as delivery vehicles for the increasingly popular freestanding inserts (fsis), which carry a great volume of coupons and other promotional materials for national advertisers.

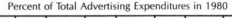

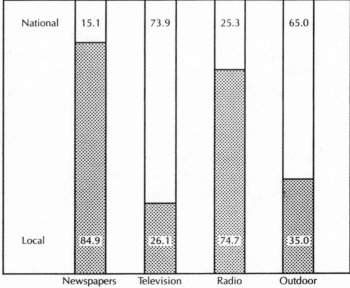

FIG. 8.3. Newspapers and radio depend heavily on revenue from local advertising. Although the majority of television and outdoor advertising comes from national advertisers, an increasing share comes from local advertisers. (*Data prepared by Robert H. Coen, vice president, McCann-Erickson Advertising Agency, Inc., New York, N.Y.*)

Percent of Total Advertising Expenditures in 1980

	Newspapers	Television	Radio	Outdoor
National	15.1	73.9	25.3	65.0
Local	84.9	26.1	74.7	35.0

ADVANTAGES

Newspaper advertising offers these major advantages:

- **Mass audience coverage.** Typically a newspaper may cover 80 percent or more of the households in a local area. This distribution provides breadth of audience with heavy concentration on higher-income, better-educated families.
- **Flexibility.** Advertisers can place ads in individual newspapers in areas where the advertised product is distributed, even adjusting the message to match specific buying preferences and individual markets. Also, ads can be placed in newspaper sections that are compatible with the advertised product or service. Travel services, for example, can place ads in travel or vacation sections and appeal to an interested and more selective audience.
- **Local, thorough readership.** Local news and photos generate high interest, with studies showing that seven out of ten adults read a newspaper on an average weekday.
- **Timeliness.** Ads can be placed on short notice, often just two to three days in advance.
- **Copy adaptability.** Because the ad can be read and referred to more than once, advertisers are able to provide detailed product information. Ads with more text to read—called **long-copy advertisements**—are used effectively in newspapers.

DISADVANTAGES

Newspaper advertising also has disadvantages:

- **Short life.** A newspaper is generally thrown away after it is read. Today's paper is considered dead when the next one appears.
- **Inferior reproduction.** Newspaper reproduction (printing quality) does not match the quality offered by most magazines. Advertisers generally do not regard newspapers as a medium that will enhance a product's perceived quality.
- **Expense.** To achieve national coverage through newspapers, an advertiser must use many papers. Also, newspapers are not regarded as a **selective medium,** targeted to a specific audience. Thus, the cost of reaching individual prospects may be quite high.

TELEVISION

Television is generally considered to be without equal as an exciting, high-impact medium, and many advertisers believe that it is the most effective of all the mass media. More than 1,500 commercial television stations beam programs into more than 98 percent of American homes, and the typical family has its set turned on slightly more than seven hours each day. The Television Bureau of Advertising estimates in the mid-1980s indicated that advertisers were investing nearly $20 billion in television, with nearly 74 percent of the total contributed by national or regional advertisers (see Figure 8.3). Some $5 billion was spent by local advertisers.

Although network television viewership is being increasingly challenged by cable television and by videocassette recording for subsequent playback, television retains the ability to deliver the largest audience of any medium. An estimated 120 million people watched the 1987 Super Bowl telecast, and advertisers paid as much as $600,000 for a 30-second announcement during the program.

Television time is classified as network, spot, and local. **Network** refers to full sponsorship, alternate sponsorship, or multisponsorship of network-originated programs. **Spot** refers to the purchase of programs or announcements on several stations without regard to network affiliation. **Local** refers to the purchase of programs or announcements on one or more stations in a single market by businesses in that market.

Another option is cable advertising. By the mid-1980s, approximately 7,300 cable systems were operating in the United States, reaching approximately 50 percent of the nation's television households. Operating systems served some 19,000 communities, and that number is increasing yearly. More than 1,000 cable systems accept advertising on their local origination channels.

ADVANTAGES

The advantages of television are as follows:

- **Audience size.** Prime-time network television offers the advertiser the largest audiences of any medium.
- **Breadth of audience.** With a coverage of more than 98 percent of all households, television reaches people of all ages and a wide range of demographic characteristics. It reaches more children and young people than newspapers do, but evidence suggests that television is less popular among highly educated people.
- **Audience selectivity.** Television can offer selective audiences to advertisers who wish to reach a segmented market. By carefully se-

lecting program content and time periods, the advertiser can reach audiences that are predominantly male, female, or sports-oriented, for example.

- **Exclusive features.** Television is unique among the media in that it combines sight, sound, and motion. These features allow an advertiser to gain a viewer's involvement in the advertising message, making television ideal for demonstrating product features and benefits.
- **Market penetration.** Television probably penetrates more homes in each market than do newspapers, but its exposure is considerably different. Readers can digest the entire contents of all newspapers available in a market. However, they can view the offerings of only one television station at a time, and the message is fleeting. Unless the viewer has taped the program, the message cannot be reviewed.
- **Program compatibility.** The advertiser can relate the content of the program to the product, and popular entertainers can be used as commercial presenters. Their involvement usually heightens interest in the commercial.

DISADVANTAGES

Some of the disadvantages of television are these:

- **Initial cost.** Television is an economical medium on the basis of cost per viewer reached, but the initial cost is high and beyond the budget of many advertisers, both local and national. In the mid-1980s, the average cost for a 30-second network commercial was $120,000. Advertisers paid as much as $15,000 for similar spots in major markets. Spots can be purchased, however, for as little as $10 on stations in smaller markets.
- **Production costs.** Commercials that compete effectively for the attention of viewers can easily cost more to produce than the cost of the broadcast time. On the other hand, low-budget commercials often look cheap and do little to help the company or product image.
- **Short life of advertising message.** The broadcast advertisement lives only 10 seconds, 15 seconds, 30 seconds, or 1 minute, in most situations.
- **Simple messages only.** The brevity of the broadcast commercial makes it difficult for the advertiser to present detailed product information.
- **Clutter.** The tendency to crowd three or four commercials, a station break, and public service announcements into the short time periods within and between programs is annoying and confusing to many viewers. This "clutter" often results in product misidentification.

MAGAZINES

Magazines offer advertisers many ways to reach specific audiences by surrounding a message with editorial material of interest to the reader. As was mentioned in Chapter 6, the *Consumer Magazine and Agri-Media* edition of the Standard Rate and Data Service directories identifies nearly 1,500 consumer magazines in 70 editorial classifications (see Figure 8.4).

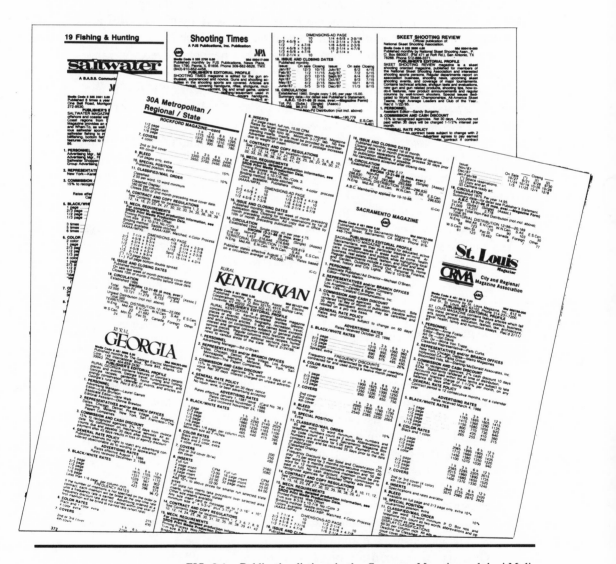

FIG. 8.4. Publication listings in the *Consumer Magazine and Agri-Media* edition of *Standard Rate and Data Service* are divided into a number of classifications that can help publicists select media. Examples from two of those classifications are shown here.

For example, more than 240 magazines are directed to farm and agri-business readers. In addition, more than 2,500 business-to-business publications are written for highly selective audiences. This wide range of magazines enables advertisers to select those that reach the specific types of readers who constitute the advertiser's target markets.

As was also mentioned in Chapter 6, business publications may be classified as either horizontal or vertical. **Horizontal publications** are aimed at individuals, such as engineers or personnel officers, doing the same kinds of work in many different industries. **Vertical publications** are aimed at all individuals employed in the same business, such as everyone in the petroleum industry, from a vice president to a new employee.

Television has made it increasingly difficult for consumer magazines to compete for advertising to reach large national audiences. *TV Guide* and *Reader's Digest,* however, are two magazines that offer large audiences. *TV Guide* delivers nearly 16.5 million copies each week and claims some 39 million readers. *Reader's Digest* delivers more than 17 million copies with an audience of 50 million adult readers. Also, both magazines offer numerous geographic and demographic breakouts to advertisers that may not have national distribution.

Many other magazines also offer national, geographic, and demographic selectivity. For example, *Time* magazine offers more than 220 ways to buy audience segments in the United States alone, making it a valuable and effective marketing tool for many advertisers.

ADVANTAGES

The advantages of magazines include the following:

- **Audience selectivity.** Magazines enable advertisers to achieve coverage of segmented markets with a minimum of waste. By selecting appropriate magazines, advertising messages can be aimed at men, women, professional people, certain income groups, or other specific audiences. In general, magazines deliver audiences of readers that are above average in terms of income, education, social position, and buying power.
- **Long life.** Magazines may be kept around the home or office for weeks and are often reread or used for reference. Subscribers also pass copies to other readers, thus extending the life of a magazine as well as increasing the audience.
- **Quality of reproduction.** Magazines are printed on quality paper, use color extensively, and generally lend prestige to an advertiser and its products or services.

DISADVANTAGES

Magazines have these disadvantages:

- **Limited market penetration.** Magazines deliver national and regional audiences, but they do not offer the extensive penetration possible with newspapers and television.
- **Lack of timeliness.** Since advertisers must plan anywhere from two weeks to as much as several months in advance, magazine advertising usually lacks the immediacy of newspapers or the broadcast media.
- **Lack of flexibility.** Some magazines have long closing dates for publication insertion orders and for production materials. This limits the flexibility to change advertisements on short notice.
- **Cost.** The cost of running advertisements in national magazines with millions of readers is high, even though the cost per individual reader may be quite low. Also, the advertiser must prepare appropriate printing materials, and the cost of preparing color advertisements can be thousands of dollars. Although the overall cost of advertising in a more selective magazine with limited circulation will be lower, the cost per reader will be much higher.

RADIO

More than 10,500 AM and FM stations are broadcasting in the United States, where nearly 490 million radio sets are in operation. Approximately half of the radios are located out of homes; thus radio is known as the everywhere medium. People listen to their favorite radio stations at home, at work, on the way to work, in their cars, and while jogging, and nearly always they are doing something else when listening.

Radio lost the stature of a leading national advertising medium as television gained popularity. Today, national network radio is limited. However, radio is the preferred medium for many local advertisers. It is used as an alternative to television for advertisers with limited budgets and as a complement to television and other advertising media.

ADVANTAGES

Radio offers advertisers a number of advantages:

- **Audience selectivity.** By selecting stations with a certain program format, advertisers can readily reach an audience that matches buyers of specific products.

- **Low cost.** The cost of radio advertising is low, so most local advertisers can afford to use radio. On a cost-per-thousand (CPM) basis, radio is considerably cheaper than other mass media.
- **Personal communication.** People listen to radio stations with which they can identify. Thus radio advertising can communicate with loyal listeners in a personal and intimate way.
- **Flexibility.** Because radio scheduling deadlines are short, copy changes can easily be made to keep messages timely. Also, low production costs add to the flexibility of radio.

DISADVANTAGES

The disadvantages of radio are the following:

- **Lack of visual image.** Radio cannot offer visual images. It is the only major medium that lacks this capability. Therefore, skillful writers must encourage the listeners to use their imaginations to create visual images appropriate for advertising messages.
- **Short messages.** Because audiences listen to radio when they are doing something else, messages are limited in time and need to be simple. Providing extensive or detailed information is difficult.

OUTDOOR

Outdoor advertising is commonly regarded as a supplementary advertising medium. For a number of years, expenditures for outdoor advertising have remained at a level of less than 3 percent of total U.S. advertising expenditures.

Approximately 600 outdoor advertising companies or plants are responsible for about 275,000 signs located in major markets across the nation. The cost of an outdoor location is based on the number of potential viewers who pass the location daily.

The advantages of outdoor advertising include geographical flexibility, broad audience reach, repetition, strong product identification, and a relatively low cost per impression. Disadvantages are a lack of audience selectivity, the speed with which the sign is passed, and the inability to express anything beyond the shortest message.

DIRECT MAIL

Direct mail follows only newspapers and television in terms of dollars invested in advertising. Not only is direct mail used to support other advertising media, but it is also used increasingly by firms involved in direct marketing. Because of its unique ability to deliver a message to a specific individual in a carefully targeted audience, many firms use direct mail as their major advertising effort.

Direct mail offers a number of unique advantages to advertisers. The advertiser can pinpoint the target audience, personalize the advertising message to a single person, use a wide variety of formats for special impact, and measure the response to an individual message or offer with remarkable accuracy. The disadvantages of direct mail include its high cost for each individual message (postage rates, or the cost of delivery, add considerably to the cost of the mailing), problems in securing quality mailing lists, problems in maintaining complete and accurate mailing lists, and the potential turnoff of those who do not wish to receive direct-mail offers.

Advertising Costs

How much does it cost to advertise? As with most other items offered for sale, the price depends largely on the kind and quantity purchased—that is, the kind of media used and the amount of advertising purchased.

Advertising costs are determined primarily by the size and the selectivity of the audience reached by the selected media. Basically, the advertiser is purchasing an opportunity to send an advertising message to people who will read, watch, or listen to the advertisement. The advertiser is purchasing an audience that has been selected to match the advertising objectives.

As was mentioned earlier, the total amount spent on advertising in the United States equals about 2 percent of the gross national product. This figure—2 percent of gross sales—is often used as a rule of thumb for establishing an advertising budget. Some firms spend only a fraction of 1 percent of gross sales; others spend 10 percent or an even higher amount. But many fall in the bracket between 1 and 4 percent of gross sales. Entertainment, cosmetics, and drug companies are most likely to be on the high side. Automotive and business-to-business advertisers are normally on the low side.

Certainly, at any one time an advertiser will spend more than at other times. A person may wish to establish a store or introduce a new service or line of merchandise. A merchant might also use advertising to help level out business cycles. Also, if an advertising program is well planned, a business person may choose to advertise more in periods when business is ordinarily slow and advertise less in times of ready sales.

Where to spend the advertising dollar to do the most good is the big question. Below are some of the cost yardsticks an advertiser uses in making advertising decisions.

NEWSPAPERS

Newspaper advertising is usually sold at the column-inch rate. A column inch is an area 1 column wide and 1 inch deep. Therefore, a paper 7 columns wide with 20-inch-long columns offers for sale 140 column inches of advertising in a full-page ad. (See Figure 8.5 for an illustration of a newspaper rate card.)

Advertising
Rates & Information
Effective Oct. 1, 1987

Times-Republican

135 West Main • P.O. Box 1300 • Marshalltown, Iowa 50158 • (515) 753-6611 / Iowa Wats 1-800-542-7893

1. PERSONNEL:
Denis Crotty, Advertising Director

2. REPRESENTATIVES:
Represented nationally by
The Papert Companies

Chicago	312-822-9116
Dallas	214-969-0000
Detroit	313-357-3933
Kansas City	913-432-6600
Los Angeles	818-990-3475
Memphis	901-278-5390
Minneapolis	612-338-1958
New Orleans	504-455-2417
New York	212-687-4750
San Francisco	415-982-3947

3. TERMS AND CONDITIONS
a. Local Retail, Classified, and Plus advertising rates are subject to 1¼ % per month late charges when left unpaid by the 28th of the month after publication.
b. All local rates are non-commissionable.
c. National ad rates are commissionable with terms of 15% and 2%.

4. ADVERTISING RATES
a. RETAIL RATES (LOCAL)
Yearly Contracts
(Rate Per Inch)

Total inches, 12 month contract

65	$ 5.90
129	5.63
194	5.42
517	5.28
1,549	5.15
3,007	4.48
6,709	4.29
12,385	4.02
24,769	3.82
Open Rate	6.65
Auction Rate	6.00
2 or more insertions	4.81
Transient Rate	7.10
Professional Card	per month 118.50

Political, Per Contract, Cash in Advance

b. CONSECUTIVE WEEKLY RETAIL (LOCAL)
(Rate Per Inch)

Minimum Inches per Week	13 Weeks Consecutively	26 Weeks Consecutively	52 Weeks Consecutively
1½ "	$5.46	$5.41	$5.35
3½ "	5.41	5.35	5.27
6 "	5.32	5.25	5.18
10 "	5.19	5.14	5.06
20 "	5.07	5.00	4.95

c. WEEKLY CONTRACT CLASSIFIED (LOCAL)
(2 Line Minimum Daily)

	Per Line Rate	Per Inch Rate
13 Consecutive Weeks	$.50	$3.82
26 Consecutive Weeks	.48	3.71
52 Consecutive Weeks	.45	3.23

d. NON-CONTRACT CLASSIFIED (LOCAL)
$1.04 per line, $4.65 per inch

*Figure cost of your advertisement from the following table counting 4 average words per line.
Effective October 1, 1987 (Two Line Minimum)

Ad Size	1 Day	2 Days	3 Days	6 Days	12 Days	26 Days
2 lines	$ 2.08	$ 4.16	$ 5.16	$ 8.26	$14.45	$ 28.90
3 lines	3.12	6.24	7.74	12.38	21.67	43.34
4 lines	4.16	8.32	10.32	16.51	28.90	57.79
5 lines	5.20	10.40	12.90	18.13	36.12	72.24
6 lines	6.24	12.48	15.48	24.77	43.34	86.69
7 lines	7.28	14.56	18.06	28.90	50.57	101.14
8 lines	8.32	16.64	20.64	33.02	57.79	115.58
9 lines	9.36	18.72	23.22	37.15	65.02	130.03
10 lines	10.40	20.80	25.80	41.28	72.24	144.48
11 lines	11.44	22.88	28.38	45.41	79.46	158.93
12 lines	12.48	24.96	30.96	49.54	86.69	173.38
13 lines	13.52	27.04	33.54	53.66	93.91	187.82

e. CITY BRIEF (LOCAL)
Minimum charge 2 lines .... $2.25 per line

f. CARDS OF THANKS/IN MEMORIAMS
80¢ per line

g. BOX ADS (CLASSIFIED)
Box number ads (ads requiring responses to be directed to the Times-Republican)
$2.00 service charge (advertiser picks up response)
$4.00 service charge (responses mailed to advertiser)

h. COLOR ADVERTISING (LOCAL)
— Color Advertising Rates —

Black + 1 color...$ 65 up to 1 page . .$105 for 2 pages
Black + 2 colors..$105 up to 1 page . .$150 for 2 pages
Black + 3 colors..$145 up to 1 page . .$210 for 2 pages
Color Stock .... Price available

i. T-R PLUS...TMC Publication
The T-R Plus is a non-subscriber full size newspaper delivered by U.S. Mail to 9,000 + homes within a 30 mile core of Marshalltown to give 100% unduplicated coverage.

Display pick-up rate, per col. inch $1.00
Classified pick-up rate, per col. inch .... .65
T-R Plus only rate (display/classified) 6.65

In a small community like Hampton, Iowa, the *Hampton Chronicle,* with a circulation just under 4,000, might charge an advertiser $2.45 per column inch. A full-page ad (168 column inches) would cost $411.60 on a one-time basis. In Denver, an advertiser might choose to run an advertisement in the *Denver Post.* A one-page advertisement would have a total of 132 column inches at a cost of $76 per column inch. The total cost of a one-page advertisement would be $10,032, but the advertising message would go out to a

---

COMBINATION CONTRACT RATES
Times-Republican
and
T-R Plus
Per Inch Rates

Sizes Per Wk.	Monthly Open	6 Wks. Consecutively	13 Wks. Consecutively	26 Wks. Consecutively	52 Wks. Consecutively
2½ "	$7.65	$6.13	$5.96	$5.90	$5.85
5"	7.60	6.07	5.90	5.85	5.77
10"	7.55	6.02	5.70	5.64	5.58
20"	7.49	5.97	5.58	5.51	5.46
40"	7.44	5.91	5.53	5.46	5.41
60"	7.39	5.86	5.47	5.41	5.35
80"	6.92	5.33	5.26	5.11	4.96
129"	6.65	5.22	5.15	5.00	4.85
258"	6.44	4.47	4.40	4.25	4.10

Guaranteed Delivery to over 23,000 households.

j. Television Programming
The TV Log is a weekly TV listing of all area cable and network channels available at regular contract rates. Advertisers must agree to run for 6 consecutive months.

— Classified Cable TV Rates —

Open Rate . . . .$3.50 for the first line, $2.50 each additional line

k. PREPRINTED TAB INSERTS
Rates Per Thousand

Tab Pages	Open	6x or 800" Contract	12x or 1500" Contract	18x or 2500" Contract	24x or 3500" Contract
4 or less	$27.00	$26.00	$25.00	$24.00	$23.00
8	35.00	32.00	31.00	30.00	29.00
12	42.00	39.00	38.00	36.00	34.00
16	46.00	44.00	42.00	40.00	38.00

Over 16 page tabloid rates are available on request.

For full size inserts double pages to get tabloid equivalent.
Cost of insert will be divided by account ROP rate per inch and inches obtained used to retire contract.

l. SPECIAL PRODUCTION CHARGES
Screening or line PMT
6" x 9" . . . .$ 4.50
9" x 12" . . . .$ 5.50
12" x 18" . . . .$ 7.50
Full page $10.50

m. DISCOUNTS (LOCAL)

T-R MORNING STAR
½ RATE
If your ad runs the week before or after a Saturday, repeat your ad in the T-R Saturday Morning Star for ½ rate.
(10% pick-up discount does not apply)

— Pick-Up (Repeat) Ad Discount —

Published advertisement may be published a second time with no copy changes at 10% less per column inch during a one-week period.

n. NATIONAL RATES (per inch)
Open Rate $7.98
6 page Newsplan 7.58
13 page Newsplan 7.18
26 page Newsplan 6.78
52 page Newsplan 6.39

NATIONAL COLOR RATES
Black and 1 color . . . .$ 80.00
Black and 2 colors 125.00
Black and 3 colors 175.00

INSERT RATES
Use local rates and add on commission.

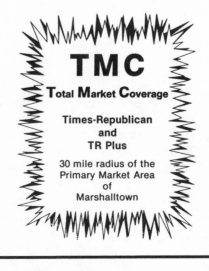

TMC
Total Market Coverage

Times-Republican
and
TR Plus

30 mile radius of the
Primary Market Area
of
Marshalltown

FIG. 8.5. This rate card, from the *Times-Republican* in Marshalltown, Iowa, shows the cost of advertising in a daily paper that claimed a readership of more than 40,000 at the time the rates were in effect. (*Courtesy of* Times-Republican, *Marshalltown, Ia.*)

circulation of over 230,000. Obviously, the full page in the *Denver Post* costs much more. However, if the two newspapers are compared by the cost per thousand subscribers (CPM), the advantage would be with the Denver newspaper.

An advertiser might wish to compare the cost of a one-page ad in the *Denver Post* with the cost of a one-page ad in a competitive newspaper, the *Rocky Mountain News*. As a tabloid newspaper, the *Rocky Mountain News* would charge $5,687.50 for a one-page ad. (That's 70 column inches at a cost of $81.25 per inch.) Because the *Rocky Mountain News* has a circulation of just over 345,000, the CPM would be $16.49. The CPM for the *Post* would be much higher—$43.62.

MAGAZINES

Almost all magazine advertising is billed by the page or fraction of a page. A full-page black-and-white ad in a consumer news magazine with a circulation of 4.5 million may cost more than $70,000. A full-color ad in that same magazine costs much more—up to $110,000. However, a page ad in a business magazine with a circulation of approximately 60,000 copies may cost only around $6,500. The cost of an advertisement depends primarily on the magazine's circulation and the selectivity of the audience reached.

The standard measure that advertisers use to compare the relative cost of magazines is also the CPM. This is calculated by multiplying the full-page cost by 1,000 and dividing the result by the magazine's circulation:

$$\frac{\text{cost of ad} \times 1,000}{\text{circulation of magazine}} = \text{CPM}$$

For example:

$$\frac{\$70,000 \times 1,000}{4,500,000} = \$15.55$$

When comparing magazines, an advertiser might find a range in CPM from approximately $6.50 for *Reader's Digest* to more than $128 for a business magazine with a circulation of 110,000. In general, the CPM is highest for limited-circulation magazines directed to highly selective or segmented audiences. The advertiser may decide, however, that the higher CPM is well worthwhile because waste circulation is held to a minimum.

RADIO AND TELEVISION

The advertising rate structure of the broadcast media is far more complex than that of the print media. Rates are based on potential audience, units of time, and time of day. Broadcast audiences fluctuate greatly throughout the day, and the fluctuation is more pronounced among television viewers than among radio listeners. Television is primarily a nighttime medium, and radio a daytime medium.

Network and station rates are scaled to take into account the general patterns of viewership or listenership. The greater the number of viewers or listeners, the higher the rate. Thus, the most expensive time on television, known as **prime time,** is from 7 p.m. to 10 p.m. (CST). Peak radio listenership, on the other hand, normally comes during **morning drive time** – the hours between 6 a.m. and 10 a.m.

As was mentioned earlier, by the mid-1980s the average 30-second prime-time network television announcement cost approximately $120,000, with spots on top-rated series costing more than $220,000. Thirty-second announcements on individual TV stations ranged from $15,000 in top-rated specials in major markets to as low as $10 in the smaller metropolitan markets. In contrast, radio spots cost from $1,000 or more in major markets to less than $1 in small towns.

In planning an advertising campaign, the advertiser decides on the target audience to be reached – the specific kind and number of viewers or listeners. Program ratings determined by independent media-rating organizations are then studied to help select television and radio programs.

An advertiser wishing to buy broadcast time can contact the local station and work with the sales manager or a station sales representative. An alternative is to rely on the services of an advertising agency or an independent media-buying service. Advertising agencies usually receive their pay in the form of a commission from the media that run the advertisements. Media services may charge a fee or operate on an incentive basis.

If the advertiser decides to work directly with the local station, the first step is to request availabilities (a list of specific commercial spots by program or time periods that may be available for purchase). Then the rates for the spots are negotiated. Because broadcast time is perishable, it may be possible to purchase spots at reduced rates as the broadcast date approaches. Newspapers and magazines, on the other hand, generally publish rate cards, and the advertising rates are seldom negotiable.

Summary

If a publicist is called on to plan or supervise an advertising program, many expert services are available, usually at no cost. The advertising departments of the various media are staffed by well-trained, experienced professionals whose main job is to assist advertisers. The publicist can take questions and problems to these experts. The publicist should be frank with them, supply them with accurate complete information, and ask their advice and assistance. Usually, help from such experts is extremely valuable and well worth the publicist's time and effort.

Exercises

1. Would the manufacturer of a computer software firm find it appropriate to schedule advertisements in both horizontal and vertical publications? Explain.
2. At a library with appropriate journalism reference books, refer to a recent volume of the *Consumer Magazine and Agri-Media Rates and Data,* a publication of Standard Rate and Data Service, Inc. Select two magazines that interest you or that you regularly read. For each magazine, do the following:
   a. Determine the circulation of the magazine.
   b. Figure the cost of a one-page black-and-white advertisement. (Use the cost for a one-time insertion.)
   c. Figure the CPM (cost per thousand) based on the magazine's circulation.
   d. Which magazine offers the greatest cost-effectiveness to an advertiser? Explain.
3. Assume you are the manager of a clothing store for children. You decide that you will place the majority of your advertising budget in the local daily newspaper. Explain some of the reasons why you think this is a wise decision.

Suggested Reading

Bovée, Courtland L., and Arens, William. "The Advertising Business," "Print Media," "Electronic Media," and "Local Advertising." Chapters 3, 13, 14, and 17 in *Contemporary Advertising*. 3d ed. Homewood, Ill.: Irwin, 1989.

Cohen, Dorothy. "Print Media: Newspapers and Magazines," and "Broadcast Media: Television and Radio." Chapters 18 and 19 in *Advertising*. Glenview, Ill.: Scott, Foresman and Co., 1988.

Russell, J. Thomas; Verrill, Glenn; and Lane, W. Ronald. "Using Television," "Using Radio," "Using Newspapers," and "Using Magazines." Chapters 8, 9, 10, and 11 in *Kleppner's Advertising Procedure*. 10th ed. Englewood Cliffs, N.J.: Prentice Hall, 1988.

Surmanek, Jim. *Media Planning: A Practical Guide*. Lincolnwood, Ill.: Crain Books, 1985.

Weilbacher, William M. "The Printed Media" and "The Broadcast Media." Chapters 13 and 14 in *Advertising*. 2d ed. New York: Macmillan Publishing Co., 1984.

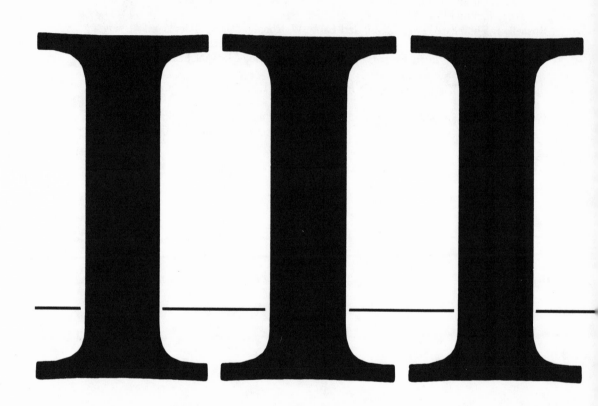

Creating Publicity Messages

ARMED with a knowledge of the fundamentals and the available publicity channels, the publicist is ready to generate messages for the selected audiences. The chapters in Part III provide general guidelines for understanding the elements of news, developing a writing syle, and creating news releases and stories for print and broadcast.

9
Gatekeepers
and News Values

JEROME L. NELSON

IN the rumor game, the first player reads a message that is then whispered to the second player, who whispers it to the third player, and so on. If you've played this game, you know how different the message at the end can be from the one that started things off. Even with the best of intentions, players make subtle changes as the message flows along. The more players, the more changes, and usually the original message gets seriously mangled.

Given this phenomenon, it's surprising that information coming to us by radio, television, newspaper, or magazine is as accurate as it is. News and information flow to us in much the same way as the messages in the rumor game move from player to player. The message the announcer reads or the reporter writes may be different in treatment—in the way the content is handled—from the original, but the odds are great that the meaning and the facts are essentially the same.

One reason for this accuracy is that **gatekeepers**—the players in the news-and-information game—share a set of values which they use to assess messages that come to them. If you, as a news-and-information user, know the values that gatekeepers share, you should be able to make more reasoned criticisms of media performance. If you are called upon to be a publicist or act as a news source, a knowledge of these values should make it easier for you to get media professionals to accept your messages.

Gatekeepers

Imagine news and information as flowing from some source. Simply put, **a gatekeeper is a person who can change or stop the flow of information before it reaches its intended receiver.**

Most of us think of gatekeepers as the professional journalists who work in the news-and-information network. But by definition, sources of news and information may be gatekeepers, too. In fact, the newspaper carrier who didn't deliver your newspaper could be a most important gatekeeper.

The fact is, the news-and-information network is huge. Thousands of people are directly involved in seeing to it that you get a daily allotment of news and information over the air or in print.

GOING THROUGH THE GATES

Think for a moment about what happens when a story breaks (a newsworthy event occurs) in some faraway place—the Middle East, for example. Say an assassination takes place in Tel Aviv. A nonjournalist witnesses the event and calls in the information to a news bureau. A reporter follows up and writes the story. An editor checks the reporter's work, perhaps making a few changes and then moving the story along via telephone, cable, or satellite to the United States. There, another editor decides what part of the story, if any, to send along for American readers or listeners. Finally, your hometown newspaper or broadcast station picks up the story, and a local editor decides what part of the story, if any, will be used.

Simple, right? Like the rumor game. Consider this: The editors of the *New York Times* receive approximately 2 million words daily from widely scattered sources. One way to grasp this number is to imagine a 200,000-word novel (longer than most today). The *Times* editors receive and make decisions about roughly ten full-length books every day. From the 2 million words, they select roughly 180,000 for publication, a bit less than one book. Of the 180,000 words, fewer than 8,000 end up on the front page. Every day, all year, the information flow is affected by decisions, decisions, decisions.

The gates controlling the flow of news and information open and close. Some stories get shut out altogether; some are severely trimmed; some go through virtually unchanged.

Let's look at the process (see Figure 9.1). For a moment, walk a mile or two in a publicist's shoes and consider gatekeeping at the source. Let's say you're the publicity person for the local garden club that wants to get a message to the general public. As the publicist, you consult with the club

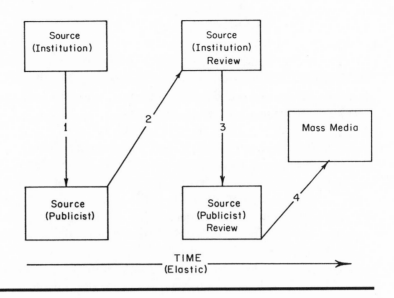

FIG. 9.1. Gatekeeping at the source. At each gate three decisions are possible: stop (the message is not forwarded); edit (the message is changed before being forwarded); go (the message is forwarded without alteration).

officers and other members who know a great deal about the particular message that's to be sent. You learn as much as you possibly can about it. You make sure your goals for the message (or for an entire campaign) are precisely and specifically stated. Then you write the story. When it's finished, you show it to the officers and members with whom you've talked. Some changes are suggested; some facts need to be omitted, and others need to be included. You write a new story and check it again with the officers and members. Finally, after editing and discussing, discussing and editing, you are done with the writing job, and you can send the story to the mass media.

Incidentally, you don't have to be working with an organization to go through this process. You yourself can function as the officers and members with whom you check out a first draft. In fact, it's a good idea to let a story cool off for a time and then read it over carefully for errors and omissions.

An important thing to consider here is the time element. For the publicist at the source, the pressure to turn out a fast story is not usually as great as it is in the newsroom, and weeks can be spent creating the finished product that gets sent to the mass media. The critical element is not time but accuracy. Does the message say exactly what you want it to say? Have you done everything you can to ensure that the editor will "buy" it? Is it consistent with the goals you have set?

POINTS FOR PUBLICISTS

Editors get hundreds of letters every day containing what the senders think of as news releases. For most of these messages, the reception process is swift—open, scan, and dump. In seconds, an experienced editor generally can judge the value of what has come through the mail. If you are a message sender, your time is worth something, and postage costs money. Preparing material for somebody's wastebasket isn't very gratifying.

Assume for the moment the editor finds a story in the mail that may possibly be used. He or she passes the story along for a rewrite. Sometimes few changes are made; other times the story is cut down or amended in various ways. When this has been done, another editor examines the story to see if it can be used in that day's paper or an upcoming newscast. The story could be stopped cold at this point. Assuming that it continues, on a newspaper it will be marked for typesetting and a headline will be written for it. Then it will be set into type. Occasionally a makeup editor will discover there is no room for the story and stop it. Or the newscast announcer, glancing at the clock, will find that time has run out and the story doesn't get told.

It's important to consider the time element again. What may have taken weeks for a source to prepare gets a lightning-fast reaction in daily newspaper or broadcast newsrooms. There the whole process probably will take less than one 8-hour shift. For weekly newspapers and magazines the process can take longer, but the media response in most cases will be faster than the time spent by the source.

A word about English. Editors tend to discount stories that aren't rendered in standard English. When you write for publication or broadcast, you need to watch your language. Manuscripts that contain flaws in grammar, punctuation, and spelling most often are rejected. (Chapter 10 discusses the basic elements of writing in more detail.)

News Values

One way to maximize your odds for success and keep your news releases out of an editor's wastebasket is to learn what the journalist thinks is news. You should also find out what kinds of messages your potential editor finds appealing. The best way to do this is to read the journalist's publication or to listen to the material the editor puts on the air. This activity can be invaluable if you're serious about success.

Editors reveal their likes and dislikes in many ways: how they "play" or place material, select content, and fix length. If you tailor your messages to their likes, your odds for success increase.

Of course, editors have their eccentricities, and you can appeal to these, but some values are shared by nearly all professional journalists. Knowing these values will help you place your stories and understand why some stories make it and others don't.

WHAT IS NEWS?

Study your local newspaper. You're bound to see that many different kinds of material are included in the broad category of news. Political happenings, sports, crime, social events, business deals, and many other reports are described as news. Again, if your goal is successful communication with the professionals, it will help you to have a practical working definition, like this one: **News is the report of an event or a situation which has significance or interest or both.**

You'll notice immediately that news is a **report.** The bank robbery itself is not news; the *report* of the bank robbery is. The world hunger problem isn't news; the *report* of world hunger is. In a sense, that would be correct, because the journalist has to deal with a problem, a situation, or an event before it becomes news.

The important thing to remember is that you, acting as a source, have the power to make news. All you have to do is convince the journalists that your messages are worthy stories. To help do this, consider some of the other concepts contained in the definition of news.

One criticism of the American press has been that it is too much event-oriented. Something has to happen, the critics contend, before the press will act. In the 1960s, it was argued that Watts, a black ghetto in Los Angeles, had to explode before the press there discussed problems that many observers believed helped incite the disastrous riot. Press coverage of the war in Vietnam sustained similar criticism.

Such criticism may be valid. It's impossible to say with certainty today what might have occurred in Watts if the problems of people living there had been explored by the press. If the community had been made aware of the problems, it might have acted to correct them, thus preventing the violence.

An analysis of media content today might suggest that the press has at least begun to report problems in the absence of events to hang them on. For example, more feature stories on consumer difficulties and grievances are found in the media now. Nevertheless, events are still critically important to editors as they consider a potential package of news.

If, as a publicist, you want to take on a problem or situation, sometimes you can create an event to provide a base for the story. The event doesn't have to be earthshaking. Something as simple as a press conference or a speech may be used as an event upon which to base problem- or situation-oriented stories.

But don't ignore a problem or situation just because you can't think of an event to use for a news peg. By definition, situations can be news. If the problem is significant enough, a journalist may be convinced it should be covered.

SIGNIFICANCE

If you'll recall some of the propositions inherent in our idea of participatory democracy, you may be able to get a firm grip on the concept of **significance.** One proposition is that robust and freewheeling discussions of ideas are necessary because if there is free debate, the truth will emerge. Furthermore, the press in a free society has a duty to provide citizens with information they need to make wise political decisions. So, any event or situation that adds to the continuing debate or provides some needed information is, almost by definition, significant. According to such precepts, virtually any information about any branch of government is significant.

Some critics argue that the media focus too narrowly on these precepts, saying for example that ecological problems didn't become news until such concerns intruded into public affairs. So, too, critics say, consumer concerns were largely unreported until advocates like Ralph Nader hurled them into the public arena with legal action and congressional testimony.

Like the criticism that the press concentrates too much on events, these concerns also may be valid. If they are, it is up to journalists to define more broadly the area of debate. Clearly politics and government are not the sole concerns of people today, and you can affect media output by letting journalists know what you think should be covered.

On a day-to-day basis, however, journalists don't think in terms of philosophical premises. Like most of us, they deal in practicalities. To journalists, **significance is the likelihood an event or a situation will have or has had some effect on members of a medium's audience.**

If an event or situation is significant, a story about it will be significant. Note that this statement does *not* say the event or situation or story will be interesting. It simply assumes a similar or parallel quality between the event or situation and the story. Note also that the journalist apparently cannot affect this quality; either something is significant to some degree, or it isn't. Although we may hope that reporting the story will draw it to public attention, that action will render it neither more nor less significant than it already is. The journalist can only point out to the audience how significant an event or situation is.

Admittedly, journalists have no really good way to measure significance. They do measure it grossly by head-counting. The more members of the audience an event or situation has affected or will affect, the more significant the story is. Therefore, an event that affects all of an audience is more significant than one that affects only a part of it. A story about an increase in individual income taxes will generally be more significant than one about an increase in excise taxes. More people in a given audience are likely to pay income taxes than to pay excise taxes. If a medium attempts to serve an entire state, an event that affects people throughout the state will be more significant than one affecting only the people in one city.

THE AUDIENCE FACTOR

The **audience** is a key. Journalists think constantly about their audiences. If, in the estimation of the journalist, an event or a situation is not significant or interesting to the audience, the event or situation goes unreported. If you want to be successful as a publicist, you must make sure your message affects or interests the audience. The larger the audience for your message, the more likely the journalist will be to accept and use it.

The media usually carry reports of traffic fatalities, such as the one reported in this radio story lead:

> A Yourtown attorney died early today when the car she was driving slammed head-on into a bridge abutment on Nearby Road.

The lead tells us quite a lot. It answers, in general terms at least, these questions: What happened? where? when? to whom? But is the story significant?

To answer the last question, you need to determine how many people in the Yourtown audience are or will be affected by the event. Think about that. Aside from the attorney's family, friends, and clients, who in the audience will be affected? Many people? Few?

Here's another lead:

> Milk prices rose 5 cents a quart today in all Yourtown grocery stores.

Which of the two news leads is the more significant? Obviously, the story about the boost in milk prices is the more significant, according to our definition. More people in the audience will probably be affected by the price increase than by the attorney's death.

It should also be obvious that **significance may have little to do with interest.** That anyone would say a traffic death is insignificant may seem surprising. Remember that when the concept of significance is used, it refers to either actual or potential effects on members of a medium's audience. Seldom is an individual death significant in these terms. It does not follow, however, that all stories about traffic deaths are insignificant. A story that shows the relationship between fatal car accidents and the absence of traffic control at a particular intersection might be very significant. Such a story could go beyond an individual accident to discuss the broader problem of traffic safety for a community.

Much the same thing may be said about stories reporting crimes. An individual story about a person being arrested, tried, and convicted of shoplifting might be interesting. A story about the problems created by shoplifting in a community could be significant.

An individual traffic death or shoplifting conviction can become the news peg upon which a good writer can hang a significant story. Remember, significance or insignificance is inherent in the event or situation; the writer cannot affect it, although the story may herald the importance of an event or situation to the audience.

A writer can do a great deal about the interest a story will have, however. To put it another way, although writers can't make merely interesting stories significant, good writers can make significant stories interesting.

WHAT IS INTEREST?

Many times, all other things being equal, a significant story will be chosen over one that is merely interesting. This means that a seemingly routine story out of city hall will bump a bright feature about a ten-year-old baton twirler. Of course, editors try to achieve a balance between what they assume their audience wants and what they believe the audience should have (accurate information with which to make wise political decisions). Stories that are both significant and interesting gladden editors' hearts.

Interest is the probability that readers or listeners will seek out a story. Unfortunately, this factor is impossible to measure. We can determine that an audience has heard or read a story, but no foolproof method is yet available to predict *if* it will hear or read a story.

Over the years, journalists have concluded that certain elements make a story interesting. The inference is, if these elements are included, the story will be interesting; that is, readers and listeners will seek it out.

News Elements

The elements of news interest most often agreed upon are timeliness, proximity, prominence, unusualness, human interest, and conflict.

TIMELINESS

All news is either timely or current or both. **News is current if it contains a reference to yesterday, today, or tomorrow.** "Current" means "now" or perhaps "recently" or "soon" (see Figure 9.2). You may infer the extent to which journalists in your own community value this element by examining the content of the media. How many news stories in your hometown paper contain some clue that the news is current? How many items broadcast by your favorite radio station fail to contain some reference to today, the recent past, or the near future? Consider the following news lead:

> Plans for a new municipal swimming pool were studied Monday night by the Yourtown City Council.

The words "Monday night" tell us the story is current.

Chuck-wagon dinner planned

The East Central Chapter of the Iowa Head Injury Association will hold a chuck-wagon dinner from 4 to 7 p.m. Sunday, Sept. 20, at the Knights of Columbus Hall, 5977 Mount Vernon Rd. SE.

Tickets are $5. They are available at the Hobby Hut at Westdale Mall, at the Art Supplier at Lindale Mall, at Armstrong's Department Store, or from any member of the Head Injury Association. Children under 6 years will be admitted free.

Besides the dinner, there will be performances by country and popular music groups, including Wild Oats.

The dinner will follow a 10K run at Kirkwood Community College, held earlier in the afternoon. The run is co-sponsored by Kirkwood and the Iowa Head Injury group.

In October, head-injured people from around the state will attend a special Head Injury Week at Camp Courageous in Monticello.

All proceeds from the fund-raising events will go for camperships and for providing services for head-injured people and their familes in this area.

For more information, call the Iowa Head Injury Association, 363-0689.

FIG. 9.2. A publicist's news release is *current* if the story contains a reference to a recent time. In this news release the time and date of the event are provided in the first paragraph of the story. (*From the* Cedar Rapids (*Iowa*) Gazette)

A story is timely if it is appropriate to the time it is published. We seldom read Christmas stories in July or tales of Independence Day in December. If we do, some element other than timeliness brings such news to the surface. Ordinarily we read stories about planting in the spring and about harvest in the fall (see Figure 9.3). Look at this news lead:

> Elementary school teachers whose classes contain more than 25 pupils are probably working too hard and are therefore inefficient, a state official says.

Summer's hot weather affects garden plants

Special to The Messenger

The recent hot weather has discouraged many outdoor activities, including gardening. While many of us retreated to the air conditioned comfort of indoors, fruits and vegetables had to cope with several days of high temperatures. Problems caused by the high temperatures may appear on various vegetables in the garden.

Sunscald occurs on tomato and pepper fruits exposed to direct sunlight. Initial symptoms are shiny white or yellow areas on the side of the fruit exposed to the sun. Later,

the affected tissue dries and collapses, forming a slightly sunken, wrinkled area. Secondary organisms invade the affected area causing that portion of the fruit to rot. Sunscald increases during periods of high temperatures.

Sunscald is usually less severe on tomato plants grown in wire cages. The upright growth habit provides shade for the developing fruit. Also, control foliar diseases of tomatoes and peppers which may defoliate plants and expose the fruits to direct light.

FRUIT CRACKING appears as a

radia or concentric cracks at the stem end on tomato fruit. Heavy rainfall or a thorough watering following a long, dry period promotes rapid fruit growth. Mature tomatoes ripening during this period of rapid fruit growth often crack. High temperatures contribute to cracking. Large-fruited varieties, such as "Beefsteak," are generally more susceptible to cracking.

Cracking my be reduced by providing uniform soil moisture levels by mulching and watering. "Avalanche," "Heinz 1350," "Jetstart" and "Supersonic," are less prone to cracking.

FIG. 9.3. This feature story appeared in late August, fulfilling the news value requirement *timeliness*. Editors would not be likely to print this story at any other time of the year. (*From the* Fort Dodge (*Iowa*) Messenger)

Although the lead doesn't contain a time cue, it seems safe to say that the timing of the story is appropriate. Clearly, it's not inappropriate. Now study this lead for a broadcast news story:

> The manhunt continues today for two armed men who shot and killed Yourtown Mayor Fred Albion here last week.

The writer includes two "current cues" in the sentence. Presumably a hunt for armed killers would continue until some closure occurred. Also, the word "today" has been inserted to stimulate or maintain interest. This technique is common in continuing or second-day stories.

If you're able to make your message current or timely, your odds for success at having it printed or broadcast climb.

PROXIMITY

Proximity refers to that which is nearby. Imagine a store in your hometown. Now think of a similar-sized store in a nearby community. If both stores burned to the ground the same night, which would you expect to learn most about from your hometown media? If you say the one in your hometown, you may understand what journalists mean by proximity. Something that occurs close to home is more likely to be reported than something that happens far away.

Include the element of proximity to increase the probability your message will be used. The job of the publicist is made much easier if stories are fashioned to include this element (see Figure 9.4).

UNI exhibit opens with reception

CEDAR FALLS — The work of 24 Kansas artists will be showcased in an exhibition opening in the University of Northern Iowa's Gallery of Art Aug. 31.

"A Kansas Collection" will open with a reception from 7 to 9 p.m. that evening and will be on display through Sept. 24. The reception and exhibition are open to the public free of charge.

The exhibit, a collection of 47 contemporary two- and three-dimensional works, opened at the new National Museum of Women in the Arts in Washington, D.C., during April, coinciding with the formal opening of the major new arts facility.

Artwork in the exhibit was selected from more than 2,000 entries by some 200 Kansas artists.

Located in the Kamerick Art Building, the UNI Gallery of Art is open from 9 a.m. to 4:30 p.m. Monday through Thursday, 7 to 9 p.m. Monday, and 1 to 4 p.m. Saturday and Sunday. The gallery is closed Fridays.

For more information, call the UNI Gallery of Art at (319) 273-2077.

FIG. 9.4. This announcement of an upcoming event appeared in the Waterloo, Iowa, newspaper. The town is in *proximity* to Cedar Falls, Iowa, where the event was to take place. Editors of papers farther away from the college would be much less interested in printing the information, because it would not serve a large percentage of their audience. (*From the* Waterloo (*Iowa*) Courier)

BURGER CELEBRATES AT DRAKE

Former Chief Justice of the U.S. Supreme Court Warren Burger will speak at the Des Moines Convention Center on Oct. 26 as part of the dedication ceremonies for the Neal and Bea Smith Law Center. The center is Drake Law School's new legal clinic at 24th Street and University Avenue.

David Walker, recently appointed dean of the Drake law school, said Burger's speech is part of a weeklong celebration commemorating the signing of the U.S. Constitution Oct. 25 through 29.

"[Burger] will be speaking on themes that interrelate — constitutional governance, the achievement of the constitution, legal education and the need for people, not just lawyers, to be educated about law and the Constitution," Walker said.

The celebration will include a visit by the 8th Circuit Court of Appeals and other public lectures and forums raising various constitutional issues.

FIG. 9.5. The news element *prominence* is evident in this release announcing a former chief justice of the U.S. Supreme Court as the featured speaker at an upcoming event. Locally prominent people highlighted in a release also increase its chances of publication. (*From the* Des Moines Business Record)

In recent years, nationwide telethons have been broadcast to collect funds to fight various diseases and to help pay the bills of political parties. One story about the Democratic party's telethon began:

Twenty-five volunteers worked
21 hours for the Democratic telethon
here this weekend.

The writer provided a local angle and made a national story proximate for a local audience.

PROMINENCE

Prominence refers to people and things that are well known. Although prominence generally applies only to people, some corporations, companies, and landmarks have become prominent, too. Journalists assume that stories about prominent people will be interesting (see Figure 9.5).

Almost anything the president of the United States does, no matter how mundane, is reported. Other personalities from politics, sports, and entertainment are also carefully covered. A quick scan of most newspapers will usually uncover at least one story about a prominent public figure or public official.

Two girls who live in the same college dormitory get the sniffles at the same time. One gets headlines; the other is ignored. One is the governor's daughter.

On the local level, one way to insert prominence into your stories is to consult well-known local personalities—the mayor, council members, priests, ministers, rabbis, and teachers—and then include their views about your situation in your message. For example:

> Yourtown Mayor Jim Sittwell to-
> day endorsed a Tea Rose Garden Club
> proposal to plant trees along Main
> Street.

Prominence enters the story with the mayor. Do you think it would make a difference if the mayor opposed the proposal?

UNUSUALNESS

One problem with unusualness is everyone has a different definition for it. What constitutes the odd, the out-of-the-ordinary, the strange, for you? I might not agree. Still, with some care, the unusual can be made to work for the individual who is trying to make news (see Figure 9.6).

Do you wanna race a duck?

No one cried "Fowl!" when Robert Duck took home $4,300 in winnings after his trained ducks waddled to victory in the recent 8th annual Great American Duck Race in Deming, N.M.

Duck is neither an employee of Ugly Duckling Rent-a-Car, which cosponsors the event with the Deming Chamber of Commerce, nor is he a relative of the company's president, Tom Duck Sr., who does have a brother named Donald.

No one's feathers were ruffled because it was the sixth consecutive victory for Robert Duck, who runs the Bosco Jewelry Co. in Albuquerque when he's not training the fastest ducks in the West.

"I heard about the race in 1980," he said, "and I thought, since my name is Duck and I had two ducks as pets, it would be fun. In the first year, out of 186 ducks, we won third place."

Determined to become the dominant Duck, he built a track much like the Deming track, which is 2 feet wide, 16 feet long and has 2-foot-high walls. Duck's is a stamina-building 24 feet long.

"What I do is buy about 50 day-old ducklings each spring, and when they're about 2 months old, I start running them," Duck explained. "Ducks don't like to be held, and once you let them go, they run away from you. You play on that. They learn that at the end of the track, they're free.

"The ducks have numbered leg bands, and I have a computer spreadsheet, Lotus 1-2-3, to keep track of their times. The slow ones don't race."

This year's grand champ was a Duck duck named Oliver South. "I told him if he didn't win," Duck said, "he'd go through the shredder."

Duck had 10 birds in the competition, including Tammy Faye—"she's a great racer but she gets makeup all over you"—and Oral Rodriguez—"I told him if he didn't make finals, the Lord would call him home." Oral did and was spared.

In attacting 45,000 visitors to Deming, a town of 12,000, the duck race has been good for business.

Said Tom Duck Sr.: "We haven't had so much excitement around here since Pancho Villa came across the Mexican border in 1912."

Clarence Petersen

FIG. 9.6. Opinions vary as to what constitutes the news element *unusualness*. The promoters of the Great American Duck Race did not pass up the opportunity to accent their version of the name game when submitting this story to the editors. (*From the* Chicago Tribune)

If hail falls, that's not unusual. If baseball-size hail falls, that's newsworthy. If brothers get together, that's routine. If brothers who haven't seen each other for 25 years get together, that's worth a story. If brothers who haven't seen each other for 25 years meet unexpectedly while waiting for a ride in a hot-air balloon, that might produce headlines.

Any story that produces a "Gee whiz!" probably is unusual. How many stories can you recall from the last time you read your newspaper? How many have you heard on the radio or on television?

Unusualness is an exception to the rule that writers can add the elements of news interest to a story. Writers can't really make something unusual, but they can point out that something is unusual and thus create interest.

HUMAN INTEREST

Human interest is another element whose definition varies from person to person. To most journalists, **human-interest stories are designed to arouse emotions in the audience.** The human-interest element may reside in the event or situation itself, or it may result from the writer's overt attempt to evoke some emotion, be it laughter, tears, rage, or even nostalgia. The hope of the writer is that readers will be able to empathize with the persons involved in the event or situation (see Figure 9.7).

Program allows kids to 'fly'

Gifted and Talented Program helps art students to excel

By SUE MENTON
Free Press Staff Writer

MANKATO — Kjel Johnson thinks maybe reading has something to do with his artistic ability.

Kjel, a sixth-grader at Roosevelt Elementary School and the son of Jill Johnson of Mankato, is one of 50 elementary students who have been participating in special art classes that are part of the District 77 Gifted and Talented Program (GTP).

Although most of the GTP classes are for students who are gifted academically, several are for those who have demonstrated unusual ability and interest in specific areas, including art, music, theater, and leadership.

THE FOURTH, fifth, and sixth graders in the special-talent classes "are highly motivated," said their teacher, Carolyn Nafstad, "but are not necessarily high-potential in other areas."

Students' work will be exhibited at the Carnegie Art Center beginning Monday evening, when the youngsters will be at the center with their projects, through the end of May.

Nafstad said it has been especially rewarding to work with the four groups of children in the art classes.

"They want to learn, and they learn so quickly," she said. "It makes it so interesting to me as a teacher. I never hear, 'Do we *have* to do this?' or 'When are we going to be done?' "

The regular elementary art teachers are limited in what they can accomplish, she said, since they only have blocks of 50 minutes. Most projects have to be started and completed within a single period.

IN NAFSTAD'S classes, which meet weekly for 1½ hours, "we have the luxury of no time restrictions. We might take four periods for a project."

She said these youngsters tend to work more slowly than the average student. "They are more meticulous. They like to plan things more thoroughly."

Kjel said he appreciates that extra time. "In a regular art class, the teacher spends so much time explaining things, and we're rushed to get things done," he said. "Here we have as much time as we need. We can work at our own pace."

One of Kjel's favorite pieces is a gnome with its hands clasped behind its back, which he modeled from clay. He said he likes drawing and painting, too, but especially likes clay because "you can do so much more with it. To draw this gnome," he said, turning his figure around, "I'd have to draw his front, his back, both sides, and the top and bottom."

HE SAID the gnome figure came from J.J.R. Tolkien's book, "The Hobbit," which is part of the "Lord of the Rings" series.

Kjel said he enjoys imagining, then drawing, the characters that he envisions while reading.

"That's the neat thing about books without illustrations: You can get your own ideas. Whatever you can imagine in your mind, you can draw.

"If you let your imagination fly," he said, "you can do anything."

FIG. 9.7. *Human interest* in news stories is accomplished by highlighting people as well as issues. This story could be written by simply telling about the gifted program, but it's inherently more interesting when personalized with one student's experience in the special art class. (*From the* Mankato (*Minn.*) Free Press)

A story about a tax increase might make a listener angry even though it contained no specific element of human interest. If the story were personalized, however, and the broadcaster tried to make the listener feel the pathos of an old man losing his home to confiscatory tax rates, it would contain human interest. Adventure yarns and stories devoted to children and animals generally ooze human interest.

Note that the element of human interest must be an obvious one. The writer, either through the material itself or the treatment of it, clearly attempts to evoke an emotional response in the audience. Examine this news lead:

> Not since the Barbary pirates threw their captives into the dungeons of Tripoli 170 years ago have American sailors known such terror or suffered such torture.

Can you decide what emotion the writer is trying to evoke? Here's another example:

> A Paris hairdresser who used to stroll the boulevards in shoulder-length hair had his locks shorn the other day. Then he put on a big hat stuffed with francs, which he proceeded to smuggle into Switzerland.

Human interest and the unusual seem married in that opening. Here's another human-interest lead:

> A former Yourtown high school football star soberly told grim-faced legislators today how he played in last year's state championship game "high on speed" and other hard drugs.

The writer attempts to create additional interest in a story on an investigation of drug and alcohol abuse through the use of personalization and human interest.

To use human interest properly requires skill and practice. Some writers describe scenes so vividly we seem to be able to experience precisely what they did when they observed the event.

All of the devices of fiction are available for use in adding human interest to a story, but it is critical to remember that news deals with facts, not fiction.

CONFLICT

People enjoy conflict, at least from a distance. Our fiction and drama teem with it. In news and information, too, **conflict helps stir and maintain interest** (see Figure 9.8).

Panel rejects smoking ban

WASHINGTON (AP) — A congressman who was twice thwarted in attempts to ban smoking aboard commercial airliners is promising to continue the effort until in-flight cigarette use is snuffed out.

"I think · this cause will ultimately win," Rep. Richard Durbin of Illinois said Wednesday after the House Appropriations Committee rejected his anti-smoking measure on a 23-11 vote. "I'm not giving up on it."

Durbin, a Democrat, proposed an amendment to the 1988 transportation appropriations bill to deny federal money to any airport serving air carriers who allow smoking aboard their planes.

In effect, it would give airlines a choice: bar smoking aloft or lose landing rights at federally subsidized airports.

The measure was the first such ban to be submitted since Congress received a series of reports concluding that second-hand smoke increases the risk of lung cancer and respiratory diseases to non-smokers.

"This is a deadly serious issue," Durbin told the committee. "It is not just a question of whether or not it is an inconvenience."

The National Academy of Sciences and Surgeon General C. Everett Koop recommended last year that cigarette smoking be banned on all domestic airline flights.

In March, however, the Federal Aviation Administration rejected such a move and said it is enough to separate airplane cabins into smoking and non-smoking sections.

The Appropriations subcommittee on transportation rejected Durbin's amendment June 11, contending in-flight smoking is a policy question, not a money matter, and should be considered by another committee.

It drew similar criticism Wednesday in full committee, mostly from lawmakers from tobacco-producing states.

"We stay in our backyard," Rep. William Natcher, D-Ky., told Durbin.

Committee Chairman Jamie L. Whitten, D-Miss., objected to it on procedural grounds, and Rep. Bill Hefner, D-N.C., called the proposal frivolous.

Durbin, meanwhile, said he may resubmit the amendment.

FIG. 9.8. The ongoing conflict between the rights of smokers and non-smokers surfaces again in this news story about the smoking policies on commercial airlines. Publicists representing each side of the issue are sure to follow the course of events closely, producing their own news releases to attempt to influence the eventual legislative result. (*From the Associated Press*)

Finding conflict where none exists is probably inappropriate, but it's fair to point out conflict if you find it. Man against man, man against himself, man against nature – these conflicts are interesting. Attorneys waging wars of words in courtrooms, doctors battling disease, men at war – they make interesting stories. Your messages will be more interesting to readers if you're able to include the element of conflict in your stories.

Summary

Gatekeepers all along the news production line, from interested observer or unwilling participant to television news anchor, affect the information that is fed to the mass media. Among professional journalists, however, a fairly standard system has evolved whereby the news value of a situation or an event is judged.

News is the report of an event or situation that has significance or interest or both. Although degrees of significance and interest in a situation or event may be debatable, one or both elements must be present if a story is to be news. Interest is usually present in one or more of the following modes: timeliness, proximity, prominence, unusualness, human interest, and conflict.

As a publicist, you must develop a cold, calculating eye for spotting news qualities. News releases do not become more newsworthy simply because you take pride in their creation. If you realistically measure the content of your messages against the backdrop of news values, you will most likely see those messages in print or on the air.

Exercises

1. Read the stories on the front page of your local newspaper. Identify the news values present in each story. Which are the dominant values—the most important ones for each story? Do you agree with the editors that the stories are worthy of placement on the front page? Why or why not?
2. Compare the stories on the front pages of three different newspapers for the same day—a daily from a metropolitan area, a daily from a medium-sized city, and a weekly or semiweekly from a small city. (Be sure the small-city paper publishes on the day you choose to do this exercise.) Discuss the news value criteria used by each paper. How are they the same? How are they different?
3. You have been named the publicity coordinator for a local grade school's upcoming carnival. Because the yearly event has become so popular, the carnival site has been moved to the high school this year. Also, the proceeds for this year's event will be donated to the family of one of the school's students who recently underwent an expensive kidney transplant. List at least three different messages you will want to send to the media. What news values will you rely on to get your messages printed or on the air?

Suggested Reading

Harriss, Julian; Leiter, B. Kelly; and Johnson, Stanley. "What Is News?" Chapter 3 in *The Complete Reporter.* 5th ed. New York: Macmillan Publishing Co., 1985.
Mencher, Melvin. "What Is News?" Chapter 3 in *News Reporting and Writing.* 4th ed. Dubuque, Iowa: Wm. C. Brown Publishers, 1987.
Stephens, Mitchell, and Lanson, Gerald. "News Judgment." Chapter 7 in *Writing and Reporting the News.* New York: Holt, Rinehart and Winston, 1986.

10 *Establishing an Effective Writing Style*

CHRISTINE FRIESLEBEN GOFF

EACH day, thousands of news releases are mailed to the media by publicists representing the largest corporations down to the smallest local organizations and clubs. To put the numbers in perspective, consider one metropolitan editor's remarks concerning news releases. He estimates that his paper receives more than 600 pieces of publicity each day. Of that number, he speculates there might be 15 releases he would consider usable, and perhaps only half of those would ultimately find their way into print. For that particular paper, that means only slightly more than 1 percent of the information proffered by publicists reaches the intended audiences. Or to put it more bluntly, 99 percent of submitted releases end up in the wastebasket. Other estimates of release use range from 5 to 10 percent—not quite as bleak as the above editor's estimate but not impressively high either.[1]

In recent years, a number of studies have examined the perception of news releases, especially from newspaper personnel. Editors have consistently indicated they are not satisfied with the publicity messages they receive. More often than not, one reason is the publicist's poor writing skills. Although this may not be the main complaint—lack of localization of the release's information heads most lists—one study cites poor writing style as a complaint of 22.7 percent of the editors surveyed.[2]

1. Bill Baxter, "The News Release: An Idea Whose Time Has Gone?" *Public Relations Review,* Spring 1981, 28.
2. Ibid., 30.

143

Fierce competition exists among publicists for print and broadcast exposure. Editors' dissatisfaction with the releases they receive indicates that publicists could avoid sabotaging their own efforts if only they would adhere to proper rules of spelling and grammar and develop an effective writing technique.

Style Considerations

In some respects, "style" is a vague word. If you were to ask three people to define "style," chances are you'd get three different answers. That's because style—the end result of how words are chosen and sentences are structured—is individual to each writer. Style can't be developed by reading a list of directions and closely following each instruction. Certainly grammatical considerations must be kept in mind. In fact, a good grammar text should be included in every writer's personal reference library. (Other deskside references include a good dictionary, a thesaurus, and a news stylebook.) But a writer's style cannot be labeled right or wrong, nor should it necessarily be labeled good or bad. Instead, writing style is judged by its effectiveness. Some writers are very effective, some moderately effective, and others ineffective. Because of the competition among news releases vying for print or broadcast consideration, being among the most effective writers makes perfect sense.

E. B. White, a writer whose words and sentences are so artistically constructed that they strike like lightning, once said this about style:

> Who can confidently say what ignites a certain combination of words, causing them to explode in the mind? Who knows why certain notes in music are capable of stirring the listener deeply, though the same notes slightly rearranged are impotent? . . . There is no satisfactory explanation of style, no infallible guide to good writing, no assurance that a person who thinks clearly will be able to write clearly, no key that unlocks the door, no inflexible rule by which the young writer may shape his course. He will often find himself steering by stars that are disturbingly in motion.[3]

If this sounds as if only the greatest literary masters have developed style, it is not so. Writing is not great because authors deemed great have written it. Writing is great because of how the words are organized, what they say and mean to the audience, whether they evoke a response, strike a chord, or cause a pondering of meaning. Even though there is no recipe for success, some guidelines, when applied, contribute to each writer's style.

3. William Strunk, Jr., and E. B. White, *The Elements of Style* (New York: Macmillan Publishing Co., 1972), 59.

BE ORGANIZED

The first requirement of good writing is the most obvious one, but it is sometimes the hardest for beginning publicists to master. Before starting any piece of writing, the publicist has to be sure where the end is going to be. In other words, have a specific plan. If you don't know where you're going with your message, your readers will get confused and give up reading. If, however, readers sense a direction in the article, they often will continue reading. This, of course, increases your chances of getting the intended audience to respond to your message in the way you would like them to.

If the word "outline" paralyzes you and elicits unpleasant memories of English composition, relax. You don't have to have three drafts of an outline before you begin writing. But you must have *some* plan, a definite direction in mind to help you focus your points more clearly.

The easiest technique to use simply requires you to keep like ideas together. For example, read the following opening paragraphs of a release:

> A group of Greenville community business leaders will meet Thursday night at the high school to discuss a program to help teenage parents work part-time while continuing to study for their diplomas.
>
> Recent studies reveal startling statistics about the large numbers of teen parents who quit school to raise a child. Without a high school diploma they are not able to rise above low-paying, low-status jobs.
>
> In response to these rising numbers, many schools are beginning to develop programs aimed at preventing adolescent pregnancies.
>
> Studies reveal that only 50 percent of teen mothers are likely to graduate from high school and teen fathers are less than 40 percent as likely to have a diploma.
>
> American educational systems have been urged by community and religious leaders to address the teenage pregnancy dilemma before the numbers reach epidemic proportions.

Here the publicist has the readers jumping between two separate issues—one that addresses how to help teen parents work and study at the same time, and another that addresses preventing adolescent pregnancies. Notice that no meeting time is given in the first paragraph. This information is lower in the release, but by jumbling ideas between the first and last paragraphs, the publicist risks losing some of the readers targeted to attend the meeting. The publicist could prevent confusion by dealing with the work-study issue in its entirety before discussing prevention programs.

BE SPECIFIC

Again, E. B. White cautions: "When you say something, make sure you have said it. The chances of your having said it are only fair."[4]

Sometimes publicists know exactly what they want to accomplish in a particular release, but what they actually write down is not clear. They assume that readers will know exactly how to respond, given certain information. If that were true, publicists' jobs would be exceedingly easy.

Let's use the above release to emphasize this point. What if the main objective of the release is to have community residents attend the meeting to discuss how the schools should tackle the delicate issue of preventing adolescent pregnancy? Suppose business leaders were being invited because they have a close association with the issue and can explain their work-study program to parents.

The publicist can't assume that people will flock to the school that night based on the information presented in the first sentence of the release. To begin with, that sentence refers to community business people. It's correct to assume if there's a meeting for community business people and you are not one of them, you are not invited. So right away the very people the publicist wants to attend the meeting have stopped reading. To correct this problem, the publicist's lead should read something like the following:

> Community residents are urged to attend an open forum at the high school Thursday night, Oct. 6, to discuss the role of schools in addressing the problem of adolescent pregnancy.

Now the publicist has the attention of the primary audience to which the release is directed. If you are writing a release, you can help yourself stay on track by asking, "What exactly do I want to accomplish with this piece of publicity?" If you know the answer to that question and organize accordingly, specific writing should follow naturally.

BE CONCISE

Researchers have long since established that there is an inverse rela-

4. Ibid., 72.

tionship between sentence length and reader comprehension. Because there is little chance that the goals of any piece of written publicity will be realized without complete reader comprehension, you will want to adhere to the principles of conciseness in your writing. (One way to accomplish reader comprehension is by writing readable prose. Formulas that test the readability of a message are discussed later in this chapter.)

Simply put, concise writing means saying what you want in the shortest number of words possible. Although "concise" doesn't necessarily mean "short," the tendency in publicity is to lean toward shorter sentences and paragraphs. Long sentences tend to wander, and wandering sentences breed deflated meaning. At times the long, cadenced sentence is effective, and if so, it should be used. After all, you want to avoid a release full of short, choppy sentences just as much as one filled with long, confusing ones. The key is to balance your writing style. Here are some considerations that will help you accomplish conciseness:

LIMIT EACH SENTENCE TO ONE IDEA

Sentences overloaded with information are as effective as a boat trying to find the harbor in a fog. Readers don't like to be confused. If they are constantly required to reread a sentence to ferret out the meaning, they are likely to quit reading. Therefore, publicists are encouraged to compose sentences that communicate only one idea at a time. For example, read the following sentence:

> Smith attributed the enrollment jump, in part, to an effort over the past two years to make more classes available to part-time students at night and on weekends, and in part to the college's new marketing campaign that began last fall with the specific goal of increasing its enrollment.

That sentence has 49 words and covers two separate points. To clarify the writing, each point should be dealt with individually, like this:

> Smith attributed the enrollment jump, in part, to an effort over the past two years to make more night and weekend classes available to part-time students. In addition, the college began a new marketing campaign last fall with the specific goal of increasing its enrollment, he said.

AVOID RUN-ON SENTENCES

Closely related to the one-idea-to-a-sentence advice is the caution to avoid run-on sentences. Run-ons are the result of writers forgetting to use one punctuation mark—the period. Run-ons differ from the first sentence in the above section in this respect: Although that sentence contained two ideas and was confusing to the reader, nothing was grammatically wrong with it. Run-ons, on the other hand, scream for some grammatical relief. For example, read the following sentence:

> Enrollment at the Northeast campus this semester increased 14 percent from last spring to 6,305 students and the Southeast campus enrollment grew nearly 19 percent to 705 students while the Northwest campus enrollment soared by 78 percent to 353 students and the Southwest campus enrollment was up 25 percent to 1,236 students.

Any reader courageous enough to make it through that sentence should be awarded with one year's free tuition at the campus of his or her choice! To avoid confusion, each campus's enrollment figures should be dealt with separately, like this:

> Enrollment at the Northeast campus this semester increased 14 percent from last spring, to 6,305 students. The Southeast campus enrollment grew nearly 19 percent, to 705 students. The largest jump in enrollment occurred at the Northwest campus, where it soared by 78 percent, to 353 students. The Southwest campus saw an enrollment increase of 25 percent, to 1,236 students.

Publicists should be aware of sentence length at all times. If you have written about 25 to 30 words without using a period, it's time to find a place to insert one.

ELIMINATE UNNECESSARY WORDS

Some writers tend to load up sentences with unnecessary words and phrases. Simple attention to detail in the editing process should help eliminate them. Watch for phrases that can be reduced to one word, such as these:

Wordy	Better
at this point in time	now
held a meeting	met
due to the fact that	because
voted to appoint	appointed
in the near future	soon
future goals	goals
in the event that	if
costs a total of	costs

The list is endless. The point is, it is easy to use unnecessary words in your writing unless you consciously avoid them.

Perhaps more subtle than the above examples of wordiness are redundant phrases. For example, here's another sentence from the enrollment release:

> The state's troubled economy also appears to be sending more unemployed workers back to the classroom to take courses that will help retrain these out-of-work persons for other jobs, school officials said.

Two phrases in that sentence reemphasize what has already been said. First, someone going back to the classroom is obviously going to take courses. Also, since the persons have been described as unemployed, the phrase "out-of-work persons" isn't necessary. Thus, the sentence could be effectively tightened this way:

> The state's troubled economy also appears to be sending more unemployed workers back to the classroom for retraining, school officials said.

The principle is simple. Don't repeat words or phrases unless they strengthen what you want to say.

AVOID CLICHÉS AND SLANG

A cliché is a much-used expression, such as, "Don't look a gift horse in the mouth" or "He who laughs last laughs best." These expressions might be effective in a conversation, but they only draw attention to themselves when written for journalistic purposes. Clichés are too often used as a crutch when the writer can't think of anything more specific to say. An occasional cliché might be effective, but overusing them makes stories old and stale.

"Slang" refers to words and phrases that are "in." In fact, "in" is a slang word. Anyone who doesn't know that the contemporary definition of "in" is "popular at the time" will be completely confused by any sentence that uses that word in its slang form. Read the following sentences:

> The students trashed the experiment.
>
> The instructor described the author's best-seller as a really good read.
>
> The basketball players were told to get their act together or surely they would lose the game.
>
> Field-trip participants were told that lunch would be a brown-bag affair.

The problem with slang is this: Because the publicist can't be sure everyone in the target audience has heard the new use of the word, there is a chance of confusing at least some of the readers. Therefore, it is wise to be, if you'll pardon the cliché, better safe than sorry and stick with conventional words and phrases. Thus, the above sentences would be more useful if written:

> The students abandoned the experiment.
>
> The instructor recommended everyone read the author's newest best-seller.
>
> The basketball players were told to concentrate on defense or they would surely lose the game.
>
> Field-trip participants were told to bring their own lunch.

See Chapter 12 for an additional discussion of the perils of slang.

USE THE ACTIVE VOICE

Publicists should use the active voice (subject/verb/object) in preference to passive voice (object/verb/subject) for the single reason that it *is* active. Passive sentences, which put the receivers of the verb first, are cumbersome and awkward. The active voice lends vitality to your writing. Read each of the following sentences in the passive voice, then in the active.

PASSIVE

More room for additional student services is provided by the new building that opened on campus last fall.

ACTIVE

The new building provides more room for additional student services.

PASSIVE

A highlight on the Blackhawk calendar for 15 years has been the Winter Carnival.

ACTIVE

The Winter Carnival has been a highlight on the Blackhawk calendar for 15 years.

PASSIVE

Also available at the park concession will be food, beverages and souvenirs.

ACTIVE

Food, beverages and souvenirs will also be available at the park concession.

Occasionally, you may use the passive voice for variety. But the rule of thumb is to construct your sentences to suggest action and thereby quicken the pace of the reading.

USE TRANSITIONS

One imperative device that contributes to effective style is the proper use of transitions, connecting words and phrases that weave the parts of a story into a whole. Sometimes—in fact, very often in short publicity pieces—there is a natural progression of ideas, and the information is self-explanatory. But in longer stories—the publicity feature, for example—the writer must help readers move from sentence to sentence, paragraph to paragraph, beginning to end, without confusing them. To achieve unity among diverse ideas, the writer incorporates transitional devices into the text.

Sometimes the transition can be a single word or a short phrase that moves the reader from one thought to the next. **"However," "therefore," "meanwhile,"** and **"on the other hand"** are some such examples.

Another common transitional device relates ideas by repeating a key name, word, or phrase mentioned earlier in the text. Read the paragraphs below to observe this technique:

Officials at Middle City Zoo expect there'll be some fun under the *boardwalk* soon.

> And to that end, **they** are hoping critters, folks and snow will show up in bulk for the second annual Zoo Fest, which this year is dedicated to raising $50,000 for a sightseeing *boardwalk* over the zoo's African exhibit.

The first transitional device above takes the reader back to the word "officials" in the first sentence by using the pronoun "they" in the second. If the first sentence of the release had read, "There'll be some fun under the boardwalk soon," the pronoun "they" in the second sentence would have had no antecedent and the reader would have wondered, "Who are 'they'?" The other repeated word, "boardwalk," is linked to the reference in the lead sentence.

A third type of transitional device, called the transitional sentence, is most often used when an issue not previously mentioned is introduced. Worded correctly, the sentence prevents an abrupt shift to the new idea. The key to making this transition work, however, is to provide some concrete information about the new point instead of simply inserting a vague reference to it. The following example begins with a poor transitionary sentence and is followed by one that relates more specific information to the reader.

> The report also investigated the status of women in administrative positions in coeducational colleges and universities.

> The report also revealed that a mere 8 percent of coeducational colleges and universities are headed by women.

Unrelated sentences crash into each other like bumper cars. Subtle transitions will prevent the collision of ideas. Although transitions come naturally to some writers, other writers must consciously strive to incorporate transitions into the text to produce publicity messages with maximum effectiveness.

SHOW–DON'T TELL

Imperative among the techniques that contribute to an effective style is descriptive writing. Publicists who want the maximum benefit from each publicity piece incorporate visual writing into the message. Writing visually does not require the talent of a literary genius, but it does mean the publicist must be more perceptive in gathering information and presenting it to the audience in ways that make the writing come alive.

Vague generalities do little to create a detailed picture in the mind of the reader. So the first requirement in learning to write visually is to *think* visually. For example, if you write, "A person entered the room," the readers must rely on their own imagination to picture that person. If you write, "A man entered the room," you have eliminated some of the mystique, but chances are, there are as many cloudy approximations of that man as there are readers. Now, if you write, "A priest entered the room," you have given the readers a visual picture that matches your intention.

The key to descriptive writing lies in the choice of words, particularly nouns and verbs. Although the tendency often is to layer adjective upon adjective and insert an adverb next to each verb, the astute writer realizes that they do little to reflect specific meaning. Many qualifiers are as clear as muddy water. Words such as "big," "little," "fat," "thin," "early," "late," "a lot," or "few" are mere abstractions of a writer's intent. Readers must guess what each of those words means, and chances are that not many will guess correctly.

Nouns and verbs, on the other hand, can be more selective. Instead of lifeless nouns and limp verbs, choose words that are strong, vivid, concrete, and interesting. Perhaps this idea can be best illustrated by several examples:

ABSTRACT

The *staff does everything* required to produce a school newspaper.

CONCRETE

The **52-member student** staff **reports** and **edits** the stories, **designs** the layout, and **sells** the advertising for the school newspaper.

ABSTRACT

The players *had something to drink* after they *were done.*

CONCRETE

The **football** players **gulped Gatorade** after they **completed the day's practice session.**

ABSTRACT

Day care for *older* people *is on the rise.*

CONCRETE

Day care for **elderly** people is **filling gaps** nationwide, **providing a social life** for them and **respite** for the people who care for them.

ABSTRACT

She was *old, polite,* and *animated.*

CONCRETE

The woman's hair was **white and thinning at the temples.** Her eyes had **sunk deep into their sockets,** and the wrinkles beneath them **rippled** toward her **hollow cheekbones.** Her manners were **above reproach,** just as they always had been from the earliest days of her youth. She had **arthritis** now, but still she **flung her arm forward** and **pointed her finger** as she **scolded** me for not watching my diet more carefully.

It's not hard to see how much color is injected into a sentence through the use of specific nouns and expressive verbs. But you must not purge *all* adjectives and adverbs from your text. In fact, some can be quite effective. For instance, the phrase "death came with savage swiftness" conveys a powerful image to the reader, as does the opposite portrayal—"he slowly dwindled under the unrelenting attack." If you choose adjectives and adverbs carefully and for a specific purpose, they can be just as forceful as precise nouns and verbs.

The following two paragraphs of a publicity feature, which appeared in the *Chicago Tribune,* combine all four categories of words—nouns, verbs, adjectives, and adverbs—to succinctly describe a phobia that strikes women more often than men:

Going to the store for a quart of milk may be a terrifying experience for some women. For those plagued by agoraphobia, the simple act of opening the door and moving outside the confines of their home can mean intense anxiety.

Agoraphobia is a powerful, unrealistic fear of ordinary places or experiences. A woman with the disorder may find herself on a city street, inside a church or at the supermarket when she is suddenly struck by an overpowering sense of being trapped in a threatening situation where help or escape is impossible.

Good writing, then, is more than just putting the proper facts before a particular audience. The effective writer presents those facts in a way that helps readers see—or if appropriate, hear, feel, taste, or smell—them for themselves. Publicists who fail to use the power of visual writing resign themselves to sentences that lumber along—right into the editor's wastebasket.

A Readability Yardstick

As was mentioned earlier, clarity and simplicity are keys to understandable writing. One way publicists can determine the level of difficulty (or simplicity) of their material is to apply a readability formula to a writing sample.

Readability studies are concerned with whether readers will be able to read and understand the writing being evaluated. Research reveals that readers who fail to get much meaning out of what is read, or readers who find the reading too difficult, usually stop reading.[5] Studies have also found that readable material results in an increase in readership, something a publicist should take to heart.[6] It would be to your advantage to heed readability measurement results and coordinate your style to a particular audience.

Several formulas have been developed throughout the years, but the two most commonly used are Rudolf Flesch's Reading Ease formula and Robert Gunning's Fog Index. Although both of these readability yardsticks were developed years ago—Flesch's in 1948 and Gunning's in 1963—they remain the most widely used formulas to date.

Flesch's contributions to the field of readability are innumerable. He was the first researcher to develop formulas suitable for measuring adult reading matter. His first formula, developed in 1943, was simplified and replaced by a 1948 version and revalidated in the 1970s. We will discuss the 1948 version here. Figure 10.1 gives the directions for applying the formula, which appears in Step 4 of Figure 10.1.[7]

The Reading Ease score will put your piece of writing on a scale between zero (practically unreadable) and 100 (easy for any literate person). Table 10.1 shows the Flesch readability index by style description and school grade.

Table 10.1.   Flesch Readability Index by Style Description and School Grade

Reading Ease score	Description of style	School grade
90 to 100	Very easy	Fifth
80 to 90	Easy	Sixth
70 to 80	Fairly easy	Seventh
60 to 70	Standard	Eighth to ninth
50 to 60	Fairly difficult	High school
30 to 50	Difficult	Some college
0 to 30	Very difficult	College graduate

5. George R. Klare and Byron Buck, *Know Your Reader* (New York: Hermitage House, 1954), 63.
6. George R. Klare, *The Measurement of Readability* (Ames: Iowa State University Press, 1963), 15.
7. Rudolf Flesch, *The Art of Readable Writing* (New York: Harper and Brothers, 1949), 250.

FIG. 10.1.   Instructions for applying the Flesch formula.

Choosing the material. If the passage to be tested is reasonably short—one to two pages—apply the formula to the entire piece. Otherwise, taking samples is more practical. To sample, use a strictly numerical scheme. For example, beginning with the first paragraph, use every third paragraph to figure the readability score.

Step 1. Count the total number of words in the piece. If sampling, count the material in the designated paragraphs in 100-word groups. Count contractions and hyphenated words as one word, and count as words any numbers or letters separated by a space. (For example, "1918," "C.O.D.," "shouldn't," "part-time," and "$9,362" all count as one word.)

Step 2. Figure the average sentence length in words. With a whole piece of writing, divide the total number of sentences into the total number of words. If sampling, count the number of sentences in each 100-word sample. Then add the total number of sentences in all samples, and divide by the number of words. (For example, if you have four 100-word samples containing 6, 9, 7, and 3 sentences, divide 400 words by 25 sentences, for an average of 16 words per sentence.)

In counting sentences, *follow the units of thought* rather than the punctuation. Usually sentences end in periods; but independent clauses separated by colons or semicolons, like these, should be counted as individual sentences. Don't break up sentences that are joined by conjunctions like "and" or "but." For example:

What is the root of all evil? Money. (Count as two sentences.)

Champion the right to be yourself; dare to be different and to set your own pattern. (Count as two sentences.)

There were two reasons to postpone the trip: the weather was bad, and the accommodations were scarce. (Count as two sentences.)

There were two reasons to postpone the trip: the weather and the accommodations. (Count as one sentence.)

She attended the meeting, but she did not participate in the proceedings. (Count as one sentence.)

"I'm sorry I can't help you," he said as he gathered his papers and prepared to leave. (Count as one sentence. In dialogue, the words outside the quotation are considered part of the sentence.)

Step 3. Figure the average word length in syllables. Count all the syllables, and divide by the total number of words. This figure is represented in the formula as number of syllables per 100 words, so put a decimal point in the hundreds column of the number of total words. For example:

Word count = 342
Syllable count = 476
476 ÷ 3.42 = 139.18 syllables per 100 words

Count the number of syllables in symbols and figures according to the way they are normally read aloud: for example, two for "%" (percent); four for "vegetable" (veg-e-ta-ble); six for "1947" (nineteen forty-seven); five for "$25" (twenty-five dollars).

As a shortcut, count all syllables except the first in words with more than one syllable. Then add the total number of words tested.

Step 4. Insert the number of syllables per 100 words (word length, *wl*) and the average number of words per sentence (sentence length, *sl*) into the following formula:

$$206.84 - .85(wl) - 1.02(sl) = \text{Reading Ease}$$

Remember, the numbers provided in the formula are constants. The only unknown information that must be inserted into the formula is the word length and the sentence length of the piece of writing being examined.

APPLYING THE FLESCH FORMULA

Although the formula might look complicated, it really is not hard to apply. Let's find the Reading Ease score for the news release in Figure 10.2. As you read the release, notice the slash marks and numbers on the script. Their meaning is as follows:

- The slash marks (/) indicate separation of sentences.
- The circled numbers at the end of each paragraph indicate the word count for that paragraph.
- The numbers above words are the syllable count of multisyllable words only. (Multisyllable words are words with more than one syllable.) The numbers are tallied and boxed to the left of each paragraph.

Here's what we have so far:

Total sentences = 18
Total number of words = 229
(Insert decimal point in hundreds column: 2.29)
Average number of words per sentence = 12.72
(229 words divided by 18 sentences)
Total number of syllables = 351
(229 single-syllable and first syllable of multisyllable words plus 122 extra syllables in multisyllable words)
Number of syllables per 100 words = 153.28
(351 syllables divided by 2.29)

Now if we insert the average number of syllables per 100 words (153.28) and the average sentence length (12.72) into the formula, we get:

CHARTER COMMUNITY HOSPITAL
1818 48th Street
Des Moines, Iowa 50310
(515) 271-6000

FOR IMMEDIATE RELEASE

Flowers can be "great medicine" for hospital patients. Indeed, flowers

[12] convey a message of warmth which says, "We hope you're feeling better." (22)

Joan Roberts is the director of nursing at Charter Community Hospital.
"Flowers play a large role in transforming a hospital room into a brighter,
cheerier environment," she says. "Fresh flowers really have a positive,

[34] therapeutic effect on recovering patients." (39)

[4] One patient in a Des Moines hospital agrees. (8)

"It's great receiving flowers from my relatives and friends because I
know they're out there thinking about me," says the patient. "Also, I
enjoy the comments I get from the nurses. When they tell me how pretty

[15] they are, it makes me feel really good." (45)

Studies have shown that nursing home patients spend more time at the

[9] table when flowers are present; they eat more and talk more to other residents. (26)

Leah Woodring, Charter Hospital's Guild president, says volunteers enjoy

[15] delivering flowers to the patients. It's the most pleasant part of the day. (22)

Des Moines florist, Jim Boesen, says mixed-cut flower arrays seem
to be the most popular for hospital patients. But shops also send out

[16] foliage plants, flowering plants and planters, he says. (31)

"Hospitals also send flowers to their physicians, employees and their
families in times of sickness and need," says Boesen. "Flowers really do

[17] boost one's morale. They are a great way to send a warm, caring message." (36)

[122]   (229)

FIG. 10.2. A news release with the Flesch formula markings applied.

206.84 − .85(153.28) − 1.02(12.72) = Reading Ease

Solving the equation gives us the readability score of the news release:

206.84 − 130.29 − 12.97 = 63.58

It's wise to round off the decimal. Change the score to the next highest number if the decimal is above .5; otherwise simply drop the decimal. Therefore the Reading Ease score for the news release is 64. According to Table 10.1, a score of 64 is standard, certainly acceptable for the mass media audience likely to receive that message.

One comment about interpreting scores on the chart. If the identified audience has few homogeneous characteristics, readability scores should be somewhere in the 60-to-80 range. On the other hand, if the audience's characteristics – especially the educational level – are identifiably similar, strive for readability scores in areas appropriate for that particular audience. Although researchers disagree about the correlation between reading levels and educational levels, there is some evidence that the two are, on the average, related.

For example, if a particular news release is targeted for publication in a newspaper, readability scores should be in the 60-to-80 range. However, if the targeted audience consists of grade-school children, the scores should be above 80. But if the targeted audience is a group of engineers with doctoral degrees, a readability score in the 30-to-50 range would be acceptable.

READABILITY LIMITATIONS AND BENEFITS

Despite the many advantages of using a readability formula, it's important to remember that the results provide an evaluation of writing style only. No attempt is made to label a style good or bad. Only the level of reading difficulty is determined. Other factors that contribute to the comprehension of reading material include the content (what is being discussed), the format (ink, paper, typography, and illustrations), and organization (headings, subheadings, graphs, tables, and so forth). Therefore, if you begin to "write to a formula," you risk losing sight of the many other factors that go into good writing.

What formulas do promote, however, is awareness. Publicists who are mindful of the need for reader comprehension center their attention on the factors of writing style that cultivate comprehension, such as sentence length and choice of words. Formulas also encourage writers to compose clear statements, which are the result of clear thinking.

Skill development takes time and effort. The conscientious publicist is willing to take that time and put forth that effort. When readability formulas take their proper place in the development of an effective writing style, the result will be messages that are widely read and fully understood.

Summary

Jotting down a message on a piece of paper is a relatively easy task. On the other hand, writing a message to a print or broadcast audience in anticipation of a specific response requires a great deal more care. Loosely organized thoughts and haphazard writing stand little chance of surviving the editor's perusal, much less of being delivered to the intended audience.

Style is not necessarily easy to develop, but with commitment to the ideals of good writing and attention to the details that promote good writing, a publicist will soon master the elements necessary for effective expression.

Exercises

1. Choose three samples of writing you find particularly effective. One should be a news story from a local newspaper; one, a feature story from a magazine; and one, content from a brochure. Analyze the style of each selection, and explain which writing techniques are used to contribute to that effective style.
2. Now choose three samples of writing from the same three areas described in Exercise 1 that you consider to be less effective. Identify the writing techniques that you think contribute to the content's weaknesses.
3. Using the Flesch readability formula given in this chapter, find the Reading Ease score of one content selection from Exercise 1 and one content selection from Exercise 2. Discuss the role of the readability scores in relation to your identification of the content as effective or not effective.
4. Find ten sentences—from any print source—that you think have apparent construction weaknesses such as those discussed in this chapter. After identifying the weaknesses, rewrite the sentences into more acceptable units of thought.

Suggested Reading

Callihan, E. L. *Grammar For Journalists.* 3d ed. Radnor, Pa.: Chilton Book Company, 1969.
Flesch, Rudolf. *How to Test Readability.* New York: Harper and Row, 1951.
Rivers, William L. *Writing: Craft and Art.* Englewood Cliffs, N.J.: Prentice-Hall, 1975.
Strunk, William, Jr., and White, E. B. *The Elements of Style.* New York: Macmillan Publishing Co., 1972.

11 *Writing for the Print Media*

JEROME L. NELSON

NOW that you have some insight into journalists and their news values, and you are aware of the attention to detail needed in grammar, spelling, and style, you are ready to learn how to produce publicity messages. It is helpful to begin by discussing two important journalistic functions: the **observation** function and the **reportorial** function.

Before Writing

One of a journalist's primary jobs is observation. Writers look at the world around them, hunting for the stuff of news. When they find it, they collect it as quickly as possible and then "write it up."

How do journalists know when they have fulfilled the observation function? Almost everyone has heard of the "five Ws and H": Who? What? When? Where? Why? How? Journalists know they have completed the observation function when they can answer each of these questions in some detail.

For example, a person's name answers "Who?" But journalists need more than just a name to answer that question. The requirement to answer the question *in some detail* demands that more information be gathered. **A complete identification includes the name and at least two of the following three elements: age, address, occupation.**

161

Journalists also collect other information that might be useful in writing a story. The kind and amount of additional information depends in part on the type of story the journalist expects to write. For example, probably less information would be needed to answer "Who?" for a story on the opening of a physics laboratory than would be needed for a profile on a physicist.

Journalists routinely collect many times more information than is needed to answer the five Ws and H and produce a story. The reason is simple: It's much better to have more information than you'll be able to use than to find you don't have enough. Under time pressure, discovering holes in your bag of information can be frustrating and embarrassing. (See Chapter 4 for a complete discussion on information-gathering techniques.)

The Two Basic Story Forms

Once the observation function has been fulfilled, the reportorial function remains. You will have completed the reportorial function when you produce an inverted pyramid story—one of two basic story forms you'll have to know.

Although newswriting allows as much creativity as any other prose, two story forms serve almost any reporting assignment:

1. The **straight** or **spot** news story, which reports events that have occurred or are about to occur and is written in the inverted pyramid form.
2. The **feature** story, which reports ideas, discussions, interpretations, background, or human-interest matters without necessarily focusing strictly on past or future events.

The volume of the daily spot news report is staggering. You'll recall how large it is from our earlier discussion of gatekeepers in Chapter 9. In considering the audience, you need to recognize that audience members have a limited amount of time available. This means the audience places two conflicting demands on the journalist: It wants to be fully informed about items in which it has an interest, and it wants to be concisely informed.

THE INVERTED-PYRAMID STORY FORM

Over the years, a particular story form has evolved that in many cases responds to these two demands. This form is the **inverted pyramid** (see Figure 11.1).

SUMMARY LEAD

ELABORATION OF LEAD

DETAILS BECOME

LESS AND LESS

IMPORTANT

AS STORY

UNFOLDS

•

FIG. 11.1.   The inverted pyramid story form.

In terms of impact, the inverted pyramid is the opposite of the modern short story. The short story saves the climax for last. The inverted pyramid story hits you with the news—the climax—at the very beginning.

Think about this for a minute. Which form is closer to the pattern you've been using all your life to tell others what has been happening? If you're like me, when you've seen something happen, you just blurt out the story, using something like an inverted pyramid form. For example, when I saw a fender bender near the office one day and started telling the secretary about it a little later, I didn't say: "It was foggy this morning and cold. I was shivering as I stood at the corner of Lincoln Way and Beach, waiting in my usual patient way for the traffic light . . . " I'm eccentric, but not that eccentric. What I started with was this: "Hey! I saw a car crash at Lincoln Way and Beach this morning." Except for the "hey," the sentence gets right to the news, and that seems natural. That's what the inverted pyramid does: It gets right to the news.

The inverted pyramid story begins with the most important details and ends with the least important details. For readers, the advantage of this story form is that those who want just the basic facts can get them by reading the first few paragraphs. Readers or listeners who want more details can stay with the story a little longer.

The inverted pyramid story appeals to editors, too. When information comes from public relations sources, one criterion editors use to judge its acceptability is whether the story is rendered in a usable form. The inverted pyramid facilitates trimming from the bottom up, which is done when there is not enough space available for the entire release. This speeds up the gatekeeping process, and editors like that.

When you have gathered information for a story, sifted through it, and analyzed it, you come to know which details are important and which aren't. Of the important details, you know which are more important than others. You know which are most important. And these facts emphasize the advantage of the inverted pyramid form for the writer. Once you know your story, it practically writes itself as you proceed from most important to less important to least important details. Figure 11.2 is a sample publicity release developed in the inverted pyramid style.

THE NEWS STORY LEAD

The most important element of any straight news story is the beginning, or **lead.** The lead may be a sentence, a paragraph, or several paragraphs long. Most often it is a single paragraph composed of a single sentence that summarizes the whole story. For example:

> A two-day seminar for Iowa producers of beef-cattle seed stock will be held November 29 and 30 in the Scheman Building.

This lead relates the important facts. It answers four of the five Ws.

Who – Iowa producers of beef-cattle seed stock
What – will hold a two-day seminar
When – November 29 and 30
Where – Scheman Building

It does the whole job in fewer than 25 words. For some readers or listeners, the information in the lead might be enough. For a producer of beef-cattle seed stock, a longer story would probably be necessary.

A **summary lead** such as the one above may introduce almost any story from the most to the least significant. Consider this lead:

> Richard Milhous Nixon, 37th president of the United States, resigned from office Thursday night. Vice President Gerald R. Ford, a 61-year-old former Michigan congressman, will be sworn in as president at 11 a.m. today in the Oval Office of the White House.

This typical summary lead topped a story on one of the most momentous news events of the past quarter of a century. Note that the lead answers four Ws – who, what, when, and where.

HOOVER PRESIDENTIAL LIBRARY ASSOCIATION, INC.
TELEPHONE 319/643-5327
P.O. BOX 696   WEST BRANCH, IOWA 52358

For more information:
Tom Walsh (319) 643-5327

FOR IMMEDIATE RELEASE

WEST BRANCH -- A gallery of the Herbert Hoover Presidential Library-Museum has been transformed into a pine forest for a new exhibit on First Lady Lou Henry Hoover's 27 years of involvement with the Girl Scout movement.

The exhibit opens Sunday, March 1. It was created as part of a national commemoration of 1987 as the 75th anniversary of the founding of the Girl Scouts in 1912. On Sunday, March 29, more than 2,000 Girl Scouts from throughout eastern Iowa and western Illinois will be in West Branch for a special 75th anniversary ceremony.

Among the items exhibited within the case which is surrounded by the artificial forest is one of the many styles of Girl Scout uniforms worn by Lou Henry Hoover between 1917 and 1944.

Lou Henry Hoover joined the Girl Scout movement in 1917, working closely with founder Juliet Lowe to raise money and to increase membership. She served two terms as the Girl Scout organization's president, personally raising $300,000 for program development and leadership training. Lou Henry Hoover also sponsored the first national cookie sale in 1935.

The Girl Scouts credited Lou Henry Hoover's enthusiasm, prestige and untiring commitment to scouting as an important influence in membership increasing from 13,000 in 1917 to 840,000 in 1944, when she died at age 69. Today, there are nearly 3 million Girl Scouts.

The new Girl Scout exhibit will remain on display through mid-summer. The Hoover Library-Museum is located just north of Interstate 80 exit 254 in West Branch. Hours are 9-5 daily.

-30-

FIG. 11.2.   A news release written in the inverted pyramid style.

Here's another lead—again following a momentous event:

> Hindus enraged by the assassination of India's Prime Minister Indira Gandhi took to the streets of New Delhi today armed with staves, rocks and firebombs, and more than 200 people were reported injured in northern India as news of Gandhi's death swept through the country.

All of the five Ws and H are covered. The lead uses 45 words, perhaps a few too many for a really good opening sentence. One way to solve the length problem is to break the lead into two sentences:

> Hindus enraged by the assassination of India's Prime Minister Indira Gandhi took to the streets of New Delhi today armed with staves, rocks and firebombs.
>
> Elsewhere in northern India, more than 200 people were reported injured as news of Gandhi's death swept through the country.

Although straight news leads generally are composed of single paragraphs of one sentence each, they need not be. Complicated stories may require that the general rule be bent.

Recall that the inverted pyramid story moves from the most important to the least important detail. You may think of the summary lead as a special case of the inverted pyramid story. Summary leads begin with the most important detail, the answer to the key question in the five Ws and H. For most stories, this means the lead will be organized to answer: what happened, when it happened, where it happened. This isn't always the case, of course, as you can see from the Nixon lead above. It goes like this: who, what, when, who, what, when, where.

If you'll recall from the discussion of news values in Chapter 9, Nixon's prominence dictates that the lead be organized that way. For most stories, what/when/where is the most likely order. Summary leads may begin with answers to any of the five Ws and H, however.

Once more, remember that the task of the newswriter in handling straight news is to decide which is the most important detail in the information gathered and then to build a lead and organize an inverted pyramid story accordingly. The rationale is simple: Just give 'em the facts.

THE FEATURE STORY FORM

Feature stories take forms unlike the inverted pyramid story form, and they may be motivated differently, too. Feature stories aren't necessarily linked to events just past or soon to be. They may be as light as dandelion seed, or heavy and serious. They may describe problems with roots in the past and possible solutions in the future. They may deal with potential problems that could arise if something isn't done. They may be just for laughs.

A good publicist takes advantage of the benefits of feature releases. They are a valuable addition to regular news releases in that they provide more exposure for the company, organization, or issue represented. Features allow more depth of message and provide limitless possibilities for creativity in the manner in which the material is presented to the target audience.

For professional feature writers, just relaying the facts isn't enough. Generally they will seek to arouse, to evoke emotion, too. Although feature writers are definitely not producing fiction, they may employ all of the techniques of fiction in the story. In fact, the **suspended-interest feature** takes exactly the same form as the short story, in which **the climax comes near the end.**

Sometimes, when the writer uses a current event as a news peg for a feature, the first few paragraphs of the story may even take an inverted pyramid form. But the point to remember is this: **The feature story form is variable and depends greatly on the content with which the writer is working.** The form for a serious story on prospects for the local economy, for example, will not be the same as the form of a light piece on a two-headed calf.

TYPES OF FEATURE STORIES

Although the list is not intended to be exhaustive, some categories of feature stories are described below.

The human interest story describes people and evokes strong emotion (see Figure 11.3). Such features are designed to make readers laugh or cry, to feel "all good inside" or to "get mad." Like the short story, a good human interest story strives for unity of effect. It seeks to evoke one dominant emotion. We discussed the news value that leads to a human interest feature in Chapter 9.

Another type of feature also falls into the human interest category. **The bright is a story designed to make readers laugh or smile.** Brights are supposed to be funny. As with other human interest stories, brights demand skill and discipline.

One hot day in Boone

by FINN BULLERS

Josie Pestotnik stepped out of the house early on Independence Day. She always goes out early in the morning to feed the cat. The air was cool. The early morning sun was creeping into the sleeping town of Boone, Iowa. Bright yellow rays filled the yard. She was up before most of the neighbors.

Josie didn't put her glasses on.

The dew glistened on the freshly cut grass of the yard DeWayne Pestotnik had just spruced up the day before. This was a special day — it was Josie and DeWayne's 47th wedding anniversary. As Josie stood on the backstairs, birds chirped a pleasant good morning.

There were to be a lot of fireworks.

A bank of evergreen trees outline the Pestotnik property at 134 W. 5th Street. The trees provide a cool place for an animal to escape the sultry Iowa heat.

Josie stood looking over the back yard at 7 a.m. She was not alone on the stairs.

"I didn't have my glasses on, and I didn't know what it was. And I called DeWayne, and I said, 'Would you come and see what this is?' So I come back and got my glasses.

"I found it laying on its side. No hair at all. No hair at all on its tail or anything. It just looked like some kind of freaky animal. And its eyes bulged clear out its head. This one was clear out, and the other partly out, and it had a wire around its neck real tight, like they had choked it to death and then drug it.

"No hair left on it at all, and all I could tell was — it had big feet and a little bit of white *right there*." Josie points to her chest.

"But no hair at all. Just a little white fuzz."

Josie waited at the steps for DeWayne. She called out and looked down. "I still didn't know what it was. Well, I didn't believe it was. And I still couldn't believe it was." DeWayne glanced down at the black pile by his wife's feet.

"By God, it's the cat," he said.

"Well, it was picked up sometime Wednesday evening the third," DeWayne says. "Sometime, I suppose, between midnight and 6 o'clock in the morning it was drug to death behind a car, and they brought it home and laid it out there on our steps, our back steps.

"There it was."

Josie went to pieces. She cried hysterically. "It was just a part of us, that's all, you know. I don't know who would have it in for the cat. I really don't."

Josie pauses for a moment to dab at her eyes with a tissue, but only for a moment. "Now, I let DeWayne do most of the talking because I get a little excited." But she continues. "It just took us as a blow, you know. Like I say, the cat was gentle and just, just a nice old cat to pick up, you know, and you could look in his eyes, and he wouldn't do anything, shoot."

DeWayne cuts in before his wife starts up again. He's a hard-baked grandfatherly type guy who would be embarrassed   t you know he's an ol' soft Pestotniks are the type of that don't spe k kindly busts" and v   lon or me' fee

FIG. 11.3. Publicists should not overlook the potential of the human interest story to communicate a point to the selected audience. (*From the* Iowa State Daily)

How-to stories show readers how to do something (see Figure 11.4). The range of topics is as wide as the imagination of writers. Everything from how to keep your spouse happy to how to repair a leaky faucet or make sure you won't be audited by the Internal Revenue Service falls into the how-to category. The story form requires that writers know what they're talking about well enough to explain it to the readers.

Profiles are short biographies (see Figure 11.5). They explain people and, in some instances, organizations. You might see a profile on consumer advocate Ralph Nader or on Amnesty International. A prerequisite of a good profile is solid, thorough reporting. To explain someone, a writer must know that person exceedingly well.

Hints for coping with senior year crazies: The college application process

Applying to college can be as painful as paying for it. The pressure is on from the moment a college-bound senior starts school in the fall, and it mounts until he or she receives notification of acceptance or rejection in the spring.

During this eight-month period, even the most supportive of families can show signs of stress. Parents typically fear that their children won't: 1) take the application process seriously; 2) write an application good enough for admission; or 3) let their parents know what they are doing or thinking.

At the same time, their children live in dread that: 1) they won't get in anywhere; 2) everyone — family, friends, teachers — will perceive them as failures; and 3) their parents won't understand their problems or be able to help them if they do.

Intense anxieties such as these can easily lead to screaming matches, slammed doors and battered feelings. Frequently the issues underlying family fights are not at all related to the alleged bone of contention.

For example, when a mother cautiously asks, "How are things?" and her high school senior responds with, "All you ever do is nag, nag, nag," the anger probably has less to do with nagging than with fears of separation and inadequacy.

"When parents can see through to the core issues and gain some perspective on them," explains psychiatrist Carole Schaffer. "they are better able to respond in an appropriate and healing way."

Here are some suggestions to commonly faced problems between parents and seniors:

• **Closing the credibility gap** — Students frequently tune out their parents at application time because they fear their parent's advice will be out-of-date, unrealistic or simply incorrect.

One mother recounts how her daughter rejected her advice by exclaiming: "What *do* you know about college? You went to an all-girls school. No one goes to an all-girls school anymore!"

Parents can turn this situation around by making an effort to understand the admissions process and by recognizing that things probably are very different from when they applied for college.

• **Setting up ground rules** — Parents can often help diffuse tensions by reaching mutual agreement on specific rules. For example, parents and seniors might agree to meet with each other on a weekly basis to discuss what progress has been made and what remains to be done on a set of applications.

A mutual arrangement of this type can go a long way towards alleviating the problems arising from "crazed" parents who feel the need to impulsively pump their children for information and seniors who clam up or withdraw in response.

• **Seeking help from an objective third party** — When parents run into problems they can't solve by themselves, they need to know where help is available and that it's "okay" to use it.

In some cases, parents may not have the expertise or knowledge to advise their child. One father recalls how inadequate he felt when his daughter asked him to help her on her essay: "I was never very good at writing. How could I possibly help my daughter organize her thoughts!"

In other cases, parents may be willing and able to help but, because the emotional environment at home has dinintegrated beyond repair, the child may reject any solutions parents offer.

In all instances, parents should know that there are resources available. In the school, parents can turn to guidance counselors and teachers. Outside of school, there are writing specialists who can help students with their applications, as well as counselors who can given personalized advice on college selection and admission procedures.

For their children's sake, it's important that parents put the application process into perspective. A sense of humor and an acknowledgement that life will go on regardless of where their child goes to school will help make senior year less crazy.

FIG. 11.4. How-to feature stories such as this one are a popular and effective way to provide the readers with specific suggestions about how to do something. (*From the* Grinnell (*Iowa*) Herald-Register)

Jack Shelley RETIRES FROM SECOND CAREER

When Jack Shelley speaks, people listen... and have listened for 47 years.

There isn't a better-known radio voice around Iowa and the Midwest than Shelley's. His was a voice people grew up with, as he gave them news of the Great Depression, a world war and their hometowns. Later his face became as well-known as his voice as television news evolved from a novelty to an essential element in people's lives. He went to where the news was being made and made his stories meaningful for national and local audiences.

That was the first half of Shelley's career—30 years as radio and television news broadcaster with WHO in Des Moines, the last 25 as news director. The second bought him to Iowa State in 1965 when Jim Schwartz, new head of the journalism department, convinced Shelley to leave WHO to build ISU's broadcast journalism program. He retired from that career at the end of Spring semester, 1982.

Shelley has always had a flair for public speaking. That reason, plus better pay, influenced this print-media-trained journalist to leave his reporter job at the Clinton Herald and enter the fledgling world of broadcast news in 1935, the year he graduated from the University of Missouri. It's a decision he's never regretted, even though at the time, newspaper editors thought radio news was "not the thing for a journalist to do," he says. From a 50,000 watt, clear-channel radio station, Shelley's news broadcasts carried over a large portion of the nation for 30 years.

Shelley assigned himself to cover World War II for WHO. He was one of a handful of war correspondents representing individual radio stations to cover both the European and Pacific theaters. He interviewed hundreds of "local boys" at the fronts in Begium, Luxemburg and Germany in 1944 and '45, sending their stories home to anxiously waiting audiences of families and friends. He was interviewing near the front in the biggest German counter offensive of the war—the Battle of the Bulge.

He switched from Army to Navy credentials to continue his interviews in the Pacific as the war drew to a close in 1945. There he covered his two biggest stories.

He was at the right place at the right time to provide the world with the first broadcast interviews of pilots and crews of the two planes that dropped atomic bombs on Hiroshima and Nagasaki. And he was aboard the battleship USS Missouri in Tokyo Bay to cover the Allies' acceptance of the unconditional Japanese surrender.

Five years later he was at Yucca Falls, Nev., as part of the press corps to cover one of the early "public" atomic bomb tests. He was one of 20 newsmen chosen by lot to be in the trenches with the "guinea pig" servicemen, less than two miles away from where the Hiroshima-type atomic bomb was detonated. His tape recorder was one of a few to withstand the shock of the blast and his report of the test was broadcast throughout the nation.

One of the early leaders of broadcast journalists' organizations, Shelley has been a staunch defender of First Amendment guarantees of freedom of the press. He helped found the Iowa Broadcast News Association, an organization that in 1971 honored him by establishing the Jack Shelley Award.

He is past president of the international Radio-Television News Directors Association, which he helped found, and of the nationwide Associated Press Radio and Television Association. He was president of the Iowa Freedom of Information Council in 1981 and a member of a committee appointed by the Iowa Supreme Court to advise it on the use of cameras and recorders in court trials.

He received the "Broadcaster of the Year" award from the Iowa Broadcasters Association in 1980, the Honor Medal from

16

the University of Missouri School of Journalism (an award later received by such journalism giants as Walter Cronkite, Chet Huntley and David Brinkley) and the "Mitchell Charnley Award" of The Northwest Broadcast News Association at the University of Minnesota.

In 1982 Shelley was honored by ISU for his academic contributions with an "Outstanding Teacher" award and received a Faculty Citation from the ISU Alumni Association.

You can't help but drop a few more names when telling Jack Shelley's story.

There was the time when he and Catherine were married; the entire WHO radio staff attended the ceremony and gave them a sendoff at the Des Moines airport. A young associate named Ronald Reagan, then WHO's sport director, played a major part in the going-away festivities. "The story has grown a little since then," Shelley notes. "Ronald Reagan was not my best man." The 40th President remembers Jack Shelley, however, and sent him a congratulatory letter and autographed photograph showing Reagan at a WHO microphone, for a recent Iowa Broadcasters Association Convention banquet honoring Shelley.

Shelley learned journalism from another person whose name is prominent in Iowa history—H.R. Gross, WHO news director. Gross later served 26 years in the U.S. House of representatives.

Early in his career Shelley made his own breaks in the news business. As a young Depression-era graduate of the University of Missouri, he stood before an Inland Daily Press Association convention in Chicago appealing to publishers and editors to give jobs to journalism graduates, saying many would work for little or no money just to get experience. The late Warren Eastman, managing editor of the Clinton Herald, was impressed by the speech and later offered him a job—but not for nothing. Shelley was paid $15 a week.

Admittedly, there have been times when Shelley has been a bit glib on the air. In one instance, however, his wordiness helped save the biggest story of his career—the interviews with the A-bomb plane crews.

"I got a half-' 'r interview ·   10 c
on ʑ ·ld v   ·oʳ ˈᵍ m   . Jˈ
biˈ   ˈ   ˈor
tˈ

FIG. 11.5. A well-written profile story is a valuable publicity technique. The focus of the feature is a person, perhaps an upcoming speaker or a member who belongs to the organization. Profile stories can generate a response, explain a position, or improve the image of the organization. (*From the* Newsletter, *Iowa State University Department of Journalism and*

The background story is designed to update, interpret, or explain the news (see Figure 11.6). Sometimes called a think piece, the background story not only gives readers the facts but also attempts to place these facts in perspective so the audience can understand an event or a situation. Publicists are often considered by journalists to be the best possible sources for background information and stories on events and situations.

A common goal unites the members of this group

A "club" of unique membership met recently to train new members and recertify current ones. By some standards, its dues are rather high.

The club, or more correctly, program, is Reach to Recovery, the American Cancer Society's peer visitation program for mastectomy patients. To belong, a woman must have had breast cancer surgery, making her eligible to make a one-on-one visit in the hospital to a new post-op patient. The training, or certification session, equips her to address the non-medical questions and concerns of a patient who is in a first-in-a-lifetime experience.

The patient finds it invaluable. Here, she thinks, is someone who, when she says she knows how you feel, *knows* how you feel. The vistor has a credibility that is impossible to be duplicated by a male physician or a nurse who hasn't faced the same surgery. Feedback on the program is overwhelmingly positive.

Jan Miller, state coordinator for Reach to Recovery, said, "It is one of ACS' most thriving programs. Linn county was the first unit in the state to have it in 1969. Last fiscal year we saw 102 patients and this fiscal year, which just ended, we saw 135, an increase of around 30 percent. With our newly-trained volunteers, we now have a pool of 20 women making regular visits."

With the increased use of mammography, a low-dose x-ray of the breast, more breast cancers are being found earlier, which may be one factor in the larger statistics. Although the figures are negative in one respect, the cancers being found earlier is positive in the other respect.

The training session always includes a presentation by a physician. Dr. Robert J. Brimmer, local surgeon who frequently performs mastectomies, spoke at this one, focusing on the risk factors involved in the development of breast cancer. Sex is the first highest risk factor (99 percent of breast carcinomas occur in the female; only one percent in males), with age being the second (85 percent in the 40-100 age bracket, 66 percent in the 50-100 group.)

Other risk factors include a personal or family history of breast cancer; being over the age of 50; childless, or having had a first child after the age of 30.

FIG. 11.6. One of the most popular publicity tools, background stories clearly state an organization's position or goals for the audience. (*From the* Cedar Rapids (*Iowa*) Gazette)

Humanistic stories might belong in any one of the categories mentioned above. The humanistic story is written according to a particular formula that is often credited to the *Wall Street Journal.* The formula goes like this:

1. Focus on an individual or individuals.
2. Make a transition to a larger issue.
3. Report on the larger issue.
4. Return to the opening focus.

The formula leads to a story such as this one:

> John and Mary Smith couldn't believe the bill from their credit-card company. The minimum monthly payment amounted to $3.50 more than John's monthly take-home pay.
> The Smiths' experience isn't unique. Dozens of young married couples have virtually charged their way to bankruptcy in recent months . . . .
> . . . On the advice of their attorney, the Smiths cut up their cards and placed themselves in the hands of a financial adviser.

The content between the ellipses would detail the issue of young couples' lack of money-management skills and the availability of financial advisers to help them correct this problem. Figure 11.7 is an example of a humanistic story following the *Wall Street Journal* style.

THE TIME FACTOR IN FEATURES

Since feature stories don't depend on spot news events, they have a relatively timeless quality the straight news story doesn't enjoy. If a spot news story isn't published within a reasonable time after the event it reports, the story grows stale and old. If the news story is about a coming event and is told too soon, the audience forgets. Spot news has a "right now" quality that can't be ignored.

The feature story, on the other hand, can be published almost anytime. Some forms, like the how-to, are truly timeless; they can be published anytime. Others need to be published at an appropriate time. For example, a story on collecting sap from maple trees should be told just before the sapping season begins, and tornado safety stories seldom appear in winter.

Women Living in Poverty Tell Their Story

by KARLA WATKINS MURPHY

Deb and her four children live in a small two-story house in a quiet neighborhood. It's the first house they've ever lived in that has central heat.

Recently she sat in her cozy kitchen in Ames, munching a slice of bread and honey. "Up until last winter we always lived in places with wood stoves or Coleman propane heaters," Deb said, laughing with a shrug. "I don't know what to do with a furnace. I have no idea.

"OUR FIRST winter here I worried about leaving the children alone in the evenings. I was afraid the heat would go off and they'd all freeze to death, or that there would be a fire. I didn't realize until a friend told me that with furnaces, you don't have to worry about it as much."

Deb, 33, is one of a growing number of women heads of households now living at the poverty level ($12,049 a year for a family of five such as Deb's). According to Census Bureau statistics, two out of three poor adults in the United States are women. In Iowa, 28 percent of persons living in families with female heads of households live below the poverty level. This involves nearly 50,000 women and children statewide.

Deb receives Aid to Families with Dependent Children, food stamps and housing assistance. Her three school-aged children receive free lunches at school. These benefits total about $10,600 annually. According to the Bureau of Labor Statistics, it takes $25,407 a year to maintain a family of four at an "intermediate" standard of living — $14,807 more than Deb subsists on with a family of five.

DEB MANAGES to feed her family on the $30 a week she receives in food stamps. "I make a lot of casseroles," she said. "We have macaroni and tuna, macaroni and cheese, macaroni and macaroni."

In another part of Ames, Bev McGuire, 50, heads another household. She and her 16-year-old son share an apartment with her unemployed 24-year-old daughter and infant grandson. They live in low-income housing. The apartment is immaculate and homey. Handmade quilts and wall-hangings decorate the rooms. It's one of the nicer places they've lived. They, too, live at the poverty level.

McGuire sat at her kitchen table, crocheting an afghan. Shares of green yarn slid through her fingers, forming loops while she talked.

"I've lived in mobile homes, apartments, dumps, places that to think back on it now, I wonder, my God, how did I live through that? Because I'm not that kind of person," McGuire said. "I can't stand filth."

THERE are two major reasons for the growing numbers of women and children living in poverty, according to a study conducted by Hariette McAdoo, a professor in the research department of Howard University's School of Social Work, and Diane Pearce, research director of the Center for National Policy Review at Catholic University of America.

Employment is not necessarily an antidote to poverty for women. A woman can expect to earn 60 percent of what a man does, according to the study.

And despite their low earning potential, 85 percent of American women can expect to support themselves (if not also their children) at some time in their lives, whether through divorce, desertion or death.

McGuire has had two heart attacks. She has an artificial heart valve and a pacemaker. She shook her head and smiled.

"In five years? I'll be dead. I'll be dead from a heart attack. From too much work. From too much stress. From too much worry," she said.

"I'VE TRIED to think of a way I can offset it, but I can't," she said. "I really don't   a way. I'm tire⌐ I a 'ire   ⌐hti·
d   ɔ·

FIG. 11.7. An example of a humanistic feature story. (*From the* Iowa State University Daily)

Copy Preparation

The road to successful release publication is dependent not only on attention to news values, content, and good writing style but also on sending the release to the editor in the proper format. Editors appreciate releases that come to them in a recognizable form. Although they might have some variations, releases that can be immediately spotted as such stand a better chance of being published. Figure 11.8 is an example of what a print release should look like.

```
                        Name of Organization
                              Address
                   (Or use letterhead stationery)


        (Name of person to contact for more information)

        (Phone Number) day:
                      night:


                                      (RELEASING INFORMATION)








              Your copy for print media articles should look like this.  It

        must be typed or word processed.  Use unlined 8 ½" x 11" copy paper

        or letterhead stationery, but not erasable bond.  Editors do not

        like the flimsy quality of bond paper; it is hard to write on.

        Double space the copy and write only on one side of the paper.  Do

        not put more than one story on a page.

              Paragraph frequently.  Edit your copy carefully.  Be sure to

        recheck  all names, dates, places and other vital facts for accuracy.

        Also read your copy for spelling and grammar errors.

              Do not carry your writing too close to the bottom of any page.

        If a story is carried over to the next page, type "-more-" at the

        bottom of every page except the last.  When the story is complete,

        write "-30-" (or "end" or "##") below the last line.


                              -more-
```

FIG. 11.8. This news story form is one of the most common. Although the content of the release is most important, following an acceptable copy form improves the chances that an editor will read your release – the first step toward publication.

If the company, organization, or group you represent has letterhead stationery, that may be used. Some groups that send out releases on a regular basis have special news release stationery. But neither is absolutely necessary.

Do not write a headline for your story. The editor will take care of that. Also, remember to use the day of the week and date rather than "yesterday," "today," "tomorrow," "last week," or "next week"—even in dated copy. You want to avoid any possible confusion about the time element of your release. (An exception to this rule is the broadcast news release, which you will learn about in Chapter 12.)

```
News Copy Form
2-2-2-2-


        Although you do not need to put your name on any page after the

first, you do need to number each additional page and indicate the

story's content with a one- or two-word reference  called a

slugline.

        The basic objective in journalistic writing is to convey the

meaning you intend to the audience.  It requires both clear

thinking and clear expression on your part, and a constant awareness

as to how the readers will interpret your words.  The publicist who

is always mindful of these points will produce releases with the

best chances of publication.


                        -30-
```

Be sure to time the release carefully. Send your copy to the editor early enough that is has a fair chance at publication, but not so early that the editor will likely forget about it before it can best be used.

A number of releasing information options indicate when the editor may use the release, but two are the most common. **"FOR IMMEDIATE RELEASE"** means the editor may use the information from the day it arrives until the message is obsolete. **"FOR RELEASE MONDAY, MARCH 16"** is a date-specific release. It is most commonly used when the information is tied to a particular event—the announcement of scholarship recipients at an awards banquet, for example.

One last feature of the news release may increase its chances of publication. Either provide photographs or suggest picture possibilities to the editor. If you do the latter, make sure you say when pictures might be taken, and then see to it that everything is in order when the photographer arrives. (See Chapter 14 for a full discussion of photographs.)

Summary

Two basic story forms are regularly used by journalists. The inverted pyramid story revolves around a spot news event. It begins with the most important information and ends with the least important. The feature story, on the other hand, does not conform to the rigid style of the spot news story but is written in one of several different forms. A dominant news value in features is human interest.

When the publicist submits a release to the print media, it should be in an acceptable format, and if possible, photographs should be sent or picture opportunities mentioned to the editor.

Exercises

1. Find three examples of spot news publicity releases in your local paper. Analyze the strengths and weaknesses in each release. Is the information adequate? If not, what's missing? Is the release a good example of an inverted pyramid story? If not, how would you change it to make it better?

2. Write a publicity release based on the following information: The Norwood Historical Society members are sponsoring a flea market and bake sale. They have been collecting donations for the past several months in preparation for this event. The following is a partial list of items that will be sold: furniture, including both large and small items; small appliances and household goods; children's clothes; toys; garden accessories; hand tools; bicycles and tricycles; and lots of

knickknacks. A solid-oak four-poster bed (circa 1900) will be raffled off at the conclusion of the sale. The bake sale will run simultaneously with the flea market. The money raised at the flea market will be donated to the city to purchase signs for the Norwood Walking Tour of Victorian Homes. The society sponsored the same event last year and donated about $500. Raffle tickets for the bed will be $1 each. The mayor has promised to stop by and lie on the bed until 100 raffle tickets are sold. He will arrive around 10 a.m. The sale date: Saturday, May 4. Place: Southside Park. Time: 8:30 a.m. until 5:30 p.m.

3. Write a feature story for your local paper about the benefits of CPR training. Your purpose is to generate an interest in the community so residents will enroll in one of a number of classes that will be offered within the next several months.

Suggested Reading

Newsom, Doug, and Wollert, James A. "Stories From Public Relations Sources." Chapter 13 in *News for the Mass Media: Media Writing*. Belmont, Calif.: Prentice-Hall, 1985.

Nolte, Lawrence W., and Wilcox, Dennis L. "The Press Release" and "The Feature Story." Chapters 8 and 9 in *Effective Publicity*. New York: John Wiley and Sons, 1984.

Simon, Raymond. "The Basic Press Release" and "Timing and Dating Releases." Units 1 and 2 in *Publicity and Public Relations Worktext*. 5th ed. Columbus, Ohio: Grid Publishing, 1983.

12 *Writing for the Electronic Media*

KENNETH L. EICH

THE age of electronic news gathering (ENG) in television began in the mid-1970s when news operations switched from filming stories (which required time-consuming transporting and processing of the film before the developed product could be edited and broadcast) to videotaping stories for instantaneous playback, if necessary, by microwaving them to the station during a newscast. Radio had relied on live reports from the scene for many years before, either by two-way communication from station mobile units or by telephone to the station.

Unfortunately, some broadcast and cable operations try to be the electronic newspaper of the air. Problems arise because broadcast information cannot be communicated effectively in print media format or style.

Broadcast scripts, whether for news, advertising, or public service announcements, must be written for the ear rather than for the eye. The audience will only *hear* the information as it's being presented—without the chance to reread any part that's not clear the first time, as can be done with printed messages.

Many broadcast writers follow the **KISS** principle (or a variation of it), meaning "keep it short and simple." Words, sentences, paragraphs, and entire scripts should be relatively short and simple.

For example, news releases for electronic media should be no longer

178

than one side of one page of double-spaced, typewritten copy. According to a 1977 survey conducted by Ohio State University, releases not used by broadcast stations are often too long, which usually means they're not written in acceptable broadcast style. Copy for ads and PSAs should run no more than 30 seconds. By the mid-1980s, almost nine out of ten broadcast commercials were 30 seconds, and the trend was toward even shorter spots. Figure 12.1 is an example of a 30-second broadcast spot.

```
                      INFORMATION SERVICE
            IOWA STATE UNIVERSITY              AMES, IOWA 50011
                 OF SCIENCE AND TECHNOLOGY          Ph: 294-4777


                                        EXTENSION NEWS
                                        Home and Family Radio
                                        News Feature


                    (For use during Fire Prevention Week Oct. 9-15)


          Take Fire Safety Home                         (time  :30)

              The fires we rarely hear about are the ones in which the most

          people die.  Home fires cause more than 5,000 deaths each year, says

          Iowa State University Fire Service Education instructor George Oster

          (Oh´stir).

              Fire Prevention Week serves as a reminder to take fire safety

          home, he says.  Install a smoke detector in each sleeping area, test

          detectors monthly, plan escape routes from bedrooms and conduct a

          home fire drill.

              For more information contact your fire department or Fire Service

          Education at ISU.


                                        ###


          source:  George Oster  (515) 294-6817

          tbp  9/30/83
```

FIG. 12.1. The PSAs that most broadcast stations air are no more than 30 seconds in length. However, publicists can provide the program director with several shorter—say, 10-second or 20-second—scripts in addition to the 30-second option, giving the station the opportunity to choose the PSA that best accommodates its program schedule.

Common Shortcomings of Broadcast Releases

Many news releases are not used by broadcast media because the releases have one or more of the following shortcomings:

Too long. As was just mentioned, news releases and other broadcast copy should be limited to one typewritten page. Type on only one side of a sheet of paper, and double-space the copy. There should be 65 characters between the right and left margins, with each full line of copy accounting for 4 seconds of airtime. Print media news releases should be edited to conform to broadcast writing style, including the omission of unnecessary details and the use of conversational language (more about these points later).

Too old. News releases for broadcast should preview an event rather than rehash it several days later.

Too dated. News releases for broadcast should consider the frequency of news and not restrict their use to the morning, afternoon, or weekly newspaper's publishing deadline.

Too self-serving. News releases, especially if broadcast, can sound as if they are a paid commercial for an individual or group instead of emphasizing the local community news angle. Save your superlatives for PSAs; news copy must be more objective or neutral.

Some Specifics of Broadcast Writing

USE SIMPLE LANGUAGE AND SHORT SENTENCES

Writer Samuel Langhorne Clemens, better known as Mark Twain, began his career as a newspaper correspondent. He was paid according to the number of words in his stories, and he is quoted as saying, "I never write 'metropolis' when I get the same pay for 'city.' " Broadcast writers should keep this in mind and use short, simple words instead of long, cumbersome ones.

Journalism professor Irving E. Fang of the University of Minnesota developed his **Easy Listening Formula** (ELF) as one way to help measure the effectiveness of broadcast writing. The ELF is easy to use and helps keep sentences short and simple. Here's how to apply it:

In any sentence, don't count any one-syllable words. Count each two syllable word as 1, each three-syllable word as 2, and so on. The total count for any sentence should not exceed 20. If the count is higher, the sentence probably has too many words or too many long words and should be rewritten.

Don't read last paragraph first

By BILL GREER
The Sunday Courier and Press

Hi! I want to learn how to write, and my mom said you could tell me where to start.

Well, hmpf, now! A lot of guys who have much more on the ball than I do have tried that for a long time. But so far as I can learn, no one as yet has found that one quick, best way to teach the art of how to write.

It takes time, and lots of it. Just to put down your thoughts on a line is of course not hard, but to do so in a way that what you want to say comes through in the end *just the way you think it* is quite a feat.

Bill Greer is a columnist for *The Sunday Courier and Press* **in Evansville.**

But this, my friend, can be taught. So if you will, let's take a look.

There is first of all, one thing that will be

of great help to you at all times. And that is to read, read, read — to glue your eyes on all the words you can get your hands on, in all the spare time which you may have.

You must do this, for you've got to learn that there is more than one way to say what you wish: You can choose from both a "right" way and a "wrong" way, though who is to judge this, I cannot say.

You must learn that there is "good" and "poor" and just plain "bad" prose, and that as a rule, it is the one who has read the most who can best choose from them.

When I taught a class like this one time, I tried to get folks to put their thoughts down in the most clear way they knew how.

I was sure that would be hard for some, for they thought the way to write was to take a lot of big words and show me that they knew how to use them.

That is not the case, though. What I told them was this: Be brief. Use all the *short* words you know, and save the long ones back in the rear of your brain for some day when you need them to read a work that is not so clear as you can do.

The tongue we speak has all the words we need to say any thought that comes to us, and that truth is one of the great and rare things in life.

The more man grows, it has been said, the more pure his speech grows — at least when it comes to those things that are of most need in his life. Look at what short words we use in speech all the time.

Our main "time" words, in fact, are hour, day, week, month and year. Our "life" words are those like eat, drink, sleep, dream, work; love, like, hate, fight;

come and go, up and down, here and there, start and stop, and so forth.

The sports fan runs, jumps, kicks, swims or vaults; throws, hits, bats, strikes, bunts, drives or putts; tries to make a goal and not foul out.

What's more, the world in which we live is hot or cold, wet or dry, round or flat.

It gives us food and drink: Bread, milk, fruit; meats like pork and beef, grains like wheat, corn, rye and oats; beans, beer, wine, cheese and salt.

We could jot down lists of such short words for a lot more things that fill our lives, too.

But what, in the end, is the gist of all this?

I have said here that one who writes must do so in the most clear way he can, if what's in his mind is to come through for all to read just as he means for it to do . . . as he "hears" it in his own thoughts.

It's not the big words that can do this job, but the small ones.

Our world needs a whole lot more folks who can put down their thoughts — or speak their mind, if you will — in a clear way. And if these words of mine are of help to you, who knows what great gifts you may some day give the world?

For in all of our days, we have grown by just one means: That has been when men who thought great new truths spoke them for us in the most pure, the most clear, the most plain way that could be done.

If you have doubts as to this, look once more at the words you have just read. And then if you would still write, take heed.

They say to you as best I can, what I know of how to write. And while this of course is not all you need to know, it is as good a place for you to start as I can think of.

P.S.: The entire column above is written in words of only one syllable. ☐

FIG. 12.2. Writing doesn't have to be remedial to be effective. This article is composed of simple words and short to moderate-length sentences, but the message is entertaining and understandable just the same.

Journalist Bill Greer once wrote an article that is an excellent example of the ELF formula at work (see Figure 12.2). The entire article, reprinted from *Scripps Howard News,* was originally published as a newspaper column. It consists entirely of one-syllable words and has an ELF score of zero.

ELIMINATE UNNECESSARY INFORMATION

Omit unessential details from broadcast copy, even though the print medium's version of that same news release or advertisement might be considerably longer. The reason is obvious. Readers can absorb much more information through reading (and rereading) a story than they can by merely listening to that same story over radio or television. Remember, the broadcast listener does not have a copy of the script to refer to if the information is unclear.

In addition to eliminating unnecessary information, it's helpful for a broadcast audience to hear necessary details, such as key names, locations, and phone numbers, more than once within a radio or TV story.

WRITE ATTENTION-GETTING LEADS

It's particularly important for the lead, or beginning, of any broadcast script to use an ear-catching fact that will grab the audience's attention. If your lead is not attention-getting, the audience is not likely to pay much attention to the rest of your copy.

WEAK LEAD

The United Way begins its annual fund drive next week to raise money for various agencies.

MORE EFFECTIVE LEAD

Building a new community center is one of the goals for this year's United Way fund drive. (By the way, notice that the ELF score for this sentence is 7.)

Your broadcast copy should also make clear *why* your message is important. In addition, you should tell the audience *how* to participate or otherwise become involved in your activity, event, or organization.

WEAK AUDIENCE PLEA

Please contribute to the United Way. Volunteers are also needed for this worthy cause.

MORE EFFECTIVE AUDIENCE PLEA

Contribute to the United Way to help build a better community for all of us. Contact the local United Way office to volunteer your services.

WRITE SIMPLE DECLARATIVE SENTENCES

Avoid information overload for the ear by limiting each sentence to one complete thought. Divide compound and complex sentences into two or more sentences in order to make that information easier for the audience to hear and understand.

COMPLEX SENTENCE

The Jaycees' annual Halloween party will be on the last Saturday in October and their annual distribution of Thanksgiving baskets will take place on the day before that holiday.

BETTER

The Jaycees' annual Halloween party will be on the last Saturday in October. Their annual distribution of Thanksgiving baskets will be on the Wednesday before Thanksgiving.

Generally, write simple, declarative sentences using the basic subject/ verb/direct object/indirect object (who says what to whom) structure. Don't separate the subject from the verb or the verb from the object by inserting long, modifying phrases or clauses.

SEPARATED SUBJECT AND VERB

The Jaycees, who formed their local chapter nine years ago with only six members, announced today that their annual membership drive resulted in 23 new members from various area businesses.

BETTER

The Jaycees say 23 new members joined their organization during the latest membership drive. The local chapter began nine years ago with six members.

Most broadcast copy is written in the active voice (the subject of the sentence acts upon the object of that sentence), not the passive voice (the subject of the sentence is acted upon by the object of that sentence). Read aloud the two parenthetical examples in the previous sentence to see and hear how the active voice is more direct, more simply constructed, and easier to understand. The passive voice is more appropriate to emphasize the receiver of the action in a particular sentence, but that's the exception to the general preference for the active voice in broadcast writing.

Keep in mind broadcast writing is more conversational and less formal than print writing. Use contractions liberally. They're (not "they are") more conversational and natural-sounding over the air. As mentioned at the beginning of the chapter, you must write for the ear, not the eye. Hear how your copy sounds by reading it aloud.

ATTRIBUTION FIRST IN BROADCAST

Put the source of the information (who says so) first for broadcast, not last as in some print media. The broadcast writer must make clear who is speaking in a radio or TV script and who is the source for the information being communicated. Broadcast copy should not sound as if the on-air announcer or the station is asserting something that really should be attributed to the proper source.

INCORRECT

The right to own guns is one of America's most cherished freedoms, according to the National Rifle Association.

CORRECT

The National Rifle Association says the right to own guns is one of America's most cherished freedoms.

PARAGRAPH FREQUENTLY AND LOGICALLY

Write broadcast copy in a logical sequence, using separate paragraphs to indicate a switch from one topic to another. If your broadcast script has two main points, finish with your first point before beginning your second. Avoid shifting from one point to the next and back again, as is done in some print media. The listening audience cannot follow such switches, although they might be perfectly clear to a newspaper or magazine reader.

It's preferable to limit your broadcast copy to one or two main points and communicate them clearly, rather than skim over half a dozen or more ideas and fail to communicate because of information overload. As was mentioned earlier, if you repeat your main points, such as the time and place of a fundraising event, the broadcast audience is much more likely to remember them.

AVOID JARGON, CLICHÉS, AND SLANG

Translate jargon into everyday English. If your audience has to try to decipher what's being said, you're failing to communicate.

The following editorial once appeared in the *Des Moines Register*. Headlined "Creative Misrepresentation," it's a good example of the follies of jargon:

In the Des Moines trial of four officials of Iowa paving firms charged

> with bid-rigging on road projects, a defense attorney contended that it wasn't really bid-rigging; it was "horizontal allocation of markets."
>
> Sure. And shoplifting is vertical merchandise repositioning. Forgery is creative cursiveness, mugging is profitable interfacing employing a manual fund-transfer mode, and inciting to riot is multidimensional persuasion through verbal stimuli.

In an article in *Editor and Publisher,* Roy H. Copperud put it more succinctly: "The difference between gobbledygook and plain English is the difference between 'terminate the illumination' and 'turn out the lights.'"

Avoid clichés (like the plague). They are not colorful, but rather color-*less,* expressions because they're overused.

Also avoid slang expressions, although they may be "cool" or "totally awesome," to use two examples that may or may not mean anything to you. And that's the point. Not everyone is familiar with slang, especially since it can be regional and is often generational, usually being most popular with teenagers and young adults. Imagine an elderly couple sitting in the comfort of their retirement home and reading the following passage:

> Hey, man, if you don't know what was going down when things were way out, far out, and even outta sight, well, maybe you were into doing your own thing or finding your own space and were so uptight or so mellowed out that it was too much hassle to get your act together, even if it was real bad, fer sure. You dig my rap?

Never assume your audience will know what you mean when you are tempted to use slang. Say what you mean clearly.

Broadcast Script Enhancements

In addition to writing in broadcast style, you should provide something extra in your copy for the electronic media whenever possible. Radio prefers the actual sounds of newsmakers or events, while television wants pictures and sounds to communicate more effectively. If such audio and video are lacking, the electronic media often relegate that news or PSA copy to a minimum amount of airtime, if they use it at all. If your release is just a straight script, called a **reader,** chances are that it will be limited to 15 or

20 seconds. If a tape is available, it could run from 40 seconds to 1 minute or longer depending on its newsworthiness.

Radio and television want an articulate spokesperson who represents and speaks for an association or organization. A spokesperson should not be microphone- or camera-shy. Such a person must be able to provide a clear, concise statement, explanation, or testimonial as part of the message the group or organization is trying to publicize.

Figure 12.3 is an example of a news release for print media. Although the publicist has no guarantee that the receiving editors will use the release, the information is presented in an acceptable print style. Notice that it follows the inverted pyramid form, as is detailed in Chapter 11.

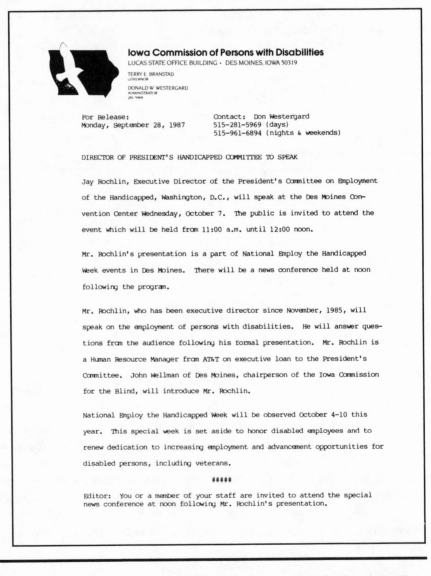

Iowa Commission of Persons with Disabilities
LUCAS STATE OFFICE BUILDING · DES MOINES, IOWA 50319

TERRY E. BRANSTAD
GOVERNOR

DONALD W. WESTERGARD
ADMINISTRATOR
281-5969

For Release:
Monday, September 28, 1987

Contact: Don Westergard
515-281-5969 (days)
515-961-6894 (nights & weekends)

DIRECTOR OF PRESIDENT'S HANDICAPPED COMMITTEE TO SPEAK

Jay Rochlin, Executive Director of the President's Committee on Employment of the Handicapped, Washington, D.C., will speak at the Des Moines Convention Center Wednesday, October 7. The public is invited to attend the event which will be held from 11:00 a.m. until 12:00 noon.

Mr. Rochlin's presentation is a part of National Employ the Handicapped Week events in Des Moines. There will be a news conference held at noon following the program.

Mr. Rochlin, who has been executive director since November, 1985, will speak on the employment of persons with disabilities. He will answer questions from the audience following his formal presentation. Mr. Rochlin is a Human Resource Manager from AT&T on executive loan to the President's Committee. John Wellman of Des Moines, chairperson of the Iowa Commission for the Blind, will introduce Mr. Rochlin.

National Employ the Handicapped Week will be observed October 4-10 this year. This special week is set aside to honor disabled employees and to renew dedication to increasing employment and advancement opportunities for disabled persons, including veterans.

#####

Editor: You or a member of your staff are invited to attend the special news conference at noon following Mr. Rochlin's presentation.

FIG. 12.3.   A news release for the print medium.

However, the release in its print form would obviously not be acceptable for radio or television. It's too long and too detailed, and it employs too cumbersome a writing style for broadcast delivery. By highlighting the key details and providing an excerpt from a tape-recorded interview, the story can be used on the air. Figure 12.4 details a broadcast version of the print release.

```
HANDICAPPED WEEK                                  TOTAL
YOUR NAME                                         TIME: 60
9/28/87                                           SECONDS



        Next week is National Employ the Handicapped Week.  In Des

Moines, the Iowa Commission of Persons with Disabilities will

sponsor a news conference as part of the week's events.

        Commission administrator Don Westergard (WEST-er-gard) says

the week is designed to honor disabled people, including

veterans:

        WESTERGARD CUT 1 "GET MORE JOBS"  20 SECONDS

        (TAPE SUMMARY:  HE SAYS THE WEEK ALSO FOCUSES ON
                        TRYING TO HELP DISABLED PEOPLE
                        GET MORE JOBS SO THEY CAN REACH
                        THEIR FULL POTENTIAL IN SOCIETY.)

        Westergard says the director of the President's Committee on

Handicapped Employment will speak at the Des Moines Convention

Center on October 7th.  Jay Rochlin's (ROCK-lin's) speech will

begin at 11 o'clock and his news conference will follow at noon.

——DASH——

        Employ the Handicapped Week runs from October 4th to the 10th.

                                ###
```

FIG. 12.4. The release in Figure 12.3 has been rewritten in broadcast style. Note that the publicist also sent a tape recording—called an actuality—to enhance the chances that the script would be used on the air.

Summary

Radio and television have built-in time limits for gathering, producing, and airing news, commercials, and public service spots. Your awareness of these restrictions and your willingness and ability to help make the broadcaster's job easier should increase the chances of your message being used effectively.

Above all, remember that providing an audiotape or videotape of a spokesperson from your organization or group adds credibility and interest to the news release. Strong broadcast news operations are not content to merely duplicate coverage by the print media. The availability and believability of a spokesperson may help determine whether your release is broadcast and how much airtime is devoted to it.

Exercises

1. Find a news release in your local newspaper. Choose one that is at least 5 column inches long, so it contains enough information for this exercise. From the information provided, script a one-page broadcast news release. Type the release on only one side of a sheet of paper, double-space the copy, and follow the suggestions for broadcast writing outlined in this chapter.
2. Script a one-page broadcast news release on a local newsworthy topic. Follow the same procedure as above, and be sure to include your contact person's name and telephone number at the top of the release.
3. Script a series of three public service announcements about a local group, organization, or community event. Limit your PSA lengths to 30, 20, and 10 seconds. Type each one on a separate sheet of paper. Use a 65-space line for broadcast copy, with each full line counting as 4 seconds.

Suggested Reading

Bland, Michael. *The Executive's Guide to TV and Radio Appearances.* White Plains, N.Y.: Knowledge Industry Publications, 1980.

Blythin, Evan, and Samovar, Larry A. *Communicating Effectively on Television.* Belmont, Calif.: Wadsworth Publishing Co., 1985.

Garvey, Dan, and Rivers, William. *Broadcast Writing.* White Plains, N.Y.: Longman, 1982.

_____. *Broadcast Writing Workbook.* White Plains, N.Y.: Longman, 1982.

Hilliard, Robert L. *Writing for Television and Radio.* 4th ed. Belmont, Calif.: Wadsworth Publishing Co., 1984.

Mayeux, Peter E. *Writing for the Broadcast Media.* Newton, Mass.: Allyn and Bacon, 1985.

Orlik, Peter B. *Broadcast Copywriting.* 3d ed. Newton, Mass.: Allyn and Bacon, 1986.

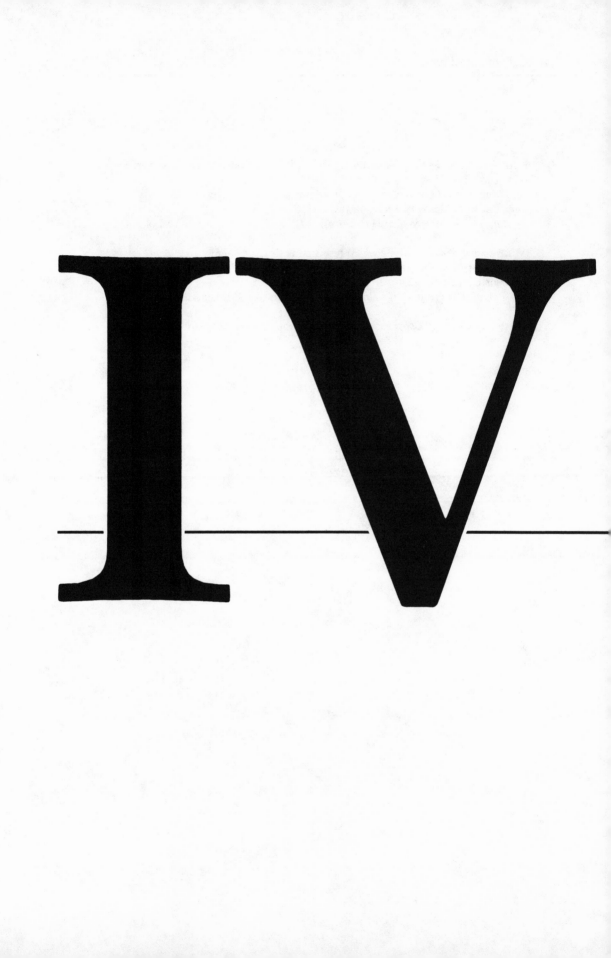

Additional Publicity Tools

A PUBLICIST can exercise a number of publicity options in addition to messages transmitted to the mass media. By taking advantage of those options, the publicist can effectively and creatively control the messages targeted to selected audiences. The chapters in Part IV discuss the advantages and limitations of controlled media and the techniques of photography and layout and design for publications and advertisements.

FIG. 13.1. Buttons, bumper stickers, mugs, and other mementos accomplish one of a publicist's goals—to get an organization's name and message to the public. (*Ross Fuglsang*)

FIG. 13.2. Clothing articles, especially T-shirts, are a popular publicity tool. Mass-distribute items with an imprint of an organization's name, and the result is walking billboards for hundreds of people to see. (*Ross Fuglsang*)

Controlled Publicity Devices

WALTER NIEBAUER

A NYONE who has worked in publicity for any length of time can tell you about the problems of trying to place information in the mass media. For example, consider what can happen when you send a two-page news release about a coming event to your local daily newspaper. Although you may consider every syllable essential, the two pages end up as a one-paragraph item on page 10 of section 3. Perhaps someone at the newspaper has erred, and incorrect information is printed, or as often happens, the information never makes it into the paper. On occasion, a notice appears after the event has occurred.

In terms of Berlo's S-M-C-R model of communication, discussed in Chapter 2, you have little control over the message, channel, or receiver after you submit your information to the gatekeepers of the mass media. However, viable alternatives to the mass media are available for disseminating your message and are collectively referred to by publicists as **controlled** media. They are controlled in the respect that the publicist has control over the content, the audience that receives the content, and the channel for conveying the message. In other words, the publicist controls all the elements in Berlo's model, although the degree of control varies widely with each medium.

Controlled publicity devices constitute a vast and varied field of information-delivery possibilities. In fact, the possibilities are too vast and varied

193

even to attempt a comprehensive list of them. Some examples are listed below for starters, and you can add to them. Note that the categories are somewhat artificial and that some of the items could be moved to another category under certain circumstances. For example, do posters belong under print or visual? From a practical standpoint, the answer is not important. What is important is to be aware of the immense possibilities (see Figures 13.1 and 13.2).

> **Print.** Personal letters, columns, newsletters, letters to the editor, brochures, fliers, bulletins, direct-mail pieces, newspaper inserts, bill inserts, banners, posters, booklets, manuals, pamphlets, shopping bags, table tents.
>
> **Visual.** Skywriting, sidewalk art, displays, exhibits, photos, slide shows, filmstrips, balloons, bumper stickers, buttons, T-shirts, caps.
>
> **Audiovisual.** Person-to-person communication, meetings, speeches, demonstrations, theater-type presentations, puppet shows, closed-circuit television, videos, cable television presentations, multi-image shows (see the special section on multi-image later in this chapter).
>
> **Electronic.** Public address systems, telephone calls, elevator sound systems, hot lines.

Most people have never considered many of these outlets as media. But if you think for a moment, you can see how they can be used for publicity. In fact, you probably can recall instances when the devices were used to publicize something, but at the time you didn't recognize them as publicity. For example, nearly all of the thousands of running events that take place in the United States each year offer T-shirts to participants. The T-shirts typically display the name of the event and the race sponsors.

If an event is staged to benefit some worthy cause—say, to raise funds to construct a community swimming pool—and your organization is one of the sponsors, how does a T-shirt publicize your organization? First, it lets people know your organization exists. Remember, publicity means "to make public." Obviously, the less known your organization is, the more important such publicity efforts are. Second, a T-shirt goes beyond mere publicity. By sponsoring an event for a worthy cause, your organization is also saying something about itself: it cares about the community and wants to help improve it. Not only have you publicized your organization, but you have also improved its public relations by boosting its image.

Selecting Controlled Media

Given the vast array of controlled media available, which should the publicist use? The answer depends on the characteristics of the people you are trying to reach with your publicity. As was mentioned in previous chapters, one of the publicist's first jobs is to define the audience as exactly and narrowly as possible. The more narrowly the audience is defined, the better the chances of the instrument's success.

For example, if you can narrow your audience to students who enroll in specific university courses, probably a simple bulletin requesting course instructors to announce an upcoming meeting will work just fine. For perhaps only 50 cents in copying expenses, you can reach your targeted audience effectively and efficiently.

How about the opposite situation, when you want to attract as large a part of the student population as possible? Perhaps you are promoting a campus dance marathon to benefit the Muscular Dystrophy Association. The idea is for students to obtain pledges for the length of time they dance. You might think this is the time to employ as much mass media—or uncontrolled—exposure as possible. After all, you're not interested in controlling your message. You're interested in attracting as many dancers and pledgers as you can.

To a certain extent, this is true. Comprehensive mass media exposure is certainly desirable in this situation. However, most seasoned publicists will tell you that unless what you are publicizing is an eagerly anticipated, regularly scheduled event, most of the mass media coverage will come after the event, which does your organization little good. Because you usually cannot count on mass media coverage, you must have some alternatives.

Another problem with the mass media approach is that it implies all students are the same. Many town businesses make that assumption when they advertise their wares in a student newspaper. A scan of most student newspapers will turn up advertisements apparently aimed at the "average" student. Successful publicists remember the adage, "A message aimed at everyone will probably reach no one." Consequently, messages aimed at all students are rarely successful.

Once again, it is the publicist's job to separate the population of students into smaller, more distinct audiences, what marketers call **segmenting** the audience. The student population can be segmented into any number of audiences, depending on the criteria appropriate for your project. For example, you can segment the group by gender, marital status, age, year in school, living situation, major, and so forth. In fact, if you had the need, you could select only left-handed, blond females from hometowns with names that begin with vowels! Obviously, this degree of segmentation is rarely necessary.

For the dance marathon, you might decide to segment by living situation—dorm dwellers, fraternity and sorority members, on-campus married students, and off-campus dwellers. Having segmented your audiences, which of the controlled media will reach them most effectively and efficiently? A glance at the different audiences should tell you that no single approach is likely to work equally well in all cases, which is why you segmented the audiences in the first place.

To select the appropriate controlled media for each audience, you must first determine if audience members share certain activities or routines that might suggest possible publicity opportunities. In the case of the dorm dwellers, you might note that they check their mailboxes once a day, eat in the dormitory cafeteria two or three times a day, use the communal bathroom at least once a day, and have monthly dorm meetings, although attendance is frequently poor.

Given this information, which of the controlled media might attract the attention of this audience? Since students check their mail each day, you might insert fliers in all the mailboxes. By doing so, you are almost certain the message will reach most of the audience—but not at all certain that it will be read or retained. Students are inundated by junk mail and fliers, and therefore the competition for their attention can be fierce. However, since fliers are usually relatively inexpensive, stuffing mailboxes is probably worthwhile as long as other approaches are also employed.

A flashy poster, banner, or perhaps even a manned booth located in the vicinity of the mailboxes might be more effective (see Figure 13.3). A booth is especially effective because it allows you to monitor the reactions to your publicity effort and make changes if necessary.

A booth and a poster might also be appropriate for the cafeteria line if the setting lends itself to such approaches. In addition, you might add table tents and, if possible, a public address announcement. For the bathrooms, how about posters or fliers on the inside doors of the stalls?

At this point you've addressed all but the dorm house meetings, which, as noted above, often are not well attended. A normal reaction might be that you've done enough, so let's ignore the meetings. However, if anyone attends the meetings, who will it be? Probably the house officers, some of the most influential and most popular house members. If you can persuade the officers to back your project, perhaps they will persuade other house members to participate. You might even suggest a competition among dorm houses, with trophies or pizzas to those who bring in the most pledge money during the dance marathon. The competition approach, in fact, has been one of the most consistently successful approaches for events such as this one. An event almost always will be better attended if there's something in it for the attendee.

If you carry out all these elements of the publicity plan, you can be

FIG. 13.3. Fliers, announcements, and posters can easily be missed if they are mounted in areas overcrowded with other information items. Instead, post the message in a high-traffic area frequented by audience members. (*Robyn Hepker*)

reasonably sure you have communicated with your audience. Obviously, if the publicity budget cannot support all the elements, you must decide which efforts will most effectively reach the most people. And remember, use your imagination.

But also use common sense to determine if the medium you choose is appropriate. For example, it is eminently appropriate for a society for the prevention of skin cancer to pass out sun hats at the state fair. It would not be appropriate for a nudist colony to promote itself by selling T-shirts.

We've now come a long way from thinking of publicity as something you try to achieve only through the mass media. In our example, and in most publicity situations, controlled media are better choices than mass media. The perception often is that placing announcements in the mass media is more prestigious than circulating some mundane fliers, but in many cases the fliers are much more effective. And after all, our primary concern is results.

Developing a Medium

When you employ controlled alternatives in your publicity efforts, you are essentially developing your own media from scratch. Consequently, for maximum effectiveness you must go through the same steps you would follow to develop your own radio station or daily newspaper.

We'll use the newsletter to illustrate the procedure because the newsletter is one of the more complex controlled media, and the considerations that go into its development encompass those that apply to virtually all the other media. For this discussion, a newsletter is defined as printed information, other than a newspaper or magazine, circulated at regular intervals. Printed information not circulated at regular intervals generally would be called a brochure or a flier.

AUDIENCE

We've already discussed the first, and most important, consideration – the audience. Everything else builds on the characteristics and needs of the audience. The more restricted and better defined the audience is, the more successful the newsletter is likely to be.

PURPOSE

The second consideration is the newsletter's purpose. Although every newsletter has a purpose, that purpose is not always apparent. The lack of a well-defined purpose makes a newsletter difficult to write and difficult to read because there is generally no consistency or continuity. It also makes the newsletter difficult to evaluate, as is discussed below.

What might the purpose be? Newsletters can be designed to educate, inform, recruit, explain, interpret, or report, or they may serve a combination of purposes. However, the list begs these questions: Educate about what? Inform about what? The answers to these questions form the third consideration in the newsletter's development. A purpose statement should include all three considerations: the audience, the purpose, and the content.

For example, if you decide to develop a newsletter for a flower-arranging club, the purpose statement might be "to inform students interested in flower arranging about upcoming meetings, to report about new materials being used in flower arranging, and to recruit new members."

Getting organization members to agree on the newsletter purpose statement is important for two reasons. First, it fosters consistency in the materials presented in the newsletter; therefore recipients will know what to expect and will eagerly look forward to receiving it. Second, it helps determine the types of items needed and saves the editor from having to battle with other members over the content.

DISTRIBUTION METHOD

The method of distribution also needs to be considered. For example, if the newsletter is to be mailed, it can be prepared in at least three ways:

1. A blank space can be left on the newsletter for the address and stamp.
2. A wrapper with space for the address and stamp can be put around the newsletter, as is often done with newspapers.
3. The newsletter can be inserted in an envelope and mailed.

The last two methods have no special production requirements, but they are more expensive and time-consuming (see Figure 13.4). Therefore the method of distribution must be a consideration in time and money budgets.

FIG. 13.4. The self-mailing newsletter can be efficiently used by many organizations. Before producing a newsletter, wise publicists visit their local post office to find out about postal costs and regulations. (*Robyn Hepker*)

Selection of a mailing method should also take into account the effort the reader has to expend to get at the newsletter. This may seem trivial, but consider how you sort your mail. Most people spend only a few seconds going through unsolicited mail such as your newsletter. In those few seconds, the reader decides whether a piece of mail will be read more thoroughly or will be thrown away. Most people can also tell a great deal about their mail without actually opening it. There are clues, such as a familiar return address or a handwritten or computer-generated address.

If for whatever reason, you suspect that your potential readers are not likely to go to the bother of opening an envelope, one of the other mailing methods would be more appropriate. If you must mail the information in an envelope, you might consider sending a Mailgram. Mailgrams look very much like telegrams but are less expensive. They are useful in certain situations because, as studies reveal, their appearance almost guarantees that the receiver will at least open it.

AUDIENCE USE OF THE MEDIUM

How the editor expects the audience to use the newsletter also affects the production of the newsletter. For example, if the newsletter is intended to be tacked to a bulletin board, it should be designed like a poster. Thus, it should probably be larger than the standard 8½-by-11-inch sheet of paper and should have all the pertinent information on one side.

TIME AND MONEY BUDGETS

Other considerations are the time and money available to put the newsletter together. Generally, the less time and money available, the less ambitious the newsletter will have to be—unless you have access to facilities and skilled personnel to help ease these constraints.

Elements of a Medium

The considerations necessary for developing a medium affect the physical elements that make up the medium. Although the elements vary according to the medium, they most commonly include the following:

- Content and length of the message
- Paper or other printable material

• Color of paper and ink
• Style of lettering
• Graphics — photos or illustrations

The newsletter example will be used to illustrate how the developmental considerations and the physical elements interact. You will notice that some of the interactions are redundant, meaning that more than one consideration may have the same effect on an element. Such redundancy is to be expected because several of the considerations are also interrelated.

AUDIENCE AND PURPOSE

How do the closely related considerations of audience and purpose affect the elements of a newsletter? Obviously, they affect the content; in essence, they define the content.

These same two considerations, especially audience, also affect the length of items. Consider the attention span of people of different ages and under different conditions. Generally, the attention span lengthens as people grow older, although only to a certain point. Therefore, the younger the audience, the shorter the message should be (see Figure 13.5).

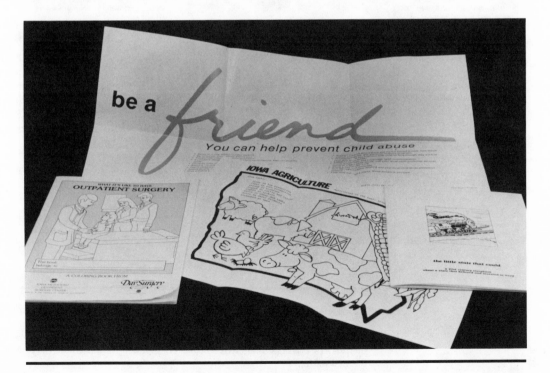

FIG. 13.5. Foldout posters, coloring books, and storybooks with short messages are popular publicity devices for many organizations. Appropriate items can be designed to fit almost any budget. (*Ross Fuglsang*)

WOMAN'S HOSPITAL NEWS

VOLUME 12 NUMBER 3   A MONTHLY PUBLICATION OF WOMAN'S HOSPITAL OF BATON ROUGE   APRIL, 1982

My first experience with perinatal loss occurred when I was a young adolescent. It involved my first horse, a beautiful palomino named Dixie.

Dixie was much too old to be bred, but we bred her anyway, and we eagerly awaited the birth. The filly was born under a fig tree in our back yard, and when she was born she had a incurable disease. She died at three days of age and I was distraught.

I wanted to protect my horse from the whole awful experience. I insisted that the filly be buried right away, and a very wise old man that worked on our farm firmly refused.

He said, "You'd better let that horse see that dead foal, or she'll keep on looking for her."

So we brought the foal to the mare, and she nudged her and tried to get her to move, and she somehow seemed at peace when she finally walked away from the dead filly.

— Dr. Evelyn Hayes

The death of a baby is one of life's greatest tragedies, evoking the deep sorrow of all touched by the death.

But parents experiencing stillbirth, miscarriage or neonatal death are often left alone to deal with their grief, left by family members and friends who feel confused and helpless, afraid to even express their sympathy.

While the great number of pregnancies results in the birth of a healthy child, there are exceptions. One in 10 pregnancies ends in miscarriage. Of the 7,499 deliveries last year at Woman's, 46 infants died before leaving the hospital, and 50 babies were stillborn.

As health care professionals come to understand more about grief and mourning, many of the traditional beliefs on the subject are changing.

More than 100 nurses, doctors, social workers, psychologists and other professionals attended the hospital's March 3 workshop entitled, "Perinatal Loss," sponsored by the Education Department.

One person who found the workshop particularly helpful

THE DEATH OF AN INFANT: COPING AND HEALING

was Connie Walters, RN, head nurse on the Fourth Floor, where women who have experienced a loss are cared for.

The Fourth Floor is generally reserved for gynecological patients.

"We think the woman who has miscarried or lost her baby is better able to recover on the Fourth Floor for several reasons. We don't restrict visiting hours at all so her family can be with her whenever she wants.

"Also, the patients are not constantly reminded of babies, and the floor is much quieter, and this gives them the chance to get the rest they need," Walters said.

"Usually I've found if you give the patient a chance to talk, that's all she needs. It's a matter of being there, allowing them to express their feelings," she said.

Women who give their babies up for adoption are also on the Fourth Floor, and also go through a difficult mourning process.

"They've lost something that will never be regained," Walters said, "and they have already formed a very strong bond with their baby. You'd be surprised how many send toys or blankets or clothes to the nursery to be sent with the baby. It's a very emotional event."

Walters says many women do not want to talk with anyone, but are helped by the presence of someone sympathetic. "I've sat in patients' rooms for 10 or 15 minutes, with no one saying anything, and that's uncomfortable. But eventually they'll start talking, or crying. I don't think I've found anyone who didn't eventually want to talk."

Speakers at the workshop were in agreement with Walters' approach: caring, talking, and giving patients the opportunity to express any feelings.

This is often difficult for health care professionals, who were taught or have come to feel they should protect their patients from any painful experience.

Dr. Evelyn Hayes, chief of obstetrics at Woman's, said, "I used to focus more on the intellectual cause of the stillbirth, or miscarriage, or

Continued on Page Two

FIG. 13.6.   Publicists must pay more attention to detail when newsletters are distributed to an audience with broad characteristics. Because members are not necessarily anticipating the message, the design must capture the readers' attention and intrigue them enough that they continue reading the newsletter.

Also, the less interested your audience is in what you have to say, the shorter your items should be. If, however, your newsletter is the only source of information on topics of great interest to your audience, articles can be as long as you have room for (see Figure 13.6).

The newsletter's audience and purpose affect the choice of paper, color, lettering, and graphics in basically the same way. All these elements serve as attractors, or bait, to lure reluctant readers into your newsletter, to grab their attention. A thorough discussion of layout and design of publications appears in Chapter 15.

DISTRIBUTION METHOD

The attraction qualities of a newsletter can be critically important when you consider the method of delivery. For example, if a newsletter or a brochure is going to compete with dozens of others on a large display rack or bulletin board, serious consideration should be given to its ability to attract attention.

Attractiveness is not synonymous with garishness. Clever publicists will tell you that in developing a medium to attract attention, more thought and less paint will often do a better job. Think about the types of envelopes that attract your attention. If you're expecting a check from the federal government, you'll probably be attracted to any envelope in your mail that looks like the plain brown envelopes the government typically uses. The same principle applies to the Mailgram's similarities to the telegram.

Some organizations go to great expense to develop a color that will consistently be identified with the organization. There's the readily recognizable American Express green and the vivid orange roof that identifies Howard Johnson's restaurants and motels.

A final comment about the method of delivery and paper selection: One of life's irritations is receiving a mailing that has all but disintegrated. Make certain that your paper has a reasonable chance of surviving delivery, whatever the delivery method may be.

Take a clue from some of the successful commercial delivery methods. For example, *National Geographic* magazine is printed on paper sturdy enough to survive the mails. But in keeping with the high-class style of the society that produces the magazine, it is wrapped in an even sturdier paper to prevent the magazine from becoming torn or wet—both of which are near tragedies to subscribers.

Producers of weekly shoppers have gone as far as sealing their product in see-through plastic to prevent wetness as it sits on a doorstep and also to prevent the paper from being scattered all over town. These well thought out delivery methods make big public relations points with readers.

AUDIENCE USE OF THE MEDIUM

How readers are expected to use the medium and how that affects newsletter elements have already been covered indirectly in the preceding discussion. For example, expecting your audience to read your newsletter quickly, say during a short train ride, has nearly the same effect on the length of items as sending information to readers who you expect will not study your information carefully. Both audiences should receive newsletters with short items.

An example will illustrate what can happen when insufficient attention is given to how the medium will be used. The setting is the University of Wisconsin–Madison campus during the late 1960s. Student groups seeking attendance at various events ran into competition from a myriad of posters on campus bulletin boards. To solve the problem, one of the organizations began silk-screening its posters in the psychedelic colors and designs popular in those days.

As might be expected, the posters gained attention, and attendance at the organization's meetings grew. As might also be expected, other organizations began to produce silk-screened posters in order to compete for student attention. Within only a few weeks, the campus bulletin boards took on the look of modern art exhibits; indeed, the posters were 8½-by-11-inch works of art.

Oddly enough, as the poster art became increasingly refined, attendance at events plummeted. The reason was quite simple. Although event organizers correctly reasoned that the artsy posters would attract attention, they were incorrect in anticipating the kind of attention. As it turned out, many students thought the posters were great for papering the walls of their apartments or dorm rooms. In other words, the better the poster, the less chance it had of surviving on a bulletin board long enough to deliver its message. The event organizers had grossly misjudged how the medium would be used by the target audience.

TIME AND MONEY BUDGETS

Undoubtedly, the considerations that most limit the newsletter are the amount of time and money available. As a consequence, the editor must usually make some compromises between the ideal product and one that will stay under budget and still be delivered on time. Within this context, the editor must address the critical question, Is the added expense worth it? To put it another way, will spending more money and time to produce a better newsletter yield dividends sufficient to justify the added expense?

As a general rule, the more captive your audience, the less money needs to be spent on newsletter production. In fact, some of the most poorly produced newsletters are those intended for very narrowly defined audiences that have few alternative sources of information on the specific topics. The looks of such newsletters could be improved, but why spend the time and money to do it when they already serve their stated purposes effectively?

What then are the time and money considerations an editor must be concerned with in choosing the various elements that go into the newsletter? Obviously, time and money are involved in researching, writing, and editing copy. The most common method of obtaining copy for newsletters is to assign topics to members of the organization. This is a good way to give members a vested interest in the product and also to share the workload and keep costs down. If this approach is used, it is critical that all writers understand and agree to the purpose of the publication. Some newsletters with widespread distribution and large circulations also employ free-lance writers, adding to the cost of content production.

The major time expenditure for the editor comes, not in editing and preparing the copy for production, but in corresponding with writers, coordinating copy flow from writers through production, and making sure all deadlines are met. Time limitations make it important for the editor to develop a comprehensive production schedule that ensures meeting the deadlines.

Time is generally not a major problem in finding or selecting the appropriate paper for the newsletter, but cost certainly is. Paper costs vary tremendously, depending on the size, weight, texture, color, and amount purchased. Consequently, it is to the editor's advantage to carefully weigh the costs against the potential benefits. Doing this is especially important when dealing with printers in larger cities, since they often have a wide variety of paper stocks from which to choose.

Most often, however, the newsletter is printed at a local copy center, whose paper selection is not likely to be extensive, although special papers might be ordered. In such instances the paper choice is a relatively simple compromise.

As a final note on paper costs, it is no secret that the printing business is highly competitive in many communities. Thus, the editor can often make significant cost savings by comparing paper costs from several sources. If you are a new customer, and the paper source sees a potential long-term commitment, you may well be able to get a good deal. Shop around.

Color is another element that requires serious cost considerations. Anytime a newsletter is printed as anything other than black on white, extra cost is involved. If a second color of ink is involved, the cost basically doubles because the newsletter requires a second run through the press. A second color also requires a second layout, so those costs must be considered.

However, what was said above about shopping around for the best paper prices goes double for printing. Printers have expenses to pay whether their presses are in operation or not. This is why small-town weekly newspapers print such things as No Trespassing and For Sale signs and rifle targets when they aren't printing the newspaper. In short, printers will do almost anything to keep their presses rolling, so it pays to find a printer who is in a slack period. In larger cities you can almost always find a printer who will do the same job at close to half the price another printer would charge. (Printers' charges are also discussed in Chapter 15.)

The type and lettering elements of the newsletter can also range from very inexpensive to very expensive. If the content is typed, the cost is minimal, but typesetting by a professional can be one of your greatest expenses.

The widespread availability of computer typesetting and word-processing equipment since the early 1980s has dramatically changed copy production. Before that, if you wanted something other than typewritten copy and headlines, you had to rely on hand-rubbed letters, an office headline machine, or professional typesetters and headline setters. Although thousands of type styles are still available through these methods, they tend to be expensive and time-consuming.

Today, inexpensive computer software makes it possible to design your own type style or copy someone else's. Professional-looking copy can be produced without the time and expense of working with a professional typesetter (see Figure 13.7).

The graphic elements of the newsletter run the gamut from line drawings to photographs, although technically the copy and headlines are also considered graphic elements. Naturally, the time and money involved depends on how fancy you want to be and how much professional help you contract. Where drawings and other artwork are concerned, however, there are some ways to cut costs.

For example, clip art books contain drawings designed to be cut out and pasted directly onto the newsletter layout. Some clip art books cover a wide variety of subjects, and others concentrate on specific subjects, such as horses or flowers. A little searching can usually turn up some useful clip art for a newsletter.

If clip art doesn't fit the bill, and original artwork is required, consider contacting the art department at the local college or perhaps even the high school. Students in most art classes are looking for something to put in their portfolios and often will do a superb job at a minimal cost.

Using photographs in a newsletter can be expensive. They require special procedures to prepare them for the newsletter, and the newsletter will often need to be produced on an offset printing press. Normally, photos do not reproduce well using common copying processes. Therefore, the editor should always carefully consider the benefits of including a photo against

FIG. 13.7. Computer typesetting and graphic programs are increasing in popularity and availability. Many organizations find that computer-generated newsletters, such as this one, are cost-efficient and less time-consuming than working with professional typesetters. (*Robyn Hepker*)

the cost and production time involved. If photos are used, check around to see who will do the preparation at the lowest cost. The variation in costs may astound you. (See Chapter 14 for a full discussion of photography.)

One last comment about the esthetics of using drawings and photos: Sooner or later most newsletter editors come to the realization that there's no sense in using a second-rate graphic, because it tends to detract from, rather than add to, the publication. So the rule is, do them well or don't do them at all.

Evaluation

Without a definite purpose statement, it is impossible to measure the medium's success. It's the same problem you have when someone comes up to you at a New Year's Eve party and asks if you had a successful year. Unless you set some goals and objectives at the beginning of the year, there's not much you can answer.

Notice that the purpose statements constructed earlier contain objectives and goals that can be measured. For example, surveying new members of the flower-arranging club will tell you if the newsletter was a factor in recruiting new members.

Surveys or some other sort of evaluation are important when using controlled media, especially if you plan to use the same type of media on a continuing basis. Evaluation will tell you if a medium has been successful in serving the stated purpose and can also indicate how the medium might be altered to make it more effective. Why continue to spend money and time on something that doesn't work?

Sometimes, despite all the time, money, and energy spent on a project, it still fails. If that happens, in all likelihood a mistake was made in defining the audience or in stating the purpose. The best thing to do is to survey the intended audience for clues about the problem and then go through the entire procedure again from the beginning.

Summary

Used properly, controlled media eliminate most of the disadvantages of the mass media. For example, it may cost more to reach your audience through controlled media, but the efficiency and effectiveness more than make up for the added expense.

The major points to remember when using controlled media are these:

- Controlled media enable the publicist to regulate which audience receives which message.
- Selection and development of a controlled medium depend on these factors:
    - Audience
    - Purpose
    - Distribution method
    - Audience use of the medium
    - Time and money budgets
- Evaluating the effectiveness of a controlled medium is essential.

Multi-image: The New Frontier

BILL GILLETTE

A hush falls over an audience of nearly 2,000 people as the large auditorium darkens. A low drumbeat starts from a side speaker. A second speaker located near the front of the auditorium picks up the beat, and in quick succession a third speaker and then a fourth join in, surrounding the audience with sound. The beat climaxes as a brass horn fanfare fills the room.

A color photograph of the Grand Canyon spreads across a 40-foot-long, 10-foot-high screen. The familiar notes of the *Grand Canyon Suite* fill the room with quadraphonic sound. Color panoramas flow across the screen only to be quickly replaced by multiple images of wildlife, flowers, and prehistoric Indian paintings. Each image or multiple of images is perfectly timed with the music. Some images appear for only a fraction of a second. Others seem to flow across the screen in waves.

The music complements the images. Dynamic passages of music are matched by slides showing the Colorado River pounding its way through rapid after rapid. Slower, more pastoral music is matched by photographs of the Grand Canyon at sunrise, at sunset, swathed in fog, or dusted with the first light snow of autumn. The show lasts only a few minutes, but during that time the audience is taken through a multi-image experience involving hundreds of 35mm slides synchronized to the music and sound effects.

Across the hall from the auditorium, smaller groups of people work on video instructional programs shown on a TV monitor. A morning-long seminar comes packaged in ¾-inch videocassettes. After viewing the tape, each member of the group receives a ½-inch videotape to continue the instruction at home. Each group leader also receives a slide tray with 80 slides and an audiocassette marked "manual" on one side and "automatic" on the other. With the proper equipment the audiotape will run the slides automatically; if such equipment is not available, the manual side has the traditional beeps that signal the operator to advance the slides.

Both experiences—the Grand Canyon production and the video

209

seminar—are part of a relatively new field known as multi-image. Using 35mm slides, a sound track, and sophisticated programming devices, multi-image is a way of getting a message across to an audience of just a few or several hundred. Multi-image communicates with sound and photography in a package that can inform, instruct, or persuade—without breaking a budget or requiring years of specialized training.

Multi-image is the use of two or more images on one or more screens accompanied by a sound track that includes music, narration, or sound effects. Although today's producer often uses computer-assisted programmers to run multiple projectors, the field of multi-image probably began with the lantern slide shows of nearly a century ago. However, the field today is riding on the wave of technology. Producers may use a microcomputer to control 20 or 200 slide projectors, or they can use a small dissolve unit (described below) to control 2 projectors tied electronically to a tape recorder. Regardless of the level of complexity, many elements of multi-image remain the same.

Sight and Sound

Multi-image involves the use of 35mm color slides as its basic visual element. There are variations on this approach, but the 35mm color slide dropped into a slide tray and shown through a standard slide projector is the basic building element of multi-image. Multi-image differs from traditional slide shows in that it involves two or more projectors presenting the viewer with two or more photographic images at the same time. The screen is black only if the producer wants it that way. Usually the screen of a multi-image show is filled with images dissolving into each other at rates sometimes faster than the eye can catch. The second important element of multi-image is the sound track, which often consists of music mixed with narration and sound effects. Synchronized with the visuals, it becomes an integral part of the production.

The Dissolve Unit

In the past, the slide-tape show was a familiar part of both business and education. Today, the slide-tape program has been transformed by a device known as a **dissolve unit.** Whether operating numerous projectors or only two projectors, the dissolve unit has three main functions: It turns the projector lamps on and off at a given rate, called the **dissolve time;** it tells the projectors how long to stay on, called the **wait time;** and it tells the projectors when to cycle the slide trays.

The beauty of the dissolve unit is that the operating cues can be recorded on tape to run the show automatically.

The multi-image program can also be copied on videotape, eliminating the need for slide projectors, dissolve units, and an operator when playing the show. Thus an operator can use the projectors, a large screen, and a tape recorder when the program is shown to large groups and can use the videocassette and its accompanying small screen for small groups. All of this can usually be done for only a fraction of the cost of a film or video production.

Multi-image Considerations

What must you consider when developing a multi-image production? The first consideration always is to determine what you want to communicate and to whom. For instance, if you are trying to motivate an audience of several hundred to do something, multiple projectors provide the opportunity to use many screens. With several projectors focused on each screen, dozens of images can be shown at one time, or one panoramic shot can take up all the screens. Thus, multi-image may be the answer for a large audience.

A second consideration is the cost and ease of production. Although large-screen multi-image shows can have six-figure production costs, most shows use two to six projectors and are relatively inexpensive to produce. Suppose you need to produce a show to motivate people to join an environmental group. A two-projector program could easily be put together with slides donated by members of the group. Using a dissolve unit, a small audiovisual tape recorder, music with a nature theme, and some narration, you could produce a low-cost, effective show for both small and large groups.

Consider, for example, a university's need to communicate its role to a wide variety of audiences. A film or a videotape could be produced, but both of those options involve considerable cost. In addition the videotape limits the audience size to a number that can easily see the video screen. A film is easily shown, but to be effective it must be professionally done. Film and video also have the handicap of being difficult and expensive to update. If the production is to be used over a long period of time, perhaps for several years, and is to be shown to a variety of groups under a variety of conditions, multi-image is a good solution.

For instance, the university could use slides from its information-service slide library and have its photography staff take more-specific slides. The slides could be accompanied by taped messages from the university president, professors, and students. The program could be produced in-house or by an outside producer. The program could be shown to large audiences and be videotaped for small groups. By changing slides, the producer could easily update the program. The costly reshooting and reediting necessary for updating video or film would be avoided.

Multi-image, then, is often a good choice when flexibility of presentation is a requirement and when cost is a factor. There are other considerations, though, when contemplating the use of multi-image.

The ability to present several images simultaneously on the screen by using multiple projectors allows "before and after" shots to be shown at the same time so the audience can make an instant comparison. Several parts of a whole can be shown on the screen. The viewers could, for instance, see an overall shot of a machine and its individual parts at the same time.

Multi-image can overwhelm an audience with spectacular views. A panoramic shot of the Grand Canyon filling a screen 40 feet long and 10 feet high can excite even the most sophisticated viewer. By using several projectors, each with a slide filling a different area of the screen, a producer can create a visual analogue to a person's thought process. Many images appear on the screen, some for only a fraction of a second and others maintaining a background image for longer times. Such visual stimulation matches the way people view objects and perhaps the very way they think. How well it's done depends on the producer's talent and imagination.

How to Begin

All that's needed to get involved in multi-image is a willingness to create and to innovate. The Association for Multi-Image International, headquartered in Tampa, is a good starting point for the newcomer. Besides having regional chapters, the association sponsors a yearly international competition. Eastman Kodak also provides information on multi-image, ranging from brochures about producing one-projector shows to books detailing the process of producing multiple-projector shows. Scores of companies produce multi-image equipment and are willing to discuss their equipment and multi-image production with anyone interested in the field.

Although few colleges or universities offer multi-image courses, the incorporation of such courses into the curricula seems to be just a matter of time. The use of multi-image by both industry and educational institutions is rapidly expanding, and the need for people with a knowledge of the field is apparent. The need for visual literacy in virtually every field of communication has never been greater, and people trained in visual communication have a bright future. Multi-image is a good place to start.

Exercises

1. Identify an event or organization that you want to publicize. Then:
   a. Define as narrowly as possible the most important target audience.
   b. Select two or three controlled media that you believe will effectively and efficiently reach the target audience.
   c. For each medium selected above, list the following information:
      • The purpose
      • The likely time and money budgets
      • The delivery methods
      • The expected audience use of the medium
   d. For each of the selected media, explain how the elements of the medium will be affected by the considerations listed in Part (c).
2. Identify a controlled medium you have been exposed to recently. Drawing from this chapter's discussion of considerations and media elements, evaluate the medium's effectiveness. How would you change the medium to make it more effective?

Suggested Reading

Ashurst, Brian. *Editing and Producing the Newsletter.* 1982. Available from 42 Village Dr., Carmel Valley, CA 93921.

Beach, Mark. *Editing Your Newsletter.* Portland, Oreg.: Coast to Coast Books, 1982.

Nolte, Lawrence W., and Wilcox, Dennis L. *Effective Publicity.* New York: John Wiley and Sons, 1984.

MULTI-IMAGE INFORMATION

Association for Multi-Image International. 8019 N. Himer Ave., Suite 401, Tampa, FL 33614.

Eastman Kodak Co. Rochester, NY 14650.

14

Good Photos Can Help Tell Your Story

ROBERT C. JOHNSON

PICTURES are increasing in number and improving in quality in almost all forms of mass communication. Journalists have found that good pictures attract attention, arouse interest, and represent a powerfully effective means of telling a story in a way that words alone cannot.

Television is the medium that perhaps has done more than any other to make twentieth-century America picture-conscious. Now that the viewing public can be transported almost instantly to the scene of a news event and watch it unfold, people no longer are satisfied solely with word descriptions of what is going on around them. They want to see what the people and places in the news look like. They expect pictorial reports in virtually all mass media and on all manner of topics.

Recognizing this growing demand for pictorial communication, the professionals who work for newspapers, television stations, and magazines are eager to obtain and use as many pictures as possible. This means there are outlets for your publicity pictures; you have the opportunity to convey a favorable impression of your organization, your project, or your company. But conveying that favorable impression depends, at least to some extent, on how much creative effort you invest in getting a good picture—one that is worth publishing.

Taking the Picture

Whether you take the picture yourself or have a photographer from the newspaper or television station carry out the assignment for you, you will want that picture to say what you intend. A professional photographer can help you arrange the subject matter and adjust lighting. Exposing the picture correctly and producing a satisfactory print are the photographer's responsibilities, but the work will be eased considerably if you have a clear idea of the picture's purpose and can explain it to the photographer.

If you take the picture yourself, you must select and arrange the subject matter, plan the background, and create lighting effects so the picture will carry out its purpose. Any camera you use should have a lens capable of producing an 8-by-10-inch enlargement that is sharp and clear from corner to corner. This generally rules out snapshot and instant cameras, with their simple lenses, but almost any adjustable camera that uses 35mm or larger film will work if you use it properly.

When you cannot do the photography yourself, arrange to have the newspaper or television station send a staff photographer. This minimizes your costs, but you will have to sell the people you contact on the news value of the event and the worth of the picture before they can justify assigning a photographer. Wherever possible, you should start working with the media at least one week ahead of the time you want the picture taken so the assignment can be fit into a photographer's schedule.

If the picture is for a newsletter, brochure, magazine, or some publication that does not have a staff photographer, you may be able to hire a newspaper or television station photographer to take the picture on a freelance basis. Another possibility is a local portrait or wedding photographer. Even an amateur who has access to a darkroom and produces photographs of good quality can do the work for you. You should expect to pay the photographer's expenses and up to $20 for the first print of each picture ordered. Additional prints of individual pictures should cost less, provided they are ordered at the same time as the first print.

In general, it is safe to publish *news* pictures without obtaining releases from the persons pictured. You should, however, obtain a written release from every person whose image appears in pictures used for advertising, promotion, or illustration of news-editorial pieces (see Figure 14.1). Although libel, slander, or privacy lawsuits arising from the use of someone's picture are rare, you should protect yourself by having a signed release in your files before publishing any photograph. (See Chapter 18 for a detailed discussion of these legal issues.)

City_____, Date_____

For value received, I hereby consent that the pictures taken of me by _____, proofs of which are hereto attached, or any reproduction of the same, may be used or sold by _____ for the purpose of illustration, advertising, or publication in any manner. I hereby certify and covenant that I am of legal age. (A parent or legal guardian must sign for a minor.)

_____
Signature of model or subject

_____
Witness

FIG. 14.1. An all-purpose release form recommended by the Photographers' Association of America.

Strive for Technical Quality

Before a picture can be reproduced with any degree of success in a publication or on television, certain mechanical and technical requirements must be met. Perhaps the most important of them is picture clarity. The images must be sharp and distinct. If the picture is blurred or fuzzy, one or more of several errors is responsible:

1. **The camera was moved when the shutter was snapped.** Practice releasing your camera shutter gently and slowly, just as the crack marksman squeezes away a rifle shot. The slightest poke or jab at the shutter will jar the camera sufficiently to blur the entire picture, even at relatively fast shutter speeds.
2. **The subject moved at the moment of exposure.** Try to catch your subject during a relaxed moment when sudden or violent movements are unlikely. One way to do this is to have the subject concentrate on a point away from the camera but plausible to the story you want to tell, so that you can take several successive exposures without disturbing the basic composition of the picture.
3. **The camera was not focused properly.** The photographer who persists in prolonging the focusing operation unnecessarily is a trial to everyone, but focusing the camera carefully is important. On a camera with a ground-glass focusing screen, one way is to adjust the focusing knob forward and backward through the point of

sharpness, narrowing the range each time until you are right on target. The camera with a range-finder system seldom presents a focusing problem. Just remember to perform the operation!

One of the reasons technical excellence is so essential is that some quality is inevitably lost whenever a picture is reproduced in newspapers or magazines or on television. For the continuous-tone photograph that you carry around in your billfold or purse to be reproduced in any medium, the tones in it would have to be broken into a pattern of dots or lines. (Look closely at the illustrations in this chapter.) In the process both tone and clarity are reduced somewhat.

The photograph that reproduces best is one that has a full contrast range from jet-black to clear white, with most of the picture area composed of the various shades of gray between these two extremes. There also should be visible detail in the picture's shadow areas as well as texture in the white areas. If you think about it, you will realize that the shadows cast by objects seldom are completely black and that even pure-white shirts or blouses have visible folds and fabric patterns. The technically excellent picture will faithfully portray such nuances of tone.

As you judge a picture for reproduction purposes, look for **tonal separation** between the objects that are important to the photograph's story. If there is only slight contrast, the objects will tend to blend together in the reproduction process and become nearly indistinguishable from one another. Also, pictures that look muddy or washed out will probably be unacceptable for publication, as will prints that are full of dust specks and scratches.

Preparing Pictures for Publication

Here are some mechanical considerations you will want to observe as you take, select, or prepare pictures for publication:

1. **The white borders around the edge of the print should not be cut off.** The editor may want to use this space to indicate the exact area of the picture to be reproduced.
2. **Don't write on the back of a picture.** Almost any mark on the reverse side of a print will leave an impression on the surface and show up in the reproduction process, even though the surface impression may not be visible to the eye.
3. **All legends, identifications, or instructions that are to accompany a picture should be typed on a separate piece of paper.** Use rubber cement to fasten the upper edge of the paper

to the back of the print so the message is visible below the picture. Adhesives other than rubber cement tend to wrinkle the photograph (see Figure 14.2).

4. **Avoid bending the picture, because surface cracks will show up in reproduction.** If you are sending a photograph by mail, sandwich it between two pieces of stiff cardboard and label the envelope **"Photograph: Do Not Bend."**

5. **Most large newspapers and magazines prefer 8-by-10-inch prints.** Some smaller daily and weekly newspapers, however, are not equipped to change the size of a picture in the engraving process. For this reason, check with the publication to see if you should submit the pictures in the exact sizes they will be when published and what sizes are wanted. Another possibility is to measure the paper's column width and then submit prints that are

```
PS36.MASTPS P:12                    EDIT                    PG:1        LN:7
█....T....T....T....3.....:.....4....v....5.....:.....6.....:.....7..:....).....:...
Hello, Mary, and WELCOME!  I've heard so many good things about you
-- it's nice we could meet in person.

My name is Personal Services/36.  That's quite a mouthful, so just
call me PS/36 for short.  I'm one of many programs that runs on the
IBM System/36 computer.

As you may know, the S/36 is a multi-talented machine.  It can have
lots of users, all doing various jobs with different programs.  You
may have learned this in some other S/36 Skillware.

                    hold your finger on Shift
                    and press Roll Up
%pa
```

On the first screen of Manpower's Personal Services/36 training program, the machine greets the trainee and introduces itself. It uses humor and easy-to-understand language to make the operator comfortable right from the start.

FIG. 14.2.   By typing the caption on the lower half of a sheet of paper and attaching it to the back bottom of the photo, an editor can simply unfold the caption and read it while looking at the picture. (*Manpower, Inc.*)

one, two, and three columns wide, thereby offering the editor a choice.

6. **If the picture is to be used on television, a color slide in a horizontal format is best because it conforms quite closely to the rectangular shape of the television screen.**

7. **For the print media, pictures should be printed on smooth glossy photographic paper.** A textured surface will not reproduce well. Toned or antiqued prints may look nice on the wall, but they cause a loss of quality when reproduced.

8. **Television stations use 35mm color slides, but magazines and newspapers may not be equipped to reproduce them.** The cost of reproducing color pictures in print is extremely high. Before submitting color pictures to a magazine or newspaper, check with the editor. Also, find out the publication's requirements for the type and size of film. Generally, magazines want a **transparency** or **color positive** film 2¼ inches square or larger. Newspapers, on the other hand, usually want a color negative and a color print.

9. **Today, film has been replaced by videotape and live remote coverage.** In the past, television stations relied on 16mm motion picture film for coverage of local events. Although most stations still have the capability of showing 16mm film, they no longer have the equipment to shoot or process it. The costs of hiring an outsider to shoot, process, and edit 16mm film are prohibitive for most organizations.

   Videotape technology is changing almost daily. At present, there is little standardization in the industry. The equipment and tape used for broadcast are significantly different from those designed for home use. The chances of a station's being able to use videotape recorded on a home videotape deck, even the portable varieties, are slim. Always check with the production staff of the specific station for which you are preparing material before you undertake any filming or videotape project.

   Your best bet is to sell the people at the station on the news or public service value of the event so that the professionals will give your organization or event the coverage you desire.

Pictures Must Tell a Story

Although these technical and mechanical considerations are of great importance, observing them will not necessarily guarantee a picture that will interest an audience or convey a message. In the final analysis, **the**

subject matter—what it is and how it is presented—determines the communicative worth of a picture.

Happily, no eternal rules govern how any particular subject should be photographed. If they did, all pictures of a given type would come close to being exactly alike. As a matter of fact, that happens all too frequently—even in the absence of such rules. How often, for example, have you seen group shots or award presentations when picture after picture looked the same? Or how many times have you seen the little knot of basketball players with arms stretched upward toward the ball or hoop? When each successive picture begins to look like the previous one, no one can blame the audience for ignoring the photograph or giving it only a passing glance. Taken with a little planning, a few props where possible, and some imagination, however, those same pictures can offer new, interesting, and informative experiences for the audience (see Figure 14.3).

You don't need to be a veteran photographer to blend these ingredients

FIG. 14.3. A good picture tells its story in an original or unique fashion without distorting the message. Avoid the overworked lineup arrangement and look for a creative way to convey the message. (*ISU Information Service*)

into the picture-taking process, although the more practice you get, the better you should become. Just observing two fundamental principles can improve almost anyone's photography in only a matter of hours:

1. **Put action into your pictures.**
2. **Keep them simple.**

USE IMAGINATION TO SHOW ACTION

Perhaps the easiest and most useful way of getting action into your pictures is to include people or animals or both (see Figures 14.4 and 14.5). If you are photographing a machine, for example, show its operator as well, and show that person turning a dial, pushing a button, or engaging in some other normal activity. Even having a person wipe sweat from his or her brow might be logical. Two considerations are important:

1. **The action must be plausible to the situation.**
2. **The action must be of a kind the camera can portray.**

In few circumstances is it plausible or desirable to have persons looking into the camera. That is the sort of action you don't want. If the person is

FIG. 14.4.   Human beings are interested in other human beings. When an editor is faced with a choice between a picture that includes a person and one that does not, the decision is generally an easy one. The human element suggests action and adds a sense of reality. (*ISU Information Service*)

FIG. 14.5. When the subjects in a picture are looking at the camera, the reality and natural atmosphere of the photograph are lost. The picture becomes another example of individuals having their pictures taken. One of the most difficult jobs a photographer faces is keeping the subjects interested in what they are doing and not in what the photographer is doing. This example is extreme, having been taken from behind the persons involved, but it illustrates the point. It also demonstrates the effect of carefully choosing the foreground of the picture. (*Jim Brandt*)

supposed to be driving a tractor, operating a lathe, or removing a cake from the oven, he or she ought to be paying attention to that chore and not gazing into the camera lens. Otherwise, all the realism is lost. The person becomes someone having his or her picture taken rather than a person performing a task.

The second consideration—action the camera can portray—is equally important. Reading, for example, is a mental process rather than a physical one. The camera can show a person in the act of reading, but the picture will be more interesting if that person is shown turning a page or frowning in puzzlement over some difficult passage in the book. The suggestion of physical action is what makes the difference.

   The entire person or animal does not always have to be in the picture. In fact, when you are photographing rather small objects, just showing the upper torso of a person, a face, or even a hand will be enough. For example, if you wanted to photograph a fisherman tying a fly or a homemaker sewing on a button, these rather intricate operations would become almost meaningless in a picture that included the entire person. Instead, try a close-up of the key objects, and include just the face and hands, locating them as strategically as possible. The human element will introduce action, arouse interest, and provide a means of establishing the relative size of the central subject matter—the fly or the button. The world's largest ear of corn will look just like any other ear of corn unless some comparison is made in the picture (see Figure 14.6).

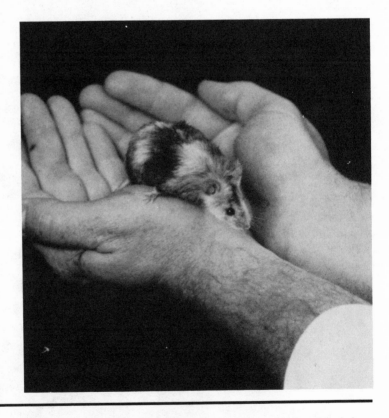

FIG. 14.6.   When the size of an object is important to a picture, include an object of known size. Subjects may be made to appear very large by selecting a very small object for direct comparison. A tiny rodent seems even smaller in a large, muscular hand than in a tiny, delicate hand. Objects can also be made to look larger by placing them nearer the camera than the object of known size—a photographic trick familiar to most fishing enthusiasts. (*ISU Information Service*)

Finally, the reality you are trying to portray in a picture by using living creatures to introduce action can be lost if they are not in a realistic situation. That is, under most circumstances, you should not expect a farmer to be feeding hogs in his best suit. Unless he is cautioned against it, however, he might show up wearing a dress suit because he is going to have his picture taken.

FIG. 14.7. Simplicity is one of the most important factors in a good picture. When setting up a picture, avoid clutter in the foreground and the background. (*Robyn Hepker*)

CUT CLUTTER FOR IMPACT

The second basic guide to setting up effective pictures—simplicity—is achieved in part by getting the subjects as close together as possible, positioning the camera as close to the subjects as possible, and selecting a camera angle that eliminates everything that does not contribute to the meaning of the picture (see Figures 14.7 and 14.8).

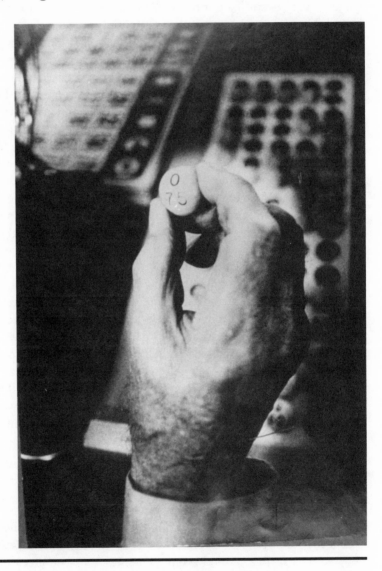

FIG. 14.8. Another way to simplify a picture is to move the camera in close to the subject. An interesting picture can usually be made even more appealing by taking it from a close viewpoint rather than a distant one. This method brings out textures and details otherwise overlooked by the casual viewer. (*Robyn Hepker*)

When an individual looks at a group of persons or objects, they are seen as part of a larger panorama. The objects can be separated by a considerable distance, but they will appear to be unified because the human eye can cover the intervening space with great speed and remarkable efficiency. In a photograph, however, the space effect is eliminated. The scene becomes a restricted one, and instead of having a reasonable unified group, you are likely to have a series of disconnected individuals. The spaces between persons or objects may seem insignificant to the eye, but they stand out in a photograph like the gap left by a missing tooth.

This principle applies to all pictures, not just to those involving groups. If you were photographing a woman and her prizewinning cake, for example, she normally would hold the cake at about waist level—a pose that looks perfectly natural to the eye. In a photograph, however, her face would be at the top of the picture and the cake at the bottom, leaving too much unused space between the two. The picture would lack unity. In fact, instead of a single picture you have two: one of the head and one of the hands and cake. To achieve unity, you might have the woman hold the cake up to her face—so close that she undoubtedly would protest. This might not look natural to the eye, but it would be effective in the finished picture. Another way of solving the problem would be to raise or lower the camera enough so that very little space existed between the face and the cake, even though the actual distance between the two objects was considerable.

One of the most difficult impulses to overcome in photography is the one that motivates you to make sure that everything is in the picture. When Grampa decides to take a picture of little Ralph opening presents on Christmas morning, his first move is likely to be step backward to make sure that he gets all of little Ralph and his package in the picture. Then he takes another step back to include the Christmas tree, then another step to get Uncle Charlie and Aunt Mabel in the picture. The result may be an interesting picture for the family album, but it would quickly find its way into an editor's wastebasket. What the editor is more likely to want is a picture characterizing the emotions of a child on Christmas morning. So instead of backing up, move in closer—then move closer still. In our example, all you would need is the expression on the boy's face and a recognizable fragment of the Christmas present. The expression conveys the meaning. Everything else merely distracts from the main point.

Moving back is easy, but it takes real courage to move in close and sacrifice all those things that it might be nice to show in the picture. If you think the editor might want a picture of the family, move them in close to the boy so they form a unified group. Then take a close picture of the group.

Even when a simple picture can be taken from some distance away, the picture is likely to be more interesting if taken from a closer viewpoint. Closeness emphasizes detail—detail that people fail to notice in their busy everyday lives. If the picture is of a loaf of bread, a shot taken from 6 feet away will show the bread, but one taken from 3 feet away will show the loaf and the texture of the bread itself.

BEWARE OF THE BACKGROUND

The background against which a picture is taken is probably the greatest source of confusion in pictures. The human eye is extremely selective, seeing only a very small area at a time. Look at an object, even something as small as a pencil. You see the pencil after your eyes have moved from end to end and side to side. The eyes examine small parts of the object, and the mind puts the image together. This is especially significant for the photographer because the eye sees only what interests it and ignores the unwanted or the distracting. A camera lens, however, is not nearly as selective as the human eye. If something exists in what is being viewed by the camera lens, the film records it, whether it is related to the subject of the picture or not.

To make things worse, the camera has only one eye and consequently cannot perceive depth. If there is a telephone pole 40 feet behind a man when his picture is taken, that pole in the finished photograph will look as though it is growing out of his head. The consequence is that an unwanted object steals interest from what the photographer was trying to say in the picture. Almost anything in the background can dominate and confuse a picture if it has no business being there. Distractions as common as a light switch on the wall or a No Parking sign can ruin an otherwise good photograph.

Safe backgrounds for most picture situations are a bare wall, a clear sky, and an open ground. If you use a wall, move your subjects 4 to 5 feet away so they will not cast confusing shadows on the wall. If you decide to use the sky, select a spot where the horizon is relatively free of trees or buildings, and take the picture from a low viewpoint (see Figure 14.9). If you wish to use the ground, pick up any litter that might be scattered around, and take the picture from a high angle (see Figure 14.10).

Often the background can help tell the story. To carry out that function, however, the background must be well organized, and everything in it must relate to the picture (see Figures 14.11 and 14.12). Avoid any background that seems uniform at first glance but actually is made up of little patches of light and dark. That includes trees, shrubbery, radiators, venetian blinds, patterned draperies, and the like. Backgrounds of that sort make pictures seem cluttered.

In general, if you are taking a picture of a dark object, place it in front of a relatively light background. If you took a black-and-white photograph of

FIG. 14.9. A low camera angle frequently can be used to eliminate background clutter. The low viewpoint places the subject against the sky rather than against trees, crowds, power poles, or other unrelated objects. (*ISU Information Service*)

FIG. 14.10. One of the best ways to eliminate a cluttered background is to shoot the picture from a high camera angle—perhaps from a chair, a nearby window, or a ladder. Sometimes a high camera angle can be achieved by holding the camera above the head. In any case, such an angle often simplifies a picture and reveals an intriguing perspective. (*Hugh Zike*)

228

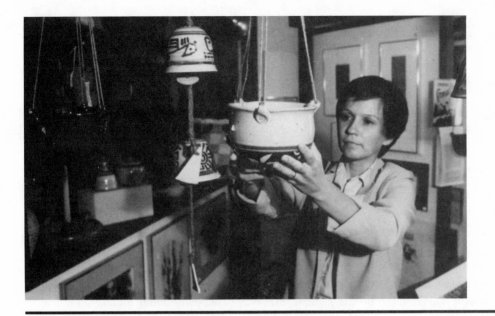

FIG. 14.11. Sometimes the background of a picture can help tell the story, but the background must be carefully chosen. Anything that does not contribute to the meaning or the character of the subject should be removed or avoided by shifting the camera position. (*ISU Information Service*)

FIG. 14.12. The foreground of a picture can also be used to tell the story effectively. Initiative and imagination resulted in a photograph with drama and personality rather than a mundane record of the back of a crowd peering into a balloon. (Also see Figure 14.5.) (*Rick Jost*)

a black Angus cow in front of a dark red barn, for instance, you would have trouble deciding where the animal ended and the barn began. The reverse situation is also true. If you arranged to photograph a blond woman in a white coat against a light background, your picture might turn out to be a face and two hands floating around in space.

PLAN LIGHTING TO FIT THE SCENE

In addition to keeping your pictures simple and loading them with action, learning as much as you can about lighting and composition and applying that knowledge will do much to make your pictures more meaningful and psychologically interesting to those who see them.

As you consider the lighting question, you must decide what mood you want the picture to portray. Do you want the subject matter to have a strong and forceful appearance, or would it be more appropriate to convey the impression of softness and gentleness? If you decide on the former, set up the picture in bright sunlight or light the subjects with incandescent light bulbs (see Figure 14.13). In both situations the light will be intense and direct, resulting in bright highlights and strong shadows. That type of lighting is appropriate for machines, buildings, persons at work, and the like. It

FIG. 14.13. Lighting is almost as important as subject matter in a good photograph. Strong lighting conditions, such as those found in direct sunlight, lend feelings of strength and forcefulness to the persons or objects in the picture. These feelings are primarily the result of the sparkling highlights and dark shadows produced by bright sunlight. (*Cindy Allen*)

would not be the lighting to use for a picture of a young child with a new puppy, where you wanted to create the effect of gentleness and affection. To do that, select a spot in the shade, take the picture on an overcast day, or use fluorescent lighting (see Figure 14.14). Those lighting conditions produce relatively less contrast between highlights and shadows.

FIG. 14.14. When the contrast between highlight and shadow is reduced, the subject takes on a soft, warm, and gentle feeling. Pictures taken on overcast days or in the shade will have soft lighting and delicate qualities. (*Larry Thiel*)

Another aspect of lighting that may be subject to control is the angle at which the rays strike the subject. If persons are in the picture, have them face directly toward or away from the light source (see Figure 14.15). Thus, you will avoid harsh, ugly shadows and lines on their faces. If, on the other hand, you are photographing an object such as a cake, a building, or a machine, the picture will be more interesting if the light strikes that object from a side angle. Side lighting creates the highlights and shadows that separate the various planes of the object in space, giving the picture volume and providing the illusion of depth. This type of lighting also brings out surface texture, illustrating for the viewer whether the subject being photo-graphed is rough, smooth, shiny, or dull (see Figure 14.16).

FIG. 14.15. It is usually best to have persons face directly toward or away from the sunlight. This avoids shadows that frequently form unattractive patterns on faces. (*Savas Tumer*)

FIG. 14.16.   With inanimate objects, on the other hand, it is usually better to have the light skim across the surface. This results in patterns of highlight and shadow, creating the illusion of three dimensions in a two-dimensional photograph. Such lighting also brings out the surface texture of the subject. (*ISU Information Service*)

PLAN COMPOSITION FOR MOOD, STORY

Although "composition" is a term about which volumes have been written, it is used here to mean the arrangement of images within the picture. As you compose a photograph, you should be less interested in the arrangement as seen without the camera than you are in the arrangement as seen through the viewfinder. When you are doing the camera work yourself, study the scene carefully through the camera's viewing system. As you do so, move the subjects to be photographed, the camera, the lighting, or all three until you are satisfied with the arrangement (see Figure 14.17). If someone else is taking the picture for you, cut a small rectangular hole in a cardboard sheet, close one eye, and study the arrangement from the camera position. Again, shift things around until you like what you see.

FIG. 14.17.   A single camera cannot perceive or record depth in a picture. When images of objects touch or coincide with each other, the illusion of depth is often lost. Even though there may be great distances between objects in a scene, they may seem to merge in a photograph, such as the illusion created here of the road projecting from the child's ear. Depth and distance can be suggested in a two-dimensional picture by carefully arranging foreground articles and objects to enhance scale and perspective. (*Robyn Hepker*)

One quality that people like to see in pictures is repetition of lines, shapes, or objects, so long as there is some variation in the pattern. If, for example, you were taking a picture of the woman who won the county fair pie-baking contest, you might show her in the foreground holding the prize pie, while in the background would be a table holding all the other pies in the contest. You could tell the story by photographing just the woman and her pie, of course, but the picture would have greater appeal with the pie repetition feature added.

Remember also that human interest is as important in pictures as it is in news and feature stories. In photographs, human interest is the reaction of the picture's subjects to the situation. That reaction in turn evokes an emotional response from the people who see the picture. Both the situation and the reaction within the picture must be clear before it conveys human interest (see Figure 14.18).

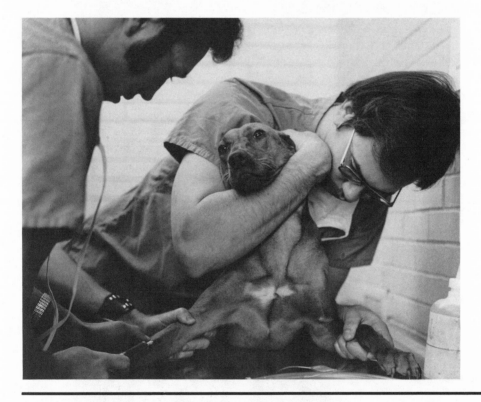

FIG. 14.18. Human interest is difficult to define, but its presence in a picture is very nearly guaranteed by an expressive animal. The human interest photo calls up human emotions—empathy, sympathy, anger, outrage, pity—with its remarkable two-dimensional power. The most forceful and memorable photographs generally possess strong elements of human interest. (*Amy Armbrust*)

You might find some other aspects of composition useful in setting up a picture. One is the shape of the picture itself. In general, the picture's shape ought to fit the subject. That is, if you are photographing a tall object, such as a silo or a grain elevator, the photograph probably will be more effective if it is taller than it is wide. Similarly, if you are photographing a horizontal scene such as a bean field or an arrangement of food on a dinner table, a horizontal picture will best fit the subject matter. It is also widely believed that a rectangular picture, either horizontal or vertical, is more interesting to the viewer than a perfectly square picture.

When you are free to arrange your subject matter, a vertical arrangement in a vertical picture is thought to convey an impression of dignity or strength (see Figure 14.19). A horizontal grouping in a horizontal format, on

FIG. 14.19. A picture with a vertical orientation of objects or with strong vertical lines conveys a feeling of dignity and a sense of respect. (*Deb Schultz*)

FIG. 14.20. Pictures composed with horizontal lines or with a horizontal arrangement of images tend to produce a quiet or restful feeling. (*Candice Cavanaugh*)

the other hand, will convey a restful or quiet mood (see Figure 14.20). A diagonal arrangement through either a horizontal or vertical picture will suggest action to the viewer (see Figure 14.21). For example, if you wanted a picture of a conveyor loading corn into a grain bin, the picture would suggest more action if it were based on a diagonal line. You could position the camera so that the wagon and the bottom of the conveyor were in the lower left corner with the conveying device running diagonally to the upper right corner where the corn was falling into the grain bin.

FIG. 14.21. Diagonal lines or a diagonal arrangement of objects will enhance the feeling of action and movement in a picture. (*Richard Anderson*)

Another way to make your publicity pictures more attractive to editors and viewers is to arrange the subjects in a spot with natural framing. The simplest example would be to pose a person in a doorway and use the doorjamb as your framing device. The framing you decide on does not need to be as obvious as a doorway, and the subject matter does not always have to be completely framed on all sides. Sometimes, just the corner of a building at the edge of the picture is sufficient. A common framing device is a tree (see Figure 14.22). Usually, the trunk is located at the edge of the picture on one side and the lower limbs and leaves complete the frame at the top.

FIG. 14.22. Providing a picture with some sort of natural frame is another way of getting reader or viewer interest. A tree, a doorway, or nearly any object can serve as a frame. (*Ron Davis*)

Summary

You are responsible for the pictures you want to place for publicity purposes, whether you actually operate the camera or not. Keep them as simple as you can, and load them with plausible action so they will seem real to both editors and viewers. Where possible, use lighting, repetition, and natural frames to emphasize the subject matter.

You also are encouraged to read carefully the instruction booklet accompanying your camera and the instruction sheet accompanying the film you buy. Both provide reliable information that can be combined with the picture-making guides discussed in this chapter to improve both the technical quality and the content of your photographs.

Exercises

1. What are the benefits of using photographs with publicity articles? Can a photograph ever detract from the story? Explain.
2. Invite several photographers from the local media to visit your class and bring samples of their work. Ask them to share some pointers that would help make your publicity photos acceptable to the medium each photographer represents. If your class has done any publicity stories with photos, ask the guests to comment on your work.
3. Review some of the publicity releases and feature stories you have written to date. For each one, think of an appropriate photograph that would have enhanced the written work. Describe the content of that picture and what techniques you would use to obtain a plausible photo.

Suggested Reading

Bethers, Ray. *Photo-Vision.* New York: St. Martin's Press, n.d.

Blaker, Alfred A. *Photography, Art and Technique.* San Francisco: W. H. Freeman and Company, 1980.

Craven, George M. *Object and Image.* 2d ed. Englewood Cliffs, N.J.: Prentice-Hall, 1982.

Davis, Phil. *Photography.* 5th ed. Dubuque, Iowa: Wm. C. Brown Publishers, 1986.

Eastman Kodak Co. *The Joy of Photography.* Rochester, N.Y.: Eastman Kodak Co., 1982.

Fox, Rodney, and Kerns, Robert. *Creative News Photography.* Ames: Iowa State University Press, 1961.

Kerns, Robert L. *Photojournalism.* Englewood Cliffs, N.J.: Prentice-Hall, 1980.

Rhode, Robert B., and McCall, Floyd H. *Introduction to Photography.* 2d ed. New York: Macmillan Publishing Co., 1971.

Swedlund, Charles. *Photography.* 2d ed. New York: Holt, Rinehart and Winston, 1981.

Time-Life. *Library of Photography.* New York: Time-Life Books, 1972.

Upton, Barbara, and Upton, John. *Photography.* 3d ed. Boston: Little, Brown, 1985.

15 *Designing Publications*

MARCIA PRIOR-MILLER

W HEN you select existing print media as channels for publicity, the proven ability of each magazine or newspaper to reach a particular segment of the broad public is a key factor for your choices. After selecting the media, you then adapt your writing or selection of accompanying artwork to the style of the individual medium. Beyond that, you have no further concern for the visual presentation of the materials you provide. The format of each publication is determined by editors and art directors, as are the sizes of paper, sizes and styles of typography, or other production considerations.

In the professionally designed publicity campaign, mass media are used primarily to raise awareness. Other media over which the publicist can have greater control are used to complement the mass media. Thus, information can be edited and designed for presentation to specific audiences, in the environment right for that message, at the exact time that the publicist desires.

When placed together with typed copy, photographs and illustrations constitute two of the major elements that you, as a publicist, use to prepare materials for printed reproduction. The process of preparing those materials for printing involves two steps in addition to writing: (1) design and layout and (2) production.

Nonprofessional publicists, as well as some professionals, often view the design, layout, and production processes as something of a mystery. The mystique rises from the fact that laying out pages for controlled materials involves making visual decisions. Conventional wisdom says these design decisions are skills that artists, but not writers, can master.

239

Not so. More than one publicist with no budget to hire a professional designer has discovered an innate flair for producing printed materials that are visually appealing and effective publicity tools. Some publicists have also learned that hiring a graphic designer does not guarantee that printed materials will capture the qualities essential to effective communication of the messages unique to a publicity campaign.

The publicist's success and the graphic designer's occasional failure in developing effective printed publications illustrates the often overlooked need to integrate the design process with the larger publicity plan. Effectively designed and printed materials for publicity campaigns involve not one but three primary phases: First, as a publicist, you will use the publicity plan to build the foundation for the design process. Second, you will prepare dummies, or prototypes, which illustrate the design concept for the publication. Third, you will supervise the production and printing of the publication.

Phase I: Planning Printed Media

When faced with the need to develop a publication, you may be tempted to focus immediately on the artistic and technical aspects of designing and laying out the pages of the publication. How can you make it good-looking, if not exquisite? What colors should you use? What typefaces should you select, and how much should you spend on production and printing?

If you jump too quickly into making these decisions, you may ignore the critical process of planning how each of the choices will enhance the publication's role in the total publicity plan. If you ignore the planning process, you may be disappointed in the final product, regardless of whether you or a hired professional designs the printed piece. Worse, the piece may fail to meet the very need for which it was included in the campaign.

A lack of adequate planning can produce disappointing results in several ways. Understanding them highlights the value of designing from the publicity plan.

A highly respected graphic designer tells the story of being hired to design a brochure to attract clients to a counseling center. The executive director of the center told the designer he wanted a brochure printed in blue and brown ink on white paper. A naturalistic illustration of two linking hands was to be placed on the front panel.

Having received these suggestions for developing the brochure, the graphic designer proceeded to query the director about the intended audience, the objectives for the brochure, and the ways the brochure would be distributed to and used by that audience. The director's answers revealed the audience to be a highly educated, sophisticated university community who might not be attracted to other, similar counseling services. The designer immediately recognized that a more effective visual approach to this audience would include, among other visual tools, abstract art and subtle blends of contemporary colors in ink and paper. However, his efforts to help the director recognize the need to match the design to the values and unique characteristics of the audience were not successful.

In this case, the director of the counseling service was satisfied with the designer's work, but the designer was not. He knew that the design the director had insisted on would never accomplish what a brochure designed to appeal directly to the audience could have.

Publicists who are too specific in their directions for the design of a publication are often satisfied with a designer's work when they shouldn't be. Others, seeing the result of such specific directions, are disappointed but don't understand why the designer was not able to produce a piece that met their real expectations. They don't realize that designing printed materials is more than putting a photograph, typography, and colors of ink and paper together so they look good. Just because a piece is visually appealing does not mean it will be an effective piece for a particular audience. So, too, what appeals to one audience may be entirely inappropriate for another.

At the other extreme are publicists and designers who view the creative process as something that should have no constraints put on it. The resulting lack of direction, while not regimenting design, also does not provide a sufficient framework for ensuring that the printed piece reaches its intended objectives.

Good graphic designers and publicists recognize the critical difference between graphic art and fine art. Fine art, like good literature, is a form of self-expression. Graphic design is not. It is a tool for communication. If a graphic design interferes with the message that is to be communicated, the design fails, no matter how visually pleasing it may be.

Thus, a key to developing visually pleasing and effective printed materials is to bring the best results of planning to the choice of specific designs. Whether you work with a budget that allows for hiring outside writers and designers or you must produce controlled publications yourself, the planning process provides the critical antecedents to the design and layout of any printed piece.

Plans for publicity can guide the design process in a number of ways. Ultimately, each publicist and graphic designer verbalize these guiding principles in ways that are most functional for each situation. At a minimum, having completed your plans for publicity, you should be able to articulate answers to each of the following questions. Some of these considerations have been discussed in previous chapters but are reiterated here to give you a total view of the elements that determine a publication's design. Figure 15.1 illustrates one group's planning process for a publicity publication.

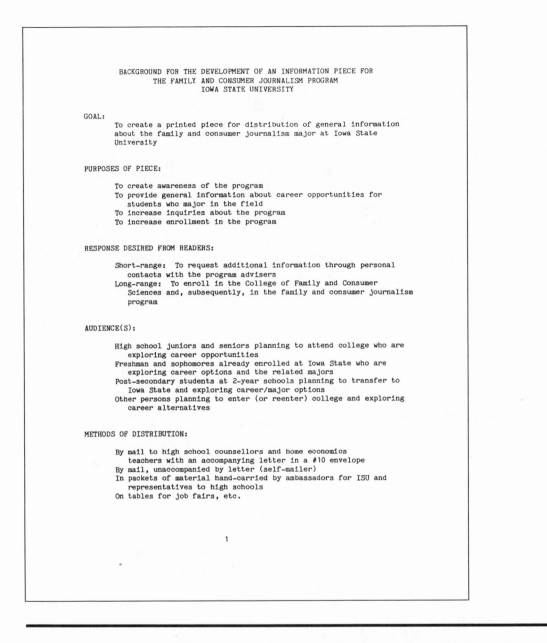

BACKGROUND FOR THE DEVELOPMENT OF AN INFORMATION PIECE FOR
THE FAMILY AND CONSUMER JOURNALISM PROGRAM
IOWA STATE UNIVERSITY

GOAL:

To create a printed piece for distribution of general information
about the family and consumer journalism major at Iowa State
University

PURPOSES OF PIECE:

To create awareness of the program
To provide general information about career opportunities for
students who major in the field
To increase inquiries about the program
To increase enrollment in the program

RESPONSE DESIRED FROM READERS:

Short-range: To request additional information through personal
contacts with the program advisers
Long-range: To enroll in the College of Family and Consumer
Sciences and, subsequently, in the family and consumer journalism
program

AUDIENCE(S):

High school juniors and seniors planning to attend college who are
exploring career opportunities
Freshman and sophomores already enrolled at Iowa State who are
exploring career options and the related majors
Post-secondary students at 2-year schools planning to transfer to
Iowa State and exploring career/major options
Other persons planning to enter (or reenter) college and exploring
career alternatives

METHODS OF DISTRIBUTION:

By mail to high school counsellors and home economics
teachers with an accompanying letter in a #10 envelope
By mail, unaccompanied by letter (self-mailer)
In packets of material hand-carried by ambassadors for ISU and
representatives to high schools
On tables for job fairs, etc.

1

FIG. 15.1. Every decision about how a publication will look should be
based on how the piece will be used. Organizing your thoughts on paper
before starting ensures that you know where you are headed. This background sheet shows how one group determined the focus of a brochure.

```
IMAGE:

        The antithesis of "suzie homemaker"; that is, family and
            consumer journalism is a major for persons interested in careers
            in the business world and in the media

        Upbeat, sophisticated, business-like but not staid;
            contemporary, in tune with the times.  Something which juniors and
            seniors in high school and freshmen/sophomores in college would
            identify with and be attracted to

COST LIMITATIONS:

        Projected budget for an initial three-year run is about $650,
            for all costs:  writing, preparation of visuals, design and
            layout, production and printing (including paper, etc.), as well
            as postage for mailing 2,000 copies

        Current options for funding may cut that figure in half.
            Therefore, all design decisions should be based on a maximum
            budget of $325, excluding costs of mailing

DESIGN LIMITATIONS:

        A realistic design will probably include one run of the press
            (i.e., 1 color of ink).  Piece must fit into a standard #10
            envelope, and be of such weight that together with one piece of
            ISU letterhead can still be mailed for $.22

        Copy will be light to medium in length; recommendations for
            artwork are requested

        Copy will be written to fit the design.  Design should allow
            for subheads.  Headline/title should incorporate an appeal to the
            reader.  That appeal may serve as a verbal link for the design
            and later focus of the copy
```

```
                                    2
```

HOW OFTEN WILL THE PUBLICATION BE PUBLISHED?

A closely related question that should also be asked is, What is the desired life span for the publication? Is the publication a one-shot piece to be distributed when needed, or is it a periodical? A newsletter distributed weekly or perhaps a monthly magazine?

If the publication is a one-time flier, folder, booklet, or other publication, you should evaluate how to keep the information and the design approach current over the life of the publication. If aspects of either the information or the design will be outdated before the desired life span of the publication ends, you will want to design accordingly.

There are many ways to adjust for the desired life span. You could create a publication with inserts that could be changed as needed. Or you might use a multiple-step approach: Develop one publication to elicit requests for a second or third. This approach can also be an effective method for reducing costs. A less expensive publication can identify the people who are most interested in additional information that may be presented in a larger, more expensive format.

A short life span may invite the use of less expensive paper, but long-lived publications need more expensive paper, because of its durability and visual appeal. Newsprint and daily newspapers are an ideal match of paper to life span. Newsprint can also be an effective choice for many other types of publications.

The design for a newsletter or magazine needs to provide identity while allowing for the flexibility and ease of production that regular deadlines demand.

WHAT IS THE PURPOSE OF THE PUBLICATION?

Another more active way of asking this question is, What should the piece accomplish? Although this question appears to be the simplest to answer, it is often the most difficult. Because it can be difficult, publicists are sometimes tempted to avoid answering it. However, that can be an expensive mistake.

Three tips may help. First, think on paper. Write down as many publication objectives as you can think of.

Second, from that list, identify one primary purpose. There may be other, secondary purposes, but few good publications can do everything equally well. Therefore, it will help to set priorities.

Finally, be as specific as possible. Most publications are designed to provide information, but information for what purpose? To raise awareness? To create a positive impression? To build loyalty to an organization? To invite a response? If so, what kind of response? Does the publication need to include a return card or coupon?

Another way to weigh multiple purposes is to identify short-term and long-term purposes. Knowing the long-term use may help define the design for the short term as well.

WHO IS THE AUDIENCE AND HOW WILL THAT AUDIENCE USE THE INFORMATION?

Early decisions about the mass media to be used for publicity may have already led to the identification of the audience. The audience for collateral publications may be the same. Many times, however, the audience will differ in ways that may have a significant impact on the publication's design.

As with the identification of purpose, the more specifically you can define the audience, the better the design can be crafted for that audience. Any campaign may have both primary and secondary audiences. If so, it may be appropriate to ask whether a single design can accommodate the differences in those audiences.

The values of an audience, as well as other psychological factors, may be as important as demographic information in understanding how your audience will receive and use the publication. So, too, lifestyle and the need people have for information determine how they will use the publication.

Busy people need information that is easy to read, digest, and apply in their lives. As your audience receives increasing amounts of information, your need to present information in clear, concise ways becomes increasingly important. If a reader has to work too hard to understand your information, your message may get lost.

Publicists can learn valuable lessons from advertisers that well understand how people's need for information affects their receptivity to it. As was mentioned in Chapter 13, people who are looking for information can be reached with attractive but relatively low-cost publications. However, people who aren't looking for information may be harder to reach. For them, more-expensive, flashier design techniques may be necessary.

With a little creative thought, you may even be able to design a publication in ways that will suggest its use. That is, you may be able to help determine how your reader uses the publication. Are you willing, for example, to have it thrown away after the first reading? Or could a creative design invite keeping it for future reference, as a poster or a keepsake? If you are designing a business card, for example, making it into a Rolodex card might invite the recipient to place it with other frequently dialed telephone numbers rather than dropping it into a pile where it will be forgotten.

Finally, the size of the audience is important. The major costs of producing publications are incurred in the setup charges—that is, the initial planning, the design, and especially the preparation of materials for printing. Thus, in general, the greater the number of pieces that are printed, the lower the cost of an individual piece (the unit cost). This reality of production, prepress, and press costs translates into opportunities to use more-expensive, unique design approaches when more copies are needed. As the number of copies drops, the less feasible it may be to use special techniques.

HOW WILL THE PIECE BE DISTRIBUTED?

If a publication is to be mailed, it may be mailed alone (a **self-mailer**) or included in an envelope with other materials. Weight and postage costs then become as much a part of the planning as other factors. The extra postage that may be required for nonstandard sizes and large envelopes can upset the balance of a budget. If the publication must fit into a specially designed envelope, that too must be accounted for in the design.

Publications that are not mailed invite many other design considerations, such as the environment in which the publication will be displayed or distributed. If, for example, the piece is a poster on a heavily used bulletin board, a design to attract a passerby may need high visual appeal—quite different from that used for a poster in a less competitive setting.

WHAT IMAGE SHOULD THE PUBLICATION PROJECT?

Typefaces, colors of ink and paper, and illustrations and other artwork are all capable of setting an infinite variety of moods and tones—whimsical or businesslike, personal or impersonal, contemporary or traditional. Images can be powerful, both for establishing a setting for the information in the publication and for telling your audience who you are as an organization. If you determine the level of quality or sophistication you want a publication to have, decisions about each design element will follow more easily.

WHAT ARE THE AVAILABLE RESOURCES FOR DEVELOPING THE PUBLICATION?

In an ideal world all beautiful things would be available to a publicist at all times for the ultimate design options. Unfortunately, that is the ideal. Publicists must work with real budgets, real photographers, and real printers. Design plans must always be tempered by a careful evaluation of what is available or can be made available through creative use of those resources.

Responses to the question of resources might include the potential budget and the photography or artwork that has already been or can be prepared. To a great extent, these resources will determine whether a publication is primarily photographic, typographic, or a blend of both. If specific pieces of artwork need to be included, such as maps or floor plans, for example, they should be prepared early on so they can be incorporated into the design of the publication.

Another group of resources that has a major impact on design are the typesetters, printers, and other suppliers whose services may be used for production. Beyond these basics, any number of resources might provide creative alternatives for the design. Perhaps you have access to word processing and computer graphics or to illustrators and photographers whose talents you could draw on.

COULD ANY OTHER FACTORS AFFECT THE PUBLICATION DESIGN?

The publicist should consider every possible use of the publication. Any one of these uses might define parameters for the publication or suggest a creative format or design approach. The possibilities are as endless as the number of situations for which controlled publications are designed. For example, information to be filed in a folder for later use might be designed as the file folder.

When you concentrate on articulating the characteristics of the audience, how that audience will receive and use the information, and how you want it to respond to the information, a graphic designer's creative energies can be focused in the best possible ways—and the most imaginative. If your time or budget dictates that you design and lay out the publication with only a printer to assist you, the same approach to planning will lead to stronger, more creative design decisions. It will also enable a printer to help you select typography and paper alternatives to enhance your concepts.

Phase II: Executing the Design

Answering each of the questions outlined in Phase I may have stimulated ideas for the visual presentation of the publication. With those ideas in mind, the second phase of publication development can begin.

Regardless of whether you execute the design and layout or work with the assistance of a graphic designer, the publication should pass through several steps before it goes to a printer. When working with a designer, be certain to allow time for sufficient communication with both the designer and the printer.

STEP 1: WRITE COPY AND DEVELOP A DUMMY OR A PROTOTYPE

Turning the conceptual decisions of the planning phase into a design begins with three complementary steps: deciding in broad terms which written and visual materials need to go into the publication, deciding on a format, and preparing a model, or dummy, of the proposed publication.

Writing copy for controlled print materials sometimes precedes developing the design. At other times, the order is reversed. Most often, the process is enhanced when the design and writing are done concurrently. That way the parameters set by the materials that must appear in the publication help determine the design, and the design concepts help determine the copy and the visuals to be prepared.

The model for the publication, referred to as a **dummy** or **prototype,** is simply a sample of the final piece (see Figure 15.2). The term "dummy" is typically used to describe a rough execution in the size, shape, and often the colors of the publication. The term "prototype" indicates a more finished model that looks as much like the final product as possible.

FIG. 15.2.   Making a prototype takes the guesswork out of how a piece will appear in print. This prototype was made for the brochure that was planned in Figure 15.1.

To make a dummy, cut a piece of paper to the desired full size of the final printed piece without any folds. Then, fold or cut the paper to the size and shape it will take when it is ready to be distributed. Any pockets or flaps or other special features in the format should be built into the dummy.

Next, indicate on the pages (or on the panels of a brochure) where the type and photographs or illustrations will be placed. The techniques used by most publication planners include multiple straight lines to indicate where blocks of text copy will be placed, boxes for photographs, and sketches for illustrations. Letter the headlines and titles, either freehand or by tracing from a catalog of typefaces available from your chosen printer. This step requires artistic skills. Selecting a format, arranging artwork and typographic elements on the page, and choosing colors and textures of paper and ink are decisions that draw on the best of innate and learned visual skills.

Decisions about design can be based on the most basic design principles. They are the same as those used by all artists: balance, proportion, sequence (sometimes called rhythm or movement), unity, and contrast. Add to these the somewhat elusive quality called style or flair to provide the visual environment for the message, and printed pieces can be developed to appeal to the whole spectrum of audiences, purposes, distribution methods, and audience uses without exceeding even the most limited budget.

Although the principles of graphic design are the same as those used by other artists, the media of design are not. That is, rather than using the watercolors or oils that painters or illustrators might select, or the fabrics and furniture that interior designers choose, graphic design manipulates typography and artwork (photographs and illustrations). Colors and textures are provided in these elements and in the choices of paper and ink. Some resources for learning how to apply the basic design principles to print media are provided at the end of this chapter.

In the early stages of planning a design, making multiple dummies is a good idea. They will allow you to explore various ideas to see which are the most appealing and which might best reach the target audience.

Some people like to work with and present only one idea to the people who make the final decisions on design. They do this, among other reasons, to force acceptance of the design that is, in their judgment, the best design. You can avoid some of the problems that can rise from this approach by preparing, or having your graphic designer prepare, two or three different designs or variations on a basic concept. From the two or three dummies, you and organization representatives can select one concept to develop into the final product. If you remain open to suggestions for the design, another, even better concept may emerge.

If the publication must be mailed, review any proposed design in light of postal costs and regulations concerning size. You may wish to take the dummy, and later the prototype, to the postmaster to check sizes and weights. Such sessions will allow adjustments in the design to keep postal costs within your budget.

STEP 2: MEET WITH ONE OR MORE PRINTERS

Once an idea emerges as being the best solution for a publicity need, you should meet with a printer to discuss available papers, typefaces, and inks and projected production costs. In most cases, you will need to meet several times with the chosen printer. The first visit should be very early in the planning of a publication, before much work is done on a dummy. The printer can give you an idea of the time and the costs involved in producing your piece. The schedule must allow for ordering paper if it is not in stock and for producing, proofing, and printing the publication. The printer can provide samples of available typefaces, inks, and papers—critical bits of information for deciding what a printed piece will look like and how complicated the design might ultimately be.

The printer will also tell you the preferred times to get estimates and bids for producing the publication. The first meeting with the printer is the best time to begin asking questions about prices, because costs will be based on how the work will be divided among the printer, the graphic designer, and you.

Printers are usually willing to give an estimate—that is a ballpark projection—of the cost for a design when it is still in the initial stages. Such estimates may change if major changes are made in the design. The final bill for the piece may be higher than the estimate if many changes are made. Other printers provide only bids—locked-in costs of producing the piece. Be sure to clarify whether you have a bid or an estimate from the printer.

Whether you are on a tight budget or a generous one, it is wise to check with the printer to determine the impact of design changes on an estimate. What may seem a small change to you may represent a significant difference in the cost of production. On the other hand, some changes are much less expensive than you might expect. Estimated costs allow the flexibility both you and the printer need as you move through the design, production, and printing stages. However, you should not expect a printer to absorb costs incurred by a design that is radically different from that on which the estimate was based. As you work with printers on publications, you will learn which changes in design have the most impact on costs.

Many publicists like to work initially with two or three printers to get competitive estimates and to take advantage of the strengths of each for different types of publications. Seldom is it necessary to obtain estimates from more than three printers. Experience often shows that the best printer for any job is the one who can provide the best blend of quality work, service, and cost. To base the selection of a printer solely on the lowest cost estimate is not always a wise decision.

STEP 3: FINISH PREPARING THE MANUSCRIPT AND PROTOTYPE

Whether the preparation of the copy for the brochure preceded or followed the design process, you will need to finish writing the copy before the design can be completed. Correct amounts of space can thus be provided for text, captions, and headlines as well as for artwork.

A manuscript for controlled media should be prepared in the same way releases are prepared for the mass media: typed, double-spaced, on one side of unruled 8½-by-11-inch white paper. In addition, you should label each part of the copy to indicate where it should be placed in the publication. Called **keying,** the labeling is often done by designating a section on a manuscript page as "Copy A," for example. On the prototype, "Copy A" is written where that section of copy is to be placed. This process is followed until each page or section of manuscript is keyed to the position it should have in the prototype.

Although preparing a prototype is a step that can be skipped, including it is a good idea when time and resources allow. The more carefully you plan a publication and the more detailed the execution of the prototype, the more certain you can be of the appearance of the printed piece.

To prepare the prototype, you may want to get from the printer a sample piece of the paper you have selected for the publication. After cutting and folding the paper to the final format (size and shape), indicate on the prototype the final design decisions: the specific placement of artwork, the location of any folds, and any special production steps, such as perforation of an area.

Also, indicate on the manuscript the final decisions about typeface choices, showing the sizes and the styles for the text, and the placement of photo and illustration captions, headlines, titles, and any other printed portions of the publication.

STEP 4: GAIN THE APPROVAL OF ALL INTERESTED PARTIES

If you are working with a graphic designer, you may want to meet with the designer once or twice before the final prototype (sometimes called a **comprehensive**) is completed. These sessions can save both you and the designer the frustration of investing large amounts of time in designs that do not satisfy the needs of the publicity campaign, and the meetings allow time to make revisions and introduce new approaches. You should also allow time for the persons for whom the materials are being prepared to review the copy and the design.

The review process can be an insecure experience for someone just learning how to do publicity. The desire to do things well can cause you to set unrealistic expectations about the ability of one person to see every angle and anticipate every question.

The experienced publicist welcomes the review process precisely because it is almost impossible for one person to catch every error or to see every subtlety of design or editorial development. A colleague may see something that, when pointed out, seems incredibly obvious but was easy for you to miss because you had to consider so many other details as you put the publication together. After materials have been reviewed and adjusted to meet differing needs and goals, you can have increased confidence that the printed piece will meet your own high standards and satisfy the goals of the publicity plan.

Phase III: Production

The third phase of designing a publication is the technical production of the piece. This phase includes preparing the manuscript for typesetting, marking artwork for reproduction, and preparing camera-ready copy for reproduction. It also requires preparing a written order for the printer's work (see Figure 15.3).

How much and which parts of this phase are handled by you, and which by the graphic designer and the printer, will be determined in great part by your respective knowledge and skills and by the services the printer provides. The technology available to you in your own office or community may also be a factor in making these decisions.

Almost all the commercial printing done today is done by offset lithography—usually referred to as **offset printing.** This method allows great flexibility in the reproduction of all types of publications. For very simple pieces, you may be able to prepare the copy and most of the artwork using a high-quality typewriter or word processor, clip art, and transfer type available at most art and office supply stores. A local copy shop can reproduce the piece within minutes.

More-complicated pieces of printing require the preparation of a **mechanical** using typeset copy and specially prepared artwork. A graphic designer will, in most cases, be trained to order type for the manuscript and to prepare the mechanical, or camera-ready copy, for the publication. You may simply provide the designer with the manuscript, indicating how many copies need to be made and when the printed pieces are to be delivered.

If you are executing the design yourself, you may want to work more closely with the printer during this last phase to know how much of the final preparation you will be doing and how much the printer will complete. If you delegate all production work to the printer, the printer will include the cost of mechanical preparation in the estimate for the printed piece.

The printer will, upon request, provide opportunities for you to inspect the work as it progresses. Called **proofing,** these checks on the prepress production of your publication are important. You should ask for and take advantage of them. Many mistakes in the copy and in the placement of elements can be corrected with minimal or no expense before they appear in print.

```
PRINTING SPECIFICATIONS

PROJECT:        Family and Consumer Journalism Brochure

DELIVERY:       November 30

CONTACTS:       Career Planning and Placement    Journalism/Mass Communication
                131 MacKay      555-0864          117 Hamilton    555-0479


SIZE:           folded -  8-1/2" x 3-3/4"
                flat -  8-1/2"  x 14"

SPECIAL
FOLDING
INSTRUCTIONS:   (front panel; 18.5 picas; other 3 panels: 21.5 picas)

TYPE PAGE:      48.5 picas x 82.5 picas

COLORS:         Base ink:      black
                Second ink:


PAPER:          70 lb. Classic Natural White

BINDERY:        3, as per prototype

TYPOGRAPHY:     Display:

                Display caps:      72 pt. Bookman Light Italic and Swash
                Major Headlines:   48 pt. Bookman Light Italic
                                   36 pt. Bookman Light Italic
                Secondary Display: 28 pt. Helvetica Condensed
                Subdisplay:        18 pt. Helvetica Italic and Roman

                Text:              10/12 Helvetica
                                   9/11 Helvetica
                Initial cap:       18 pt. Helvetica


ARTWORK:        5 halftones
                rules on panels, as per prototype


QUANTITY:       2000


DELIVERY:       131 MacKay, between 8 a.m. and 5 p.m.


PRINTING SPECIFICATIONS
```

FIG. 15.3.   A work order with specific instructions must accompany the final design of a publication piece so the printer knows exactly what to do.

You should check with the printer about the costs associated with making corrections. Do not assume that mistakes will be corrected without a charge. The general rule is that mistakes that were in materials you provided the printer or that you approved at an earlier stage of production will result in additional charges when you request corrections. On the other hand, you are not charged for mistakes the printer made while producing the printed piece, unless you saw a proof, missed the error, and gave the go-ahead for the next phase of production.

If you have time, and even if you think you don't, you should check materials after corrections are made. Sometimes new errors creep into the copy when a correction is made; sometimes a designer or printer misunderstands what you meant the correction to be. Be ready to go to the printer immediately to make these checks if the printer has no representative to bring proofs to you. If you delay, you may cause the printer to miss the deadlines you agreed on.

No publicist's role in the production of printed materials is complete until the piece is off the press. It is your responsibility to keep on top of all deadlines: yours, the graphic designer's, and the printer's. If anyone is running late, you need to know so you can negotiate with everyone whose work may be affected by the delay. Finally, one last check of the printed piece provides you an opportunity to evaluate the work of the printer as well as to learn from the final presentation how to improve your work when you plan future publications.

Summary

The best publications for publicity purposes are not designed and laid out in a vacuum. Instead, they are the culmination of careful planning for providing information to specific audiences, thereby meeting the publicity goals and the audience's need to receive and use the information.

Whether working alone or with a professional graphic designer, the publicist remains involved in the process from the time the early decisions are made about the design concepts, through the development of the prototype of the publication, and until the printer has taken the final printed piece off the press.

Careful study of the quality of the final printed piece enables the publicist to gradually learn how planning can enhance both the artistic execution and the technical preparation of printed pieces.

Exercises

1. Design and lay out a publication to use for a specific publicity purpose. First, prepare a written description of the concept for the publication, using the guidelines provided in this chapter. Then prepare a dummy or prototype on which the typefaces to be used for headlines and titles are drawn or traced. Next, indicate the placement of copy, artwork, and photographs.
2. Using Figure 15.3 as a guide, write printing specifications to obtain estimates for the prototype completed in Exercise 1. Indicate the general categories and the

specific requirements for each printing operation on which the estimate is based. (It may be necessary to consult with a printer for specific guidelines.)

3. Begin a publication design and layout idea file. Collect a group of brochures, logos, clippings of typography, graphs, paper samples, and other examples of photographs, artwork, or layouts that you find especially attractive. Divide the samples into groups based on how you anticipate using them. Label and file the samples accordingly.

Suggested Reading

DESIGN AND LAYOUT

Conover, Theodore E. *Graphic Communications Today.* St. Paul: West Publishing Co., 1985. Basic to intermediate.

Crow, Wendell C. *Communication Graphics.* Englewood Cliffs, N.J.: Prentice-Hall, 1986. Basic to intermediate.

Moen, Daryl. *Newspaper Layout and Design.* Ames: Iowa State University Press, 1984. Basic to intermediate.

Nelson, Roy Paul. *Publication Design.* 3d ed. Dubuque, Iowa: Wm. C. Brown Publishers, 1983. Basic to intermediate.

White, Jan V. *Mastering Graphics: Design and Production Made Easy.* New York: R. R. Bowker Co., 1983. Advanced.

TYPOGRAPHY

Craig, James. *Designing With Type.* Rev. ed. New York: Watson-Guptill Publications, 1980. Basic.

PRODUCTION AIDS

Craig, James. *Production for the Graphic Designer.* New York: Watson-Guptill Publications, 1974. Basic.

International Paper Co. *Pocket Pal.* 13th ed. New York: International Paper Company, 1983. Basic.

Lem, Dean Philip. *Graphics Master 2.* 2d ed. Los Angeles: Dean Lem Associates, 1977. Basic to intermediate.

ART SYNDICATES

Inx. 137 Fifth Ave., New York, NY 10010.

San Francisco Chronicle Features. 870 Market St., San Francisco, CA 94102.

ANNUAL TALENT DIRECTORIES

The Art Director's Index to Photographers. John S. Butsch and Associates, 415 W. Superior St., Chicago, IL 60610.

The Creative Black Book. Friendly Publications, 80 Irving Pl., New York, NY 10003.

DRY TRANSFER TYPE

Chartpak. One River Rd., Leeds, MA 01053.

Formatt. Graphic Products Corp., Rolling Meadows, IL 60008.

Letraset. Letraset U.S.A., 40 Eisenhower Dr., Paramus, NJ 07652.

Prestype. 194 Veterans Blvd., Carlstadt, NJ 07072.

Zip-a-tone. 150 Fencl Ln., Hillside, IL 60162.

BOOKS, CATALOGS, AND PERIODICALS

Dover Pictorial Archive Book Catalog. Dover Publications, 180 Varick St., New York, NY 10014. Free; write for it on your letterhead. Most books listed contain hundreds of pieces of copyright-free art.

Dry Faces Directory of Dry Transfer Lettering. Art Direction Book Co., 10 E. Thirty-ninth St., New York, NY 10016. Fee involved.

Herbert Shprentz Co. P.O. Box 83, Irvington, NY 10533. Send for free catalog of books containing copyright-free art.

16 *Ad Copy and Layout*

KATHERINE TOLAND FRITH

ADVERTISING is a powerful form of communication. It differs from other forms of publicity in that it is nonpersonal communication that is essentially paid for and usually persuasive in nature. Advertising can be about products, services, or ideas. However, unlike other forms of publicity, the sponsor for the advertising communication is always identified.

As was mentioned in Chapter 8, American businesses spend more than $100 billion each year in newspaper, magazine, television, radio, and direct-mail advertising as well as other promotional materials. Since media space is usually expensive, the first step for most organizations planning an advertising campaign is to conduct research that can help determine the most effective advertising strategy.

Advertising Research

Advertising research may be identified as product research, consumer research, market research, motivation research, and media research. These five major forms of research can help the advertiser answer these questions:

- Who is the target audience for the message?
- What are consumer attitudes toward the product, service, or idea?
- What will motivate the consumer to buy the product or respond to the service or idea?

257

- When is the most appropriate time to schedule the advertisement?
- How long should the advertising continue?
- What media are the most efficient vehicles for the advertiser's message?

PRODUCT RESEARCH

Product research deals basically with a product and its competition. The research is designed to provide the advertiser with information about consumer attitudes toward the product's quality, uses, benefits, price, and other distinguishing characteristics.

CONSUMER RESEARCH

Consumer research takes an in-depth look at the people whom the advertiser wants either to buy and use the product or to respond to the service or idea. Here the research may consider such demographic data as marital status, age, income, sex, religion, race, and occupation.

MARKET RESEARCH

Market research helps the manufacturer determine the appropriate geographical areas and outlets for product distribution. Market research can provide the advertiser with information such as the per capita income of a certain area or the number of families in the area. Simmons Market Research, one of the largest research companies in the United States, conducts market research for agencies and advertisers. (Information on how to contact Simmons is given at the end of this chapter.) Other good sources of secondary research data are U.S. government publications, industry trade journals, and association newsletters.

MOTIVATION RESEARCH

Motivation research is largely psychological research that attempts to uncover deep-seated, unconscious consumer motivations. The research is usually conducted by trained psychologists who are competent in dealing with the subconscious and finding the real reasons for consumers' actions.

MEDIA RESEARCH

Media research is designed to help the advertiser determine the appropriate medium to carry the message and be read, watched, or heard by potential buyers. Most research of this type is conducted and paid for by the separate media.

For example, a newspaper might conduct a survey to determine characteristics of its market area, such as number of people and households, income, occupation, number of business outlets, and so forth. Additional surveys might focus on the characteristics of the newspaper's readers and their reading habits. Other media would conduct similar research.

Large advertising agencies have considerable research available for the development of the advertising. However, local or retail advertisements are usually prepared by an employee of the business, and local advertisements are often based on hunches or intuition. At both the agency level and the local level, research is crucial to the success of the advertisement.

The Advertising Message

Whether an ad is prepared by an agency, a small business, or a volunteer for a nonprofit organization, the same general approach should be followed. First, clear objectives should be established. Often, the objectives are stated in a copy platform, a one-page strategy that defines the following:

1. Who the target audience is—the specific group of people toward whom the advertising is aimed.
2. What the message strategy is—specific details about the content of the ads.
3. What the media plan is—specific recommendations on which media should be used.

After the objectives and strategy are determined, then and only then does the copywriter begin the task of phrasing the advertising message. An effective copywriter writes short sentences with specific nouns and active verbs. Words should be short and familiar and kept to a minimum. Only those words that tell the sales story or explain the organization's cause need be included.

An ad should begin with a headline that is a short, interesting statement about the benefits of the product or service. The headline attracts the reader and directs his or her attention to the main text of the message. The body copy should amplify the headline and be a logical progression of believable information. At the end of the copy, a course of action should be suggested, such as "Call for more information about blood donation" or "Stop by and test-drive the new Mazda."

In advertising, some latitude is possible in the use of partial sentences or unusual capitalization to stress a sales point, but in general, the copy should follow the basic rules of good grammar. Unusual grammar tends to draw attention to itself and interrupts the copy flow that has been so carefully formulated.

The copy should be written on a one-to-one (personal) basis, without seeming contrived. Although a million people might be exposed to the message, each individual receives it alone. If the copywriter writes as if he or she is selling the product, service, or idea to one person, many people will buy.

Guidelines for Effective Advertising

Advertising professional Morton Levinstein once cited eight guidelines to effective retail advertising.[1] Although his remarks were directed toward retail merchants, they are equally helpful to any publicist engaged in creating an advertisement to promote an organization, a service, or an idea.

1. The purpose of advertising is to sell, not to satisfy the personal ambitions of the advertising person, the artistic aspirations of the artist, or the vanity of the firm. Advertising should try to sell, not call unnecessary attention to itself, its cleverness, or its flamboyant originality.
2. Every advertising person should assume that customers do not want to read the advertisement. Therefore, make reading it as easy as possible.
3. People are primarily interested in themselves. Therefore, show how your product or service can help them.
4. Make ads simple and easy to read. It is better to have only three important statements in an ad than to have six important ones mixed in with fifteen that are not.
5. Ideas are important in advertising. Give your ads plenty of thought. Have definite reasons for doing what you do. Space is expensive. If you cannot give a good reason for running an ad, don't run it. When you have something worth saying, that is the time to advertise.

1. Morton Levinstein, "Eight Ways to Strengthen Your Advertising." *Automotive Retailer,* June 1946.

6. Be yourself. Give your ads a personality. Let them express the individuality of your store so the people who read the ads will feel that your store is composed of human beings and not just bricks, showcases, and store fixtures. The publicist should attempt to do the same in projecting the image of an organization.

7. Don't be dogmatic. All rules can be broken, including these. The only hard and fast rule in advertising is that there is no hard and fast rule. Be flexible in your thinking. Don't be afraid to try something different.

8. Don't use advertising to cover up your past mistakes. Good advertising will not help sell bad merchandise. Such advertising is expensive because it will not produce results, and it also gives people the wrong impression of your store. Sell the merchandise that people want to buy, at the time they want to buy it and at the price they want to pay for it.

Art Direction

Whereas the copywriter uses words to communicate with the selected audience, the art director uses visuals. This creative team works together to produce an ad that grabs the audience's attention, builds interest, creates desire, and ultimately requires action. In other words, the headline, text, and visuals must work together as a unit to involve the reader and make a key sales point.

In an advertising agency, the art director makes sure all the visual elements of the ad communicate with the reader. Therefore, the photograph, the typography (the style and arrangement of printed letters), the colors, and even the white space (any area of the ad not filled with art or copy) are all carefully planned.

If you so choose, a professional ad agency can design and write your organization's ads. If, on the other hand, you want to do your own ad work—or need to, because of budget restraints—be sure to fuse the visual and verbal elements of an ad to adequately communicate the message to the target audience.

Laying Out the Ad

The task of laying out an ad may bewilder the nonadvertising professional. But the publicist should remember that the major function of the

FIG. 16.1. This ad for a day surgery center follows a rather standard layout design. But the creative blend of the headline, illustration, and text material portrays an ad whose message is not standard but individualistic. (*Courtesy of CMF&Z, Inc.*)

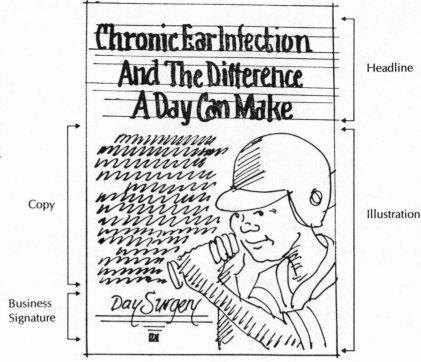

Headline

Illustration

Copy

Business Signature

layout is to make the ad as easy to read as possible. Accomplishing this calls for an emphasis on simplicity.

Leaf through any newspaper or national magazine and you will find that the layout of most ads is quite standard. Each contains one main headline, a dominant illustration, a copy block, and a trademark or business signature (see Figure 16.1). Such sameness in a layout does not mean the professional who prepared the ad lacked talent or imagination. It means, instead, that the most effective layout is the one that is most simple.

To prepare an ad for the print media, use the following procedure (refer once again to Figure 16.1):

1. Use a piece of paper (called a layout sheet) large enough to accommodate the ad and still leave room in the margins for instructions to the printer.
2. Draw in the borders to the exact size of the ad.
3. Paste proofs (trial impressions of the artwork) in the exact position desired in the final ad. If proofs are not available, indicate the position and size of illustrations by blocking out the area.
4. Letter in the headlines and any other copy that will use large type in approximately the same size you want it to appear in the final ad.
5. Indicate where the body copy will be placed using straight or zigzag lines that are horizontal and parallel.
6. Indicate the position of the trademark, product name, or company name.
7. On a separate 8½-by-11-inch sheet of paper, type the copy (see Figure 16.2). Do not try to type the copy line for line on the layout; the printer will handle this for you.

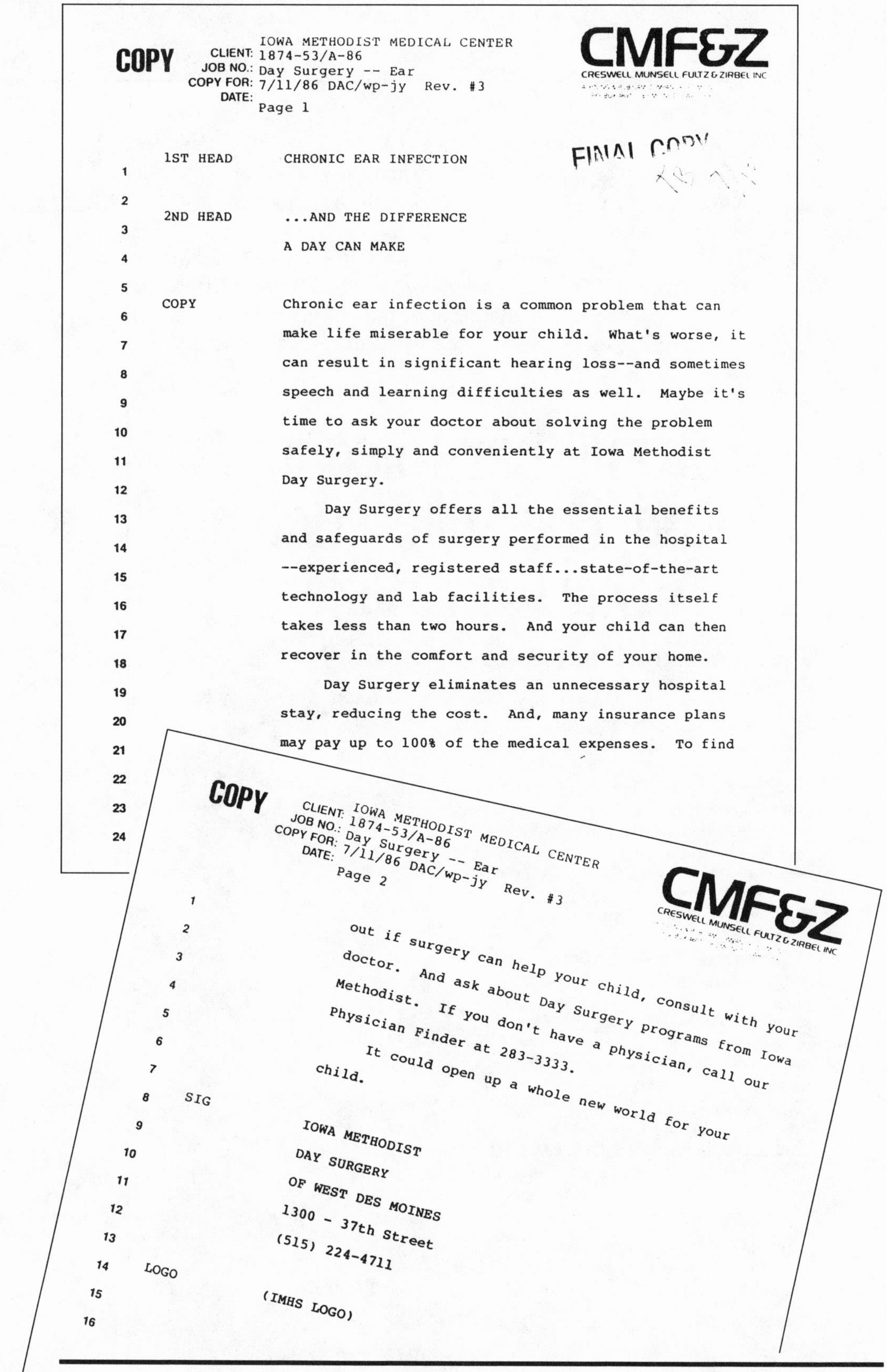

COPY

CMF&Z
CRESWELL MUNSELL FULTZ & ZIRBEL INC

FINAL COPY

1 1ST HEAD   CHRONIC EAR INFECTION

2

3 2ND HEAD   ...AND THE DIFFERENCE

4   A DAY CAN MAKE

5

6 COPY   Chronic ear infection is a common problem that can

7   make life miserable for your child. What's worse, it

8   can result in significant hearing loss--and sometimes

9   speech and learning difficulties as well. Maybe it's

10   time to ask your doctor about solving the problem

11   safely, simply and conveniently at Iowa Methodist

12   Day Surgery.

13   Day Surgery offers all the essential benefits

14   and safeguards of surgery performed in the hospital

15   --experienced, registered staff...state-of-the-art

16   technology and lab facilities. The process itself

17   takes less than two hours. And your child can then

18   recover in the comfort and security of your home.

19   Day Surgery eliminates an unnecessary hospital

20   stay, reducing the cost. And, many insurance plans

21   may pay up to 100% of the medical expenses. To find

22

23

24

COPY

CMF&Z
CRESWELL MUNSELL FULTZ & ZIRBEL INC

1

2   out if surgery can help your child, consult with your

3   doctor. And ask about Day Surgery programs from Iowa

4   Methodist. If you don't have a physician, call our

5   Physician Finder at 283-3333.

6   It could open up a whole new world for your

7   child.

8 SIG

9   IOWA METHODIST

10   DAY SURGERY

11   OF WEST DES MOINES

12   1300 - 37th Street

13   (515) 224-4711

14 LOGO

15   (IMHS LOGO)

16

FIG. 16.2. The copy for an advertisement is submitted on a separate
sheet or sheets of paper. The printer's instructions (not shown here) indicate the size of the headlines and body copy for copyfitting purposes.
(*Courtesy of CMF&Z, Inc.*)

8. Other pertinent information, such as the name of the advertiser, the medium, the date of the ad's insertion, and the size of the ad should be included in the upper left-hand corner of the copy sheet.

Figure 16.3 shows the finished ad as it ran in the chosen medium, a newspaper in this case. Notice that the photo is different from the rough draft of the ad. The change was made because the original illustration was no longer appropriate; when the ad ran, the baseball season was over.

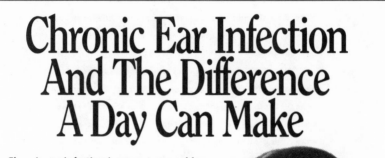

Chronic Ear Infection And The Difference A Day Can Make

Chronic ear infection is a common problem that can make life miserable for your child. What's worse, it can result in significant hearing loss — and sometimes speech and learning difficulties as well. Maybe it's time to ask your doctor about solving the problem safely, simply and conveniently at Iowa Methodist Day Surgery.

Day Surgery offers all the essential benefits and safeguards of surgery performed in the hospital — experienced, registered staff...state-of-the-art technology and lab facilities. The process itself takes less than two hours. And your child can then recover in the comfort and security of your home.

Day Surgery eliminates an unnecessary hospital stay, reducing the cost. And, many insurance plans may pay up to 100% of the medical expense. To find out if surgery can help your child, consult with your doctor. And ask about Day Surgery programs from Iowa Methodist. If you don't have a physician, call our Physician Finder at 283-3333.

It could open up a whole new world for your child.

IOWA METHODIST
Day Surgery
OF WEST DES MOINES

MHS

1300 - 37th Street   WDM   (515) 224-4711

FIG. 16.3.   The ad as it appeared in the newspaper. (*Courtesy of Day Surgery, a service of Iowa Methodist Medical Center*)

Type Selection

"Type" (or "typeface") refers to the distinctive designs of printed letters, numbers, and punctuation marks that appear in advertisements. Certain typefaces are more suitable for women's items; others denote masculinity. Some can help promote a feeling of prestige or the urgency of a sale, and still others can help create a mood or setting for the product or service being advertised. The subject of typefaces is too complex to cover in this book. However, in many cases printers will help publicists make type decisions. (See the Suggested Reading list at the end of Chapter 15 for a book about typography.)

The size of type you use, of course, will depend to a large extent on the size of your ad. Type sizes are relatively easy to understand. The height of type is measured in points; there are 72 points per inch. Therefore, the printer's 72-point type is 1 inch high from the top of the ascender to the bottom of the descender (a capital letter is about $11/16$ inches high), 36-point type is $1/2$ inch high (cap height about $3/8$ inches), and so on. The text type you are reading right now is 10-point type and is about $9/64$ inch high. Typically, 8- or 9-point body type is used in a newspaper's news section.

As was mentioned in Chapter 13, several microcomputer software products are available that provide many of the graphic artist's tools, including a wide range of typefaces in various sizes. In addition, layout programs allow the user to combine text, typography, and graphics. Some are designed to feed directly into electronic typesetting, but all can be used with a dot-matrix or laser printer to produce a finished layout. Indeed, the availability of do-it-yourself publishing software has revolutionized the publicity industry, especially for the nonprofessional publicist.

Broadcast Advertising

Too often public relations nonprofessionals overlook broadcast advertising when organizing their publicity campaigns. It is a mistake to do so. The better publicity campaign has a mix of controlled and uncontrolled messages, and radio advertising offers a controlled option that can accommodate most organizations, even those with small budgets.

Radio station personnel will help with commercials in any way your organization wishes. If you want the advertising personnel to write and produce the commercial, they will. If you want to write the script and let the station produce the ad, that can be arranged, too. If you have the equipment and know-how and want to do everything, that's another option. In general, the nonprofessional publicist is content to write the ad's script and leave the production to the professionals.

The mechanics of writing scripts for broadcast are covered in Chapter 12. As far as content is concerned, the message should relate to the experiences of the listeners. The choice of music and sound effects will also have a bearing on the ad's success; those with the best techniques will capture the audience's attention. An example of a radio script for a 30-second commercial is shown in Figure 16.4.

RADIO COPY

CLIENT:	IOWA METHODIST MEDICAL CENTER	
JOB NO.:	1874-6-86	
COPY FOR:	Neighborhood Clinic	
LENGTH:	:30	
TITLE:	"Catman"	
SPOT NO.:	IMMC-86-0533	
DATE:	5/9/86 DC/wp-cr Rev. #1	
	Page 1	

CMF&Z
CRESWELL, MUNSELL, FULTZ & ZIRBEL INC
A YOUNG & RUBICAM COMPANY · DES MOINES CEDAR RAPIDS
PO BOX 4807 DES MOINES IOWA 50306 (515) 246-3500

FINAL COPY KB 5/14

```
1                    (MUSIC UP)

2   ANNCR:           Accidents and illnesses are never convenient...

3   WOMAN::          (CALLING FROM A DISTANCE)

4                    Watch the cat, honey!

5   MAN:             What caaaaaat

6   SFX:             (Cat howling and crash)

7   ANNCR:           That's why Iowa Methodist Neighborhood clinics are.

8                    Close to you, open ten to ten, seven days a week,

9                    and the doctor is always in.  For routine and

10                   urgent medical needs, make us your first stop.  We

11                   can help you get well...sooner!

12

13                   Iowa Methodist Neighborhood Clinics...

14                   Southeast 14th at Lacona

15                   On 35th, across from Valley West Mall

16                   And at 4631 Merle Hay Road, just 1/2 mile south of

17                   I-80.

18                   (MUSIC OUT)

19

20

21

22

23

24
```

FIG. 16.4. A typical radio script is set up much like a standard play script. The person speaking is listed in all capital letters in a column to the left of the script. Music and sound effect cues (labeled "SFX") are written inside parentheses on the copy sheet. The underlined words denote emphasis. (*Courtesy of Iowa Methodist Medical Center*)

Summary

This chapter has outlined the major forms of research that can be used to develop a creative advertising strategy. Once this strategy is determined, the copywriter and art director develop the text and layout for the print campaign.

Good body copy has a simple yet persuasive writing style with short sentences and paragraphs. The standard layout contains the headline, one dominant visual, a copy block, and the trademark or business logo. (Chapter 15 details other layout principles.)

In many cases, these media professionals will undertake the chore of preparing the advertisement or an entire campaign. It is still important that you understand the principles of effective advertising, however, so you can evaluate their work, either as a publicist or as a consumer.

Exercises

1. Search your local newspaper to find two advertisements that you find particularly appealing and that originate from local nonprofit organizations. Discuss the merits of each ad in terms of what makes the ad effective.
2. Now search your local newspaper to find two advertisements that you think are less effective and that originate from local nonprofit organizations. Discuss the drawbacks of each ad that lessen the impact of the message. What would you do to improve the effectiveness of each ad?
3. Choose an activity or service you wish to publicize for a local organization. Based on the guidelines in this chapter, do the following:
   a. Design an ad that announces the service or upcoming activity of the organization.
   b. Write a 30-second broadcast commercial based on the same service or activity.

Suggested Reading

Book, Albert, and Schick, C. Dennis. *Fundamentals of Copy and Layout.* Chicago: Crain Books, 1984.

Bovée, Courtland L., and Arens, William. *Contemporary Advertising.* 3d ed. Homewood, Ill.: Irwin, 1989.

Burton, Philip. *Advertising Copywriting.* 5th ed. Columbus, Ohio: Grid Publishers, 1983.

Jewler, A. Jerome. *Creative Strategy in Advertising.* 3d ed. Belmont, Calif.: Wadsworth Publishing Co., 1989.

MEDIA MARKETS RESEARCH INFORMATION

Simmons Market Research Bureau. 219 E. Forty-second St., New York, NY 10017.

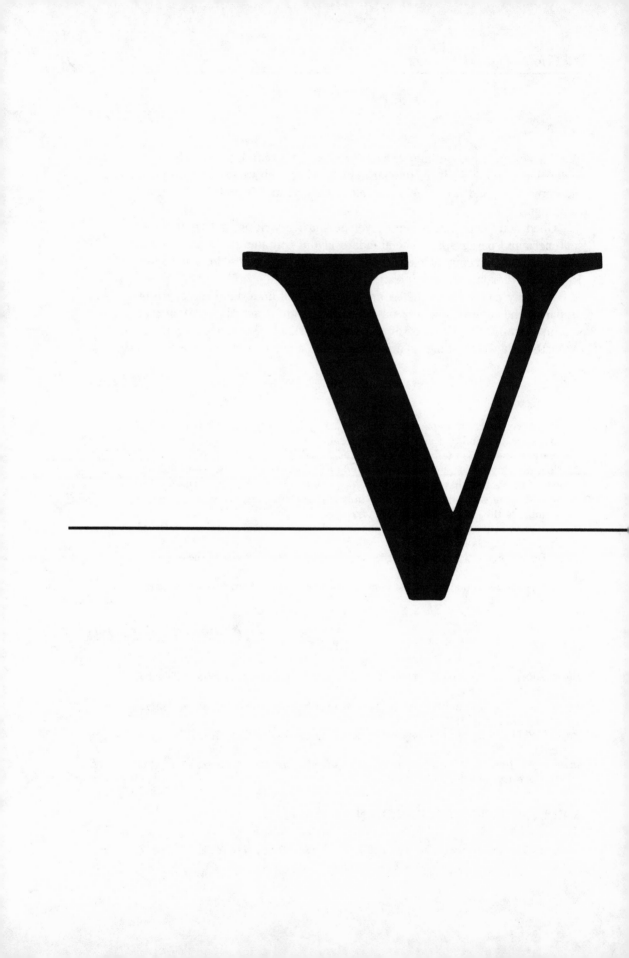

Professional and Social Responsibility

THERE IS NO effective communication without credibility. The First Amendment to the Constitution allows the publicist—indeed, anyone—to write, but it does not assure responsible and judicious writing. The chapters in Part V evaluate the role of the press in society and discuss the necessary ingredients for accountable journalism.

17 *The Press and Society*

BARBARA M. MACK

MANY view the press[1] in the United States as a small group of elite, political liberals managing vast chains of newspapers and radio and television stations dedicated to the criticism of anything conservative. To others, the press is a staunch guardian of political freedoms, dedicated to the preservation of a participatory democracy. What is the role of the press today? How has it changed over the past 200 years, and how will it change in the decades to come?

The press today is something far different from that envisioned by the founders of the United States. In the days of Benjamin Franklin and Thomas Jefferson, the press had no high-flown ideals of journalistic ethics and no dedication to objective reporting. Newspapers were tools of political propagandists, and their political viewpoints permeated every inch of type.

The development of a system of press ethics dedicated to the objective reporting of facts is largely a creature of the twentieth century and developed in part as a response to competition from the new media of radio and television and the rise of monopoly-newspaper towns. Newspapers today report on government, private industry, and the personal lives of some citizens. News reports can frustrate, embarrass, and damage, but as U.S. Supreme Court Justice Felix Frankfurter wrote:

> A free press is indispensable to the workings of our democratic society. The business of the press . . . is the promotion of truth regarding public matters by

1. Although the word "press" is traditionally associated with newspapers, its use in this chapter includes any of the print or broadcast news media.

furnishing the basis for an understanding of them. Truth and understanding are not wares like peanuts or potatoes. . . . I find myself entirely in agreement with Judge Learned Hand that neither exclusively, nor even primarily, are the interests of the newspaper industry conclusive; for the industry serves one of the most vital of all general interests: the dissemination of news from as many different sources and with as many different facets and colors as possible. That interest is closely akin to, if indeed not the same as, the interest protected by the First Amendment; it presupposes that right conclusions are more likely to be gathered out of a multitude of tongues, than through any kind of authoritative selection. To many this is, and always will be, folly, but we have staked upon it our all.

In examining the role of the American press in society, it is helpful to realize that the American press enjoys a unique degree of freedom. Other nations espouse freedom of the press in constitutions or declarations—even the constitution of the USSR contains a provision ensuring freedom of speech, press, and assembly—but the United States has been uniquely successful at establishing a working relationship between the government and the press that allows a high degree of access to government information and a high tolerance for publication of that information. Friction occurs, and government officials and the press regularly battle over what information should or should not be printed. Frequently, the courts become the arbiter of such disputes and must interpret what the constitutional guarantee of a free press means. But generally, these battles are viewed as part of a political process that has protected the press for the last 200 years.

A similar interrelationship exists between the press and its readers. In large measure, what is printed in news columns is a reflection of the desires of the majority of readers. For the press to be effective in conveying information, readers, listeners, and viewers must learn to be critical consumers of news. Friction occurs between the press and its readers, and that friction, or criticism, often is responsible for improved performance by news organizations.

One way in which the print medium and the public communicate is through the use of newspaper ombudsmen. An ombudsman is a newspaper employee who investigates the complaints of readers and responds directly to the reader or, when appropriate, through a signed column in the newspaper. Few newspapers had ombudsmen in the 1960s, but in the 1970s more and more newspapers established a formal procedure for dealing with complaints.

One experiment in dealing with complaints of newspaper fairness and accuracy was the National News Council. An unofficial body originally financed by the Twentieth Century Fund, the council began operating in 1973 and acted as an arbiter for disputes between newspapers and individuals who believed they had been wronged by press coverage. During the eleven years it functioned, the council was always controversial. It was denounced by the *New York Times,* which alleged that the council was the forerunner of a government-controlled press.

Other ways of communication are more direct: lawsuits, letters to the editor, canceled subscriptions, pickets, and public campaigns to discredit a newspaper all are ways in which readers can communicate directly with their newspaper. The press communicates with its readers, viewers, or listeners through its news and entertainment products.

But what do people really want from the press? As early as 1946, the Commission of Freedom of the Press (financed by publisher Henry R. Luce and *Encyclopedia Britannica*) created an accurate list of the expectations the public has of the press. The commission said society required of the press the following:

- A truthful, comprehensive, and intelligent account of the day's events in a context that gives them meaning.
- A forum for the exchange of comment and criticism.
- The projection of a representative picture of the constituent groups in the society.
- The presentation and clarification of the goals and values of society.
- Full access to the day's intelligence.

How well has the press fulfilled its responsibilities? What are the goals of the media, and how well have those goals been communicated to their readers, viewers, and listeners? How believable are the media?

How Trusted Is the Press?

News organizations have an insatiable curiosity about themselves and how they are perceived by the public. Surveys of the public's attitudes toward the news and those who report it are frequent and have begun to show some consistent incongruities during the last several years. Major surveys by the *Washington Post* and the *Los Angeles Times* conducted in 1981 showed that most Americans believed that the press would, at times, cover up stories or fabricate details. At the same time, both surveys said the media were generally more trustworthy than government officials.

The Press and the Government

What role should the press play in covering the government? Should it be a fierce watchdog operating as an adversary of government, or should it be the true observer, reporting what occurs but at all costs avoiding becoming an actor in the drama?

Friction between the press and the government in this country is as old as the American Revolution. Thomas Jefferson once said that if he had to choose between a free press without a government or a government without a free press he would choose the former, but it's also true that our third president often complained about press criticism of his administration.

More recently, government officials have complained loudly that the press is insensitive to a host of issues: national security, a criminal defendant's right to a fair trial, economic development, school system administration . . . the list is endless.

There have been some dark days in the press's relationship with the government. During World War II, for example, the press willingly submitted copy to government censors and largely acted as the public relations arm of the government, tossing out jingoistic support for the war effort. The press supported victory gardens and the purchase of war bonds but also supported some questionable government policies like the internment of Japanese-American citizens in relocation camps to prevent the possibility of their spying. Few newspapers questioned that government policy, which forced Japanese-American citizens to sell their homes and businesses at ridiculously low prices.

In the 1950s, the press generally was supportive of the activities of the junior senator from Wisconsin, Joseph McCarthy, as he looked for communist conspirators behind every tree and under every rock. McCarthy subpoenaed hundreds of people and grilled them mercilessly, alleging that even the most casual contact with socialist or communist political theory made someone a communist, a communist sympathizer, or a "fellow traveler" on the path to global domination by communism. For four years, McCarthy held sway in Washington, and his methods were rarely questioned by the national press corps. It was not until March 9, 1954, when broadcaster Edward R. Murrow publicly attacked McCarthy and his Red Scare tactics, that the press corps began to explore McCarthy's methods and motivation.

The 1960s marked the beginning of a new era of press-government relations. The reassessment of the role of the press grew out of one of the greatest debacles in this nation's foreign policy, and the press's role in that historic incident: the invasion of the Bay of Pigs.

In 1960, reporters for the *Washington Post* and the *New York Times* uncovered a U.S. plan to support an invasion of newly communist Cuba. The invading forces were to be Cuban refugees who had fled the country when Fidel Castro seized power in 1958, but the forces were financed and trained by the Central Intelligence Agency. Both the *Post* and the *Times* stifled the story at the request of President John F. Kennedy. Some stories were killed entirely, and others were softened to avoid admitting that the invasion was imminent.

The invasion was launched in 1961 and was an unmitigated disaster. The invading anticommunist guerrilla troops were quickly and bloodily defeated by Castro's soldiers. Kennedy was widely criticized for supporting the expensive failure and later told the *Times'* editors he wished they'd printed the entire story, perhaps averting the disaster.

The Bay of Pigs was followed by the Vietnam War, and President Lyndon B. Johnson quickly found that the aggressive press coverage of the war was an uncomfortable change from the supportive cheerleading that had marked World War II. Vietnam became known as the television war because for the first time technology allowed millions of Americans to see, from the comfort of their living rooms, film of actual combat. President Richard M. Nixon railed against the press, which by 1968 had begun calling for an end to the war. Nixon kept a "hit list" of journalists who in his view had been particularly hostile to the positions of his administration.

In fact, Nixon's ultimate battle with the press ended his presidency. Bob Woodward and Carl Bernstein of the *Washington Post* investigated a break-in at the Democratic National Committee headquarters, in an office building known as the Watergate, and uncovered a trail of dirty tricks and cover-ups involving Nixon. Two years later, under attack from the press and Congress and facing possible impeachment by the Senate, Richard Nixon resigned.

The end of the Watergate scandal didn't mark the end of government-press conflict. In 1979, the U.S. Justice Department sought a court order to prevent the publication of an article on how to build a hydrogen bomb, even though the information had been gathered from nongovernment sources, and in another case it threatened to sue reporters and editors for printing Department of Defense information leaked to the press by confidential sources. Press coverage of Latin America was attacked by President Ronald Reagan as being sympathetic to communism. In 1986, Reagan told reporters they were endangering the lives of U.S. hostages held in Lebanon by reporting that in order to pave the way for the hostages' release, America had shipped arms to Iran, a nation openly hostile to the United States. Later, the press revealed not only the arms sales to Iran but also that some of the money from those arms sales had been funneled to anticommunist rebels in Latin America. The controversy became the most serious one in the Reagan presidency to that date.

The role of the press as the watchdog for the public is easiest to understand on a national scale. Small-town publishers, however, often face difficult decisions about when to be a booster of the community and when to be a critic. The small-town newspaper is an influential institution, and publishers—who often are also the advertising managers and the chief reporters—must walk a tightrope, balancing the need for social and economic stability of the community against the need for accurate and full reporting of news stories that will irritate public officials or embarrass their fellow citizens. Publishers realize that the person who is the subject of a critical story may also be sitting beside them at the local cafe the next morning or at church next Sunday. The courageous and independent small-town newspaper publisher is a direct contradiction of another source of criticism often leveled at the press: monopoly ownership.

Monopoly Ownership

Much of the power of the American press is becoming concentrated in a dozen or so major media companies. Few major cities in this country have a daily newspaper that is not owned by or affiliated with a national communications corporation. Journalism reviews have bemoaned the sales of family-owned newspapers such as the *Louisville* (Ky.) *Courier-Journal* and the *Des Moines Register* to large newspaper chains.

Many media companies, such as the New York Times, Inc., the Washington Post Co., Knight-Ridder, Inc., and the (Chicago) Tribune Co., also are diversifying business operations to include a number of radio and television stations, outdoor billboard companies, satellite businesses, cable television operations, and magazine and book publishing. The executives of these corporations argue that the economies of scale offered by large companies mean more money can be spent on quality news operations. The ability to purchase newsprint, ink, presses, and computers in large quantities means savings that can be translated into profits for shareholders. These executives believe that editorial independence and integrity are preserved by chain ownership.

Opponents of the concentration of ownership argue that too much power has been placed in the hands of too few media executives. The free press that Judge Learned Hand envisioned was founded on the belief that the truth is "more likely to be gathered from a multitude of tongues." Few cities have competing newspapers to provide a diversity of voices. The diversity that does exist arises from competition among the various news media.

In the 1970s, the Federal Communications Commission, concerned about the number of large newspapers that also owned television and radio stations in the same cities, created cross-ownership rules that forbid the holder of a broadcast license from owning another medium of communication in the same market. A few exceptions have been allowed, but generally, a television station owner cannot own a radio station or daily newspaper in the same market, nor can a radio station owner own a television station or newspaper in the same market. The cross-ownership rules have provided some protection against monopolization of the flow of news in a single city or market, but they do not provide protection against what some critics call the cultural monopoly of the press.

The Cultural Monopoly

The vast majority of American publishers, editors, and broadcasters are well educated, white, and male. They are the heads of large businesses and often are among the most powerful members of a community. Although scientific documentation of any kind of class bias in the press remains elusive, press critics argue that homogeneous press management means a lack of diversity in the news.

In the broadcasting arena, the Federal Communications Commission tried during the 1970s to expand the cultural backgrounds of station owners by giving preference to license applications filed by companies owned by blacks, Hispanics, or women. However, this policy has not had a major impact on the broadcasting community, in part because relatively few new radio and VHF television licenses have been granted in recent years, and in part because broadcasting is such an expensive enterprise that few lenders have been willing to lend such "high-risk" groups the large amounts of money necessary to finance a new station. These groups also have difficulty purchasing existing stations because the prices for such stations in major urban markets (where most of the minority populations reside) have risen dramatically during the last decade.

The FCC has been more successful, however, in getting broadcast owners to increase the number of women and minorities employed by existing stations. The FCC's policies on employment practices demand that a station's employees be a reflection of the community's work force in terms of sex and racial mix. The standards also demand that minority and female employees be represented at all managerial and technical levels, rather than crowded into lower-paying job categories. Each year, stations are required to file a detailed employment report with the FCC. The only stations exempted are those with fewer than five employees and those operating in markets where minorities comprise less than 5 percent of the population.

The FCC measures do not ensure that the media in the United States will not suffer from the cultural bias feared by many critics, but they do indicate a growing awareness of the issue.

Advertiser Pressure

One of the oldest criticisms hurled at the press is the charge that publishers are often too sensitive to the concerns of advertisers and are willing to suppress or ignore news that might damage an advertiser.

There is fierce competition for the advertising dollar in any city large enough to support a newspaper and a radio or television station. But advertisers also need a specific advertising mix – a blend of newspaper, magazine, radio, television, outdoor, and direct mail – that allows them to sell their products to the largest percentage of the targeted audience. Because newspapers are widely circulated and have a heterogeneous readership, they are an important part of almost any mix. Advertisers may withdraw their ads for a day or so to protest a particular article, but the corresponding decline in their business usually forces them back to the newspaper within days.

The Press and Its Agenda

Many critics believe that the press exercises undue power over the agenda of government and industry. The press is capable of drawing attention to and exciting public concern toward an issue simply by giving the issue extended and widespread publicity. Some critics argue that at the turn of the century, William Randolph Hearst, a powerful California newspaper publisher, was responsible for the commencement of the Spanish-American War. His newspaper, the *San Francisco Examiner,* gave continual, inflammatory coverage of unrest in Cuba, and the phrase "Remember the Maine" became the war cry of a nation after the *Examiner* created the headline to commemorate a ship sunk in a Havana harbor.

Today's press critics argue that multimillion-dollar communications companies are still trying to set the agendas of their communities, their states, and the nation. Editorial opinions are not always expressed on the editorial pages, according to critics.

It is true that news judgment plays a critical role in determining what a community or a nation will care about. Just as the press received laurels for its coverage of issues like Watergate, it has also been accused of turning a blind eye to important issues. In the wake of the explosion of the space shuttle *Challenger* on January 28, 1986, the press was criticized for its failure to explore the efficiency and safety of the shuttle program. Media critics also said the press was unduly critical when launches were scrubbed for safety purposes, thus creating more public pressure to launch even under questionable circumstances.

But editors are trained to evaluate news through a careful process of balancing what the public wants to know with what the public needs to know. The process of making news judgments is a delicate and difficult one, fraught with perils of human frailty. But by and large, editors are honest, well-meaning people who approach their jobs with a sense of dedication and professionalism.

Press Professionalism

The development of journalism schools to educate and train professionals has been one of the most important contributions to the American press in this century. During the past several decades journalism schools have moved quickly from technical or vocational arts programs to programs that teach a sophisticated appreciation of communications and its relationship to a self-governing nation.

Today's journalism graduates most often see themselves as professionals working among highly educated and dedicated colleagues. Many of them will likely develop a special skill in a particular field—business and industry, health, education, environmental sciences, law—that enables them to be better fact gatherers and better educators.

The Press and Its Critics

Although many newspapers have developed ombudsmen to respond to the complaints of individuals, the press has been less successful at dealing with criticisms of the press as an institution.

The mass media are aware of criticism; dozens of annual colloquia, symposia, and seminars are designed to discuss the subject. But how the media determine which criticisms are justified, what changes should be made in response to that criticism, and how those changes are communicated to readers, viewers, and listeners remain elusive goals.

Even the harshest critics of the press have avoided suggesting any substantial changes in the basic structure of the press. Other countries have established government-owned media or allowed licenses of news organizations to be revoked for "unprofessional performance," but no such changes in the American press have ever been considered.

Summary

Americans are bombarded each day by thousands of messages from the mass media. Television and radio commercials, billboards, newscasts, newspapers, magazines, movies, television and radio programs all compete for people's attention. Technological advances have given the media additional power to influence lives.

News organizations wield a particular power and can effectively set the agenda for state and federal governments by focusing attention on a particular concern or issue. The agenda-setting power of the media poses a problem for many media critics who argue that the press should only observe the news and should not attempt to create controversy by challenging government policies or decisions. Opponents argue that only a vigorous, investigative press can bring to light many government actions that are hidden under layers of bureaucracy.

The growth of large, multinational communications corporations has caused concern because many people fear that consolidation of ownership of newspapers, radio, and television stations will result in limiting the amount of information citizens receive. Other critics have voiced concern that the media are too heavily dominated by Anglo values that do not correctly reflect the racial and ethnic diversity of American society.

These concerns place a special burden on the media, which operate under the protection of the First Amendment to the U.S. Constitution. Since relatively little government regulation of the media is allowed, the media have a particular obligation to develop and follow high standards of professional behavior.

Exercises

1. The Federal Communications Commission has adopted rules that limit the number of radio and television stations that can be owned by the same company. Should Congress consider similar rules that would limit the number of newspapers that can be owned by a single corporation? Why or why not?

2. If terrorists or other criminals seize hostages and demand access to radio or television, should the station owners accede to these demands? What arguments can be made for and against meeting the demands?

3. Should Congress pass legislation setting quotas for the hiring of women and minorities by newspapers? The Federal Communications Commission requires radio and television stations to report the numbers of minorities and women employed by the stations. Should newspapers report these figures as well? Why or why not?

4. If the account of a news event differed markedly between the television newscast you watched and the newspaper account you read, which would you believe? What elements of a news story give it credibility in your eyes? Why?

Suggested Reading

Bayley, Edwin R. *Joe McCarthy and the Press.* New York: Pantheon Books, 1981.

Boot, William. "NASA and the Spellbound Press." *Columbia Journalism Review* 25 (July/August 1986): 23–29.

Boylan, James. "Declarations of Independence." *Columbia Journalism Review* 25 (November/December 1986): 29–45.

Emery, Michael, and Smythe, Ted, eds. *Readings in Mass Communications.* 6th ed. Dubuque, Iowa: Wm. C. Brown Publishers, 1986. Selected recommended reading: "The Agenda-Setting Role of Mass Communication," by Chaim Eyal, Jim Winter, and Max McCombs; "Media Monitors," by Richard T. Stout; and "New Rules for a Changing Press," by Charles W. Bailey.

Harless, James D. *Mass Communication.* Dubuque, Iowa: Wm. C. Brown Publishers, 1985. Selected recommended reading: "Regulation and Self-regulation of the Media."

Salisbury, Harrison. *Without Fear or Favor: An Uncompromising Look at the* New York Times. New York: Ballantine Books, 1980.

Press Responsibility

EDMUND G. BLINN

MUCH to their chagrin, journalists have become suspect in our society. Some public-opinion surveys have placed reporters, editors, and broadcasters low on the list of professional practitioners and tradesmen in terms of respect and believability.

These findings appeared within ten years following American journalism's finest hour—when a stunningly professional performance by many of the nation's journalists brought about the resignation, in the face of impeachment, of a president of the United States. Newspaper reporters and broadcasters enjoyed, then, the respect and admiration of most of their fellow citizens. But, as always, a price had to be paid, and through their own actions, journalists contributed significantly to their resulting loss of esteem.

The Impact of Watergate

Not all Americans believed that the resignation of President Richard M. Nixon after the Watergate scandal[1] had been fairly attained. Many argued

1. "Watergate" was the term used to describe the series of related events beginning with the burglary of the Democratic party headquarters in the Watergate Building in Washington, D.C., in 1972 and culminating with Nixon's resignation in 1974.

that American journalists had disliked Nixon since the early years of his political career and that their distaste had inspired much of what was reported to the detriment of our 37th president. The pro-Nixonites claimed, for example, that the press had held their man responsible for actions that, when taken by earlier presidents, went unreported.

Journalists reported via the newspapers, news magazines, and airwaves what the Nixon supporters said. Many reporters investigated the claims by the naysayers and in the process verified some of them. With such reporting the journalists were simply fulfilling their responsibilities, but the results sometimes were damaging to the media's image.

Furthermore, the Watergate success emboldened the media, and intensive investigative reporting into all areas of American life—not just government—became the order of the day. And with fame and fortune the obvious lot of the most successful investigative reporters, younger journalists began digging for information that might reward them in like manner. The results were sometimes disastrous, and journalism writhed under the lash of public disapproval.

When it was disclosed that a *Washington Post* reporter, Janet Cooke, had falsified a Pulitzer prize–winning story about a twelve-year-old drug addict, the media engaged in soul-searching. The need for such self-examination escalated with later revelations that in a *New York Times* story a free-lance writer had reported an interview with a Cambodian rebel military leader that had never taken place, and that a *Wall Street Journal* columnist had used his insider's position to his own and his friends' profit. Grimly, the media reported these and similar events, and the readers and viewers were largely unforgiving.

The situation was such that prominent persons caught in embarrassing or illegal activities by the press found their most believable defense to be that they were victims of media overkill (trial by media), they were quoted out of context, or, like Nixon, they were subject to media vengeance. The media, as always, reported these defensive statements.

By 1984, many media-watchers were convinced that the anguish of journalists had been translated into an increased caution in dealing with sensitive matters.

Lawsuits against the Press

Further distress for journalists came as more and more libel and invasion of privacy suits were instituted against them. By the late 1970s, the United States was becoming an increasingly litigious society. Americans were more likely than ever to settle their grievances in court, and being among the most visible of institutions, the mass media were particularly vulnerable to litigation.

In the early 1980s, juries in trials of the media increasingly found in favor of plaintiffs, and some damage awards were for enormous sums. A jury awarded $9.2 million to the plaintiff in a suit against a small daily newspaper in Alton, Illinois. The newspaper was forced into bankruptcy but managed to continue publication when it settled with the plaintiffs for $1.4 million. In another case a federal jury granted Mobil Oil president William Tavoulareas $2.05 million in damages in a suit against the *Washington Post.* That judgment was later reversed, however.

Such awards tend to intimidate journalists, even though most jury awards against mass media in libel actions are reduced or overturned on appeal. Even if a media defendant wins a case, the costs of litigation are still onerous—attorneys' fees average about $1,000 a day.

When such factors as public distrust, the enormous costs of litigation, and the claim of media overemphasis of some persons charged with illegal or unethical actions exist, journalists quite naturally experience increased caution. But it is the readers and viewers who suffer most, for the result of that caution inevitably is a decrease in the amount of information available to the public. A more cautious press translates to a diminished democracy, because a less fully informed electorate is a less effective electorate.

Adherence to Journalistic Principles

Such caution on the part of journalists is largely unnecessary. Simple adherence to two basic principles of newsroom procedure has always been enough to justify publication or broadcast. Those principles are **accuracy** and **objectivity.** If a story is objective and accurate, no journalist need apologize, for the account of an event will have been fair to all parties. Fairness is the end sought by journalists with a firm sense of professionalism. However, accuracy and objectivity are not easy to attain. Journalism is practiced in an atmosphere requiring great volume and burdensome speed, and those requirements are conducive to error.

In an average day, a journalist may read and evaluate hundreds of stories containing many thousands of words and in a scant few hours must select, edit, position, and write headlines for stories. In the welter of such pressure, the journalist is fully aware that error is inevitable, although inexcusable.

Although journalists are never surprised by errors, they never cease to agonize over them. Thus, they will do almost anything to avoid charges that the errors were deliberate and designed to deceive readers. News professionals believe that as collectors and disseminators of information, they have an obligation to avoid inaccuracies. (See the Code of Professional Standards given in the Appendix.)

ACCURACY

In journalism, then, responsibility for accuracy rests with reporters, editors, writers, proofreaders, and others who make their living in the profession. But responsibility does not end with the professional. It also rests with those who supply information to the media, whether they are serving as news sources or voluntarily contributing information. The major responsibility rests with the journalist, of course, because the media are the primary disseminators of information. But the suppliers of information cannot, in good conscience, evade responsibility.

This is especially true for publicists. When serving as an interview source or writing for publication, publicists should follow this guiding rule for carrying out their responsibility for accuracy: **Make no assumptions about facts.** Writers for the media should never assume, for example, that they know how to spell a name; that they know the date, time, and place of an event; that they are quoting someone correctly; that because they were told something, it must be so; that they are citing a statistic or any other fact accurately. Facts are checked through reliable reference books, the person or persons directly involved are questioned, and everything else is done to establish beyond a reasonable doubt the accuracy of the information. No real substitute exists for being certain, and the only way to be certain is to verify, and verify again. Facts that cannot be verified should not be transmitted.

When a source is interviewed by a journalist and the subject matter is sensitive or involves many intricate details, the source may be able to assure accuracy by asking the interviewer for review privileges. This procedure allows the source to check the accuracy of the completed story or tape before publication or broadcast. If this privilege is extended, the source must adhere to one basic ground rule—that is, the information is checked for accuracy only, not for manner of expression.

Many representatives of the mass media, however, refuse to grant the review privilege, preferring to maintain complete independence from all outside pressures. Most editors place their trust in a journalist's commitment to the principles of accuracy and fairness. But other measures are available to a source who is concerned about the accurate portrayal of information. Some of those alternatives follow:

1. The source may refuse further interviews if the published material is inaccurate through no fault of the source.

2. The source may make the review privilege a condition to any interview.
3. The source may require that questions be submitted in writing so they may be answered in like manner.

These alternatives are not as satisfactory as an interview freely conducted in mutual confidence and respect by a professional journalist. The publicist should strive to develop press relationships based on that mutual respect, as problems are not likely to exist in such an atmosphere.

Even when the source and the journalist make painstaking efforts to avoid error, mistakes occur. Still, given the complexities of the business, errors are not as frequent as journalists fear—nor as news consumers may imagine—and the many checkpoints that material must clear before it is approved for release help provide a high degree of accuracy.

OBJECTIVITY

If accuracy is difficult to achieve, objectivity in the presentation of information is nearly impossible. But recognizing the impossibility of the task should not prevent one from trying. Publication and broadcast journalists gather and present information in the spirit of objectivity, although they know subjective judgments are made about what information is included in the story and what is left out. If those judgments are made on the basis of professional knowledge—that is, on the basis of what facts best tell the story—then the newsperson has performed in as objective a manner as possible, and the story will have the necessary balance. Professionalism requires that all sides of a story be published, and that assures fairness.

The publicists' task is somewhat different in this regard. The purpose of publicity is to convey specific messages to specific audiences to accomplish specific goals. Although publicists should always strive to be objective and fair, the stories they write obviously are not always balanced. Press releases pass on information reflecting the desired image of a person, a company, or an organization. If something good happens, the news is heralded; if something bad happens, the news is downplayed. The publicist can accomplish the desired goals with a subtle writing technique. But be aware that if releases are blatantly unbalanced, they most likely will not be used by the news media.

FAIRNESS

The objectivity question has long been argued among professionals, but never has fairness been regarded as anything but an absolute necessity in the practice of journalism. Many journalists believe that the attempt to be as objective as humanly possible helps achieve fairness. Accuracy and objectivity, then, are standards necessary to fairness. Certainly, few people would object to those standards as ideals. Still, it is seldom that any two persons will agree as to what is fair. Journalists soon learn this bitter lesson, but such knowledge should not deter them from adhering to a fair-minded approach to the reporting process. It has been suggested that a fair approach calls for both objectivity and subjectivity. But, pragmatically, fairness has these requirements:

1. Offering all sides of a controversy an opportunity to be heard.
2. Striving to report situations in perspective.
3. Discarding loaded words and labels in favor of facts.
4. Submerging personal biases and prejudices.
5. Paying careful attention to the context of events and situations.
6. Avoiding a participant's role in events.
7. Guarding against presenting the account with overcolorful expression.
8. Providing background information wherever necessary.
9. Attributing opinions, judgments, and disputed "facts" to the appropriate source.
10. Reserving personal opinion for the page, section, or broadcast openly devoted to that purpose.

Proper Use of Attribution

The average person often has difficulty in distinguishing opinion and fact as presented by the media. Opinion is offered in the form of advertising, editorial cartoons (even in so-called comic strips), letters to the editor, syndicated columns, and editorials. Readers and listeners should accept such opinion for what it is. But the media also publish opinion in news stories and feature articles, which causes some reader confusion.

Readers, unfortunately, frequently consider opinion in news stories and features as that of the publisher or broadcaster even when it clearly is attributed to other sources. Such articles might quote the remarks of politicians and candidates for public office, representatives of charitable institutions and organizations, persons speaking for the innumerable committees formed in support of the various sides of disputed issues, or even a football or basketball coach on the approaching season's prospects for the team. The quoted remarks are facts—that is, it is a fact the persons quoted did express those opinions. The key to separating fact and opinion in this context is to give clear **attribution** of the opinions to the persons who expressed them.

Citizens obviously need and want such expressions of opinion to be reported by news sources, and the media have an obligation to provide the information. Journalists also are expected to make clear the identity of the person or agency responsible for the opinions. Evaluation of the worth of the opinions and judgments then may be safely left to readers or listeners. Thus, such observations must be credited to their sources, clearly and unmistakably. The following are some examples:

INCORRECT

Everyone should attend this extremely important meeting of the Yourtown City Council next Tuesday evening.

CORRECT

City Councilman Joseph M. Jones said that next Tuesday's council meeting is "extremely important," and he urged residents to attend.

INCORRECT

Women are demeaned by pornography, and the legislature should recognize that fact by law.

CORRECT

Calling for a law that would forbid distribution of pornography in the state, Senator Alton J. Smith asserted that "women are demeaned by such swill."

INCORRECT

Vote for Republicans and independents in the next election.

CORRECT

The Citizens for Responsible Government chairman said he would advise voters to cast their ballots for Republicans and independent candidates in the coming election.

INCORRECT

The money collected will be used for desperately needed computer terminals at the high school. It's a worthy cause.

CORRECT

PTA President Zora Terwilliger-Lyons said the money collected will be used to purchase "desperately needed" computer terminals for the high school. "The cause is obviously worthy," she said.

INCORRECT

The concert will be the biggest, grandest event in the university's history.

CORRECT

Matthew Cortinella, concert committee chairman, said the event would be "the biggest and grandest" in the history of the university.

The examples cited above illustrate proper attribution for short statements. The principle applies to longer accounts as well. Two versions of a single story shown below illustrate the importance of appropriate attribution:

NO ATTRIBUTION

The leader of our organization spoke to a large crowd at the Union Hall Tuesday night. He was enthusiastically received by all those in attendance.

Unions are being denied their rights by management in these hard times, but only because the government has allowed that to happen.

The fault lies with our elected representatives, who work hand in glove with the oppressors.

ATTRIBUTION

Approximately 150 people Tuesday night heard a local union official charge members of Congress with working "hand in glove" with management to deny the rights of the workingman.

Albert Sorderman, chairman of Chapter 228 of the Order of Electrical Workers, said, "Management is taking advantage of these hard times to deny unions their rights, but only because the government has allowed that to happen."

But attribution may be carried too far. When facts are not subject to dispute, such as the time or location of an event, the name of the speaker, the date of an election, and so on, attribution is not necessary.

It has been said that in an average lifetime every American will at some point be subject to press attention. Thus, when a reporter asks for one person's opinion on a particular issue, it's important to understand a basic journalistic procedure. That is, in most circumstances, the reporter will seek out the opinions of other persons on the same subject. In order to be fair, the reporter must solicit all the available information. If all that collected information is reported accurately and in context, the sources should have no complaint.

Readers Demand Accuracy

Because democracy is impossible without an informed electorate, the mass media are indispensable to its practice. The people of the nation depend on newspapers, magazines, books, movies, television, and radio for the information they want and must have. They pursue that information with rigor — studies have revealed that the average adult spends four to six hours daily perusing media output.

Readers need information to order their lives, to set business and professional agenda, to plan entertainment, to learn of the agonies and ecstasies of friends, neighbors, and even strangers. They ask for weather reports, for governmental and social news, for reports of police and court activities, for sports events results, and the latest in scandals and atrocities. Readers simply have a desire and need to know.

Although professional and other specialized publications provide some of the required information, the only agencies established and equipped to give readers the bulk of general knowledge are the news media. Although error is always possible, given the enormous size of news operations, most Americans apparently realize that overall, the press's accuracy record is impressive. They still rely daily on that record to make decisions, to order their lives, and to carry out their duties as citizens.

Journalists are most concerned for accuracy as a professional responsibility, but they know there is another important reason to avoid error and partisanship. Any publication or electronic news operation with a persistent record of inaccurate reporting will soon lose public confidence. And that can mean a declining circulation or audience, reduced income because of less advertising, and thus, a threatened existence.

In addition, of course, such sloppy and thoughtless performance can inspire a costly libel suit or an equally costly invasion of privacy action. Veteran journalists are fully aware that carelessness is the foremost cause of suits for damages. Because so much printed and broadcast material is potentially libelous, particularly articles on crime and other wrongdoing, accuracy and fairness are more than ideals for performance; they are essential.

When printed and broadcast material is defamatory or invades privacy, inaccurate or unfair reporting may harm innocent persons, and the results can be costly, as was noted earlier. Even if the error or unfairness is unintentional, the consequences can be disastrous. Libel suits can result from publication of a wrong name, initial, address, or other item of identification, and the person or firm instituting suit may collect damages if the error is the result of carelessness.

THE FUNDAMENTALS OF LIBEL

Journalists and news sources should know the fundamentals of libel law. Knowledge of that law is important to an understanding and appreciation of the responsibilities of both the press and the sources of news, for both are liable when a publication or broadcast damages the reputation of a person or a firm. The plaintiff—the person or organization involved—can sue, separately or jointly, any person who had any part in the publication or broadcast: the writer, the participating editors, the publisher or station owner, or the sources of the information.

For example, if a source tells a reporter a neighbor is running a drug-distributing operation, and the newspaper publishes the story, the neighbor may sue both the source and the newspaper. If the information is not true, and that can be proven, both the source and the newspaper may be considerably out of pocket.

As a general rule, the one who publishes must pay. That means a news medium is responsible for published libel no matter in what form it appears. An actionable defamation can appear in news columns or broadcasts, advertising, cartoons, photographs, headlines, and letters to the editor.

Some states have an exception to this general rule. The courts of those states adhere to what is called the rule of neutral reportage, which provides protection for a news medium that accurately attributes even a libelous statement to an acknowledged expert on the subject of the story. The acknowledged expert may be held liable, however. Not many states have accepted the new standard, and jurists generally regard it with suspicion.

THE ELEMENTS OF LIBEL

Recognizing a libel is a relatively simple matter. Libel has three elements, all three of which must be present in order for legal liability to exist.

They are **defamation, publication,** and **identification.**

In order for **defamation** to occur, the material must in some way injure someone's reputation falsely. The words may be libelous in themselves (**libel per se**) or because of special circumstances (**libel per quod**). Many words are libelous per se, of course (thief, murderer, rapist, Nazi, communist, embezzler, prostitute), but in general, false statements that hold a person up to the ridicule or contempt of his or her fellow human beings are defamatory.

Libel per quod can exist in circumstances in which, although the printed or broadcast information is not defamatory, public knowledge creates the damaging impression. It is not libelous, for example, to publish, even falsely, that a clergyman attended a party at an American Legion clubhouse. But if it is widely known that the function featured nude performers, defamation has occurred if the clergyman was not present.

Publication exists when the presses begin to roll or a broadcast goes on the air, but the legal rule should be kept carefully in mind. That rule is that publication occurs when a third, disinterested person sees or hears the material. The Alton, Illinois, case mentioned earlier is an example of how this rule works. The allegedly libelous information that brought about the suit was never printed in a newspaper. It had been mailed in a letter to a government agency, which became that third, disinterested party.

Identification has been accomplished when an ascertainable, living person has been referred to in the offending statement.[2] Identification need not be by name, however. Should any person be identifiable to members of the public by physical description, personality sketch, photograph, drawing, address, or occupation (there is only one president of the United States, for example), this requirement is satisfied.

When all three of these elements of libel have been established, the injured party can institute a suit for damage to reputation. Whether the plaintiff is successful in acquiring satisfaction depends on the evidence presented at trial. The person alleging injury must prove the case by a preponderance of believable evidence. A jury, in most cases, will render the verdict.

LIBEL DEFENSES

If the person or persons sued for defamation decide to defend themselves in court, legal defenses are available. The defendant may plead **truth** or **privilege.** Because truth is exceedingly difficult to prove in a court of law, it is generally not the sole defense pleaded. Most defendants

---

2. Legally, a dead person may not institute a suit for defamation, nor may any living party file suit in the name of the deceased.

offer both truth and privilege as justification for publication. A defendant must prove, again through the bulk of the best evidence, whatever is pleaded in defense.

Obviously, proving truth becomes easier when the allegedly libelous material has been published in a fair and accurate manner. Privilege as a defense is always conditional, with one exception. When the defendant is a government official and the alleged defamation concerns the remarks or writings offered by that official in the performance of official duties, the defense is **absolute privilege.** A government official cannot be sued successfully for libel no matter what was officially communicated, even if the official knew that the content of the expression was damaging and false.

A **conditional privilege** exists for reporting what is presented under the absolute privilege granted to government officials. To enjoy that conditional privilege, reports of absolutely privileged information must be fair and accurate. No opinion is allowed, and the proof of accuracy rests on whether a reasonable reader would understand from the news report what would have been understood from reading the government document or hearing the government official's remarks. This privilege is granted on the basis the people should be kept informed about the actions and activities of government, which is newsworthy per se.

A further conditional privilege is extended to the publication of comment and criticism on matters of public importance and concern. This privilege is frequently referred to as the **constitutional privilege,** because it is based on First Amendment guarantees. The rationale for this defense emerged from a 1964 lawsuit filed by Montgomery, Alabama, police commissioner L. B. Sullivan. He sued the *New York Times* for libel resulting from an ad purchased by a group of civil rights leaders in which some of the information was incorrect. In its decision, the Supreme Court said:

> The general proposition that freedom of expression upon public questions is secured by the First Amendment has long been settled by our decisions. The constitutional safeguard, we have said, "was fashioned to assure unfettered interchange of ideas for the bringing about of political and social changes desired by the people. . . . It is a prized American privilege to speak one's mind, although not always with perfect good taste, on all public institutions," and this opportunity is to be afforded for "vigorous advocacy" no less than "abstract discussion." New York Times v. Sullivan, 376 U.S. 254, 84 S.Ct. 710, 11 L.Ed. 2D 686 (1964).

The court, then, ruled that a public official could not successfully sue for defamation arising from comment concerning his conduct of official duties.

Government officials do have recourse in the courts, however, if they can prove that the publication or broadcast was inspired by **actual malice,** defined by the Supreme Court in the *Sullivan* case as knowledge that the allegedly libelous statement "was false or with reckless disregard of whether it was false or not." Thus, a plaintiff who is a public official must prove that the material in question was false or that the publisher displayed no concern for the truth if the material concerned official acts or pronouncements.

The private affairs of public officials are another matter of course. Those who comment on such must prove that the private lifestyle could have a damaging effect on the performance of official duties in order to plead the constitutional privilege.

Public figure plaintiffs also must prove actual malice in order to collect damages for defamation resulting from their public activities and statements. A public figure is any person whose name or person is instantly recognizable by average citizens (referred to as an all-purpose public figure), or any person who thrusts himself or herself into the vortex of a public controversy "in order to influence the resolution of the issues involved." The second type of public figure is sometimes referred to as a limited (or vortex) public figure.

Private persons may not have to prove actual malice in order to collect damages for defamation, unless the state law under which the issue is tried requires such proof. In some states the private plaintiff has only to prove negligence with fault, which generally means that the publisher failed to check for the truth of the statement or statements in question.

In recent years, mass-media defendants generally have won libel suits, at least before courts of appeal. Juries, however, have displayed some evidence that they are not as sympathetic to First Amendment claims as are judges.

Invasion of Privacy

Juries have tended, too, to show less concern for the demands of free expression when plaintiffs have sued mass media for invasion of privacy. Appellate judges, however, are apt to examine issues in light of First Amendment provisions and thus tend to rule in favor of media defendants.

Invasion of privacy suits have become of increasing concern to journalists. More and more of these suits have been filed in recent years, to the extent that some publishers and broadcast-station owners take them as seriously as defamation suits.

Although the right to personal privacy is not mentioned in the Bill of Rights, the Supreme Court has ruled that right is implicit in these amendments: the First (the implied right of association); the Third (the right to refuse to quarter troops in one's home in time of peace); the Fourth (the right of the people to be secure against unreasonable searches and seizures); the

Fifth (the right to refuse to testify against oneself); and the Ninth (which specifies that rights not spelled out in the Constitution are not necessarily excluded).

The right of privacy is the right to be left alone, to go through life unnoticed. Pure privacy is an undesirable condition for most of us, of course. We desire attention, but on our own terms. The law of privacy seeks to set boundaries beyond which mass media may not go in penetration of that right.

Through the years, the legal right to privacy against invasion by mass communication has evolved into four separate torts. (A tort is a civil injury subject to suit for damages.) These torts are

1. Intrusion into the seclusion or solitude of an individual.
2. Publication of embarrassing private facts concerning a person.
3. Placing a person in a false light in the public eye.
4. Appropriation of a person's name or likeness for commercial purposes without permission.

Generally, journalists are in danger of violating a person's seclusion or solitude when they use subterfuge to obtain admission into someone's home—or hospital room or private office—or when they snoop with the assistance of electronic devices. Such acts of intrusion are violations of the criminal code in most states, usually involving the act of trespass, and courts have ruled that journalists may not violate the law even for the commendable purpose of gathering information for transmittal to the public. It is unusual, however, for newsgatherers to be involved in such actions.

Most violation-of-privacy suits involve the publication of information concerning private lives of individuals or the use of a person's name or likeness for commercial purposes (usually an advertisement) without consent. False-light suits, like intrusion actions, are relatively rare.

If the private information published is newsworthy, invasion suits usually fail. Satisfaction of simple public curiosity does not meet the newsworthy standard, but information in government records that are legally available for public inspection can be published without fear of tort liability.

In determining what is of legitimate public interest, the courts generally have applied the test of reasonableness, admittedly a vague standard. When that test is applied, however, judges tend to rule in favor of the public's right to know.

As was noted earlier, many invasion of privacy suits involve the use of a person's name or likeness in advertising or other promotional material without permission to do so. The courts have maintained that people have a property right in their individual identities. The best protection against such a suit is to obtain written permission for the use of a name or likeness, even if money must be paid for the subject's consent. (An example of a standard permission form is shown in Chapter 14.)

This area is of particular concern to publicists. In fact, only within the past few years has another aspect of privacy been recognized – the right of publicity. This means that if a person's name or likeness is of any commercial consequence, the publicist must bargain with that person before using the celebrity in any campaign promotion. The basis of such a requirement can be reasonably understood – to use a celebrity's name or likeness without permission is to deny that person income.

Remember, though, that an obtained consent, even if paid for, could cause a defendant to lose in court if the defendant has failed yet another test of reasonableness. One court, for example, ruled for a professional model who had been paid to sign a consent form for the use of her likeness. The court said it was unreasonable for the defendant, a photographer, to have used the plaintiff's photograph in such a manner as to portray her as a prostitute.

Journalists are seldom charged with placing persons in a false light in the eyes of the public. Such actions usually stem from the publication of biographies or television docudramas in which the facts of the subjects' lives have been substantially falsified. In one case, however, two journalists lost a false-light suit because they quoted at length a person they had never interviewed. Those quotations had the effect, the plaintiff said, of placing her in a false light. It should be noted that adherence to the professional standards of accuracy and objectivity could have saved those journalists money and embarrassment.

Truth is obviously the best defense to a claim of false-light invasion of privacy. If the defendant has published the truth, a suit cannot be successful.

Sharpening Professionalism

In response to the heightened public criticism noted earlier, many media companies have experimented with a number of devices designed to inhibit inaccuracy and prevent unfairness. Among them have been regular and systematic checks with news sources, internal bureaus of fair play, ombudsmen appointed to accept complaints and arrange for corrections or adjustments when justified, and community press councils organized to evaluate performance. In the first heat of optimism, it seemed some of these devices would contribute significantly to public understanding and trust, but some have failed to withstand the test of time.

In the 1970s, press councils began establishing agencies through which members of the public could get a hearing concerning their claims of media abuse. The National News Council, a state press council (in Minnesota), and a number of community councils all enhanced, to a degree, public understanding of the mass media. Unfortunately, the National News Council was dismantled in the early 1980s, the victim of insufficient funding and a failure to acquire support from some important media organizations. Many community councils have failed outright or become moribund because of a lack of public interest. The Minnesota council remains as almost the sole successful representative of the movement for independent evaluative agencies.

Journalism review publications, another product of the 1970s, attempt to monitor mass media performance by questioning the performance of individual newspapers, broadcasters, and publishers. Most of these review publications are funded largely by advertising, which usually has been insufficient. Although many major cities were once serviced by such publications, the *Washington Journalism Review* and the *Columbia Journalism Review* are the strongest survivors.

Although many major publications still offer ombudsmen and internal bureaus to monitor their own communication performance, the impressive initial drive toward public accountability and education has been somewhat blunted. Even the once-vigorous programs to monitor performance through regular checks of news sources have diminished in significance because of the pressures involved—the amount of time needed for such checks and the multitudinous daily activities of publication.

Summary

The best remedy for public dissatisfaction, distrust, and legal problems is journalistic professionalism. That means having a first concern for accuracy and fairness. Given the requirements of disseminating news, that concern can never result in perfection, but it can significantly alleviate the problems. Mass media consumers can aid journalistic professionalism by acting as knowledgeable critics of performance and by exhibiting an equal concern for accuracy and fairness when approached as sources of information.

Exercises

1. Organize a panel of several persons from each of the following groups: (a) news or publicity story sources, (b) publicists, (c) professional newspaper or broadcast journalists. Discuss how information is gathered for a story and how the resulting story is relayed to the audience in terms of accuracy, fairness, and objectivity. If instances of communication breakdown are mentioned by panel members, discuss how the breakdown occurred and what could have been done to avoid the problem.

2. From a daily paper, clip three publicity feature stories that contain direct and indirect quotes. Examine the quotes in terms of content and attribution. Are the direct quotes necessary and effective? Does each direct or indirect quote have proper attribution? Are there any sentences that appear to be the writer's opinion because of the use of editorial words or a lack of attribution? If so, rewrite the sentences to be more objective.

3. Divide the class into groups. Each group should research a libel case that is currently in the court system. Have the group present a synopsis of the case to the class, identifying the elements of libel and the defenses used by the defendant(s). Based on the information in this chapter and other research from media law books presented by the group, let the class discuss what the ultimate outcome of the case might be.

Suggested Reading

Gillmor, Donald M., and Barron, Jerome A. *Mass Communication Law*. 4th ed. St. Paul: West Publishing Co., 1984.

Halberstam, David. *The Powers That Be*. New York: Alfred A. Knopf, 1979.

Kreighbaum, Hillier. *Pressures on the Press*. New York: Thomas Y. Crowell Co., 1972.

Lambeth, Edmund G. *Committed Journalism: An Ethic for the Profession*. Bloomington: Indiana University Press, 1986.

Nelson, Harold L., and Teeter, Dwight L., Jr. *Law of Mass Communications*. 4th ed. La Habra, Calif.: Foundation Press, 1984.

Pember, Donald R. *Mass Media Law*. 3d ed. Dubuque, Iowa: Wm. C. Brown Publishers, 1984.

Appendix

Code Of Professional Standards
For The Practice Of Public Relations

Public Relations Society of America

This Code, adopted by the PRSA Assembly, replaces a Code of Ethics in force since 1950 and revised in 1954. The current Code of Professional Standards, including the previous Statement of Principles, was approved in 1959 and revised in 1963, 1977, and 1983.

Declaration of Principles

Members of the Public Relations Society of America base their professional principles on the fundamental value and dignity of the individual, holding that the free exercise of human rights, especially freedom of speech, freedom of assembly, and freedom of the press, is essential to the practice of public relations.

In serving the interests of clients and employers, we dedicate ourselves to the goals of better communication, understanding, and cooperation among the diverse individuals, groups, and institutions of society, and of equal opportunity of employment in the public relations profession.

We pledge:

To conduct ourselves professionally, with truth, accuracy, fairness, and responsibility to the public;

To improve our individual competence and advance the knowledge and proficiency of the profession through continuing research and education;

And to adhere to the articles of the Code of Professional Standards for the Practice of Public Relations as adopted by the governing Assembly of the Society.

Code of Professional Standards
for the Practice of Public Relations

These articles have been adopted by the Public Relations Society of America to promote and maintain high standards of public service and ethical conduct among its members.

1. A member shall deal fairly with clients or employers, past, present, or potential, with fellow practitioners, and with the general public.
2. A member shall conduct his or her professional life in accord with the public interest.
3. A member shall adhere to truth and accuracy and to generally accepted standards of good taste.
4. A member shall not represent conflicting or competing interests without the express consent of those involved, given after a full disclosure of the facts; nor place himself or herself in a position where the member's interest is or may be in conflict with a duty to a client, or others, without a full disclosure of such interests to all involved.
5. A member shall safeguard the confidences of present and former clients, as well as those of persons or entities who have disclosed confidences to a member in the context of communications relating to an anticipated professional relationship with such member, and shall not accept retainers or employment that may involve disclosing, using, or offering to use such confidences to the disadvantage or prejudice of such present, former, or potential clients or employers.
6. A member shall not engage in any practice that tends to corrupt the integrity of channels of communication or the processes of government.
7. A member shall not intentionally communicate false or misleading information, and is obligated to use care to avoid communication of false or misleading information.
8. A member shall be prepared to identify publicly the name of the client or employer on whose behalf any public communication is made.
9. A member shall not make use of any individual or organization purporting to serve or represent an announced cause, or purporting to be independent or unbiased, but actually serving an undisclosed special or private interest of a member, client, or employer.
10. A member shall not intentionally injure the professional reputation or practice of another practitioner. However, if a member has evidence that another member has been guilty of unethical, illegal, or unfair practices, including those in violation of this Code, the member shall present the information promptly to the proper authorities of the Society for action in accordance with the procedure set forth in Article XII of the Bylaws.
11. A member called as a witness in a proceeding for the enforcement of this Code shall be bound to appear, unless excused for sufficient reason by the judicial panel.
12. A member, in performing services for a client or employer, shall not accept fees, commissions, or any other valuable consideration from anyone other than the client or employer in connection with those services without the express consent of the client or employer, given after a full disclosure of the facts.
13. A member shall not guarantee the achievement of specified results beyond the member's direct control.
14. A member shall, as soon as possible, sever relations with any organization or individual if such relationship requires conduct contrary to the articles of this Code.

OFFICIAL INTERPRETATIONS OF THE CODE

Interpretation of Code Paragraph 2, which reads, "A member shall conduct his or her professional life in accord with the public interest."

The public interest is here defined primarily as comprising respect for and enforcement of the rights guaranteed by the Constitution of the United States of America.

Interpretation of Code Paragraph 5, which reads, "A member shall safeguard the confidences of present and former clients, as well as those of persons or entities who have disclosed confidences to a member in the context of communications relating to an anticipated professional relationship with such member, and shall not accept retainers or employment that may involve disclosing, using, or offering to use such confidences to the disadvantage or prejudice of such present, former, or potential clients or employers."

1. This article does not prohibit a member who has knowledge of client or employer activities that are illegal from making such disclosures to the proper authorities as he or she believes are legally required.

2. Communications between a practitioner and client/employer are deemed to be confidential under Article 5 of the Code of Professional Standards. However, although practitioner-client/employer communications are considered confidential between the parties, such communications are not privileged against disclosure in a court of law.

3. In the absence of any contractual arrangement, the client or employer legally owns the rights to papers or materials created for him.

Interpretation of Code Paragraph 6, which reads, "A member shall not engage in any practice that tends to corrupt the integrity of channels of communication or the processes of government."

1. Practices prohibited by this paragraph are those that tend to place representatives of media or government under any obligation to the member, or the member's employer or client, which is in conflict with their obligations to media or government, such as:
   a. the giving of gifts of more than nominal value;
   b. any form of payment or compensation to a member of the media in order to obtain preferential or guaranteed news or editorial coverage in the medium;
   c. any retainer or fee to a media employee or use of such employee if retained by a client or employer, where the circumstances are not fully disclosed to and accepted by the media employer;
   d. providing trips, for media representatives, that are unrelated to legitimate news interest;
   e. the use by a member of an investment or loan or advertising commitment made by the member, or the member's client or employer, to obtain preferential or guaranteed coverage in the medium.

2. This Code paragraph does not prohibit hosting media or government representatives at meals, cocktails, or news functions and special events that are occasions for the exchange of news information or views, or the furtherance of understanding, which is part of the public relations function. Nor does it pro-

hibit the bona fide press event or tour when media or government representatives are given the opportunity for an on-the-spot viewing of a newsworthy product, process, or event in which the media or government representatives have a legitimate interest. What is customary or reasonable hospitality has to be a matter of particular judgment in specific situations. In all of these cases, however, it is, or should be, understood that no preferential treatment or guarantees are expected or implied and that complete independence always is left to the media or government representative.

3. This paragraph does not prohibit the reasonable giving or lending of sample products or services to media representatives who have a legitimate interest in the products or services.

4. It is permissible, under Article 6 of the Code, to offer complimentary or discount rates to the media (travel writers, for example) if the rate is for business use and is made available to all writers. Considerable question exists as to the propriety of extending such rates for personal use.

Interpretation of Code Paragraph 10, which reads, "A member shall not intentionally injure the professional reputation or practice of another practitioner. However, if a member has evidence that another member has been guilty of unethical, illegal, or unfair practices, including those in violation of this Code, the member shall present the information promptly to the proper authorities of the Society for action in accordance with the procedure set forth in Article XII of the Bylaws."

Blind solicitation, on its face, is not prohibited by the Code. However, if the customer list were improperly obtained, or if the solicitation contained references reflecting adversely on the quality of current services, a complaint might be justified.

Interpretation of Code Paragraph 13, which reads, "A member shall not guarantee the achievement of specified results beyond the member's direct control."

This Code paragraph, in effect, prohibits misleading a client or employer as to what professional public relations can accomplish. It does not prohibit guarantees of quality or service. But it does prohibit guaranteeing specific results which, by their very nature, cannot be guaranteed because they are not subject to the member's control. As an example, a guarantee that a news release will appear specifically in a particular publication would be prohibited. This paragraph should not be interpreted as prohibiting contingent fees.

Index